Christian Armor

Christian Armor

The Rosary and the Bible

David C. Bellusci, OP

WIPF & STOCK · Eugene, Oregon

CHRISTIAN ARMOR
The Rosary and the Bible

Copyright © 2024 David C. Bellusci. All rights reserved. Except for brief quotations in critical publications or reviews, no part of this book may be reproduced in any manner without prior written permission from the publisher. Write: Permissions, Wipf and Stock Publishers, 199 W. 8th Ave., Suite 3, Eugene, OR 97401.

Wipf & Stock
An Imprint of Wipf and Stock Publishers
199 W. 8th Ave., Suite 3
Eugene, OR 97401

www.wipfandstock.com

PAPERBACK ISBN: 978-1-6667-8610-1
HARDCOVER ISBN: 978-1-6667-8611-8
EBOOK ISBN: 978-1-6667-8612-5

VERSION NUMBER 04/01/24

All Scripture quotations are from The Catholic Edition of the New Revised Standard Version of the Bible, copyright © 1989. National Council of the Churches of Christ in the United States of America. Used by permission. All rights reserved worldwide.

In memory
of mamma and papa
who first brought me to the Holy Land
—Nazareth, Bethlehem, and Jerusalem—
to reflect, discern, and worship.

And in memory of Garrett Thomas Marchetti
(2001–21)

who served our pilgrim Masses, June 2019,
in Tiberius, Nazareth, Mt. Tabor, Bethlehem,
Bethany, and Gethsemane.

Dedicated to my students,
my godchildren,
my spiritual children,
and my nephews and nieces.

In Honorem Beatissimae Virginis Mariae

Then Mary said, "Here am I, the servant of the Lord; let it be with me according to your word." (Luke 1:38)

"Lord, to whom can we go?
You have the words of eternal life." (John 6:68)

Contents

List of Tables | xix
Preface | xxi
Acknowledgments | xxv
Introduction | xxvii
Scripture Abreviations | xxix

JOYFUL MYSTERIES

I—First Joyful Mystery—Annunciation | 3
    1. Nazareth 3
    2. Mary: Chosen by God 4
    3. Eve: First Woman 5
    4. Mary: The New Eve 6
    5. Mary's Humility 11
II—Fruit of this Mystery: Virtue of Humility | 12
    Practical Matters— 12
    Humility: Path to Sanctity 12
    Pride: Way to Death 12

I—Second Joyful Mystery—Visitation | 16
    1. Ein Karem 16
    2. Mary and Elizabeth 17
    3. Baptizer and Savior in Their Wombs 18
    4. Humility and Charity 20
    5. Immaculate Conception 22

II—Fruit of this Mystery: Virtue of Charity; Love of Neighbor | 24
   Practical Matters— 24
   Truth 25
   Death 26
   Love 26

I—Third Joyful Mystery—Birth of Jesus | 28
   1. Bethlehem 28
   2. Jesus's Ancestry 29
   3. Joseph: Husband of Mary 30
   4. Roman Census 32
   5. Birth of Jesus: Promise Fulfilled 33
II—Fruit of this Mystery: Virtue of Poverty | 37
   Practical Matters— 37

I—Fourth Joyful Mystery—Presentation in the Temple | 41
   1. Mary and Joseph Present Jesus in the Temple 41
   2. Simeon's Prophesy 44
   3. Sword Pierces Mary's Soul 45
II—Fruit of this Mystery: Virtue of Obedience | 47
   Practical Matters— 47

I—Fifth Joyful Mystery—Finding of Jesus in the Temple | 54
   1. Looking for Your Child 54
   2. Finding Jesus 55
   3. Throne of the Word 55
   4. "Finding": Repeats Itself in the Joyful Mysteries 58
II—Fruit of this Mystery: Virtue of Piety | 59
   Practical Matters— 59

LUMINOUS MYSTERIES

I—First Luminous Mystery—Baptism of the Lord | 67
   1. Jordan River 67
   2. John and Jesus 68
   3. Ein Karem: Old and New Covenants 70
   4. Purity of John the Baptist 72

    5. Baptism of Jesus   74
    6. Holy Trinity   75
II—Fruit of this Mystery: Openness to the Holy Spirit | 77
    Practical Matters—   77

I—Second Luminous Mystery—Miracle at Cana | 80
    1. Wedding   80
        i. The problem   82
        ii. Significance of Wine   82
        iii. Truth in Purity   83
    2. Mary and Jesus   84
    3. Wedding Feast of the Lamb   86
    4. Mary as Mediatrix   88
II—Fruit of this Mystery: to Jesus through Mary | 89
    Practical Matters—   89

I—Third Luminous Mystery—Proclamation of the Kingdom of God | 92
    1. Two Kingdoms   92
        i. Heal the Sick   94
        ii. Raise the Dead   97
        iii. Cleanse the Lepers   98
        iv. Cast out Demons   99
        v. Beatitudes of the Kingdom   101
II—Fruit of this Mystery: Repentance; Trust in God | 101
    Practical Matters—   101

I—Fourth Luminous Mystery—Transfiguration | 105
    1. Mount Tabor   105
    2. Transfiguration   106
        i. Elijah   107
        ii. Law of Moses   109
        iii. "My Beloved Son"   111
II—Fruit of this Mystery: Desire for Holiness | 112
    Practical Matters—   112
    1. Holiness in Scriptures   112
    2. Discipline   113
    3. Striving in Virtue   114

I—Fifth Luminous Mystery—Institution of the Eucharist | 116
    1. Last Supper   116
    2. Priesthood of Jesus   122
II—Fruit of this Mystery: Eucharistic Adoration; Active Participation at Mass | 124
    Practical Matters—   124
    1. Bread and Wine   124
    2. Body and Blood of Christ   124
    3. Doubting Thomas   125
    4. Eucharistic Adoration   126

SORROWFUL MYSTERIES

I—First Sorrowful Mystery—Agony in the Garden | 131
    1. Gethsemane   131
    2. Prophesy   132
    3. Agony   134
    4. Betrayal   135
    5. Father's Will   137
II—Fruit of this Mystery: Virtue of Contrition; Conformity to the Will of God | 139
    Practical Matters—   139

I—Second Sorrowful Mystery—Scourging at the Pillar | 144
    1. Judas Betrays Jesus   144
    2. Caiphas's House   146
    3. Peter's Threefold Denial   147
    4. Divinity and Kingship   148
    5. Pilate's Dilemma   150
    6. Flagellation   151
II—Fruit of this Mystery: Virtue of Purity; Mortification | 152
    Practical Matters—   152
    Steps towards Purity   155
    1. Choosing   155
    2. Strengthening   155
    3. Sacraments   156

    4. Spiritual Reading   156
    5. Confessor   156

I—Third Sorrowful Mystery—Crowning with Thorns | 158
    1. Handed over to the Romans   158
    2. Throne of His Ancestor David   159
    3. The House of Jacob Forever   161
    4. His Reign Will Have No End   162
    5. Your Kingdom Come   165
II—Fruit of this Mystery: Virtue of Moral Courage | 166
    Practical Matters—   166

I—Fourth Sorrowful Mystery—Jesus Carries His Cross | 172
    1. Via Dolorosa   172
        1st Station: Jesus Is Condemned to Death   173
        2nd Station: Jesus Takes Up His Cross   173
        3rd Station: Jesus Falls the First Time   174
        4th Station: Jesus Is Met by His Blessed Mother   174
        5th Station: Simon of Cyrene Helps Jesus Carry His Cross   175
        6th Station: The Face of Jesus Is Wiped by Veronica   176
        7th Station: Jesus Falls a Second Time   177
        8th Station: Jesus Consoles the Women of Jerusalem   177
        9th Station: Jesus Falls the Third Time   178
        10th Station: Jesus Is Stripped of His Garments   178
II—Fruit of this Mystery: Virtue of Patience | 179
    Practical Matters—   179
    What Is Patience?   179
        1. Patience with Ourselves   180
        2. Patience with Others   180
        3. Patience with God   182
        4. Patience in Spiritual Battle   183

I—Fifth Sorrowful Mystery—Crucifixion and Death of Our Lord | 185
    1. Our Lives Forever Changed   185
        11th Station: Jesus Is Nailed to the Cross   185
        12th Station: Jesus Dies on the Cross   186
        13th Station: Jesus Is Taken Down from the Cross   186
        14th Station: Jesus Is Laid in the Tomb   187

  2. Death of Jesus 187
  3. Salvific Act 188
  4. Law and Prophets 189
    i. Exodus 190
    ii. Psalms 191
    iii. Isaiah 192
    iv. Transfiguration 192
    v. Mary at the Cross 192
II—Fruit of this Mystery: Virtue of Self-Denial | 193
  Practical Matters— 193

GLORIOUS MYSTERIES

I—First Glorious Mystery—Resurrection of Our Lord | 199
  1. Basilica of the Holy Sepulcher 199
    i. Holy Tomb 200
    ii. Women at the Tomb 201
    iii. Dark/Light 202
  First Appearance—Jerusalem: Jesus Greets Mary Magdalene 203
  Second Appearance—Emmaus: Jesus Breaking Bread 206
  Third Appearance—Jesus Shows Thomas His Wounds 207
  Fourth Appearance—Tiberius: Jesus Eats Breakfast with His Apostles 208
II—Fruit of this Mystery: Virtue of Faith | 209
  Practical Matters— 209
  Dealing with Doubt 210

I—Second Glorious Mystery—Ascension of Our Lord | 212
  1. Ascension 212
  2. Son of Man 215
  3. Jesus's Kingship 216
  4. House of Jacob 218
II—Fruit of this Mystery: Virtue of Hope; Desire for Heaven | 219
  Practical Matters— 219

I—Third Glorious Mystery: Descent of the Holy Spirit upon the Apostles and the Blessed Virgin Mary | 225
    1. Language   225
    2. Holy Spirit   226
    3. Upper Room   228
    4. Speaking Other Tongues   230
    5. Paraclete—"Counselor"   233
    6. Gifts and Fruit of the Spirit   233

II—Fruit of this Mystery: Wisdom; Love of God | 236
    Practical Matters—   236
    1. Ten Commandments   236
    2. Eight Beatitudes   236

I—Fourth Glorious Mystery—Assumption of the Blessed Virgin Mary Body and Soul into Heaven | 239
    1. Mt. Zion   239
    2. Ebionite Heresy   240
    3. Council of Ephesus   242
    4. Devotion to Mary   243
    5. Assumption of Mary   245
    6. Assumption of Mary and Immaculate Conception   246

II—Fruit of this Mystery: Devotion to Mary | 248
    Practical Matters   248

I—Fifth Glorious Mystery—The Coronation of the Blessed Virgin Mary | 252
    1. Catholic Queens and Saints   252
        i. St. Helen: Empress of the Roman Empire   253
        ii. St. Clotilda: Queen of France   253
        iii. St. Margaret: Queen of Scotland   254
        iv. St. Jadwiga: Queen of Poland   254
        v. St. Bridget of Sweden   255
        vi. Venerable Isabel of Castile: Queen of Spain   257
    2. Biblical Queens   258
        i. Queen of Sheba   258
        ii. Song of Songs 4:7, 12   259
        iii. Psalms of David   260

       iv. Queen Mother of the Davidic Kingdom   261
       v. Queen Esther   262
       vi. New Testament—Virgin Mary   263
           St. Luke chapter 1   263
           Revelation chapter 12   264
II—Fruit of this Mystery: Eternal Happiness | 265
    Practical Matters—   265

Conclusion | 267
Bibliography | 269
Subject Index | 271
Scripture Index | 285

List of Tables

Table 1: Gift and Mystery | 234
Table 2: Fruit and Mystery | 235
Table 3: Rosary Schedule | 251

Preface

A Dominican writing a book on the rosary seems fitting, given that the Dominicans wear the rosary as part of their habit. Moreover, filial devotion to the blessed Virgin Mary, Mother of God, is found in the Constitutions of the Order of Preachers.[1] The biblical themes of each mystery of the rosary has inspired Dominican preaching.

Although this writing project on the rosary and its biblical themes began in 2018, the motivation for this work can be traced to my first year at university year in Montreal, Canada.

At the beginning of my university studies, and living away from home, I continued my practice of participating at daily Mass at the Basilica of Notre Dame or at the Loyola Chapel in the Notre-Dame-de-Grace district of the city. Being a devout Catholic, I also wanted to grow in my knowledge of the Scriptures, so I joined two Bible study groups offered by Evangelical Christians: Campus Crusade for Christ and Intervarsity Christian Fellowship. I soon found myself attempting to answer their questions or responding to their criticisms of my beliefs and practises as a Catholic. Questions about the Pope, praying to Mary and the Saints, indulgences, salvation by works, purgatory, and praying for the dead, just to name a few. Although I strived to practice my Catholic faith, I could not always answer their questions, nor could I defend myself in response to their criticisms.

I enjoyed the company of some Catholic friends, but we rarely talked about our religious beliefs. My network also included several non-Christian friends to whom I explained the teachings of the Catholic Church. And I was also very close friends with an atheist; this individual referred to my beliefs as "fairy tales."

---

1. *Book of Constitutions and Ordinations of the Friars of the Order of Preachers*, Sect. 1, Ch. 1, Art. 3, Paragraph 28, I.

In the first year of studies, during the summer months, I took a course in modern philosophy covering René Descartes, John Locke, and David Hume. Questions that I tried to answer no longer concerned my Catholic faith; I was now trying to make sense of my belief in God. During that same summer that I studied modern philosophy, the religious studies department sponsored a talk by an international biblical scholar. The lecture included comparisons between Genesis and Isaiah.

I was left disturbed by the scholar's lecture; what I carried away was an argument to reduce the Bible to a mythical narrative. I began to wonder about his biblical scholarship and the "demythologizing" of the Bible. At that same event, I approached the international scholar in the faculty lounge during the reception. After my brief exchange with this invited lecturer, in the presence of some faculty members listening, I responded as a zealous follower of Christ; I ended the conversation by telling the speaker, "there is still time for your salvation."[2]

That evening I returned home, late in the dark, feeling depressed. I reached a state of total confusion. I lay on the floor in my one-room apartment, more than just crying. I was screaming in anger because I no longer knew what I believed. Did I believe in anything? I could not be sure. I was not even certain whether God existed. In the course of two semesters, I rapidly slid downhill from faith to uncertainty sinking further into an abyss.

I felt certain of my existence. I did not have to prove to myself a self-evident truth. And to exist meant that a greater being than myself gave me my existence, a being upon whom I depended for my own and ongoing existence. A being who gave life to me and who sustains me: God.

I also knew from experience that I sinned and I needed a savior. That is why God sent his Son. To save me. I could not dismiss the outstanding fidelity of Mary as she stood before her son at the cross. And Jesus entrusted me to his Mother; in fact, in my room hung Salvador Dali's "Crucifixion" with Mary looking upon her resurrecting Son.

Somehow, I understood what I believed and why. Why I was a Roman Catholic. From that late night to the early morning I experienced what I now call, "my six-hour crisis of faith." From that day onwards, I made it my responsibility to learn everything I could about Catholicism. I was nineteen years old.

Christian Armor is meant to be spiritual reading adequate for Scripture classes or rosary-themed retreats. As a personal spiritual reading, *Christian Armor* can be read one page per day to probe the rosary mystery along with the Biblical verses. This savoring of both God's Word and the

---

2. A paraphrase of my "final words."

rosary allows for Scriptural meditation, personal reflection, and thanksgiving. After the end of each mystery, with probing "practical matters," the reader is encouraged to set goals in virtue-building.

Our Lady of the Rosary, pray for us.

Rome, Santa Maria Maggiore

Assumption of Mary

August 15, 2023

Acknowledgments

I am grateful to the biblical scholarship of Jean Doutre (OP), Michel Gourgues (OP), and Rick Jaworski (CC) in their New Testament instruction, and Walter Vogels (MAfr) in Old Testament studies. These biblical scholars provided me with a deeper theological understanding of New Testament and Old Testament studies.

In Mariology, Maximo Gatela (OP) offered direction and guidance in the biblical and historical understanding of the Virgin Mary, especially the Immaculate Conception. The late Father Lawrence Dewan (OP)⁺ provided me with the foundation to Thomist Metaphysics and Ethics. In Catechetical studies, I benefitted from the teaching of John Vandennacker (CC).

I wish to thank my colleagues at Catholic Pacific College. The faculty and staff share one mission: educating and forming students in truth and love anchored in Christ and his Church.

I am very grateful to Milanka Lachman and 206 Tours who made it possible for me to go on pilgrimages to Egypt, the Holy Land, and Jordan, journeys that served as archaeological, geographic, and especially biblical foundation to understanding the rosary mysteries in connection to both the Old and New Testament.

A particular thanks to Lorraine Claire Shelstad for proofreading this manuscript, checking it for typos, grammar, and punctuation. Any errors remaining in the manuscript are my own.

My writing on the mysteries of the rosary and the Scripture started during a retreat at the Benedictine Monastery in Mission, BC, on the Feast of the Presentation in 2018; I returned to the monastery to work on the scriptural meditations. I am grateful to the Benedictine monks for their hospitality, their prayerful surroundings, and their silence to help me contemplate the Word of God. At Santa Maria Maggiore, the Apostolic College in Rome, where I spend my summer months working with the Dominican confessors,

I am grateful for the international Dominican community and the fraternal atmosphere of Dominican life. My time in Rome enabled me to pray before *Salus Populi Romani,* to reflect, re-think, and revise my chapters. In the silence of Our Lady of Oropa, a Marian shrine in the Italian Alps—not far from Turin—the prayerful surroundings provided the focus I needed for further reflection and revision on my manuscript.

The regular retreats I offer to prayer groups, my courses on Scriptures taught to university students at Catholic Pacific College, the Bible study/faith sharing groups, and my daily Biblical/Mass reflections provided the source for this book on the rosary and the sacred Scripture. Among these prayer groups I would like to mention in gratitude the Guards of Honor of the Sacred Heart, the Legion of Mary, the Padre Pio Prayer Group, and the Knights of Columbus. Among the religious congregations, I am grateful for the presence and prayers of the Carmelite Nuns, Dominican Friars, Nuns, and Nashville Sisters, the Franciscan Sisters of the Eucharist, the Missionaries of Charity, Missionary Sisters of Queen of the Apostle, and Passionist Nuns. A celibate young men's prayer group—Pier Giorgio Frassati Bible study and faith sharing—where we end by praying the rosary, have supported me with their prayers and Roman Catholic zeal.

I wish to thank my family for their encouraging and supportive presence in my life—brothers, sisters, nephews, nieces, aunts, uncles, and cousins. I always remain grateful to my Dominican community in Vancouver for being a spiritual pillar for me, their joyful presence, their apostolic energy, and their commitment to the Gospel of Christ; they are a source of inspiration. Finally, I am grateful to the many faithful Catholics, family, and friends, who have kept me in their rosary prayers.

Introduction

This work on the rosary and the Bible is divided according to the twenty mysteries of the rosary. The title of these mysteries direct the faithful to the biblical theme or biblical inspiration for the meditation. The fruit of the mysteries are also included with a practical angle: virtue-building. Prayer is fundamentally about spiritual growth which means to grow in virtue. This makes prayer concrete—connected to the reality of our lives and the world we live in.

Christian Armor presents the twenty mysteries in chronological order, beginning with the Virgin Mary in whom the Son of God is enfleshed, then the life of Jesus, the promised Savior; the ministry and passion of Jesus; and the eternal life we can hope for as faithful disciples of Jesus, Son of God.

The five joyful mysteries include: the Annunciation, Visitation, Nativity of Our Lord, Presentation, Finding in the Temple. The Five Luminous Mysteries: Baptism of Our Lord, Wedding at Cana, Preaching of the Kingdom, the Transfiguration, the Eucharist which contain the mysteries associated with the ministry of Jesus introduced by his baptism. The five sorrowful mysteries that mark the passion of Jesus follow chronologically: Agony, Flagellation, Crowning with Thorns, Carrying the Cross, Crucifixion. Meditation on the five sorrowful mysteries will also extend to the Way of the Cross. The five glorious mysteries—Resurrection, Ascension, Descent of the Holy Spirit, Assumption of Mary, Coronation of Mary—represent the fulfillment of Christ's promise to those who remain faithful to his teachings and persevere to the end.

The Scripture passages used for each of the mysteries provide the biblical focus and reflection for each of the mysteries drawing from both Old Testament and New Testament events. The Holy Spirit as the source of both the Sacred Scriptures and Church Tradition opens us to God's revelation with prayer that sustains our communication with God. References are made to the *Catechism of the Catholic Church* on doctrinal or moral issues to shed further light on the biblical text. Selected references are made to the Dominican preacher St. Thomas Aquinas; the angelic doctor has proven to be a sound reference for Christian orthodoxy throughout the centuries.

Scripture Abreviations

OT

Genesis	Gen
Exodus	Exod
Leviticus	Lev
Numbers	Num
Deuteronomy	Deut
Joshua	Josh
Judges	Judg
Ruth	Ruth
1 Samuel	1 Sam
2 Samuel	2 Sam
1 Kings	1 Kgs
2 Kings	2 Kgs
1 Chronicles	1 Chr
2 Chronicles	2 Chr
Ezra	Ezra
Nehemiah	Neh
Tobit	Tob
Judith	Jdt
Esther	Esth
1–2 Maccabees	1–2 Macc
Job	Job
Psalms	Ps (Pss)
Proverbs	Prov
Ecclesiastes (or Qoheleth)	Eccl (or Qoh)
Song of Solomon	Song
Wisdom	Wis
Sirach	Sir
Isaiah	Isa
Jeremiah	Jer
Lamentations	Lam
Baruch	Bar
Ezekiel	Ezek
Daniel	Dan
Hosea	Hos
Joel	Joel
Amos	Amos
Obadiah	Obad
Jonah	Jon
Micah	Mic
Nahum	Nah
Habakkuk	Hab
Zephaniah	Zeph
Haggai	Hag
Zechariah	Zech
Malachi	Mal

NT

Matthew	Matt	2 Thessalonians	2 Thess
Mark	Mark	1 Timothy	1 Tim
Luke	Luke	2 Timothy	2 Tim
John	John	Titus	Titus
Acts	Acts	Philemon	Phlm
Romans	Rom	Hebrews	Heb
1 Corinthians	1 Cor	James	Jas
2 Corinthians	2 Cor	1 Peter	1 Pet
Galatians	Gal	2 Peter	2 Pet
Ephesians	Eph	1 John	1 John
Philippians	Phil	2 John	2 John
Colossians	Col	3 John	3 John
1 Thessalonians	1 Thess	Jude	Jude
		Revelation	Rev

Joyful Mysteries

First Joyful Mystery—Annunciation

I—And he came to her and said, "Hail, full of grace, the Lord is with you!" (Luke 1:28)

Our Father . . . Hail Mary . . . Glory Be . . .

1. Nazareth

As we approach the crypt, pilgrims remain kneeling in meditative silence, candles and prayer unchanged for centuries. The pilgrims are moved by the presence of the mother of God. The sense of a mantle enveloping each pilgrim with Mary's love and protection covers the sacred space. The solemn mass filled the basilica with devoted voices—the pilgrim's desire to remain kneeling in thanksgiving for God's love, for Mary his chosen daughter. And to reflect on the most radical event in history: the "here" of the incarnation. This dwelling—the crypt where the angel Gabriel appeared to Mary—transmits the silence of Mary, and the awesomeness of her consent.

At her home in Nazareth, God privileged this young woman to be the mother of his Son in this sacred space. This encounter between the human and the divine through the message of an angel realizes the act of conception by the power of the Holy Spirit upon Mary; she conceives the Second Person of the Trinity in her flesh—in her womb.

The earliest pilgrim whose records date from the fourth century, Egeria, mentions a "big and splendid cave in which she lived" in reference to Mary while on her journey to Nazareth.[1] The remains of a crusader church are evident above the cave. Nazareth became inaccessible to Christians after 1187 with the Battle of Hattin and the collapse of the Latin Crusader

---

1. Egeria, *Egeria's Travels*, 96. Egeria may have been a nun from Spain. Her identity remains uncertain, but she left a valuable account of her descriptions of the places she visited in the Holy Land.

Kingdom of Jerusalem. In the early seventeenth century, the Franciscans obtained the church property and what remained of the church, thereby re-establishing the Christian presence. The present Church of the Annunciation in Nazareth was dedicated in 1969.

The visible Byzantine remains in the Basilica floor date to the mid-fifth century and contrasts with the crusader church floor with the cave to the left standing from the entrance. The *chaire Maria*—words of the angel Gabriel—inscribed over the symbolic seven steps descending to Mary's grotto suggests a baptistry of the pre-Constantinian period. The cave itself where we knelt to pray in this most sublime location holds an altar with the words, *And the Word—HERE—was made flesh.* Certainly, holy ground where one can only kneel to contemplate the encounter between Mary, the message of the angel, and "the Word Became Flesh." The floral architecture symbolizes the Virgin Mary.[2] To be united with Mary means to be united with Jesus.

2. Mary: Chosen by God

The angel Gabriel, a messenger of God, was sent to Nazareth, a city in Galilee. This is not the first time we hear of an angel performing an act that serves to deliver a message of God's divine presence—to secure the forces of goodness—a divine service, a watchful intercessor.

In the Book of Tobit, Raphael plays an active role as a messenger sent by God to intervene in the lives of Tobias and Sarah by guiding, leading, and intervening in both their lives. Tobias loves Sarah as his "sister" and future wife (Tob 5–8). In the book of the prophet Daniel, Michael is presented as the "defender" of God's faithful (Dan 12:1), and in Revelation, Michael is actively engaged in battling the "dragon"; the archangel Michael protects the combat against diabolical forces (Rev 12:7).[3]

Now the angel Gabriel appears to a woman chosen by God residing in the town of Nazareth from the house of David. The child she is being asked to conceive by the Holy Spirit is the "Son of the Most High" (Luke 1:32). The woman will give birth to a child whom she will name "Jesus."

---

2. It was the first time I celebrated mass in the upper church, June 19, 2019, and brought back memories of my first visit to the Holy Land first with my father, then with my mother, while discerning my vocation.

3. Saint Thomas Aquinas points out that angels are immaterial beings between God and man in the hierarchy of being: spiritual beings that are created so close to God, but created beings making them similar to man. Aquinas, *Summa Theologiae*, Pt. 1, qq. 50-64 for details. [Henceforth: *Summa Theologiae—ST*, Part (Pt), question (q), article (art), reply (rep).]

This child will sit on the throne of David, and the kingdom of Jesus "will have no end"—his kingdom is eternal.

In Genesis, the fallen angel, Satan, appeared as a serpent cunningly turning the first woman, Eve, and the man, Adam, against God (Gen 3). But now we find this loyal angel appearing to the woman, Mary, so she might act upon God's plan for human salvation, and the angel Gabriel waits for Mary's consent.

God has a plan to save humanity: first, to destroy the work of the enemy, the devil, and second, to bring eternal life to his human creation. This young virgin, chosen in the hill country of Nazareth, not far from the Sea of Galilee and the town of Cana, is the woman for whom humanity has been waiting for centuries—Mary's "yes."

The Virgin Mary, the angel Gabriel, and the Holy Spirit form a spiritual hierarchy, bringing Jesus, the Second Person of the Trinity, into the world. Each act according to their power: Mary's human, Gabriel's angelic, and the Holy Spirit's divine. The angel transmits, Mary consents, and the Holy Spirit acts. Mary is at the center of this triptych.

Mary's human freedom is never jeopardized but respected: to accept this divine mission, a mission that will be a battle between the forces of good and evil, that is, between Jesus and Satan, so that man can enter into God's eternal kingdom. Mary, at the bottom of the hierarchy, is now raised above the angels: Mary enfleshes the Son of God.

3. Eve: First Woman

In God's plan for our salvation, the role of the woman to crush Satan's head is already foretold in what is referred to as the *Proto-Evangelium*: "I will put enmity between you and the woman, / and between your offspring and hers; / he will strike your head, / and you will strike his heel" (Gen 3:15).

The first man and woman brought sin into the world—original sin, deadly sin, transmitted to each of us when we were conceived—a sin only conquerable by God's power, God's intervention, God's cleansing which is accomplished by Christ on the cross. Through the sacrament of baptism God's human creation is reconciled with God by the faith of the parents or personal faith.

The first woman allowed herself to be tempted by the serpent and was seduced by Satan's cunning, twisting language to the point of the woman rethinking God's words, doubting God, believing the devil was telling the truth, and drawn by the promise of god-like power: "You will not die; for

God knows that when you eat of it your eyes will be opened, and you will be like God, knowing good and evil" (Gen 3:4–5).

The man simply went along with the woman rather naively without offering any resistance or guardianship as a man should; this is his fundamental role since creation: to guard, to protect, to assert his authority. Given what the man knew of the prohibition (Gen 2:16), the man's responsibility was to intervene against the serpent who contradicted God. The man failed as guardian, his priestly role as the first created man, and protector, the kingly role entrusted to him.

The fall occurs soon after the woman examines the tree: "So when the woman saw that the tree was good for food, and that it was a delight to the eyes, and that the tree was to be desired to make one wise . . ." (Gen 3:6). The fruit satisfies instincts, senses, and intelligence, all three created by God to give thanks to God, but all three powers of the soul can be distorted to turn us away from God. These three goods potentially manifest themselves as sins: bodily lust, sensory lust, and pride. The triple-concupiscence is repeated in the First Letter of John: "for all that is in the world—the desire of the flesh, the desire of the eyes, the pride in riches—comes not from the Father but the world" (1 John 2:16).[4]

God inflicts punishment upon all three involved: the serpent who turned the woman and the man against God, the man who failed his guardian/priestly role, and the woman who allowed herself to be entertained by the seductive suggestions of the serpent. In the case of the serpent, God says, "he will bruise your head," referring to "his" heel; indirectly the woman crushes Satan by her heel, her offspring, Jesus. So, the head of Satan is crushed. We have in the *Proto-Evangelium* the new Eve and the new Adam, Mary and Jesus. The woman whom God addresses in terms of "your offspring" is also translated as "your seed." But "seed" identifies a male. In the case of the woman whom God addresses, there is no seed and there will be no seed; the woman's offspring is born by the Holy Spirit and not the seed of a man.

4. Mary: The New Eve

So, what is Mary's role? She is chosen to be mother of the "Son of the Most High," the one who will be "holy," and whom she will call Jesus for his kingdom will be without end. Mary is chosen out of all women for this role in divine motherhood; from the beginning of time, in God's divine plan, Mary

---

4. *Revised Standard Version* Catholic Edition translates "desire" as "lust" which is more consistent with the moral statement that John is making in his First Letter.

was prepared for the incarnation, the Second Person of the Trinity enfleshed in her womb. One thing was needed: Mary's consent.

The grave sin that has inflicted the world, transmitted from one generation to the next, could only be destroyed by the power of God himself coming into the world born of a pure woman, prepared to receive God in her flesh. Mary is chosen to bring the Son of God, the Savior of humanity into the world. Only divine intervention, the Second Person of the Trinity, can destroy the work of Satan.

To be saved by the Son of God who enters into the world necessitates that the Savior is born of human flesh—the flesh of a woman chosen by God—the Son of God—a divine person, co-eternal with the Godhead, one same divine substance.[5]

God knew when the time had come to bring his Son into the world. In his divine plan, God could have chosen the besieging of Jerusalem during the Assyrian Empire of the early eight century BC, or after the destruction of Jerusalem during the Babylonian invasion in the late sixth century BC, or after the capture of Jerusalem under Greek domination in the mid-third century BC. Instead, God waited and saw the time was fitting during the Roman Empire, when Judea formed a Roman province and was clearly separated from Samaria in the north—a history of division between the south and the north: the divided house of Jacob.

Judah is the house to which God made his promise; in the words of Jacob, his fourth-born son, "The scepter shall not depart from Judah, nor the ruler's staff from between his feet, until tribute comes to him; and the obedience of the peoples is his" (Gen 49:10). Jacob explained to his first three sons why the three sons dishonored him and so did not receive their father's blessing: Reuben had committed incest (Gen 35:22); Simeon and Levi carried out a wicked plan against the Shechemites making Jacob "odious" to the inhabitants (Gen 34:25–26). This leaves Jacob with his fourth-born son, Judah, who receives praise and exercises power.

This predilection of Judah, while strange because Judah is not the first born of Jacob but the fourth-born, is understood on the basis of the sins of Reuben, Simeon, and Levi, the first three of the twelve sons and twelve tribes

---

5. The solemnity of the Annunciation, March 25, is inseparable from the solemnity of the Immaculate Conception, December 8, and nine months from the Nativity of Mary, September 8. Why is the Advent solemnity of the Immaculate Conception inseparable from the birth of Jesus Christ? After all, the immaculate conception of Mary is about Mary's conception, not that of Jesus. Mary's conception is fittingly celebrated December 8 during the season of Advent in preparation for the birth of the Messiah, just as Mary herself had been prepared by God.

of Israel. In fact, Simeon will "disappear" as a tribe, absorbed into Judah, and Levi will not possess any land as he will become the priestly tribe.

When David the Bethlehemite is chosen by God after Jesse presents his seven sons to Samuel, the last-born, the eighth, is anointed king. The house of Judah and the throne of David (1 Sam 16:1–13) fulfil Jacob's prophetic blessings.

Mary is betrothed to a man, Joseph of the house of David (Matt 1:16), and Mary herself is of the house of David (Luke 1:27). God sent the angel Gabriel to a woman who is both betrothed to a man of the house of David, Jesus's spiritual father, and a woman from the house of David, from whom the Son of God will physically be born. Thus, the Davidic ancestry of Jesus is conveyed in both genealogies, Matthew's and Luke's.

The parents of Mary, Saint Joachim and Saint Anne, conceived Mary through a natural conjugal union. However, in their union a supernatural event had occurred that could only be understood and explained through Divine intervention: the Virgin Mary was conceived without the stain of original sin. Mary's soul was created united to the material flesh in Saint Anne's womb, unlike the "unnatural" fallen state because this was not how God originally created the man and woman. Mary is without sin just as God's original creation of man and woman were without sin. Mary received this particular grace for one reason: to bring the Son of God into the world. In other words, Mary's privilege is directed to an end: the birth of the Messiah, Son of the Most High: "Greetings, favored one! The Lord is with you" (Luke 1:28).[6] The sense of "Rejoice, you who enjoy God's favor," from the Greek, *kekaritomene*, literally, "full of grace" can be translated as, "Hail, full of grace, the Lord is with you!" The meaning behind this translation is that the Greek conveys Mary has already been "graced" and continues, in the present perfect in English, "you have been graced"; this suggests, "Rejoice, you who have been graced . . ." With an exceptional greeting of this kind, being "favored" as other translations give, Mary has been prepared for this divine motherhood enfleshing the Second Person of the Trinity; the fitting greeting is "most exalted one."[7]

We are all born with original sin. This is true since the fall. Original sin goes back to the first man and the first woman, Adam and Eve, who disobeyed God's command; they could eat from all the fruit in the Garden

---

6. *New Revised Standard Version* Catholic Edition has replaced "hail" used in the prayer to the Virgin Mary with "greetings"; and the significant "highly favored one" is weakened to, "favored one." The new translation (NRSVCE) seems to lose the spiritual richness of the earlier translation (RSVCE) in an attempt to "modernize" the English.

7. See, Hahn and Mitch, *New Testament*, 105, note 1:28 on "Hail."

with the one exception: from the fruit of the tree of knowledge they were prohibited (Gen 2:15-17).

Tempted by Satan, camouflaged as a serpent, both the man and the woman succumbed to Satan, listening to Satan's seducing words, who superbly confused the woman through language. The serpent was a master of rhetoric, skillfully playing with the woman's words who repeated the prohibition; so, the serpent rephrased God's command to distort God's goodness and God's intentions. The serpent successfully led the woman to doubt, then lose trust in God, and instead, to believe the words of the serpent, Satan, the great deceiver (Gen 3:1–5). From communion with God built on truth, the serpent leads to a rupture in that communion by creating mistrust between the human creation and God the Creator. By the end of the exchange the paradox is manifest: the God who creates a good world is suspected of being deceptive, and Satan, the deceitful creature, is trusted for his promise. The power of language, the skill of deceit.

This scene where the exchange occurs is disturbing because it shows how language can be manipulated in such a way that truth becomes falsehood and falsehood becomes truth. This is clearly the power of the devil to subvert our minds and thoughts so what is good appears as evil and what is evil appears as good.

This first sin which has been transmitted to generation after generation, a sin reflecting the very nature of the woundedness of humans, a wound so serious and so deep, an "ontological wound" that it can only be healed by the power of God—and God heals through his Son, Jesus Christ.[8]

The Virgin Mary was free from this stain of original sin. God intervened and protected Mary in a privileged way so that she did not experience original sin or its effects. Yet, Mary remained free to choose, just as the first woman, Eve, was free to choose to listen to God or to listen to the devil. And because one of the effects of sin is "death," Mary did not undergo the corruption of death which is due to sin as we shall see in the fourth glorious mystery.

Mary, to whom the angel Gabriel appeared, informed her that she had found favor with God, the woman whom God preserved from original sin, the woman born of the house of David, the woman betrothed to a man named Joseph, also from the house of David. Mary had been favored by God, past, present, and future.

Mary was free just as Eve was free; Eve, the woman to bring sin into the world by listening to the warped words of Satan. Mary remained free to listen to unchanging truth of God's words, the Word Mary enfleshed in

---

8. See, *Catechism*, #402–#404.

her blessed womb. Yes, Mary was free. She was free to reverse the disobedience of the first woman by saying "yes" to God, by obedience to God, by submitting herself to the promise of God, unlike the first woman who submitted herself to the promise of the devil.

The work of disobedience of the first woman, *Eva*, has been undone by the perfect obedience of another woman, whom we now invoke: *Ave! Ave Maria, gratia plena*—"Hail Mary full of grace"—in our Marian prayers and hymns. We "rejoice" as the angel tells Mary, "Rejoice!" because she has been favored, chosen by God, to bring his divine Son into the world. Mary's divine mission leads to our salvation by the Son she bears, echoing the words of God in Genesis, alluding to the woman's offspring, "he shall bruise your head . . ." addressing the serpent.

With the biblical details above, especially the comparison between the first woman, Eve, and Mary, the New Eve, people are inclined to think that if Mary was chosen by God, if she was born immaculate, without sin, then, *of course*, she said "yes" to God's plan. Did she really have any choice in the matter? Scriptures shows that Mary was free to accept or refuse God's plan.

This "yes" that follows the angel Gabriel's announcement Mary expresses in words of great trust in God's providence: Mary's faith, "let it be to me according to your word" (Luke 1:38), words expressing Mary's freedom to cooperate—or not—with God's plan, announced by the angel's message. And so, in Mary the act of conception of our Savior, the Son of the Most High, takes place at the instant of Mary's *fiat*, "let it be *done*."

God has a plan, but his will is not imposed; otherwise, one cannot freely say "yes" to truth and express "yes" to love—to love presupposes the freedom to choose, to exercise the intelligence and choose the truth presented to us.

For this reason, Eve and Mary are contrasted: both women are without sin, one at creation, the other through conception, both are free, and both choose radically opposed ends: the woman Eve desires divinity for herself, the new Eve, Mary, desires to serve the divine and offers herself.

Eve consents to Satan, introducing the sin of pride, and Mary humbly consents to the work of the Holy Spirit, and enfleshes the Son of God. Mary reverses the act of the first woman. Eve disobeyed God, believing she and the man God created could be the gods Satan promised. Only Jesus can destroy the power of Satan, crush his head, and the Son of God came into the world for this very purpose: to destroy the devil, his works, and so to liberate us.

5. Mary's Humility

In this first joyful mystery we see the commencement of the fulfillment of the prophet Isaiah in the conceiving act of our salvation. God's plan with Mary's "consent": the plan to save humanity. The fundamental moral act in this first mystery serves to combat Eve's pride which Mary's Son, the Son of God, will achieve on the cross by destroying the very one who transmitted pride into the world: Satan. Mary herself, while still carrying Jesus in her womb, upon meeting her cousin Elizabeth, conveys the sense of "humility" to identify Mary's relationship with God, "for he has regarded the low estate of his handmaiden" (Luke 1:48) in the second joyful mystery, and Jesus himself teaches us by the words, "Take my yoke upon you, and learn from me; for I am gentle and lowly in heart . . ." (Matt 11:29). Christ's teachings emphasized the value of humility. Man's spiritual well-being, which is to aim towards heavenly and spiritual goods, is obstructed when striving to fulfil worldly ambitions and sensorial gratification.[9]

The difference between Mary and Eve is that Mary was not seduced by the world expressed in her virginity; Mary is pure in that she was not contaminated by the world in any sense. As a rational human creature, Mary collaborates with God's plan of redemption through her free will. Mary exercises her freedom choosing the path of humility and her choices, in response to God's call, lead to the crushing of Satan through her divine Son.

Mary's desire to unite herself to the will of God is reflected in her one question, how this conception can occur when she is a virgin and she has "no husband" (Luke 1:34-35). The angel Gabriel informs Mary that "the power of the Most High, will overshadow you." Mary's cooperation is fundamental in this plan of salvation relying on her "yes," yet, shrouded in mystery while the world waits for Mary to say "yes" to God.

Clearly, Mary is overwhelmed but also overjoyed with this news as she knows how God continued to keep his covenantal promise with Abraham, Isaac, Jacob, the house of Judah, David the Bethlehemite and king, the prophets pointing to the Messiah being born of a virgin. Isaiah's prophesy of Jesus's birth points to Mary, "and a virgin shall give birth to a son" (Isa 7:14).[10] The time arrived for the woman to collaborate with God and his promise in a definitive manner.

---

9. Aquinas, *ST*, Pt. 2a-2ae, q. 161, a. 5, rep. 3-4.

10. *New Revised Standard Version* Catholic Edition gives "young woman." The Septuagint Greek translates the Hebrew *alma* as *parthenos*, "virgin." On the subject of "virgin," see Bergsma and Pitre, *Old Testament* (Isa 7:14), 755-56.

II—Fruit of this Mystery: Virtue of Humility

Practical Matters—
1. Humility: Path to Sanctity

Mary unites herself to God's will in an act of humility. This perfect humility teaches us to unite ourselves to God's plan for us which is to be holy (1 Thess 4:3) so we can be in communion with him, participate in divine life on our pilgrim journey towards God's heavenly kingdom, and share in eternal life.

The humility of Mary brings the Word of God into our world; Mary's act of humility anticipates and prepares us for the sublime act of humility, God who enters into the world in human flesh. Jesus, the new Adam, destroys Satan and his power.

We have the example of countless saints that witnessed the truth of humility modelling themselves after the humility of Mary, Joseph, and Jesus, receiving their strength from Christ crucified and the grace he gives us in his body and blood and the sacraments. All the saints who left behind families of wealth and power; saints who suffered as spouses or parents; saints who were executed by emperors and monarchs because of their Catholic faith; saints who persevered through difficult religious communities, the demands of their bishops, religious superiors, and even popes; saints who were tortured to death by pagans and even fellow Christians—all reflect humility.

2. Pride: Way to Death

Why does pride have such power, a grip on man that at times pride seems unshakable? We can look at the music and film industry where the "idols" are worshiped in a way that they eclipse the transcendent God. The world bows and turns into a state of frenzy by the very sight of these stars on earth who do not lead to God or truth or holiness or self-giving love. Pride motivates sexual perversion, power, and greed. When people read the events surrounding the golden calf in Exodus, the story is treated like a distant biblical event where people worshiped golden calves associated with the god Apis. And yet, the state of hysteria caused by rock music and movie idols are reminiscent of the words of Exodus, "and rose up to revel" (Exod 32:6).[11] This is the work of lust, a devilish offspring of pride. God told the serpent its offspring will be enemies of the offspring of the

---

11. Also, "rose up to amuse themselves," *Revised New Jerusalem Bible* Study Edition.

woman. The Son of God, the offspring of the woman, came to destroy Satan and his offspring: pride, lust, greed.

We know in the history of Israel, followed by Judah, pride is the sin God severely punished. Pride shows up by turning away from the true God of Israel and fornicating with false Canaanite gods. People choose gods that please them, gods that seduce, gods that serve human needs. God's wrath is especially evident in Exodus—after the worship of the golden calf—with the slaughter of three thousand Israelites (Exod 32:28). The cycles of infidelity and punishment are attributed to the fall of Israel in the north and later Judah in the south, chronologically evident in the Second Book of Kings.

Turning away from the true God, betraying God by turning to other gods with whom one fornicates like an adulterous spouse, dramatically and painfully described by the prophet Hosea, results in punishment (Hos 1:2). God corrects his people so they understand the value of fidelity, and this means overcoming pride, believing they can go elsewhere to find another, "better god" that suits their whims, to satisfy their capricious needs.

In the New Testament Judas is associated with greed because he hands Jesus over to the soldiers of the Jewish authorities (John 18:3). Jesus was not the Messiah that Judas had expected, the political liberator who would restore the earthly Israel. So, did Judas have any "use" for Jesus? What good was Jesus if he could not be the military king, the messianic king anticipated from the house of David? A king without soldiers, men unarmed, a Gospel of truth and love that offered neither power nor glory, could Jesus respond to the aspirations of Judas? It seemed better to make some money off him by delivering Jesus to the soldiers. The act of Judas was motivated out of pride that turned to greed.

Pride has affected every aspect of our lives, family strife over "possessions and ownership," work settings over salaries and promotions, and even within religious/pastoral settings over authority and status.

In Catholicism we have the benefit of the authority of our local bishop or religious superior to whom a Catholic submits himself to overcome pride. Obedience is the pledge/promise/vow that serves to shatter pride. This explains why obedience is at times painfully difficult. Yet, spiritually, obedience purifies us of pride because God's grace helps us overcome the effects of sin introduced into our lives by the first man and woman: the sin of pride.

Christians are called to witness truth and love that fosters unity, but instead, Christianity shows the sinful reality of division. We witness religious fragmentation that is hardly the work of the Holy Spirit. This is due to pride. In a Scripture class, one of my students who belonged to the Quaker denomination asked me, "So what accounts for all this division in Christianity? All these denominations?" I asked him, "What do you think?" He sat silently as the other students listened. He replied, "Pride."

This is why Catholicism strives for church unity; division is not the work of the Spirit. Paul teaches us we have "One Faith, One Baptism, One Lord" (Eph 4:5). We know the value of oneness from the biblical teaching on marriage (Gen 1:28; 2:24); we know the conjugal imagery and language expressed throughout the Old Testament and fulfilled in the New Testament by Jesus himself and the church as his bride (Eph 5:23).

The refusal to submit to ecclesial authority on doctrinal and moral issues suggests the sin of pride. Humans resist authority. We promote and reward independence so one has no need for God. Protests against magisterial teaching, whatever causes to doubt divine authority, relativizing the Word of God to create a subjective morality, and the rejection of natural law which has its source in God. These sinful human defects lead us back to original sin. We make ourselves into the divine authority. For this reason Saint Thomas Aquinas considers pride as the most "serious" of all sins.[12]

The first joyful mystery meditating on the annunciation serves to help us grow in humility. Humility strengthens us to combat pride. We can see how pride entered the world where the first man and woman listen to Satan and are tempted with Satan's deceiving words to "become like gods."

Rather than serving God and worshiping God, they succumb to the temptation of becoming like gods themselves, where they neither serve nor worship God in humility but now have complete control over their own lives and their own destiny, as if they were gods of their lives, and this is pride.

With pride, disobedience, and division we are far from the trusting humility of the Virgin Mary at the annunciation, and the radical humility of Jesus on the cross. We have turned the Word of God into language that suits us, that fits our sinful nature. Listening to the divine Word means we are converted by the teachings of Jesus and transformed by grace, his body and blood offered on the cross.

The road to sanctity is concretely lived; Jesus has already done the work for us but we need to respond not only with our lips but by our lives (Matt 7:21). We should desire to ask for the grace so that God can work in us his Spirit of truth and love, so we may be purified of our pride that distorts our lives and our relationships.

Could we be so taken in by the subtle lies and distortions we hear, like the woman and the man in the presence of the serpent, that we no longer

---

12. Aquinas, *ST*, Pt. 2a-2ae, q. 62, art. 6, rep. In turn, ecclesial authorities are expected to be coherent in their teachings, drawing from Tradition, Scriptures, and Natural Law which participates in the Eternal Law of God.

recognize our pride? If God's human creation could not see their pride—if we do not—that is equivalent to saying we do not see our sins. How can we avoid sin if we do not realize we are sinning? But the man and woman clearly knew the prohibition; the woman repeated to the serpent the words of God. We also know what God asks of us in order be in communion with him; he gave us the church and the sacred Scriptures for this purpose. God also gave us our human nature—natural law—found within the human being and helps us discern right from wrong (Rom 2:14). So, God helps us by the very nature of our intelligence; and then, the supernatural grace we receive through Christ's sacrifice on the cross and the sacraments of the church. We do know what pride looks like. And we do know the holiness we are called to live; humility is the path to sanctity.

Second Joyful Mystery—Visitation

I—*In those days Mary set out and went with haste to a Judean town in the hill country, where she entered the house of Zechariah and greeted Elizabeth.* (Luke 1:39-40)

Our Father . . . Hail Mary . . . Glory Be . . .

1. Ein Karem—"fountain of the vineyard"

After Mary conceived by the Holy Spirit as the Scriptures reveal to us in the first joyful mystery, Luke's Gospel informs us that Mary goes to visit her cousin Elizabeth. The angel also announced that Elizabeth, who "was said to be barren," also conceived and was now in her sixth month (Luke 1:36).

Mary departs from Nazareth across the Judean hill country to the village of her cousin Elizabeth, Ein Karem, about ninety miles.[1] A journey to Ein Karem displays beautiful hills stretching from Galilee to Judea. Mary carried in her womb the divine presence of her baby, this supernatural gift, the Son of God. And with anticipation, Mary journeys to share her joy and thanksgiving with her cousin. Mary visited Elizabeth because she desired to spend time with her older cousin, to be present to her, and to attend to Elizabeth's needs.

Could Mary have travelled about ninety miles without her husband, Joseph, across these hills? With Mary carrying the child of God within her womb, and Joseph knowing the responsibility entrusted to him to protect his wife and his spiritual child conceived by the Holy Spirit, most certainly Joseph accompanied Mary.[2]

---

1. 144 kilometers.

2. Even though Luke does not make reference to Joseph on this journey, we can be certain that as a faithful husband and loving spiritual father, Joseph remained close to Mary, travelling with her to Ein Karem from Galilee into Judea.

The journey to Ein Karem echoes another biblical event when the Word of God was being transported. David, King of Judah, in his religious fervor acted as a priest as he brought the ark of the covenant to Jerusalem (2 Sam 6:12). In Mary is preserved God's divine Word, his Son; in the ark of the covenant was kept the Decalogue, God's revealed Word. Judea is God's plan for both the ark of the covenant and the Word made flesh. In Jerusalem the covenant preserves the Law, and the Word made flesh leads to eternal life. The procession of the ark of the covenant is a solemn religious event where "David and all the house of Israel were dancing before the LORD with all their might" (2 Sam 6:5). The encounter between Elizabeth and Mary is a profound personal and religious event, as Elizabeth states, "For as soon as I heard the sound of your greeting, the child in my womb leaped for joy" (Luke 1:44). With Joseph, husband of Mary, following behind, and with Mary, the ark of the covenant, moving ahead, with the angels, we unite ourselves in this Corpus Christi "procession."

The mosaic on the facade next to the belltower of the Church of the Visitation depicts the second joyful mystery of the rosary: Mary on her journey into the Judean hill country to visit her cousin Elizabeth.[3]

2. Mary and Elizabeth

Besides the joy of the two cousins who are going to have babies, and the charity that motivates Mary, what else could lead Mary to travel to Ein Karem to visit her cousin? No doubt the news that her cousin who was unable to conceive and well-beyond child-bearing age announced by the angel, the same angel Gabriel who announced Mary's call to divine motherhood: the supernatural nature of their pregnancies. The angel proclaims in Luke's Gospel, "for nothing will be impossible with God" (Luke 1:37). Mary's conception of Jesus follows after the news of her cousin's miraculous pregnancy. The Scriptures tell us that immediately after Mary's consent to God's divine plan, Mary leaves to visit her cousin Elizabeth. We clearly grasp from the Scriptures Mary's charity, her faith in God. Mary shares in people's joys and sufferings. Mary offers her presence.

Mary's journey to visit her cousin is not conveyed with fear or apprehension. We sense she travels with enthusiasm anticipating her thanksgiving

---

[3]. One of the mosaics in the church looked familiar. Sitting in front of the mosaic, reflecting, I then remembered my mother. Before I became a priest, she had bought a postcard of the mosaic of the main chapel where Mary is honored by saints just as Elizabeth had honored her. The textures of Mary's pinkish robe and her blue mantle stood out in the postcard, prominently featured in the chapel's mosaic.

with Elizabeth for God's wonders, truly an amazing God. On her journey, Mary contemplates the greatness and goodness of God. Mary's journey across the Judean hill countryside with Jesus in her womb and Joseph watching, motivated by charity, is a solemn procession of thanksgiving.

We recognize in Mary a woman of faith whose exceptional courage testifies to her cooperative role in redemption, further conveyed in the encounter with her cousin Elizabeth. Mary did not remain at home knowing her own condition and the child whom she enfleshed in her womb required her total attention. Mary could have allowed the message she received about her divine motherhood, and her physical condition of being with child, to justify remaining in Nazareth. But Mary is not focused on herself; an act of charity is about the other, and Mary's thoughts are directed towards her cousin Elizabeth and the baby Elizabeth is miraculously carrying. While Mary experienced supernatural intervention in her own life, this does not eclipse the value of her cousin's personal and spiritual journey. Mary, instead, joyfully exercises charity in this visit to her cousin in Ein Karem.

Within the first forty lines of Luke's Gospel, we identify Mary as a woman of courage, of faith, of charity. God motivates Mary's actions; she finds her guiding strength in God. These virtues are reflected in Mary's profound religious disposition towards God to whom she responds with complete trust.

3. Baptizer and Savior in their Wombs

Visiting Ein Karem, one will notice another church in the town named after John the Baptist. The church preserves the memory of John's birthplace and the Benedictus (Luke 1:68–79), the hymn of Zechariah inspired by the events surrounding John's birth.[4]

The encounter between Mary and Elizabeth is sufficient to cause the baby in Elizabeth's womb to leap with joy. Two mothers entrust themselves to God. One mother carries within her womb the voice of repentance and conversion, and the other mother brings forth the Son whose body and blood save humanity. And for the baby Jesus the voice of his mother is the sweetness of her presence. Mary will remain with Jesus to his death on the cross.

For Mary knows the baby within her womb, Son of God, is the presence of her Savior. Her Savior preserved Mary from original sin in anticipation of the redemptive nature of the cross that her Son will carry, the cross he will be

---

4. In the Roman breviary, the Benedictus from the Gospel of Luke is prayed at Lauds—Morning Prayer.

nailed to, and the cross he will die on. Mary's Savior, the Son of God, saved Mary in anticipation of Jesus's redemptive act, a singular privilege Mary received to conceive the Son of God in her womb.

The leap of the baby in Elizabeth's womb leads Elizabeth to acknowledge Mary: "Blessed are you among women, and blessed is the fruit of your womb" (Luke 1:42). Elizabeth's words sound familiar to us because they are the biblical words honoring Mary as Elizabeth greets her cousin. Echoing these opening verses in the formula of this Marian prayer are the words of the angel Gabriel who at the annunciation greets Mary, "Rejoice" or "Hail," the Latin *Ave*, as Luke continues with the angel's words, "highly favored" or "full of grace" and "the Lord is with you." The words found in the first stanza of the "Hail Mary," one recognizes in the greetings the angel and in this case, Elizabeth, as she honors Mary, "Blessed are you among women."

We pray the words of Elizabeth, and we repeat the words of Luke the Evangelist: "Blessed are you among women." When we read, probe, and meditate the Scriptures, we are bound to repeat the words, to repeat the words inspired by the Holy Spirit. These sublime words have meanings that pertain to our salvation; the words are meant to be repeated each day throughout our life. They are the words of the Third Person of the Trinity communicating to us God's plan of salvation—God's saving power. Through prophetic words, supernatural events, and holy people, ultimately, through the Word made flesh, his beloved Son—we are saved.

Mary is unique among women in the role she has, to bring the Son of God into the world, and this privilege is one that comes by divine intervention. Mary is blessed because God has chosen her, has prepared her, and Mary has favorably responded.

Immediately following Elizabeth's greeting, we can appreciate why Catholics address Mary as "blessed" and "blessed is the fruit of your womb"—namely, "Jesus." At the center of Mary's blessedness is Jesus. It is clearly a Christocentric greeting and understanding of who Mary is in God's divine plan for our salvation. Mary's role is inseparable from the salvific role of her Son, the Son of God. Mary does not represent an outside observer, an accidental feature to God's divine plan; her role is essential in that Mary gives birth to a divine Person; her flesh gives Jesus his human nature, the nature by which he suffers and dies for us. Elizabeth recognizes this divine presence and the salvific role of the child in Mary's womb and immediately points to Jesus, "blessed is the fruit of your womb." Even though Mary visits her cousin who is advanced in years, the focus is on the Christ-child. The presence of Jesus in Mary's womb becomes the central "act of worship" in the visitation.

The first stanza of what becomes integral to the *Ave Maria* prayer, and therefore the rosary, ends with Elizabeth's words directed towards Jesus; the focal point of the Marian prayer is Jesus himself, the Savior to whom Elizabeth points, the Savior whom Mary carries in her womb: Jesus.

Elizabeth grasped Mary's role in salvation, and it seemed natural to Elizabeth to honor Mary in this cooperative role initiated by Mary's consent to conceive Jesus, "Son of the Most High," and to be fulfilled by Mary's divine "Son on the cross." Elizabeth approaches her cousin with humility, the same humility with which Mary embarks upon a journey to visit her cousin. The humility expressed by these two women in their love, faith, and joy anticipates their maternal roles: for Elizabeth, mother of the prophet John the Baptist, and for Mary, mother of the Savior, Jesus Christ. The women pursue an extraordinary journey with their sons in their wombs; the sons of these women will transform the world. God has prepared these women with their disposition towards humility; the two women joyfully celebrate the sons they carry in their wombs and acknowledge their Savior. The visitation is indeed an encounter of "charity." Elizabeth brings John into the world, and Mary, her Son, Jesus; they will lead to the road of truth, to conversion and salvation, respectively.

4. Humility and Charity

The humble words of Elizabeth offer a lesson in humility to those who fail to recognize Mary's role in our redemption. Elizabeth asks, "And why has this happened to me, that the mother of my Lord comes to me?" (Luke 1:43). We often have difficulty acknowledging the value of others, appreciating their presence, respecting them, unless we know that we can directly benefit. Elizabeth and Mary are two women who say little in the Scriptures, but for the few words these women utter, they transmit rich and powerful theological realities. A probing heart seeking truth, in love with God, will read this exchange of love between cousins as the words that God himself wishes to communicate to us as he works through each person to bring about man's redemption. To embrace Mary as Elizabeth does, to acknowledge her as the "mother of my Lord," requires the humility and spiritual disposition of Elizabeth. "And why has this happened to me, that the mother of my Lord comes to me?" Elizabeth's "loud cry" makes it clear that she is overjoyed and humbled by Mary's visit and her presence (Luke 1:42).

The humility of the first joyful mystery continues into the charity of the second joyful mystery; humility makes charity possible. Humility is that which combats and overcomes pride. Charity is not possible if we are filled with ourselves. The kind of love that charity demands, to exercise charity, is to love in truth; love fails to be exercised when love is self-serving. In the wombs of Elizabeth and Mary, the mothers will teach their sons about humility and charity, as Zechariah and Joseph reflect the virtues of humility and charity in the lives of John and Jesus that their boys will learn and live.

To forget ourselves takes humility—to put the others before us produces charity. And so, Elizabeth can ask, "And why has this happened to me, that the mother of my Lord comes to me?"

Could we see John the Baptist speaking any differently to his cousin Jesus than Elizabeth speaking to Mary? In fact, the words of Elizabeth anticipate the words of her son John, who will say, "I am not worthy to untie the thong of his sandals" (Luke 3:16). This mystery of relations between cousins, John and Jesus, sons of these humble women, is taken up in the first luminous mystery, the baptism of Jesus. We find the practice of virtue between these mothers that will be transmitted to their sons. This will also be the case for Zachariah and Joseph and the virtues they transmit to John and Jesus, respectively.

The miraculous intervention in the case of the husbands reveals the roles played and to be played by the father, Zechariah, and spiritual father, Joseph; both men docile to the will of God with the difference that Zechariah shows apprehension—"How will I know that this is so?" (Luke 1:18)—while Joseph conveys complete trust, "When Joseph awoke from sleep, he did as the angel of the Lord commanded him . . ." (Matt 1:24). Mary's words resemble Zechariah's, but her words reflect her trust in God highlighting that she is a virgin and she does not have a husband; yet, Mary does not ask for any sign—she simply wants to understand, "How can this be?" (Luke 1:34).

"How will I know this . . . ?" For Zechariah, he and his wife are both advanced in age, and so he is looking for a sign from the angel Gabriel. Knowing means reassurance that the angel's words will come true. This is not the case for Mary. She states a fact of her innocence: "But how can this come about since I have no knowledge of man"? Mary does not look for a sign but states the reality of her virginal state. The promises of offspring are fulfilled in both instances, although Zechariah experiences a period of being silenced since he did not believe. Instead, the angel answers Mary's question asking how this will take place. With the angel Gabriel's explanation on how the divine conception will come about, Mary consents.

Mary manifests complete trust by her humility, which further manifests itself in her act of charity journeying to Ein Karem to visit her cousin. Humility is needed to exercise charity. Humility reciprocated by Elizabeth, acknowledging and addressing Mary as blessed, while Elizabeth receives the mother of her Lord.

Elizabeth does not end with Mary any more than the second mystery stops at Mary; we prayerfully follow Elizabeth's words which are given in the biblical context of the Marian prayer, "and blessed is the fruit of your womb" (Luke 1:42). The fruit of Mary's womb is "Jesus"; all those who know and pray the *Ave Maria,* "Hail Mary," recognize Jesus is the center of the prayer just as Elizabeth's proclamation is Christocentric.

5. Immaculate Conception

To make the erroneous claim that Mary eclipses her son, or replaces her son, as some Christian denominations claim, or that Mary is some kind of divine goddess, is largely due to the ignorance of the Scriptures and tradition.[5] Prayers honoring Mary evident in these biblical passages show that reverence for Mary is grounded in the Scriptures. Marian devotion reflects the humility of Elizabeth who acknowledges her cousin as the mother of her Lord, the blessedness of the "fruit" of Mary's womb.

Roman Catholics express their devotion to the Virgin Mary, their honor for Saint Elizabeth and Saint John the Baptist because they all point to Jesus, the Savior and Son of God. This reverence for those who point to the incarnation is solemnized through feasts, solemnities, and intercessory prayers.[6]

We meditate on the Scriptures in this second joyful mystery of the rosary with its clear biblical sources; our thoughts turn not only to the events that lead us to our Savior, Jesus, events related to his conception, but these biblical passages continue into our present day. We are called to exercise courage, humility, and charity as Mary and Joseph, Elizabeth and Zechariah, who prepare us for John and Jesus by their actions. They ultimately welcomed their Savior, Jesus, into their hearts and daily lives. The mission of preparation is specifically entrusted to John the Baptist as we find in the first luminous mystery of the rosary.

Biblical events filled with deep layers of the God-breathed Word, we are called to reflect upon, pray about, and exercise in our own lives. We cannot diminish or bracket the role played by the individuals whom God

---

5. In a Scripture class of mine, students were given an assignment on Mary's role in our salvation drawing from Luke's Gospel. One of my non-Catholic students wrote that, "unlike Catholics, Pentecostals do not believe Mary is divine." I asked the student to come and see me for further clarification. In response I explained what the Catholic Church teaches about Mary; "divinity" is not one of Mary's attributes. She was grateful for our discussion; and she rewrote her assignment in harmony with Luke's Gospel.

6. In the Roman Catholic calendar, the feast of the Visitation is celebrated on May 31.

chooses, and who cooperate with God's plan; we ourselves are called to respond to this plan of holiness through courage, humility, and charity, just as these biblical figures had done anticipating the incarnation of their savior. Preparation represents an ongoing acknowledgement of who Jesus is and accepting him as Lord of our lives, just as Jesus is the center of the prayer, "Hail Mary . . . blessed is the fruit of your womb," the reason why Elizabeth humbles herself, honored by Mary's visit, "And why has this happened to me, that the mother of my Lord comes to me?"

Elizabeth's words suggest that she knows what happened to Mary, "And blessed is she who believed that there would be a fulfillment of what was spoken to her by the Lord" (Luke 1:45). We might ask, "To what does this promise refer?" Elizabeth was aware of the promise made to Mary, the conception of Mary's divine Son, the old covenant promise has been fulfilled. Elizabeth receives Mary and addresses her in terms of the fulfillment; the promise signifies the entire history of the promise made to the people of Israel: the promise of the Messiah.

With these words Mary responds to her cousin with the Magnificat. In the opening lines of the Magnificat, Mary proclaims in her visit with Elizabeth that her spirit rejoices in, "God my Savior" (Luke 1:47). The reference to Jesus as Mary's Savior caused difficulty for medieval theologians and certainly for non-Catholics today who like to say, "Mary was just like any other woman . . ." But Catholics uphold that Mary was conceived without original sin. A non-Catholic student of mine went as far as saying, "Mary was a sinner like any other person."[7] Such a statement is quite shocking to Catholic ears that are very sensitive when false statements are made about our blessed mother. As mentioned earlier in this second mystery and the first joyful mystery, Mary was born immaculate—without original sin—but she also remained sinless throughout her life.[8]

While the biblical wording "God my Savior" expresses Mary's need of a Savior, indeed like any other human, this is not because Mary sinned or because she was born with original sin. Needing a Savior like all humans, yet, Mary is chosen to be the mother of God, so she is "preserved" in advance from the original sin transmitted to all of humanity since the time of the fall. Mary, in other words, was saved by the cross of Christ, preserved from original sin at her conception, in "anticipation" of Christ's sacrifice on

---

7. I informed the student based on Scriptures we have no evidence that Mary ever sinned. And based on logic, God would not permit a woman disposed towards sin to conceive his Son. Finally, I told the student (and others in the class) I would not accept any assignments where Mary is referred to as a "sinner."

8. In the Roman Catholic calendar, the Immaculate Conception of Mary is a solemnity celebrated on December 8.

the cross. Unlike Mary, we are cleansed of original sin at our baptism—after the crucifixion and resurrection of Christ.[9]

If we return to the first joyful mystery and recognize Mary as the new Eve, one of the parallels between the two women is that they were both created without sin and remained free to choose to sin or not to sin. Eve disobeyed God while Mary obeyed God. Mary's obedience remained throughout her life in complete union with the will of God. God, who has divine foreknowledge, anticipated the offering of his Son; with his sacrifice, the Son of God was able to save Mary in advance from original sin. God's foreknowledge of Mary's willingness to cooperate in his plan of salvation meant having chosen Mary for this purpose.

Mary herself says, "From henceforth all generations will call me blessed" (Luke 1:47), and having just alluded to God who looked upon her "humiliation," she will be called blessed by "all" generations because she is the mother of the Lord. Mary's identity like her mission is Christocentric; this is made clear in Mary's Magnificat. Mary knows that the Son of the Most High enfleshed within her, that all generations will call her blessed, because the child whom she was asked to conceive by the power of the Holy Spirit grows within her womb.

And this is why we pray "Blessed are you among women" in the first stanza of the Hail Mary. Hail Mary synthesizes the biblical verses of the incarnation, God made flesh, by the woman whom God chose, Mary. The visitation reflects a time of joyful excitement; the anticipation of two women who will bring their sons into the world marking radical conversion and salvation. The visit to Elizabeth in Ein Karem signifies a time of preparation. In Mary's visit to her cousin we have the greatest virtue that Jesus will teach us, that he will live to its fullest, already expressed by the mother carrying our Savior: charity.

II—Fruit of this Mystery: Virtue of Charity; Love of Neighbor

Practical matters—

We know the love of neighbor is taught to us by Christ himself as one of the two fundamental commandments. The love of neighbor flows out of the love of God. These two commandments are reflected in the Mosaic Law, the

---

9. See the *Catechism*, #490-#493; also, Apostolic Constitution, Pope Pius IX, *Ineffabilis Deus*, December 8, 1854.

first three in reference to the love of God and the remaining seven in reference to the love of neighbor.

Ten Commandments (Exod 20:1–21)

1. I am the Lord your God. You shall not have any other gods before me.
2. You shall not take the name of your Lord your God in vain.
3. Remember to keep the Sabbath holy.
4. Honor your father and your mother.
5. You shall not kill.
6. You shall not commit adultery.
7. You shall not steal.
8. You shall not bear false witness against your neighbor.
9. You shall not covet your neighbor's wife.
10. You shall not covet your neighbor's goods.

Jesus synthesizes the Decalogue, the Ten Commandments transmitted by Moses, into his Two Commandments of Love:

Two Commandments (Mark 12:30–31)

1. You shall love the Lord your God with all your heart, and with all your soul, and with all your mind, and with all your strength;
2. You shall love your neighbor as yourself.

Truth

Truth is inseparable from love. Truth finds its perfection in love. When we follow the Mosaic commandments we follow the teachings of Jesus. Each commandment pertains to how we relate to God and to the other. The "other" can be our neighbor, a peer, a colleague, a friend, a relative, our relationships which are meant to be lived in truth following the commandments of God. Mary's visit to her cousin Elizabeth is more than just an expression of culture, duty, and affection. Mary brings good news. So does Elizabeth. The news of their offspring they both want to share is more than that of ordinary women with everyday events to discuss. They both know the divine work of God in their lives, the supernatural activity that makes these women central figures in preparation for the coming of the Baptizer and the Savior. Authentic charity presupposes humility.

Love is manifested concretely in the act of charity Mary shows towards her cousin. The person of Jesus Christ present in Mary's womb will perfectly fulfil the self-offering of love as sacrifice. We have seen that truth is inseparable from love because only truth can lead to perfect love.

Death

The absence of love is what? Hate? In fact, the absence of love is death. When love is selfish, self-interested, self-absorbed, love that does not seek the good of the other, love that holds back, this is not love. These are all signs of death. Love that is not true; false love is the same as death.

Death manifests itself in pride, greed, and lust. Each of these vices leads to a dead end if the person is not illuminated by truth. Death is non-generative and non-life giving. Death is the fall into darkness, distant from the light and darkened by error, leading to sin. Dwelling in darkness, sin spreads. Violating the natural sexual order created and willed by God leads to sexual corruption and death. When Jesus responds to the Pharisees on marriage, Jesus goes back to Genesis (Matt 19:2–6; Gen 2:24). When Paul admonishes Christian sexual misconduct, he compares them to something worse than pagans (1 Cor 5:1). Darkness and death of moral errors spread like a pandemic.

Love

True love seeks the good of the other while reciprocity and relationality are sought and fundamental to being in communion with others. Christian love is "other"-centered.[10] While the Mosaic commandments are transmitted primarily in the negative form; they tell us fundamentally what to do, to love God. They tell us to love our neighbor by not doing what is evil but respecting others and showing filial piety before God. To violate these commandments towards God and our neighbor is a violation of love. Informed by truth, love is an act that moves us towards performing deeds of goodness, "love of neighbor," as we have in the visitation.

This is our meditation on charity in the second joyful mystery of the rosary. Like Mary, we are called to be witnesses of God's love—his divine

---

10. Aquinas, *ST*, Pt. 1a-2ae, q. 28, "Of the Effects of Love."

order—otherwise what do we witness? This love is not the love of the world—a subjective experience reducing love to merely personal satisfaction. Love is the journey Mary undertakes knowing her cousin needs her company and comfort. Love is to share the good news of God's promise. Love offers the hope of salvation. Love brings joy by living in the truth.

Charity is the fundamental Christian virtue—the expression of love—that has been brutally attacked and corrupted. Satan wages a relentless battle to undermine love because of its centrality in Christ's teachings. Love is salvific. By twisting sin and making evil appear good, Satan distorts the Christian message just as Satan deceived the first man and woman twisting the words of God (Gen 3).

Since love includes the subjective experience of feelings, we can easily make subjective experience the basis of love, and the more intensely we associate love with the feeling of pleasure, we are more mistakenly led to believe love is pleasure. The disciple of Christ knows that love does not exclude pain and suffering, even moments of emptiness—the desert experience of "nothingness." And yet, both in joy and pain, God's burning love for us remains constant—God is present, and God is all we need. God is the truest and greatest love we bring to others.

Mary's actions in this second joyful mystery demonstrate charity. But they also serve as preparatory acts; she brings Jesus in her womb to her cousin Elizabeth. Elizabeth's own son leaps at the presence of the divine child, and Elizabeth will bring her son, John, into the world who will prepare the way for Jesus. Charity in this mystery anticipates the love that will consume the world. Jesus will reveal the true act of love by his life and teachings, by his crucifixion, death, and resurrection. In this second joyful mystery we meditate the connection between humility and love as Mary and Elizabeth show us: the concreteness of love anchored in truth:

Hail Mary full of grace; the Lord is with thee.
Blessed are thou among women
and blessed is the fruit of thy womb,
Jesus.

Third Joyful Mystery—Birth of Jesus

I—"To you is born this day in the city of David a Savior, who is Christ, the Lord." (Luke 2:11)

Our Father . . . Hail Mary . . . Glory Be . . .

1. Bethlehem—"house of bread"

A visit to the Basilica of the Nativity in Bethlehem reveals stones and designs in the interior of the basilica preserving its Christian history. The prominent presence of Byzantine churches of the fourth to sixth centuries followed by the crusader churches of the twelfth century reflect the faith, struggles, and battles to defend the Christian presence.

In an attempt to eradicate Christianity, the Roman emperor Hadrian replaced Christian sanctuaries with pagan gods and temples, and in the case of Bethlehem, a statue of the goddess Venus was erected. Paradoxically, these pagan sites facilitated the identification of Christian centers of devotion. The Empress Saint Helen in 326 AD, mother of Constantine, having embarked on a pilgrimage to the Holy Land, ordered in the early fourth century the building of Christian basilicas in three locations, one at the site of the Nativity, the other at Golgotha, and the third on the Mount of Olives. Already in this early stage of Christianity, the centrality of the church building and its structure, designed as the temple of worship for the Christian faithful, preserved and transmitted our religion by handing down what they received in continuity with Christian sources.

Attempts to silence Christianity have been made from its beginnings, first by the Jewish religious authorities as related in the Gospels and the Pauline Epistles, followed by the Roman emperors Nero, Marcus Aurelius, Decius, Diocletian, then the Persian Sasanian forces, followed by Arab

Muslims, continuing with Ottoman Muslims.[1] Violent attempts aiming to destroy the presence of Christian communities and their central Gospel message, "God sent his Son to save the world from sin so we may have Eternal Life," a message of truth and love, continues into the postmodern era through subtle and coercive anti-Christian narratives.

By God's providential design, the Basilica of the Nativity escaped destruction. Justinian in the sixth century rebuilt the basilica to reflect the worship and glorify the birth place of the Son of God. A visit to the prayerful church of Shepherds' Fields, just outside of Bethlehem, reminds us that in this grassy and rocky terrain, the shepherds were the first to receive the message that the Messiah was born. In the caves animals were kept where they ate from an eating trough or "manger."[2] A rather crude rough and uncorrowned setting was chosen for the birth for the Son of God. The royal pomp and pageantry expected—and rightfully so for a king—simply did not reflect the birth of the Messiah who found his warmth in his mother's arms and the feeding trough of most probably an extended room where they were staying.

2. Jesus's Ancestry

In Matthew's Gospel we first hear of the genealogy of Jesus Christ who is identified from the outset as the Son of David. Beginning with Abraham, Matthew brings us with three clear chronological divisions of generations: first, generations until David, "and Jesse the father of King David" (Matt 1:6); the second division of generations ends with the deportation to Babylon (Matt 1:11); and finally the generations in the third division ends with, "and Jacob the father of Joseph the husband of Mary, of whom Jesus was born, who is called Christ" (Matt 1:16). Matthew's genealogy emphasizes the house of David, identifying Joseph as the adoptive and legal father of Jesus (Matt 1:1-16).

In Luke's Gospel, unlike the genealogy that produces the paternal line, Luke identifies the maternal line; this accounts for obvious differences between the two genealogies. In Luke's Gospel, Nathan is the son of David, and not Solomon, the royal lineage we find in Matthew's Gospel, thus giving the Davidic ancestry as it passes from Nathan to Mary (Luke 3:31). The intimate details Luke provides from the annunciation then for the birth of Jesus suggests that Mary was Luke's direct source of information.

1. Weidenkopf, *Catholic Church*, 90, fn. 12; Samson, *Come and See*, 240.
2. At the Papal Basilica of Santa Maria Maggiore in Rome, the crypt beneath the main altar contains the five wooden pieces of the crib of Bethlehem.

For Jesus who was "descended" from David (Rom 1:1–4) means according to the flesh; this applies to Mary because Jesus was enfleshed by his mother, Mary, the incarnation account we find in Mathew's Gospel. Mary, as shown in the first joyful mystery, is the woman whose seed also crushes the head of Satan: the seed of truth overpowers the forces of evil and falsehood.

Luke informs us that Mary and Joseph were from Nazareth (Luke 1:26). We read further: "Joseph also went from the town of Nazareth in Galilee to Judea, to the city of David called Bethlehem, because he was descended from the house and family of David. He went to be registered with Mary, to whom he was engaged and who was expecting a child" (Luke 2:4–5). Nazareth was home to the descendants of the house of David calling themselves "Nazoreans," based on the words of the prophet Isaiah: "A shoot shall come out from the stump of Jesse, and a branch shall grow out of his roots. A shoot will spring from the stock of Jesse, a new shoot will grow from his roots" (Isa 11:1). At the time of Mary and Joseph, Nazareth was a hamlet in the Galilean hills where the descendants of David lived bearing this messianic name, "branch," associated with Jesse, the father of David. The inhabitants of Nazareth identified themselves as this "stock of Jesse."[3]

3. Joseph: Husband of Mary

Matthew describes Joseph as the man to whom Mary was promised in marriage, "Her husband Joseph, being a righteous man . . ." (Matt 1:19). This does not only mean "just" in the moral sense but also what is proper to a religious man: hard-working, truthful, faithful to God's laws. Jesus learned his spiritual father's trade as "carpenter" (Matt 13:55; Mark 6:3). In Nazareth, beneath the Church of Saint Joseph, we find the house and workshop of Joseph as well as archaeological evidence of a baptismal site.

Jesus is a descendant of this stalk of Jesse, this branch belonging to the Nazoreans settled in Galilee. The Davidic lineage which Jesus receives from Joseph, his legal father, is made clear immediately after Mary's conception of Jesus. We read in the angel's words of the first joyful mystery of the annunciation, ". . . a virgin engaged to a man whose name was Joseph, of the house of David" (Luke 1:27). In the second joyful mystery, Joseph, journeys with Mary, his betrothed, the woman God entrusted to Joseph and the child enfleshed in Mary's womb.

When Mary asks the angel, "How can this come to be for I know not man," Mary is essentially stating she has not ever had any sexual relations

---

3. See, Pixner, *Paths of the Messiah*, 3–4.

and this includes the man to whom she is engaged, Joseph. Our first introduction to Joseph is based on the indirect language of the annunciation: Joseph is both a religious man and a chaste man. God's plan is that the woman whom God chose to be the mother of his divine Son is betrothed to a man with the same religious and chaste principles.

So, we meet Joseph indirectly at the annunciation, and discretely at the visitation. Joseph did not let his wife go alone from Nazareth to Ein Karem on the grounds that the journey would be too demanding and even too dangerous. Even if Mary had been accompanied by others, Joseph as the guardian of both Mary and Jesus would be at their side. His presence meant as husband, he protected the woman whom he loved and married, and as spiritual father, the responsibility entrusted to him by God was to protect, teach, and love Jesus.

The chaste disposition of Joseph, reflected in his role as husband and spiritual father, is prefigured by Joseph in the Old Testament. Both the Old and New Testament Josephs are chaste men reflecting a valued and honorable life of virtue. Not only does chastity show the respect for the law of God but also the truthfulness of one's actions: to assume knowledge of the flesh that has not been approved or recognized by the community, or to take possession of a person without their consent, are injustices at the personal and communal levels. The two Josephs, Old and New Testaments, clearly manifest truthfulness in their actions; the sense of what is just before God and man. Joseph in the Old Testament understood that Potiphar's wife, the woman who sought to seduce him, was violating her marital promise of fidelity that would lead to adultery, fornicating with another man. Being already married, Potiphar's wife could not legitimately engage in a sexual union (Gen 39:7–10). In the case of Joseph in the New Testament, Joseph respected Mary's virginity before their marriage and even afterwards as we hear from Mary herself in the annunciation, and further expressed in Matthew's Gospel when Joseph expressed uncertainty about the proper course of action to take with the news of Mary being "with child" (Matt 1:18). So, Joseph, the man to whom Mary was betrothed, completes the actions of Joseph in the Old Testament in a deeper way, proving himself to be a chaste and upright man—as husband of Mary and spiritual father of God's Son.

Further parallels become evident in the life of Jesus when Joseph finds safety in Egypt for Mary and Jesus (Matt 2:13–21), just as we have in the Old Testament where Joseph plays an instrumental role in bringing his family to Egypt where the family finds refuge (Gen 46). From the words of their father, Jacob, "Go to Joseph" (Gen 41:55), we have acquired the Latin phrase, *Ite ad Joseph*, applied to the New Testament Joseph.[4]

Mary and Joseph show that God chooses ordinary but holy people to carry out his will, while both reflect refined religious sensibilities. Mary and Joseph represent a couple from the poorer families of Judah. Nevertheless, the ordinary religious couple experience the extraordinary power of God. Their religious observances of God's Law, their interior disposition towards the truth, reflects why God chose both Mary and Joseph to be the family into which Jesus is born. Jesus spent thirty years at Joseph's home in Nazareth with his mother, Mary. Jesus learned the trade of a carpenter observing and practicing Joseph's craft. Nor can we be dismissive—or indifferent—towards those whom God chooses to collaborate in his divine plan for our salvation, and whom God continues to place on our path, saints, so we can continue to witness the work of the Holy Spirit.

God's plan is evident in the interconnectedness of events: not only preparing Mary as the immaculate mother of his Son, a woman without sin, but also fundamental is Joseph's lineage. The messianic prophesy to be fulfilled is the Messiah who is from the house of David (2 Sam 7:13–14): "He shall build a house for my name, and I will establish the throne of his Kingdom forever. I will be a father to him, and he shall be a son to me." Jesus's ancestry fulfils the messianic prophesy with language that is suggestive of a supernatural nature of this fulfilment: "I will establish the throne of his Kingdom forever"; in other words, this is more than a temporal earthly kingdom. We also have the divine filiation that is expressed "he shall be a son to me," both prophecies fulfilled in Jesus Christ.

4. Roman Census

The Roman Emperor, Caesar Augustus, calls for a census, the first such census in the empire, implemented by Quirinius, Governor of Syria, around the time of Jesus's birth. Even though the Roman Empire had extended outside of Italy since the third century BC, the census providentially occurred when Mary was about to give birth to Jesus. Would Jesus otherwise have been born in Nazareth where Mary and Joseph lived among the Nazorenes? Or would Mary and Joseph have gone to Bethlehem anyway knowing Jesus is the fulfilment of the messianic prophesy as the angel informed both Mary (Luke 1:32–35) and Joseph (Matt 1:20–21). Familiar with Micha's prophesy, would

---

4. Pope Francis offers enriching insight on Saint Joseph in his Apostolic Letter, *Patris corde* "With a Father's Heart," marking the opening of the Year of Saint Joseph, December 8, 2020 to December 8, 2021.

THIRD JOYFUL MYSTERY—BIRTH OF JESUS

they have travelled to Bethlehem, "But you, O Bethlehem of Ephrathah, who are one of the little clans of Judah, from you shall come forth for me one who is to rule in Israel . . ." (Mic 5:2)? But the reality of an imperial census leads Joseph and Mary to Bethlehem, the city of David with the messianic implications for not only to the Kingdom of Judah but the fulfillment of the law and the prophets associated with the house of David; an eternal Kingdom announced by the angel Gabriel in the first joyful mystery and finding its fulfillment in the birth of Jesus in the third joyful mystery.

Jesus is born into God's chosen race, the people of Israel, with whom God first established a covenant, with Abraham, Isaac, and Jacob and to whom God revealed himself (Deut 9:28). The promised Messiah, the Son of God, is born in this Hebrew context. But the extension of the Roman empire with its infrastructure of military networks, ports, bridges, and roads reach across the Mediterranean as far as north as the Danube. At the same time as the Latin language and Roman cultural influence, there existed the widespread Greek intellectual life that can be traced to the presocratic period of the fifth century BC. This means the birth of the promised Messiah, occurred during the prominence of the Second Temple Period of the Jewish religion, the extension of Greek rational tradition, and the Roman imperial infrastructure. Each will serve the proclamation of the good news: fulfillment of the promise (Jewish faith), understanding the message (Greek reason), and universal evangelization (Roman church).

Joseph being the chosen spiritual father of Jesus, the man to whom Mary was betrothed, indicates that when the census is taken, with the journey to Bethlehem, messianic implications are evident: the birthplace of Jesus, the home of David, the Bethlehemite. For the divine incarnation to be the fulfillment of the promise, Jesus's birth, death, and resurrection need to demonstrate how they are the realization of the old covenant, the Law, and the Prophets. The roles of Mary and Joseph are fundamental: salvation comes through the house of David, Joseph's lineage and the flesh of Mary; the conception of Jesus by the power of the Holy Spirit.

5. Birth of Jesus: Promise Fulfilled

Matthew describes Joseph as a "righteous" man; Joseph learns that Mary was with child "before they came together" and resolved to distance himself from Mary and not publicly repudiate her. Joseph knew that at work in Mary was something beyond his grasp, when an angel appeared to him saying, "Joseph, son of David, do not be afraid to take Mary as your wife, for the child conceived in her is from the Holy Spirit. She will bear a son, and you are to name him Jesus, for he will save his people from their sins" (Matt 1:20–21). Joseph, the spiritual and legal father of Jesus, is part of the divine plan to fulfil the messianic promise of the house of David. Joseph, the husband of Mary, commits himself to God's work.

Mary was betrothed to a "just man"—a man of religious piety—observing the Mosaic law; hence, a man who feared God, a fitting man to be the legal father of Jesus and husband to Mary. Joseph acted as the angel instructed him. Joseph departed from Nazareth to the city of David according to the instructions of the Roman authorities and registered in the city of their tribe, Bethlehem, in Judah.

The Davidic ties to Bethlehem are first mentioned in the book of Ruth. We are told that Naomi's husband, Elimelech, passed away in the land of Moab, and ten years later Naomi's sons both died, Mahlone and Chilion (Ruth 1:1–5). Having heard that conditions had improved in Bethlehem, Naomi decided to return to her people. Instead of remaining behind with her sister Orpah, who returned to her people and to her god, Chemosh, Ruth faithfully accompanied Naomi back to Bethlehem. Ruth felt a bond with Naomi, her people, and her God: "Where you go, I will go; where you lodge, I will lodge; your people shall be my people, and your God my God" (Ruth 1:16).

In Bethlehem, Ruth found herself in a vulnerable situation as a woman without a father or husband to protect her. Ruth's precarious condition is immediately understood by Boaz who instructs Ruth as a Moabitess foreigner how to conduct herself for her own protection (Ruth 2:8–9). Boaz is portrayed as a just man and does not take advantage of Ruth's fragile situation (Ruth 3:7–9). Ruth marries a just man who respects her and loves her, while Ruth shows fidelity to the God of Israel; Boaz brings into his family lineage of a foreigner, a Moabitess (Ruth 4:13). Boaz and Ruth give birth to Obed whose son Jesse is the father of David (Ruth 4:18–22).

In this town of Bethlehem, we have the Davidic lineage: Bethlehem/Ephrathah where Jesus is born.

Luke gives us details of the birth: "While they were there, the time came for her to deliver her child. And she gave birth to her firstborn son and wrapped him in bands of cloth, and laid him in a manger, because there was no place for them in the inn" (Luke 2:6–7). We can imagine that with the census in a town like Bethlehem, the inns quickly filled up. Mary and Joseph found a place to stay where Mary could rest since her time to give birth was approaching. It's unlikely that a husband with his wife, visibly approaching childbirth would be refused hospitality especially in their family's tribal town. Joseph and Mary would have been directed to a home of family or friends further in the fields where there was a room with an eating trough where Mary could give birth in privacy and where the baby could be kept warm.

We have heard of Ruth's fidelity to Naomi; Bethlehem itself recalls the fidelity of the God of Israel. The Hebrew word *hesed* expresses "loving" and "faithful" kindness. When Naomi responds to Ruth, she refers to *hesed*: "May the LORD deal kindly with you, as you have dealt with the dead and with me" (Ruth 1:8).[5] Bethlehem, the town of "bread" from *Bet-lehem*, or "house of food," provided for the children of Israel—precisely the reason Naomi and Ruth go to Bethlehem. Ruth's departure with Naomi highlights the latter's return to her home of "bread," to the God who is faithful to his people. "Fidelity" represents not only the central theme of the old covenant but its driving force: God's promise. A covenantal oath or "family bond" between God and his people is first made with Abraham where the nations are blessed through Abraham's seed (Gen 12:1–3). Abraham's fidelity towards God is not the result of an abstract or conceptual "faith" but fidelity expressed in very concrete terms: accepting the will of God by offering to sacrifice his son, Isaac (Gen 22:6). The covenant is renewed with Abraham's son, Isaac (Gen 17:21), and Isaac's son, Jacob (Gen 28:13–15).[6] God's fidelity to his people continues in Exodus when the Israelites are delivered from slavery by God's instrument, Moses. With Moses a covenant is renewed at Mount Sinai with the blood of bullocks (Exod 24). The messianic promise of a Davidic kingdom—an everlasting kingdom—is to be fulfilled (2 Sam 7:12–13). God's promise and perfect fulfillment we hear at the annunciation, the first joyful mystery.

The Messiah was born in the midst of sheep and shepherds under the heavens illuminated by stars and a brilliant star. The immaculate mother of Jesus, Mary, contemplating the divine Messiah, and Mary's husband, Joseph, the guardian, adoring the Son of God in this first chapel, the home of the Holy Family, where the Son of God is worshiped.

When the angel announces to the shepherds a "sign," we ask, What "sign" were the angels expecting or looking for? What sign should we be thinking of? ". . . to you is born this day in the city of David a Savior, who is the Messiah, the Lord. This will be a sign for you: you will find a child wrapped in bands of cloth and lying in a manger" (Luke 2:11–12). Bethlehem, city of David, a "sign" that echoes the sign of Isaiah: "Therefore the Lord himself will give you a sign. Look, the young woman is with child and

---

5. On *hesed* in the Book of Ruth. See, Bergsma and Pitre, *Old Testament*, 342.

6. Actually, in the case of Isaac's offspring, Esau is tricked, leading to the first-born son's blessing going to Jacob (Gen 25:27–34; 27).

shall bear a son, and shall name him Immanuel" (Isa 7:14).[7] The "sign" the shepherds and the people of Judah were waiting for was God's faithful love fulfilled. This promise made to the house of David recognized the promise made to David: "I will raise up your offspring after you . . . and I will establish the throne of his kingdom forever" (2 Sam 7:12–13).

Certainly, the setting of the birth of the heir of David who will restore the Davidic dynasty with one that is greater—an everlasting one—would have taken the shepherds by surprise just as this baffles us: a "sign" of a king born without any human signs of royal pomp or majestic ceremony. A birth we can expect of a poor family no doubt but certainly not a royal one. We learn from the very start that God reaches out to those who are waiting, those whose hands are empty and hearts prepared. God keeps his promise in the vulnerability and fragility of an infant.

Not a single sign of power. Not a single sign of opulence. The sign is an eating trough, a baby in "swaddling" clothes, the sign is the house of David. The sign, ultimately the star, that brightens the dark of night. Honor and devotion to the infant Jesus is more than traditional piety. The infant Jesus teaches us God came to us, in the flesh of a baby, and began his human journey like us, as a tender child, giving himself to us to be loved, to be worshiped, to be held in our arms, to be kept in our hearts. Jesus is the light.

This smallness and vulnerability encountered in the presence of the Son of God amazes us. This is especially true for men who are drawn to the tough and powerful, the mighty warrior, a soldier on a horse in battle cry—instead, we are asked to embrace this babe. This child's flesh is depicted beautifully and symbolically in a painting of Pierre Mignard, *The Virgin of the Grapes* (1614–16). The fleshiness of Jesus with the grapes as a focus of the painting anticipates Jesus offering his body and blood, his flesh on the cross, fifth sorrowful mystery and fifth luminous mystery. With Mary and Jesus veiled together, this union of hearts further suggests the wedding feast at Cana, the second luminous mystery. The pure innocent flesh of the infant Jesus is the same flesh, unblemished flesh that will be offered as a sacrificed lamb.

God did not send his Son into the world as a powerful prince but as the prince of peace. The Son of God began his life as a baby in a manger, surrounded by animals and shepherds, a deeply religious mother and spiritual father. The poverty of the holy family disposes us to the humility and piety that leads to our salvation. This moment between mother and child, Mary the Virgin and Jesus Son of God, is expressed in the intimacy of mother and child, the love a mother experiences setting her eyes on

---

7. Young woman, meaning "virgin." See, fn. 10, first joyful mystery.

her child, and Mary knows this child is the Son of God who received his flesh from her; the divine Son, entrusted to Mary, the flesh of the house of Judah, Son of David, is that of his mother. Holding Jesus in her arms Mary was the first person to contemplate the Messiah, to contemplate the anointed one, to contemplate God-incarnate.

Joseph kneels to worship and stands to watch over, to guard the child entrusted to him by God, the child announced to him by the angel Gabriel. Joseph assumes his duty as the husband of the woman he chose to marry and as guardian of the divine child. In the midst of creation, under the blue starry sky of Bethlehem, a child is born. Perhaps this was not the birth of Immanuel that Joseph expected or envisioned, and yet, united with God's will, we see the complete trust that Joseph has in God, and the divine plan of which he became part. While Joseph may seem like any spiritual father dutifully fulfilling his role, a man of religion moves beyond religious duty: Joseph acted out of love, love for Jesus and love for Mary. Joseph's chaste disposition enabled him to see God and to discern God's plan. Anchored in the truth of the Scriptures, Joseph experienced the intensity of human love in every fibre of his body. Baby Jesus is embraced by his mother, protected by his father, kept warm by the animals, and worshiped by all, the shepherds and the angels singing, "Glory to God in the highest."

The birth of Jesus is the physical reality of God's plan to save humanity. Mary cooperates with this plan as mother who gives Jesus his flesh, and Joseph cooperates as a deeply religious husband and Jesus's guardian. The birth of the Christ child in Bethlehem means for each of us to contemplate Jesus, the Son of God, the promised Messiah.

II—Fruit of this Mystery: Virtue of Poverty

Practical matters—

I remember visiting a community of Franciscans one year over the Christmas holidays not far from Rome. Placed before the altar, baby Jesus was brightly illuminated with Christmas lights and a shining star over the crib. The community of men prayed before the Christ child in a manger. Jesus, the light that dispels the darkness. God who comes to us in the flesh of a babe. We are invited to receive and embrace of the Son of God.

The birth of the divine child, however, is now eclipsed by our neopagan surroundings marketing Christmas—or "holiday season"—as a time of shallow "gift-giving." In the noise of our cities, the congestion of line-ups in malls, frustration of finding parking space, tap of credit card purchases, text message distractions—in the midst of all this, can we actually find time to contemplate Jesus? We might squeeze Christmas Mass into our schedule, but what about our heart? Have our hearts been prepared to receive Jesus? What about attending weekday masses as we anticipate the birth of our Lord?

Making room in our hearts means purifying our cluttered minds especially from what causes sin, or sin itself. By prayer, by abstinence, by charitable acts, by sacramental confession, we can prepare ourselves for Jesus, Son of God. To contemplate Jesus means first of all opening our hearts and minds to encounter him, to receive him. Making room for him so that our hearts and minds are not like an inn so packed that there is no room for Christ. We need to rid ourselves of all the clutter. Our capacity to receive Jesus, to contemplate him is shaped by how much space we give him. We can in the silence of Bethlehem—of our own hearts—contemplate his majesty, the truth, the love that Jesus brings; God in the flesh, an infant in the arms of his mother. This detachment from the world, and withdrawal into the inner recesses of our soul, is what we mean by "poor in spirit."

"Poverty" suggests not only material simplicity but a disposition of detachment from the world. Not to be attached to the world. To be poor means the openness to attach ourselves to God, truth, and goodness. What it means to be poor has been disputed even in religious communities. How poor, how radical is the disciple of Christ called to live poverty? As one of the three evangelical councils, poverty, along with obedience and chastity, is fundamental in our spiritual lives. Jesus Christ himself from his very birth—and his whole life—remained detached from the world.

Reflecting this detachment Jesus states, "Foxes have holes, and birds of the air have nests; but the Son of Man has nowhere to lay his head" (Matt 8:20). Jesus's place of rest, his shelter, extended to his friends who invited him as in Mary, Martha, and Lazarus (John 12:1–8).[8] The poverty of Jesus clearly started from his birth where Mary and Joseph found a manger for the Son of God.

Detachment from possessions means we appreciate our things, we take care of them, but they are not the focus of our life—our goods do not enslave us. Our attachments should not be the cause of arguments or conflicts. In this spirit of detachment, we learn starting from childhood to share our possessions, otherwise we are inclined to fight over what is "mine" leading to a series of vices starting with one's own siblings, from greed to anger to hatred. And when the occasion arises that we need to

---

8. Pope Francis proclaimed July 29 as the Obligatory Memorial of Mary, Martha, and Lazarus, the friends of Jesus, to be added to the Roman Catholic calendar of Blesseds and Saints.

give up these precious possessions, we learn to do this respectfully, with sensitivity, finding where our possession can be best utilized: church fundraising activities, Catholic charities, or non-profit organizations.

A person may possess wealth and display detachment; the wealthy person can generously support the church, religious communities, and charitable causes. In fact, the church depends on donors and has always relied on generous benefactors to sustain her institutions, the formation of seminarians and religious. So the generosity of benefactors shows a spirit of detachment, helping the church and those in need.

The problem is that possessions can make a person greedy, envious, and proud, and with one's hands and stomach full, we feel satisfied, so, "Why do I need God if I have everything I need?"[9] In a course I took at university, Theology of Hope, a student from Haiti said, "The Haitians own little, we continuously suffer natural disasters, and lose the little we possess, finding ourselves continuously turning to God for help." This makes a people disposed to prayer, seeking help from God, creating a religious disposition. Paradoxically, the religious disposition is lacking in cultures where the people have plenty, their hands and stomachs full; they appear to have less need to worship, and even less motivation to follow the radicality of Christ's teachings.

Nevertheless, we should not have to wait until we are so desperate that we turn to God, but there is something in human nature that causes us to run to God only when help is needed, and often, that is when we experience difficulty and tragedy . . . when one's life has reached the bottom of a pit and darkness seems inescapable.

The attachment to people, where sin—or the occasion of sin—places the soul at risk, indicates a certain incapacity of detachment or "poverty" from certain individuals. Yet, such detachment is needed from "creatures" to preserve a chaste mind, heart, and body. How often do the faithful choose the occasion of sin—and sin—preferring an unchaste and unholy attachment over Jesus who should be our only absolute attachment? If poverty in relations, attachments, in pleasures that risk being the occasion of sin, is not part our spiritual journey, how can we truly surrender ourselves to God?

Poverty is not only detachment from worldly things but an openness to God, fulfilling our true needs, nourishing us through the sacraments, through his Word. Poverty helps purify us of vices, of greed, of envy, of pride: "I only have enough for me." Poverty teaches us to share with others, to be detached, to be generous.

---

9. Words used by a wealthy woman to express her disbelief in God.

Like Mary and Joseph who could not find a place to stay, like the baby Jesus who was born in a manger, to be poor means to find a space in the world, yet, detached, so the "room" that we make is ultimately for Jesus: to contemplate and adore him. The mystery of the incarnation has as a fruit the "spirit of poverty": the divine Son who takes on human flesh reflects God lowering himself to the condition of human needs and suffering, to fully unite himself with us. The poverty of being human means Jesus enters and participates in our world of pain and suffering, so as to meet us, embrace us, love us: to carry our sins. Poverty is associated with humility because we are placed in a position of need and dependence, and if the mighty are identified with pride this reflects their self-reliance and independence, not having any "need" for God—or anyone else. Our journey as Jesus's disciples begins with stripping ourselves of the superfluous and unnecessary, ridding ourselves of those mental distractions that waste our time and thoughts, and to being detached from our many possessions that clutter our minds and hearts. With purity, we can contemplate the babe of Bethlehem, the divine infant, Jesus. This explains why the poor show receptivity and openness to the Gospel: they are fed by the Word of God and the sacraments.

Fourth Joyful Mystery—Presentation in the Temple

I— *... they brought him up to Jerusalem to present him to the Lord ...* (Luke 2:22)

Our Father ... Hail Mary ... Glory Be ...

1. Mary and Joseph Present Jesus in the Temple

As a devout religious couple, Mary and Joseph express their religious observance according to the Law of Moses as they present Jesus, Son of the Most High, in the temple. Mary and Joseph, by following what is prescribed by the Law, show they desire to do what is right for their child knowing that following the commandments of God is to act according to truth and love. Their impulse to present Jesus in the temple, seeking for the child God's blessings, means to consecrate Jesus as prescribed by the Law (Luke 2:22). Not only as a religious couple, but as mother and guardian, they know the responsibility they have, Mary giving birth and Joseph being entrusted with God's Son, the one to fulfil the messianic promise as the angel Gabriel announced to Mary in the first joyful mystery. Mary and Joseph know that apart from adhering to the Mosaic law, and assuming the duties as parents, they have Jesus in their arms not only the future of God's people, and all of humanity, but a divine plan that far transcends them. They trust in God; they witness God's promise being fulfilled.

Mary and Joseph act in obedience: they act in truth; they act in love. They teach us not only as parents but as a religious couple, a chaste woman and man, to live in the presence of God in abandonment placing holiness which God seeks for each of us, holiness that means fidelity to God and to remain in communion with him. Mary and Joseph follow the directives of the Mosaic Law: "When the time came for their purification according to the law of Moses, they brought him up to Jerusalem to present him to the Lord (as it is written in the law of the Lord, 'Every firstborn male shall be designated as holy to the Lord'), and they offered a sacrifice according to what is stated in the law of the Lord), 'a pair of turtledoves or two young pigeons'" (Luke 2:22–24; Exod 13:2; Lev 12:8).

Is this not what parents are called to do, the earliest liturgical act they participate in on behalf of their child, presenting their baby to God? As Christians we perform this act at church, at the baptismal font, requesting baptism for the child, as an act of obedience—the holy thing to do just as Mary and Joseph who had a responsibility towards the child entrusted to them, offered Jesus to God, consecration of the child. We present the child to be baptized; not only "presented" but as Christians we have the effects of Jesus's body and blood offered at the cross in obedience to the Father, the effects of the outpouring of the Holy Spirit, that purifies the child of original sin, strengthens the child to combat against the forces of evil, and offers the child membership in the Christian community.

The sublime act of the presentation of Jesus in the temple foreshadows the responsibility of parents presenting their child for baptism; a reflection of the religious duty of parents. The supreme value attached to the child's body and soul to be placed immediately in the trust of God's cleansing love and mercy. Based on the Levitical teaching that elaborates the Mosaic teaching from Exodus, we are informed, "The Lord said to Moses: Consecrate to me all the firstborn; whatever is the first to open the womb among the Israelites, of human beings and animals, is mine" (Exod 13:1–2).

The elaborated teaching found in Leviticus states, "This is the law for her who bears a child, male or female. If she cannot afford a sheep, she shall take two turtledoves or two pigeons" (Lev 12:7–8). This clearly indicates that Mary and Joseph were a poor couple; that woman and man whom God had chosen to be mother and guardian to his Son. The cleansing purity of poverty leads to obedience, and obedience is inseparable from humility. Mary and Joseph had already combated the forces of evil that led sin into the world: pride. Unlike the first man and woman who wanted to be "like gods," Mary and Joseph bow before God, serve God, love God, with the only desire of carrying out God's will. This is not possible when purity is lacking, when pride rules; without humility we cannot have selfless self-giving love. This purity makes Mary and Joseph a simple but extraordinary couple in their united desire to fulfil God's plan as parents with the Son entrusted to them, Mary by her flesh, and Joseph by his spiritual fatherhood.

The fundamental act of obedience at the Temple anticipates both the significance of the "little ones" who are not to be turned away in their spiritual life, but rather received as Jesus taught, to be welcomed, to be baptized. The baptism of infants draws from the Catholic Church's teachings and the biblical basis of "original sin" but also the recreation of the infant in the image of Christ, and the welcoming of this recreated being in the name of the Holy Trinity into the Christian community of faith.[1] The presentation at the temple prepares us for infant baptism as conveyed and fulfilled in Christ's teachings.

The Levitical teaching asks for a lamb but Mary and Joseph are too poor to provide a lamb and instead offer turtle doves. A lamb to be sacrificed; Jesus himself. And he will offer himself in obedience to God the Father just as Mary and Joseph offer a sacrifice of turtle doves in obedience to the Mosaic Law. The presentation points to the perfect sacrifice, Jesus who presents himself as an offering; he is the Lamb to be sacrificed. Offering himself, the priest sacrificing, Jesus is to become the perfection of the sacrifice offered at the Temple; for Jesus is the sacrifice offered in obedience (Heb 9:11–12).

Holy obedience as expression of all three theological virtues—faith, hope, and charity—are reflected in the act of Mary and Joseph in the temple and will find the perfect fulfillment of the sacrifice of Jesus on the cross. The obedience of Jesus offering himself as sacrifice restores our relationship with God the Father and reestablishes the original communion with God that was lost by the disobedience of the first man and first woman; that is, only the Son of God sacrificed in the flesh of man can remove the sin radically rooted in humanity since the fall. Only Jesus can accomplish this through his obedience surrendering himself to the will of the Father. Already Mary and Joseph prefigure the obedience that Jesus will follow; only Jesus is the innocent and unblemished Lamb to be sacrificed.

Mary reflects this model of obedience for she received the message of the angel Gabriel to be the mother of the Son of the Most High, Son of God, and she accepts her mission to follow Jesus to the foot of the cross where very few of the disciples and followers of Jesus appear. Mary's journey, unlike that of Eve, will be one of perfect obedience. Two women created immaculate, but only one will follow the path of humility and obedience: Mary. And unlike Adam, perfect obedience will be offered by one man to God the Father: Jesus. The begotten Son of God washes away the sins of the world.

This consecration of Jesus—"every first-born male must be consecrated to the Lord"—is made in the presence of God at the temple. The act binds Mary, Joseph, and Jesus to God. Two young parents present their child before God; we recognize the humility and the depth of their love.

---

1. See, *Catechism*, #1250, #1265-#1267.

The sense of "obedience" of Mary and Joseph dominates the fourth mystery and the fruit of the fourth mystery.

The fourth joyful mystery demonstrates how closely linked the mysteries of the rosaries are; the fourth joyful mystery also anticipates the fifth sorrowful mystery, the crucifixion where Jesus is offered again, this time as sacrifice, the Lamb offered at the presentation. And we see the salvific link for all of humanity—children, boys and girls, men, women—all called to baptism. The first luminous mystery, paralleling the presentation, expresses the baptismal act that responds to the saving mission of Christ culminating on the cross.

2. Simeon's Prophecy

The Holy Spirit revealed to the Prophet Simeon that "he would not see death before he had seen the Lord's Christ" (Luke 2:26). Luke tells us that Simeon lived in Jerusalem, a man known to be "righteous and devout" who looked "forward" with certitude to the "consolation of Israel" (Luke 2:25). With the Holy Spirit resting upon him Simeon's prophetic mission is revealed: the Holy Spirit led Simeon to the temple arriving to encounter Mary, Joseph, and the child, Jesus. Simeon observed the couple presenting their baby and offering two turtle doves; he understood their humble status, attentive to the Mosaic law, revealing the two as a religious couple. Simeon was struck by the holy purity of Mary and Joseph reflected in their eyes, the truth and beauty that stood out in this woman and this man before him; and the child held in the mother's arms. Simeon now had the assurance that he would not die before seeing the Christ of the Lord, as he had patiently waited to "set eyes" on the Savior chosen by God and now appearing before him at the temple precisely to meet the "Christ," the anointed one. Simeon waits. He observes. And he prays.

The "Christ" from Greek and "Messiah" from Hebrew means the "anointed one," so Simeon is referring to the messianic figure—only a king can be anointed and only a priest can anoint the king. David is known to be this kingly figure and becomes the symbol for the anointed one that Simeon and the people of Israel are waiting for (1 Sam 16:13; 2 Sam 7:12–13, 16). Simeon took Jesus in his arms, saying, "for my eyes have seen your salvation" (Luke 2:30). Simeon embraces "salvation" in the flesh of a baby. Simeon recognizes in the holiness of Mary and Joseph, the woman chosen by God, and the husband, loving guardian of the mother and child, the infant before him called to "restore" Israel. Simeon's eyes penetrated beyond the human flesh and political structures of the natural order. He prophetically transcended the nature of things to the supernatural, divine order; this child was called to save, his mission "salvation," that is, to restore separated people, divided nations, a fragmented world. Simeon prophesied this "restoration" was to be fulfilled by the child held in his arms.

Simeon makes this clear in his *nunc dimittis*, "Now you are dismissing your servant . . ."; the child he set his eyes on refers not only to the people of Israel, but the prophecy to be fulfilled extends to "a light for revelation to the gentiles" (Luke 2:32).[2] The child has come to restore humanity, the house of Israel and pagan gentiles alike. Simeon speaks these words of "restoration" holding the child, Jesus, in his arms to make it clear he is referring to "this" child and nobody else. In Jesus, restoration takes place; in Jesus, the fulfillment of the Law and Prophets is realized. Restoration conveys "to unite"—to make "one."

3. Sword Pierces Mary's Soul

Prophesying with the baby boy in his arms then, Simeon blessed them and said to Mary his mother, "and a sword will pierce your own soul too" (Luke 2:25). Simeon's prophetic words are not consoling, to tell a mother who just gave birth, bringing the child to be presented before God, "and a sword will pierce your own soul too." Nor can Joseph take comfort in such a prophesy knowing what awaits his wife and the child he loves. But they both understand this child has a divine mission, and now Simeon indicates suffering is part of the divine mission. And while Simeon sees in Jesus the salvation to come, he knows the suffering Mary will experience as a mother: "a sword will pierce your own soul too."

Powerful words and a powerful image.

Simeon points to Mary: the child, her child, the Savior, will pierce her soul. We gather from this verse, in Simeon's words, Mary will participate in the suffering of Jesus. This prophesy represents the first sorrow of what Catholics traditionally speak of as the "seven sorrows of Mary." A religious art tradition of statues and paintings of the seven sorrows of Mary has followed with seven swords in her bosom beginning with this first sorrow: "and a sword will pierce your own soul too." In the Church of the Holy Sepulchre in Jerusalem the statue of the bust of Mary is pierced by a single sword going through her bosom. Mary understood the child of God was born in her womb; she would remain one with her Son in his sufferings. And Joseph observes, listening, reflecting at Simeon and his prophesies wondering about what lies ahead for

---

2. The Roman Catholic breviary employs the biblical words of Simeon known by the Latin, *Nunc dimittis*, "Now you are dismissing," in the formal night prayer of Compline.

Jesus and for Mary—his wife and God's child entrusted to him. Joseph surrendered himself completely to the will of God.

In presenting Jesus at the temple, the act of obedience which the fourth joyful mystery conveys also anticipates Jesus's obedience to his Father at the cross. The presentation signals the acts of obedience to God the Father.

Mary is immaculate; she does not know any sin. So how can a sword pierce her soul to cause such great anguish? In the Old Testament the prevailing thought the prevailing thought until the book of Job was that curses and punishment were due to sin, while good people received the blessings from God and were rewarded for their good deeds. The suffering of Job teaches us that one can be "blameless and upright" (Job 1:1) and experience unexplained tragedy. At the end, we simply cannot penetrate the mysteries of God whether blessings or suffering (Job 28:20–28).

Mary and Jesus united at the cross, Mary at the foot of the cross, her Son nailed to the cross, both sinless, both innocent, both in union with the will of the Father. Mary and Jesus teach us that truthfulness, goodness, and holiness do not exclude suffering. Jesus died a cruel death; Mary stood united with Jesus at his crucifixion. Mary in her purity and her faith saw beyond the crucifixion, aware of God's plan for our salvation, but this did not diminish her suffering as a mother seeing her son naked, nailed, and bleeding to death on the cross.

These images of the sword piercing Mary reflect images of the passion, but we cannot separate the mysteries—joyful, sorrowful, glorious, and luminous—as if they are unrelated events or disconnected stories in the life of Mary and Jesus. All the mysteries of the rosary are interconnected because one mystery anticipates another as in the fourth joyful mystery, and prophetically, the crucifixion, the fifth sorrowful mystery. The mother of our Lord, and our Lord, Jesus Christ, are tied together in the rosary beads as are each of the mysteries and their lives.

The human experience of suffering conveys the reality of the human condition. The Second Person of the Trinity is conceived in the flesh; this requires a woman who becomes the mother of Jesus. The woman God chooses for the incarnation of the Second Person of the Trinity is prepared in advance, not by her intelligence, not by her will, but by the state of her soul: immaculate. Like all of humanity, subsequent events after Mary's birth depend on Mary's intelligence and her freewill to carry out God's plan for the salvation of humanity. The mysteries of the rosary, therefore, are bound together as are the lives of Mary, mother, and Jesus, Savior.

Joseph spends his earthly life as a loving spiritual father to Jesus, a model of both manhood and virtue. Protecting Jesus, aware of his divine mission, safeguarding him from the wickedness of the secular powers seeking to kill the child. Joseph, a hard-working carpenter, a man of purity, loved and protected his wife from any harm or danger. A man obedient to God.

The Christmas season places us immediately before the reality of what it means to be "Christian": the birth of Jesus a most joyful event immediately followed by pain and suffering with the slaughter of innocent babies. Then, Mary meets the prophet Simeon, who prophesies her soul being pierced.[3]

While working in Rome I visited one of the many city museums near Piazza Barberini. I saw a painting vividly depicting the dramatic event of the babies being hunted for slaughter. The painting captures the fear and suffering of the mothers but also their protectiveness. These innocent babies, vulnerable, being ripped away from their defenseless mothers, are killed on the spot by King Herod's soldiers. Fragility. Innocence. Vulnerability. The contrast is remarkable: soldiers with bulging muscles and veiny arms holding swords who follow orders to kill innocent babies and helpless mothers. Jacoppo Negretti (1548-1628) succeeds the realism of the flesh; the penetrating artist paints the flesh of the mother and child in identical textures of smooth, soft, gentle sensations compared to the rough skin of soldiers extending their arms, ready to slaughter without mercy, to destroy innocent life by the whim of the king's command.[4] The Roman Catholic Church in her wisdom remembers these vulnerable infants as saints innocently slaughtered. Saints and sanctity from the origins of Christianity teach us the power of the Holy Spirit integral to Christian living. Joseph discovered in a dream Herod's wicked intentions. Mary and Joseph escaped to Egypt heeding the angel's warning. We commemorate these events only a few days after Christmas.

II—Fourth Fruit of this Mystery: Virtue of Obedience

Practical matters—

We began this mystery with the obedient act of Mary and Joseph in the temple offering Jesus to God according to Mosaic Law. The obedience of Mary and Joseph prepares and anticipates the salvific mission of Jesus in his own obedience to the will of his Father. We obey because we choose to obey,

---

3. In the Roman Catholic calendar, the same week as the Nativity—the "Christmas Octave"—events focus on King Herod who orders the first born males killed as he looks for Jesus (Matt 2:16). The feast of the Holy Innocents is observed on December 28th, three days after Nativity of Jesus.

4. "The Slaughter of the Innocents" is in display at Rome's Galleria Nazionale d'Arte Antica, Via delle Quattro Fontane, 13, not far from Piazza Barberini/metro station.

because a loving God is asking us to obey, to obey him, our Father, who seeks to bring each one of us to him, united with him for all of eternity.

As Catholics we obey the teachings of Jesus, the commandments of God, the laws of the church. For priests and those who belong to religious communities, obedience represents a fundamental vow or promise that is made to a religious superior or bishop. The vow or promise of obedience derives from the obedience of Jesus. The Savior calls us to follow him setting the example; Jesus paves the way. Obedience is experienced as the most difficult vow because obedience touches on our intelligence; pride obstructs obedience. The first man and woman disobeyed God because Satan appealed to their intelligence by twisting truth with cunning words, manipulating the will by the senses, reasoning with them, confusing them, until finally sight, touch, taste, and the desire to possess divine wisdom lead the man and woman to disobey (Gen 3). The first sin is manifested in disobedience. But God's plan is directed towards perfect obedience and repairs the damage caused by the first man and woman. Mary and Jesus are perfectly united to God's will and his divine plan; both followed the path of obedience out of truth and moved by love. Joseph protects, teaches, and loves the child Jesus. Joseph proves to be an obedient man in his religious observance and holiness, in particular, his chastity.

The greatest challenge to our spiritual lives is obedience to God: we find our way out of obedience by justifying and rationalizing our sins rather than acknowledging our failure to obey, our disobedience. Our intelligence needs to be informed by Scriptures, tradition, and also natural law in moral matters to be "obedient" to truth.

In the light of church tradition, Scriptures, and natural law, the human intelligence is enlightened. Where one's position differs from authority, civil or church, the moral duty is to follow one's conscience always bearing in mind that the conscience needs to be informed by tradition, Scriptures, and natural law. Saint Thomas More, the sixteenth century English Chancellor in the Court of King Henry VIII, was accused of treason. More defended himself as loyal English subject who loved the king, but he refused to take an oath placing the king's authority on religious matters above the Church of Rome. Following his conscience, More did not sign King Henry VIII's Oath of Supremacy.[5] While all the other Eng-

---

5. The Act of Supremacy was introduced by King Henry VIII in 1534 and imposed on the English people acknowledging him as the supreme head of the Church of England. Refusal to accept the oath was punishable by death. English Roman Catholics who remained faithful to the Roman pontiff as head of the church and refused to take the oath faced execution. Remaining faithful to their church, 430 Roman Catholics were executed (1534–44).

lish Bishops, with the exception of Bishop John Fisher of Rochester, signed the oath, More overcame any kind of threats, coercion, or manipulation into signing the oath adhering strictly to his conscience—even if all the English Bishops broke with Rome (with the exception of Fisher)—by signing the oath. More knew he faced execution like the Carthusian monks whom he witnessed from his jail as they walked to their execution. More, was caught between two authorities, civil and religious, and he loved his beloved king; nevertheless, enlightened by his conscience, More remained loyal to his Catholic faith and the Bishop of Rome, the Pope.[6]

Obedience, or at least "loyalty" to what is true and good, affects our day to day lives. But how do we make choices? Saint Thomas More was an educated man who was not influenced by public pressure in any way; as a devout Catholic he also experienced freedom in Christ so he could not be threatened into making decisions he did not agree with. Today, we have the mainstream media, social media, endless news feeds, blogs and electronic sources that influence our emotions and our thinking. But unless these sources reflect church tradition, sacred Scriptures, and natural law, their reliability can be questioned. God created us in his image and likeness (Gen 1:27) which means we have reason and freewill; our relationship with God and the community of believers and non-believers draws from revealed and natural truths that are unchanging. Obedience to truth is what Saint Thomas More and the martyrs of the church throughout the centuries firmly understood and adhered to.

Our obedience is to the teachings of Christ who gave his body and blood for us and obedience to the church he left us. The Office of the Papacy was mandated by Christ to preserve the deposit of our Catholic faith; and to transmit biblical moral teaching uncontaminated by the poison of errors which today is reflected in relativism, hedonism, and sexual ideologies (Eph 4:14; 2 Pet 2:2). Our obedience is not the claims made by theologians when their assertions violate church tradition, sacred Scriptures, or the natural law. Our intelligence adheres to the truth of Christ and the church Christ left us, the truth the martyrs died for, and the truth the Christian martyrs continue to die for. We follow the Saints, receptive to the power of the Holy Spirit, following in the footsteps of Jesus Christ, obediently carrying our cross as we follow our Savior.

This is the truth which we are all called to obey Jesus: "the way, the truth and the life" (John 14:6). And Mary, mother and first disciple of Christ, perfectly adheres to this truth. The obedience of the presentation expressed by

---

6. A succinct account of these events relating to England, King Henry VIII, and Saint Thomas More can be found in Karlin and Oakley, *Thomas More*, 11-19.

Mary and Joseph to the Mosaic law contains an underlying element evident in the life of Mary, the woman who says "yes" to God's will. Already in the first joyful mystery, we observed that Mary's "yes" to God's plan undoes Eve's "no" to God. These mysteries of humility and obedience, first and fourth joyful mysteries represent more than parallel mysteries; they belong to the life of Mary, Joseph, and Jesus, and sanctify the life of the believer.

The other side of obedience, the refusal to obey, is clearly evident by the acts of the woman and the man in the Garden of Eden—when our first rupture with God occurred. Clearly linked to disobedience is the sin of pride: not God's truth but man's truth; not God's way but man's way. To correct the sin of pride is the virtue of humility expressed in obedience and perfectly expressed in the obedience of Jesus. The redemptive power of Christ's blood on the cross is efficaciously present in the sacraments of the church. We are restored at our baptism.

This obedience applies to the clergy, bishops, priests, and deacons, and the religious who promise obedience to their authorities, and the Catholic laity repeat their baptismal promises at every Easter Vigil Mass by reaffirming the teachings Catholic Church, and rejecting Satan and his works.[7] By crushing the sin of pride, obedience purifies and empties the person of their ego, their "me," and cultivates the God-centeredness of obedience embodied perfectly and absolutely by Jesus on the cross, in his *kerygma*—"the emptying of himself"—as we meditate in the fifth sorrowful mystery.

Something in human nature that is inclined towards "rebelling," the child's "no" to parental instruction and guidance, seems an inherent inclination in our lives. While freedom in its authentic expression unites us with the will of God, the disordered freedom generates increasing rebellion so evident in the world of gratifying pleasures by ridding oneself of all the structures, commitments, and responsibilities that "compromise" one's self-focused rationalized freedom and even go as far as falsely employing the words of the Bible to justify sexual sins.

Obedience and freedom appear to be opposed to each other. How can one be free when there are laws to be obeyed, the law of God, Christ, and the church? Does freedom, therefore, mean being without "laws" or a "lawless" person? This is what contemporary music in western societies appears to advocate: fusing sexuality and violence in a music industry for which many "artists" and "performances" exist to serve as models of "rebellion" in the name of freedom of expression. Rebelling against social and moral norms, the blasphemy in religious misrepresentation justified as art. And the direct

---

7. See the Roman Catholic rite of baptism, "renunciation of sin and profession of faith"; and Easter Vigil liturgy, "renewal of baptismal promises."

or indirect target: Christian values. How will the youth—our future—interpret "obedience" in the light of the dominant perversions?

Paradoxically, with the antagonism expressed towards Christian religious sensibility regarded as "art," Christians are expected to be "open-minded" and "tolerant" towards these blasphemous demonstrations of crude insensitivity. A performance in Italy backed by an American gospel choir resulted in the Vatican and Italian Episcopal Conference to react, saying the sacrilege that involved baptism was hurtful and unacceptable and condemned its broadcast.[8] Catholicism that serves to influence the global moral conscience is relentlessly attacked by the mainstream media to discredit and dismiss Catholicism in the name of "freedom of expression"; this means to mock Catholic symbols and Christian values. The primal sin of the first man and the first woman, "disobedience," shows its ugly head as the devil continues to lead God's human creation to rebel against God, source of truth and love.

But we also have the disobedience of the community, the people who betray God not at a personal level but at a communal level. Moses leads a people across the Red Sea away from slavery and oppression, liberating them by God's power and prepares them to receive God's holy instructions (Exod 19:5). The people of Israel, however, instead of waiting for Moses to descend from Mount Sinai carve for themselves a golden calf, worshiping a false god they created out of gold, only to amuse themselves in eating, drinking, and the sexual perversion that followed (Exod 32:1-6). The collective disobedience is manifested, ironically, soon after the people had told Moses, "Everything that the LORD has spoken we will do" (Exod 19:8). The disobedience of a people collectively results from the coercive force that makes the individual voice and the personal response go unheard if not crushed by the masses altogether. The power of collective pressure, to seduce, especially when this involves driving forces of wealth, power, and sex, and the threatening weight of punishment and death, the overpowered individual easily succumbs.

The collective failure at Mount Sinai is redeemed by a collective sacrifice: the tribes of Israel disobey but Levi triumphs (Exod 32:25–29). The Levites rally around Moses to let him know they are with him and obey Moses's instructions to slaughter the thousands who had violated their promises to follow the Ten Commandments. The collective slaughter of the Israelites at the hands of the Levites is expressed as a sacrifice, "cost of a son or a brother."

---

8. San Remo musical performance of a sacrilegious baptism on stage in February 2022.

The Levites consecrated themselves to God through a sacrificial slaughter, thereby, receiving God's blessing and the Levitical priesthood.

The disobedience of Israel at the foot of Mount Sinai contrasts with the collective obedience of the Levites who "sacrifice" their tribes, the earlier obedience of Abraham who is willing to sacrifice his only son, preparing the people of Israel for something far greater: the pascal sacrifice of Jesus himself to save humanity.

Collective disobedience of Israel and collective obedience of Levites both at Mount Sinai first act out the sins of pride and lust and then are corrected by the virtues of humility and purity. Both are manifested at a collective level, either provoking human weakness into disobedience and sin, or building human strength in obedience to faith. We know by experience that we are weakened by the vices of others as we are also strengthened and sustained by the virtuous acts of others.

Obedience, literally *ob + audire,* means "to listen to" in such a way that one is inclined in mind, heart, and body towards God who is speaking, making his words audible. Obedience to the will of God, to obey truth, or as Paul calls it, "the obedience of faith" (Rom 1:5), means faith made concrete by acts. Such obedience inclines both the intelligence and the will to be in communion with God where true freedom is found, and only such freedom can satisfy the longing for that happiness that has its ultimate end in God.

Mary's obedience and Joseph's obedience to God, perfectly fulfilled in Jesus, Son of God, each responds to God's will, obedience to the will of the Father who is loved. The obedience to God not only reflects the love of God that unites each of them—differentiated by their mission—and with complete surrender to God's plan.

In the first instance, Mary unites herself with God's plan for our salvation. Mary places her trust in God knowing he is all-loving and only seeks our good. Mary surrenders herself having received the words of the angel Gabriel as presented in the first joyful mystery. Mary's obedience includes an inquiring intelligence, seeking to understand, as the rational creature whom God has created possesses the desire to know, as Mary asks, "How can this be?" due to the reality of her virginal state.

Guardian of Jesus, the child whom he loves, Joseph finds himself in dangerous circumstances after the birth of Jesus where once again he places his trust in God's messenger who delivers the news of Herod's slaughter of the first-born, meditated in the third joyful mystery. Joseph's life as husband to Mary and spiritual father of Jesus is characterized by trust, by holy obedience, by the purity of a man who knows that God loves him and his wife and all of humanity, and that the child entrusted to him is called to fulfil God's plan. Joseph obeys as a man of humility, a man who adheres to the will of God.

Jesus exercises perfect obedience of the old covenant but transcends this obedience because Jesus acts in communion with the will of his Father. Doing the Father's will not as obligation or moral duty but out of love the Son has for the Father: to love the Father in truth is to do the Father's will (John 6:38–40). The obedience to the Mosaic Law as a mark of fidelity to God's will in the life of Jesus, obedience to truth radically expressed on the cross as a perfect act of love. Truth and love cannot be separated. The centrality of obedience as fidelity to God as we see in the Mosaic Law finds its fulfillment in Christ but also teaches the value of obedience as followers of Christ. To obey is an act of truth. To obey is an act of love. The entire fourth joyful mystery is built around the virtue of obedience.

We recognize Eve's disobedience in contrast to Mary's obedience, the disobedience of Adam, and the obedience of Jesus; in the first instance leading to the fall of the man and the woman, and the fallen state of humanity, and in the second instance, the woman—the mother—and the man—the Son of God—cooperate in the salvation of humanity. Jesus understands the path of obedience: his salvific mission will be to follow the path of unwavering obedience to God the Father and the Father's plan for human salvation to restore man with God.

Fifth Joyful Mystery—Finding of Jesus in the Temple

I—"Child, why have you treated us like this? Look, your father and I have been searching for you in great anxiety." (Luke 2:48)

Our Father . . . Hail Mary . . . Glory Be . . .

1. Looking for Your Child

Have you ever had the experience of losing someone? Well, with smartphones it's easier to find the lost person. Nevertheless, in some surroundings even with smartphones, panic is unavoidable; in crowds and congested spaces, at a shopping center or at the airport, disappearances are frightening. When it's someone who is elderly and fragile, someone with health issues, or someone who does not speak the local language, and especially a child, a sense of urgency overcomes us—are they alright?

In the case of children, panic immediately sets in. Is the child lost or abducted? Safe or stranded somewhere? One summer as all five of my nephews and nieces were at home, my sister came to realize that her fourth child—the oldest daughter about five years old at the time—was missing. Despite calling out her name, repeatedly . . . nothing . . . nor did the other four know where their sister was—or that she had disappeared, looking confused and worried themselves. My sister checked the rooms calling out her little girl's name. No answer . . . And so, my sister went out into the street shouting out her little girls' name, praying, now in a state of panic. No answer . . . My sister called out to God for help. Another inspection of the rooms, closets, and cupboard. No answer . . . nothing. But this time she heard a faint chuckle in the bathroom closet. The little five-year-old was found playing hide and seek!

2. Finding Jesus

Jesus was twelve years old when he travelled with his mother and father to pray at the Temple of Jerusalem. Going to the temple, Mary and Joseph observed their religious duties; the presence of Jesus demonstrated the significance of transmitting the faith, handing down the divine teachings, and going to Jerusalem for the feast of the Passover (Exod 12:14-17). Above twelve years old, the adolescent boy is expected to be with his father and prays with other men in the temple. But since Mary and Joseph thought Jesus was with the other parent, Jesus would have been twelve years old (Luke 2:42).

When Mary and Joseph left the temple for Nazareth, they discovered Jesus was not with the other parent. And so, the search begins on the third day. The journey from Jerusalem back to Nazareth, travelling northeast from the land of Judah to Galilee, with their Galilean caravan, Jesus may not have been in sight. They figured he was following, and not far behind like any twelve year old playing with his friends; his parents had no reason to worry. Several days go by and Jesus does not appear; one or two days late, but a third day? Mary and Joseph become alarmed. And so the search begins on the third day.

Travelling in different parts of the world one discovers family members and extended family scattered across villages, and time goes by chatting with neighbors and friends. So, reacting on the third day as Mary and Joseph had done shows that Jesus was brought up like any child; he experienced the humanness of childhood, playfulness, and yes, even—inadvertently—causing his parents to worry. When Mary and Joseph finally make their way back to Jerusalem, however, they do not find Jesus delayed by the company of family or distraction of friends, but rather, Mary and Joseph find Jesus in the temple—with the teachers answering their questions and asking questions himself.

3. Throne of the Word

The finding in the temple places Jesus on the throne—the throne of truth, "sitting among the teachers" (Luke 2:46). A pre-adolescent—twelve years old—Jesus conveys his wisdom to teach teachers. Jesus drew their attention by his surprising knowledge as the teachers listened to him; and they "were amazed at his understanding and his answers" (Luke 2:47). This fifth joyful mystery represents the first act Jesus expresses as "teacher," the truth he advances towards the fulfillment of his mission. Even though we do not have any record of what Jesus said, we know the teachers were listening, acknowledging his religious depth and wisdom.

In this pivotal moment Jesus "sits" exercising his wisdom with authority. Jesus, who is the Word, sits on the throne, teaching truth with authority that leads to his cross, before he sits on his throne of glory at the right hand of the Father.

In this first physical separation from his parents for three days, as if anticipating his resurrection on the third day, Jesus already at twelve years old unites himself with his Father's will. The finding in the temple reveals this intersection where the vertical movement Jesus adheres to his Father's will, and the horizontal movement Jesus submits himself to his earthly authority, Joseph and Mary. We hear Mary's motherly concern: "Child, why have you treated us like this? Look, your father and I have been searching for you in great anxiety" (Luke 2:48). The intersection of duties manifested by Jesus being found at the temple reflects both his humanity and divinity, where he is called to obedience: "And Jesus increased in wisdom and in years, and in divine and human favor" (Luke 2:52).

These knowledgeable men, learned teachers, were amazed with his level of understanding. We have here the only glimpse the Scriptures gives us of Jesus, as a twelve year old. At the temple, the interest of Jesus seems to be not that of a typical twelve year old as he preferred to sit with the teachers and be in their company—religious authorities who taught the Torah and sacred writings. So, we find out something about Jesus in his reply: "Why were you searching for me? Did you not know that I must be in my Father's house?" (Luke 2:49). The finding in the temple represents a temporal marker in the life and events of Jesus: he submits himself to the will of his Father, while he deeply loves his mother, Mary, and expresses devoted respect towards his spiritual father, Joseph.

The first revelation that Jesus has come to do the will of his Father, that Jesus is not bound to the will of his parents, surfaces at the finding in the temple. The mystery demonstrates the clear vertical direction in the life of Jesus as an adolescent who grows into manhood and matures in understanding; he is one with the Father in truth and in love. As Jesus grows in knowledge, his human will is in conformity with his Father's will. The finding in the temple anticipates Jesus's mission to glorify his Father by carrying out his Father's plan for human salvation. Jesus shows that he understands the temple is his Father's house expressing his unity with the Father; the temple is the house of God, his Father. We also know Jesus will later identify the temple with his own body. This second layer of meaning takes on an eschatological sense; his resurrection and the fulfillment of his

FIFTH JOYFUL MYSTERY—FINDING OF JESUS IN THE TEMPLE

mission, prophesying the destruction of the temple: "Destroy this temple, and in three days I will raise it up" (John: 2:19).[1]

Mary and Joseph, apart from being worried parents, are confused about Jesus's behavior, physically distancing himself from them by remaining in Jerusalem and not joining them on the road back to Nazareth. Jesus acknowledges divine authority over human authority, the will of God and his obedience to God over his obedience to human authority. As Jesus returns home with Mary and Joseph, Jesus remains obedient to them but subordinates the role of Mary and Joseph to that of his Father (Luke 2:49). Nevertheless, Jesus does submit himself to Mary and Joseph: "And he went down with them and came to Nazareth, and was obedient to them" (Luke 2:51).

The finding of Jesus is related to obedience; as we pray in the fourth mystery, the presentation, which signifies our religious obedience to God, to Christ's teachings, the magisterium of the Catholic Church, but also to our earthly parents, as found in the fourth commandment. In the finding of Jesus, we find Jesus also fulfilling the fourth joyful mystery and the fourth commandment: obedience. He owes obedience to his parents, but obedience to God the Father comes first.

We are told, "his mother treasured all these things in her heart" (Luke 2:51). Mary's silence reflects a woman who shows discretion and reserve; she talks little. Mary's words remain only a few in the Scriptures, but in each scene her words are charged with meaning. Mary is a woman of contemplation, and her actions are performed with silence, not drawing attention to herself. Mary reflects. Mary ponders.

The life of Mary, mother of God, means that from the conception of Jesus she kept and treasured these events in her heart. God chose Mary, the contemplative woman reflected in her silent disposition, to give birth to his Son. The two are spiritually connected: to keep the events surrounding the life of Jesus in her heart while she contemplated her divine Son. Mary does not go about speaking of her Son like a busybody to bring attention to him or to herself. Drawing attention to himself and his divine mission was what Jesus avoided for many years. Even at the instance of his first miracle by Mary's intercession, Jesus tells Mary, "Woman, what concern is that to you and to me? My hour has not yet come" (John 2:4). This cooperation between Mary and Jesus is reflected in the second luminous mystery when Mary turns to Jesus asking for his intervention at a wedding where she unexpectedly plays an intercessory role. The silence Mary keeps we find is consistent in the

---

1. The Temple of Jerusalem was in fact destroyed in 60 AD under Roman Emperor Nero. See Weidenkopf, *Timeless History*, 44–45.

Scriptures; when Mary does speak, her words express the mission she has in cooperating with Jesus in God's plan for our salvation.

Just as in the birth of Jesus, where Mary did not fully understand how she was expected to cooperate with God's plan—"How can this be, since I am a virgin?" (Luke 1:42)—this ongoing grasping remains true for Mary's journey with Jesus. Mary put her trust in God and his message, his promise of eternal salvation, without knowing all the details how this was to come about. Mary knew that she was chosen to be the mother of the "Son of the Most High," that "a sword would pierce her soul," and now that her Son was found at the temple: "Did you not know I must be in my Father's house" (Luke 2:49). Mary knew that God's Son that she conceived in her flesh, entrusted to Joseph, and growing up at her side meant to cooperate with God's plan for our salvation but is now "concerned" looking for Jesus.

We have in the temple scene the humanity of Jesus, and yet, a child who seeks to do his Father's will. The divine bond with the Father gradually unveils itself to the rest of the world. Jesus, an adolescent, seeks to obey the will of his Father with whom his will is ultimately united.

4. "Finding": Repeats Itself in the Joyful Mysteries

* the angel Gabriel *finds* Mary ready to receive the message of the incarnation—

* Mary *finds* her cousin Elizabeth at Ein Karem, and her cousin's child leapt in her womb—

* Jesus is *found* in the manger with Mary and Joseph, then the angels announce his birth—

* the shepherds at the announcement of the Angels *find* Mary, Joseph, and Jesus in the manger—

The shepherds, the poorest in economic status with no power and no wealth, the simplest in terms of their lifestyle, lead their sheep grazing to Jesus himself, who embodies the shepherd of shepherds, who leads those who recognize his voice. To these shepherds the angels first announce the birth of the good shepherd, the Messiah. The shepherds who are attentive to their sheep have *found* the true shepherd who is born in their midst, attentive to all mankind, leading them through the narrow gate to eternal life for those who recognize his voice.

* we *find* Jesus in the most humble of settings, defying human logic; the Savior born without worldly power or material wealth; born outside a village, in a manger—

* Herod's soldiers slaughter the baby boys as they try to *find* Jesus—

* the kings who follow the star leading them to Bethlehem where they *find* Jesus, and offer him frankincense, gold, and myrrh—

* Mary and Joseph *find* Jesus in the Temple of Jerusalem, Mary, a concerned mother can only say, "Son, why have you done this to us?"

Because we are made in God's image and likeness, our intelligence is illuminated by God when we seek the truth; hence, our desire for the truth is in our nature, just as it is in our nature that our will inclines us towards the good. God helps us to find him, so long as we seek what is true and good. God ultimately leads us to the Father's divine will with whom we are called into communion. Human intelligence, therefore, is like a star illuminated by God leading us to his Son, just as the three kings found Jesus (Matt 2:10–11). Saint Thomas Aquinas tells us that the intelligence serves truth, just as the will is directed towards what is good; the intelligence that illuminates our minds in order to know what is good and so do what is right.[2] God is truth and goodness, enfleshed in Jesus Christ.

Jesus is revealed to shepherds and wise men, to those who seek him with their truth-seeking intelligence, in both the simplicity of shepherds and the wisdom of kings. God created man with intelligence so we may know the truth and be led to God. Fear and hatred seek relentlessly to silence truth, to kill Jesus and destroy the message of salvation. False prophets existed—and still exist; in the Letter of John they are called the "Antichrist" (1 John 2:18).

II—Fruit of this Mystery: Virtue of Piety

Practical matters—

"Piety": what does this even mean? We sometimes say, "She is pious." Or "He is pious"—the adjective for the noun, piety. We associate "piety" with someone who is committed and faithful to regular religious observance, attending mass on weekdays or Sundays, a specific devotion to a Saint, to the blessed Virgin Mary, adoration of the blessed sacrament, a daily

---

2. Aquinas, *ST*, Pt. 1, q. 16, art. 1.

Scripture reading, weekly or monthly participation in prayer groups; all of these belong to the life of "piety."

A statue of a saint standing in a person's house or room, a saint who signifies a cultural or national figure and nothing more, does not make the person pious. The unopened, unread Bible on the bookshelf collecting dust where it sits month after month does not make the person pious. Piety involves concrete actions, whether in regular religious observances or spiritual readings, followed by interior movement, that is, a change where the person seeks to grow and concretely advances in the life of virtue leading to further sanctification by the grace of God.

While a student at the University of Toronto, I was invited to the home of a family friend. I asked my mother's friend where she attended mass on Sundays. The woman then glanced at her calendar on the wall with the face of Jesus, and she pointed, "You see, that's where I have Jesus," her beliefs displayed a calendar with the face of Jesus. Is this piety? Not unless she actually prayed. A picture does not make a person pious. Piety is a way of life, of daily prayer and ongoing conversion. The two are inseparable: piety and sanctification. Fidelity to religious practices is intended for the person's spiritual growth.

The word "piety" relates to acts of religious expression that have their source in God. These acts convey worship of God directly, or indirectly by honoring the saints of God, recognized for their receptivity to the Holy Spirit, the Third Person of the Trinity. Therefore, a pious act is a religious one. Praying the rosary, abstaining from meat on Fridays, and praying a novena are all expressions of piety with the most sublime act of piety—participating in the Sunday mass. These acts place us in relation to God stating something about our religious beliefs. In fact, piety ties us to God which is the meaning of "religion," to "tie" or "bind"—ultimately to the source of truth and goodness in our lives, our Creator.

What is the opposite of piety? We have the English word "impious," which means, according to the Oxford English Dictionary, "showing a lack of respect for God and religion." The adjective conveys a pejorative attitude because a person fails to acknowledge the Creator and the honor that is due to the author and sustainer of life. We need to be careful the appearance of piety does not reflect the hypocrisy condemned by Jesus and the apostles: "Religion that is pure and undefiled before God, the Father, is this: to care for orphans and widows in their distress, and to keep oneself unstained by the world" (Jas 1:27). Jesus teaches, "Beware of practicing your piety before others in order to be seen by them; for then you have no reward from your Father in heaven" (Matt 6:1).

When we worship God expressed in pious acts, we are disposed towards growing in charity towards our neighbor, which presupposes interior conversion. This interior "turning" towards God, the movement of the soul, leads to exercising charity in truth that is self-giving, directed towards the good of the other as Saint James makes perfectly clear in concrete acts. This is the fundamental difference between Christian love and "love" reduced to self-interest. The conversion or "turning around" reflects the growth in life of virtue informed by truth; a disposition towards the good is acquired thereby creating a habit, that is "virtue."

In Christianity, then, piety takes on three dimensions: first, the movement towards worshiping God and honoring his saints who lived by the Holy Spirit; the second movement is an interior one of sanctification where communion with the Trinitarian God and the invocation of the saints lead to increased disposition towards virtue and the exercise of virtue; this disposition moves outwards towards others, in the form of charity perfected by God's grace. So, the three-pronged expression of piety moves from worship of God and honoring his saints to interior sanctification by grace and intercession, and finally to charity. Piety is the work of the Holy Spirit, what we recognize as one of the seven gifts of the Holy Spirit, sustained and nurtured by God's grace.

Why is the finding of Jesus in the temple associated with piety?

Piety begins in the home, where families pray and worship together, serve as an example to their children, and teach their children the value of prayer, while supporting each other spiritually. When I went to Mangalore, India, for the priestly ordination of a close friend of mine, I stayed with him and his family for over two weeks. The family included his father, mother, brother, sister-in-law, two nephews (four and six years old), and two aunts, one who belonged to the Handmaids of Mary, and the other who arrived from Dubai, his godmother. The family prayed together each evening around 8:30 pm, led by the father; we faced the altar starting with the rosary, followed by a Scripture reading (from the day). One of the family members led a decade of the rosary, including the six-year-old nephew. At the end of the prayers the elder family members blessed the younger ones making their request: "bless me." This Catholic practice in India reflects a true example of piety.

There are those fallen angels who will try to snatch the pious away from their religious observances, pious practices, by planting seeds of doubt and then confusion about what God is asking of them. These seedlings of doubt echo the serpent who cleverly seeded lies into the woman and man even though both knew God's prohibition. We must not forget that Satan hates holiness, and as the Exorcist of Rome, Father Gabriel Amorth tells us, "Mary disapproves of the work of Satan."³ Whatever Satan can do to bring the pious believer into the clutches of demonic power, step by step, leading the pious away from Mary, from Jesus, from the sacraments, from church, and finally, from God; slowly so, the pious become impious. What is sin is no longer sin, repeating Satan's lies and following his deceptive tactics.

Going on a pilgrimage—ninety miles from Nazareth to Jerusalem—means that a believer made a real effort to offer a sacrifice and pray at the temple.⁴ This holy effort, this holy desire, this offering to God reflects piety. The piety of Mary and Joseph—as with all believers following the laws of God—expresses and conveys religious observance. So piety entails personal sacrifice or self-discipline, concrete acts of virtue in one's life. If piety is not reflected in one's own personal life striving for virtue, for holiness, then the external signs are cosmetic, like beautiful liturgies in denominations that permit moral errors which violate Scriptures and natural law: "truth" precedes the "beautiful."

Virtue is concrete. Exercising piety and advancing in virtue go together; some effort is made to sacrifice certain activities on a Sunday so one can attend mass. Such efforts should become natural which signify the acquisition of virtue, the natural disposition to attend Sunday mass. This applies to weekday masses or prayer groups to worship God and honor his saints. Catholics discover spiritual growth from attending an "obligatory" Sunday mass or solemnity that over time changes to one of disposition: awaiting the spiritual richness of the Sunday liturgy in the pursuit of truth and love.⁵

My experience in Zimbabwe while teaching at a Catholic mission in Masvingo Province for three years showed me what piety looks like. I observed mothers and fathers dressed in their formal Sunday clothing, men dressed in suits and ties, women with elegant dresses knee length and ribbons in their hair, with their eight, nine, ten children ahead of them on the way to the Catholic mission, not in a car, or a bus, but walking an hour or more by foot given the location of their remote homes. Living in Africa, I also travelled through the Central African Republic where I attended mass on November 1 to observe All Saints Day. I noticed in the church numerous

---

3. Amorth, *Maria e Satana*, 53.

4. About 150 kilometers.

5. When a person misses Sunday mass or an obligatory solemnity this needs to be brought to confession since the third commandment has been violated. Each country has their own obligatory solemnities decided by the National Conference of Bishops—often transferred to the Sunday if the obligatory solemnity occurs during the weekday. Obligatory solemnities are on a fixed day in some countries are those such as the Immaculate Conception (December 8), Christmas (December 25), Mary Mother of God (January 1), the Assumption of Mary (August 15), All Saints (November 1).

FIFTH JOYFUL MYSTERY—FINDING OF JESUS IN THE TEMPLE

French soldiers attending mass and in line to receive communion. They made a point of attending mass and observing the solemnity.

My experiences in India, Zimbabwe, and the Central African Republic contrast the excuses made for not being able to participate in Sunday mass because of feeling "too tired," or the weather is "too rainy," or "too cold." I have had heard children tell me they are "too busy" to attend mass because of their Sunday activities ranging from music to dance with sports activities being the most frequent excuse. These children reflect their family values, often lifestyles influenced by the community to which they belong: individualistic, materialistic, and hedonistic. The sense of personal piety can easily be lost—and not even learned.

I do find it edifying to celebrate Sunday morning mass at 8 a.m. and notice altar servers who are waiting in the sacristy or sitting in their designated chairs to serve mass. This, no doubt, reflects the values of their home, transmitted to them, these elementary and high school students have learned the significance of being present for mass and serving mass. These children have acquired the sense of piety, the virtue of waking up perhaps as early as 7 a.m. so they can serve mass on a Sunday morning. Children will do what they observe in the home because they grow up understanding the values that matter in the home. Whether these pious practices acquired in childhood continue throughout their life raises other issues at a societal level. The point remains that parents communicate the best values they can when this includes the virtue of piety. In this way, parents also fulfil their responsibility in the spiritual instruction of their children.

A friend of mine who belonged to a non-denominational mission organization in Thailand during her evangelical days told me when I first met her that one does not need to go to church to pray to God. True, indeed; Christ teaches us himself to close our door; "go into our room" where our heavenly Father hears us in private (Matt 6:6). Christ teaches us to deepen our communion with God. However, public acts of religious observance were fundamental to the people of Israel as a people of faith living their faith as a community of worshipers. Jesus does not teach us to replace public worship with a personal form of worship. On the contrary, Jesus wants us to deepen our personal communion with God while observing worship within our community that serves to support and strengthen each other. Jesus does not promote individualism, ignoring the value of community prayer and worship. Jesus teaches, "For where two or three are gathered in my name, I am there among them" (Matt 18:20). Piety helps to strengthen others in their own faith journey. For the Catholic believer, our parish setting where we worship means belonging to a Christian community where we receive the sacraments and pray together. All of Jesus's activities had a public dimension even when he was alone with his apostles. And when Jesus prayed in anguish alone in the Garden of Gethsemane, he asked for the presence of Peter, James, and John (Matt 26:37–38).

These pious practices lead us to find Christ, our Savior, the King of kings, whom we worship on our knees. Piety also edifies others in the community; our acts convey our beliefs to those who may have a weaker faith. Piety serves, therefore, to nurture our personal communion with God but also as a worshiping community. The religious value of piety therefore functions at three levels: i.) individual observance of religious practice that places the person in communion with God; ii.) the concrete virtue that follows from such religious practices; and iii.) edifying support this provides for the believing community. Piety is where the fifth joyful mystery leads us—to the one whom we are looking for: with Mary and Joseph we find Jesus in the temple, truth who sits on the throne. For Jesus is the Word, and our piety expressed in religious observance leads to the throne of truth.

LUMINOUS MYSTERIES

First Luminous Mystery—Baptism of the Lord

I—*In those days Jesus came came from Nazareth of Galilee and was baptized by John in the Jordan.* (Mark 1:9)

Our Father . . . Hail Mary . . . Glory Be . . .

1. Jordan River

A visit to Mount Nebo in Jordan on a clear day offers the magnificent scenery of the Jordan Valley as far as the Dead Sea. From this position on Mount Nebo, Moses experienced the exhilarating view of the promised land. The Roman Catholic Church of Moses is built on the site where Moses died. The earlier presence of a church was already documented by Egeria on a pilgrimage in 394.[1]

Geographically, the Jordan River contains symbolic value for the Israelites: when Moses reached Canaan with the Israelites, he died on Mount Nebo east of the Jordan River (Deut 34:1, 5–6), so Moses never crossed the Jordan River with the Israelites although he led them to the river. Joshua standing at flood level led the Israelites across the Jordan with the priests leading the ark of the covenant (Jos 3:15–17); the prophet Elijah lived near the Jordan River (1 Kings 17:5); and the first purification in the Jordan takes place when the prophet Elisha instructs Naaman the Syrian to bathe in the Jordan and he is healed of his leprosy (2 Kings 5:9–10, 14). The Jordan was also crossed by Judas Maccabeus and his brother Jonathan Maccabeus during the Nabatean war (1 Macc 5:24).

The eastern bank of the Jordan River, bordering Israel and Jordan, marks the site where Jesus was baptized, about six miles from the Dead Sea, known

---

1. *Egeria's Travels*, 121.

as "Bethany Beyond the Jordan."[2] Beginning 650 feet above sea level on the slopes of Mount Herman in Israel, the Jordan provides the water source for the Sea of Galilee. The Jordan River flows into the Dead Sea, the lowest elevation below sea level.[3] The Jordan River is mentioned about 175 times in the Old Testament and about 15 times in the New Testament. Walking in the cool water of the Jordan surrounded by reeds, while the hot sun beats down on the pilgrims, creates the sense of life and rebirth. The significance of the baptism is conveyed by the very context of Saint John's baptism.

2. John and Jesus

The artistic interest as a religious subject involving the infants, Jesus, and John, were painted by the Renaissance artist Raphael. In his famous work, *Madonna della Seggiola with the Infant Jesus and St. John* (1513–14), the Virgin Mary holds Jesus, her head close to her son's, and young John the Baptist folding his hands in prayer at Mary's knee. The warmth of the colors, olive, peach, apricot, and Saint John's earthy gown, creates a natural innocence, especially as Mary firmly holds the fleshy, "lamb-like" Jesus. Saint John looks towards Jesus as if ready to announce the "Lamb of God." The painting captures in its harmony and beauty this relation between John and his cousin Jesus.[4]

The story of John's birth is narrated in the opening of Luke's Gospel where Luke presents the supernatural events related to the birth of the "baptizer" before introducing the "Messiah," as meditated in the second joyful mystery. Luke provides a precise time frame: "days of Herod"—around 37–1 BC. The lineage of the parents, Zechariah and Elizabeth, is clearly stated: Zechariah descended from the priestly order of Abijah and Elizabeth traces her origins to one of the daughters of Aaron. Both husband and wife belonged to the priestly house of Levi (Luke 1:5); moreover, priests serving at the temple were required to marry within their own tribe based on the Levitical law (Lev 21:14).

Elizabeth and Zechariah were advancing in years. Elizabeth, expecting her first child, proved to be a miracle. The angel instructs Zechariah

---

2. The Jordanian side is a UNESCO World Heritage site visited by Pope Francis in 2016. The Jordanian site also corresponds to the Madaba map, the sixth century mosaic floor in Saint George's Church, detailing the earliest depiction of the Holy Land. Archaeologists in 1996 excavating the area found twenty churches dating to the Roman and Byzantine periods as well as baptismal pools.

3. Measurement: 955 feet below sea level or 291 meters below sea level.

4. *Madonna della Seggiola* is on display at the Palazzo Pitti in Florence.

on the ascetic observances of his son, "he must never drink wine or strong drink" associated with the Nazirite vow (Luke 1:15), and he "will be filled with the Holy Spirit." Zechariah's son is given a mission: "he will turn many of the people of Israel to the Lord their God." Zechariah's son is also compared to the great prophet Elijah "with the spirit and power of Elijah" (Luke 1:16–17). His son will "make a people prepared for the Lord." John will grow to fulfil his prophetic role leading the people to conversion and getting them ready for Christ. The angel Gabriel reveals himself to Zechariah as the messenger of God. But Zechariah having questioned the angel, suggesting doubt as he and his wife were advancing in years, is reprimanded and becomes mute until the child is born (Luke 1:19-20). Instead, Elizabeth, having conceived, overcomes the disgrace previously caused by her barrenness. God looked favorably upon her (Luke 1:25).

The visitation, the second joyful mystery, shows parallels with the mystery of the annunciation, the first joyful mystery. The joyful mysteries start with the supernatural source of salvation opening the way to the new covenant. Contrast between Zechariah and Mary emerges in the first luminous mystery where Zechariah expresses doubt and is punished, while Mary seeks to grasp the supernatural act and is provided with an explanation. The response to Mary trying to make sense of the angel's message reveals God's miraculous intervention: the Holy Spirit will descend upon her. Akin to her doubting husband, even Elizabeth expressed living with the shame of her infertile condition, for it was perceived as a dishonor. Mary's attention is focused on the child of God she will bring into the world without expressing concern for the personal or social ramifications of her conception. And Joseph is instructed by the angel how to proceed given Joseph's state of confusion with the news of Mary "being with child."

The language employed in the first and second joyful mysteries, the conceptions of John and Jesus, conveys the two roles to be assumed by these men, prophetic and salvific, respectively. The contrast Luke provides clearly differentiates John and Jesus in terms of missions and lineage; where John is from the Levitical tribe, Jesus is from the house of David on both the side of his mother, Mary (Luke 1:27), and that of his spiritual and legal father, Joseph, also from the house of David (Luke 3:23–31). The overlapping of John and Jesus, their missions in the transition from the old covenant to the new covenant is made evident in Luke's Gospel.

In his exchange with the angel Gabriel, we encounter Zechariah perform his priestly duties in the temple of Jerusalem. Luke's Gospel reveals the issue of naming the son; Zechariah intended on following the practice of giving the child their son the father's name. Elizabeth brings their child to term telling Zechariah the name the child—"John"—though nobody in the family was named John. Unable to speak, Zechariah then writes down the name "John" (Luke 1:13; 60–63). The role of the women, Elizabeth who gives birth to the prophet, John, and Mary who gives birth to the Savior, Jesus, play a central role in the transition from the old covenant to the new covenant. John's birth and his naming, directed by God, produce a sign of God's plan: John is part of the saving mission of Jesus, Son of God.

Zechariah's prophecy clearly expresses the prophetic role his son, John, plays—one of preparation: "And you, child, will be called the prophet of the Most High; for you will go before the Lord to prepare his ways, to give knowledge of salvation to his people by the forgiveness of their sins" (Luke 1:76-77).[5]

3. Ein Karem: Old and New Covenants

In Ein Karem the beautiful church of Saint John the Baptist was erected in 1939 by the Italian architect, Antonio Barluzzi, who designed and executed the Holy Land Roman Catholic churches. Built in the location where it was believed that John the Baptist was born, excavations in 1941 unearthed ceramics dating from the period of the first century BC to about seventy AD corresponding to the lifetime of Zechariah, Elizabeth, and John the Baptist. The layers of church mosaics and architecture can be traced to the Byzantine period, fourth to seventh centuries, but it is predominantly eleventh-century construction of the crusader period.[6] The small grotto on the left side of the church where an altar has been erected is identified as the location where John was born. The beautiful interior art of the church noted by pilgrims and travelers is reflected in the design of the tiles used in the Baptist's grotto and in the floor and walls, tiles reflecting the religious culture of Spanish Franciscans who have been the custodians of the church.[7]

At Ein Karem Elizabeth and Mary meet; we meditated on this encounter in the second joyful mystery. In this meeting between mothers and cousins, the babies they carry, John and Jesus, experience the joy that charity brings. Mary entered the house of Zechariah, and greeted Elizabeth, and hearing Mary's greeting, "the child leaped in her womb" (Luke 1:41). Mary

5. The Roman Catholic breviary employs Zechariah's opening words, "Blessed be . . . " in Morning Prayer—Lauds—known as the Benedictus.

6. The Church of Saint Anne in Jerusalem, dedicated to the parents of Mary, Saint Anne and Saint Joachim, represents a perfect example of Crusader-Romanesque architecture and engineering completed in 1138.

7. The site of the church had already been identified in 1106 by a Russian pilgrim, Abbot Daniel, who mentions the church—and the grotto on the left side—as the birthplace of John the Baptist.

is the mother of Elizabeth's Lord, as Elizabeth acknowledges in her words addressing Mary, and John leaps precisely because he hears the voice of the mother of his Lord—her voice, her greeting. John's voice will be heard in the desert preparing the way for this child in Mary's womb, his cousin, his Savior. The encounter between cousins, who carry the call to conversion and future salvation in their wombs, together contain the movements from the old covenant to the new covenant, the prophets and the law, and their fulfillment in Jesus. In this meeting of mothers in Ein Karem, John leaps at the voice signaling salvation, the sign of new life and rebirth.

Events surrounding the birth of John followed by the birth of Jesus provide signs of how the two cousins are associated in the call to conversion; John, in preparation for the Savior, Jesus. Preparing the way, John calls the people to conversion, purification, and baptism and prepares them for Jesus and discipleship. John withdraws to the desert, a sign of detachment from the world, living on honey and locusts, wearing a camel hair garment and a leather belt around his waist (Matt 3:4) expressing poverty, purity, and detachment, but also a reflection of the angel's ascetic instructions given to Zechariah in John's upbringing. John's ministry and that of Jesus overlap to fit perfectly the transition of covenants, old and new, which converge at the baptism of Jesus by John (Matt 3:13–17), ending in John's decapitation, having chastised Herod for his adulterous sin with Herodius (Mark 6:17-28; Lev 18:16).[8]

Thus, the preparation of John begins at his childbirth, the ascetic radicality he lives as an adult, and finally he is ready to instruct the people on conversion and baptism in the Jordan (Matt 3:4, 11). While John had many disciples he insists that another will follow him. He baptizes with water, but the one to follow will baptize in the Spirit. John focuses on "making way for the Lord" through baptism of repentance, symbolized by the cleansing in the Jordan; he prepares the way for Jesus who is also "baptized" by John in the Jordan. The Holy Spirit as a dove descends upon Jesus showing God the Father's approval. Jesus's ministry starts with his baptism in the Jordan; and he will lead his disciples to eternal salvation. Water signifies cleansing, purification, and conversion, but with the baptism of Holy Spirit, a new meaning of water is understood: cleansing of original sin, being reborn in the Trinitarian God, and becoming God's adopted children.

Identified as a prophetic figure, John the Baptist is referred to as Elijah. What is the connection between John and Elijah? The words of Zechariah are central in John's prophetic role: "And you, child, will be called the prophet of the Most High; for you will go before the Lord to prepare his

---

8. Herod Antipas's half-brother, Philip, Herodius's husband, was still living.

ways, to give knowledge of salvation to his people by the forgiveness of their sins" (Luke 1:76–77). The mission of John anticipates and paves the way for the Lord—to prepare the people for salvation. The association with Elijah—and not any other prophet—is because Elijah was considered the greatest among the Old Testament prophets. Even the clothing John wore was identified with that of Elijah's: "'. . . a leather belt around his waist.' He said, 'It is Elijah the Tishbite'" (2 Kings 1:8).

Reference to Elijah appears in the last book of the minor prophets, Malachi: "Lo, I will send you the prophet Elijah before the great and terrible day of the LORD comes" (Mal 4:5). Malachi's prophecies anticipate both the baptizer who immediately precedes Jesus, with allusion to Jesus following John. Like the "sign," John's voice resounds with the coming of the Messiah as prophesied by Malachi.

The Gospels provide an account of John the Baptist baptizing Jesus, and in the Gospel of Mark, Jesus makes reference to Elijah (Mark 9:13). This continuity from prophet to prophet, Elijah to John, and prophet to Savior, John to Jesus, is evident, as Matthew states, "Truly I tell you, among those born of women no one has arisen greater than John the Baptist . . . For all the prophets and the law prophesied until John came; and if you are willing to accept it, he is Elijah who is to come" (Matt 11:11, 13–14). The Elijah that is to come refers to Malachi's prophesy—"he has come"—John the Baptist.

4. Purity of John the Baptist

John the Baptist lived in penance and truth; he preached, preparing the way for the Messiah whom he acknowledged as being greater than him, to the point of being unworthy to untie his sandals. John assumes his mission as the mediator between the old covenant and the new covenant. From childbirth John the Baptist was brought up according to the Nizirite vow; he later lived off locusts and honey, radically detached from the world, wearing a camel-hair garment tied around his waist (Matt 3:4).

Though John is imprisoned for courageously proclaiming what is true, John's imprisonment does not weaken his desire to proclaim the truth. John the Baptist was imprisoned by Herod Antipas, tetrarch of Galilee and Perea. Herod Antipas was the son of Herod the Great who was "king" of Judea at the time of Jesus's birth. These were client-kings of the Roman emperors. The Gospel of Luke states the reason why John the Baptist was imprisoned: "But Herod the ruler, who had been rebuked by him because of Herodias, his brother's wife, and because of all the evil things that Herod had done, added to them all by shutting up John in prison"

(Luke 3:19–20). John did not withdraw from the necessity to confront the sexual misconduct of the king violating God's laws. In keeping with his mission of preaching and conversion, John did not fear correcting the king for his actions and scandalous activities.

John the Baptist rebuked Herod for his sexual relationship with Herodias, his brother's wife. Herodias was angered by John's chastisement, and the scandal could lead to an insurrection if the prophet spoke out against the sexual immorality of the king. Herod refrained from executing John precisely because John benefited from the reputation of a prophet, although Herod personally desired to execute him (Matt 14:5). Herod understood the power of the crowd. The opportunity to deal with John arose during Herod's birthday; Herodias made strategic use of the event seeking John's execution. Herodias's daughter danced for Herod at a banquet for his birthday, and Herod being so pleased, granted her daughter, Salome, whatever she wished. At the instigation of Herodias, Salome asked for the head of John the Baptist "on a platter" (Matt 14:6–8). Herod felt compelled to comply given the oath he made to Salome; he agreed to her wish, and Herod ordered John's execution, his head brought on a platter for the perverse pleasure of the three of them.[9]

The significance of the sexual perversion on the part of Herod, Herodias, and Salome reflects the moral degeneration of an entire family, contrasted with the firm moral rectitude of John in his preaching, his living, and his death for the truth. John, who sought to purify his senses and passions, who lived a detached life, looking ahead to Jesus as the Messiah, and humbled himself acknowledging he was unworthy to tie the sandals of Jesus. John's humility and purity are contrasted to the sexual immorality, hedonism, and narcissism demonstrated in birthday banquet reflecting the multiple layers of Herod's sensuous gratification. The self-centered pleasures extended to executing an innocent man. Herod represents the archetype of sexual indulgence: though Herod knew John to be a righteous man, the passion motivating Herod's marriage to his brother's wife, the erotic pleasure brought by his step-daughter dancing before him, and bound by a foolish oath, Herod submits to Herodias's request having John's head brought on a platter.

---

9. In the Roman Catholic Church the memorial of the Beheading of John the Baptist is observed on August 29th.

5. Baptism of Jesus

The baptism of Jesus is presented in all four Gospels. In Matthew's Gospel, the baptism is prefaced by the words of John: "I need to be baptized by you, and do you come to me?" (Matt 3:14). John's Gospel indicates that John knows the identity of Jesus, who he is, but this is revealed to John by the Spirit who sent John: "I myself did not know him; but he who sent me to baptize with water said to me, 'He on whom you see the Spirit descend and remain, this is he who baptizes with the Holy Spirit'" (John 1:33). John the Baptist states his reason for baptizing Jesus: "but I came baptizing with water for this reason, that he might be revealed to Israel" (John 1:31). While John is baptizing in the Jordan, he knows that Jesus does not need to be baptized. John the Baptist acknowledges this fundamental difference between the two of them, not only suggesting humility, but affirming who Jesus is. Only after Jesus provides an explanation is John prepared to baptize him: "Let it be so now; for thus it is fitting for us to fulfil all righteousness" (Matt 3:15).

Jesus responded to John by asserting that both of them will "fulfil all righteousness." John and Jesus both share in a mission of "righteousness" that is to be fulfilled, but each with a unique role: prophetic for John, salvific for Jesus. Why does Jesus ask for baptism, the pouring of water that signifies purification and conversion? Jesus speaks of "fulfillment" referring to the Law and the Prophets. In the waters of the Jordan, the old covenant promise made with Israel is fulfilled in Jesus with the start of the new covenant opening salvation to all of humanity.

In Matthew's Gospel, we hear God the Father address the crowd. Matthew relates the event: "And when Jesus had been baptized, just as he came up from the water, suddenly the heavens were opened to him and he saw the Spirit of God descending like a dove and alighting on him. And a voice from heaven said, 'This is my Son, the Beloved, with whom I am well pleased'" (Matt 3:16–17). The Father's voice, "this is my Son," is directed to the witnesses, the listeners, where the Father expresses his love for his Son, "my Son," and that he is pleased with him. An affirmation of Jesus's mission that comes from the Father. The Spirit of God descends upon him establishing the divine nature of Jesus's mission. This is in continuity with the Spirit of God descending upon Mary by whom she conceives Jesus. The Spirit of God does not merely express designation of a mission, but the mission is inseparable from the Triune God that manifests itself for the first time in the New Testament with the baptism of Jesus.

In the Gospels of Mark and Luke, the Father addresses Jesus, his beloved Son: "In those days Jesus came from Nazareth of Galilee and was baptized by John in the Jordan. And just as he was coming up out of the water, he saw the heavens torn apart and the Spirit descending like a dove on him. And a voice came from heaven, "You are my Son, the Beloved; with you I am well pleased" (Mark 1:9–11). The language focuses on the Father, addressing the Son: "You are my Son, the Beloved." The language is personal, directed to the Son, expressing the love of the Father, and the Father is "well pleased." The relationality conveys a communion of love between the Father and the Son but also the mission to be accomplished by the Son. As with the Gospel of Matthew, the Spirit descends upon the Son to identify him as the chosen one, the Messiah, as John the Baptist attests himself. The baptism of Jesus prepares Jesus for his ministry that pleases the Father.

In Luke's Gospel, we read, "Now when all the people were baptized, and when Jesus also had been baptized and was praying, the heaven was opened, and the Holy Spirit descended upon him in bodily form like a dove. And a voice came from heaven, "You are my Son, the Beloved; with you I am well pleased" (Luke 3:21–22). Luke conveys the sense of oneness between Jesus and the people, all being baptized, even though Jesus did not need to be baptized, and John knew this. As in Mark's Gospel, however, the Holy Spirit descends upon Jesus, thereby identifying him, and separating him from all the others who were being baptized, and separated from John who was baptizing even Jesus, "You are my Son, the Beloved," affirming the relationality between Father and Son, built on love, and this love anticipates the Son's mission that pleases the Father. As with Mark, the language conveys this personal communion between Father and Son, while meant to be heard and understood by those witnessing—the ones who follow Jesus.

The baptism of Jesus followed by the sign of the Holy Spirit marks the beginning of Jesus's ministry; Jesus is the chosen one, the Messiah, for whom John prepared the people and for whom John had been prepared himself. In the waters of the Jordan, in Judea, humanity is prepared for a radical transformation, in fact, an ontological change for all those who accept the teachings of Jesus and choose to follow him.[10] The conversion begins with John baptizing in water, the symbol of new life and rebirth, but with the Holy Spirit that descends upon Jesus is the Spirit that also descends upon the church at Pentecost, the third glorious mystery.

6. Holy Trinity

All three Gospels, Matthew, Mark, and Luke, show the same development of events: i.) Jesus reaches the Jordan River; ii.) Jesus is baptized by

---

10. The "ontological" reference is to the change in the "being" of the person which occurs at baptism by being cleansed of original sin.

John although Jesus does not need baptism; iii.) after baptism the Spirit descends upon Jesus; iv.) we hear the voice of the Father addressing Jesus—"my Son." The baptism of Jesus in the Jordan River reveals the Father, Son, and the Holy Spirit and represents the first manifestation in the New Testament of the Holy Trinity: three divine Persons who are one in their divine substance while distinct in their relations.[11]

Two factors emerge at the baptism of Jesus in the Jordan: i.) the transition from the old covenant to the new covenant is marked by a manifestation of the Trinitarian God; and, ii) the Holy Trinity also marks the beginning of the ministry of Jesus. In the Trinitarian manifestation, the Gospels do not provide details. A further manifestation of the Trinity is offered with the descent of the Holy Spirit at Pentecost, the third glorious mystery. The Scriptures do not provide the terminology to express the substantial union or the divine relation of Persons of the Trinitarian God. However, the distinction of each person is clearly evident; Father, Son, and Holy Spirit, while each person is identified in relational terms of the Holy Trinity.[12]

We have the Holy Trinity revealed in the Scriptures, but the articulation of the Holy Trinity relied on church fathers in the midst of theological disputes and controversies in the early church. The Ecumenical Church Councils provided clarity by formulating the teachings of the church making Christian doctrine uniform and definitive. The "universality" of the teaching was assured by the Roman pontiff who confirmed or ratified the teachings.[13]

Belief in a Trinitarian God is fundamental to confessing the Christian faith. The Holy Spirit is the source of the Christian faith expressed in both the tradition of the church and sacred Scriptures. Interpreting the Scriptures without objective authoritative guidance, relying merely on personal interpretation, has led to conflicting interpretations leading to heterodox movements or "heresies." To claim a doctrine or teaching is Christian, we need a an objective authoritative reference besides the Bible—what Roman Catholics call the magisterium—the "teaching office of the church."

---

11. See *Catechism*, #252–#253. Also, "the Father generates, the Son is begotten, the Holy Spirit proceeds," as stated, "The divine unity is Triune," *CCC* #254.

12. See *Catechism of the Catholic Church*, #245, #251. This is an example of where, "Show me in the Bible . . ." does not always work when Christian doctrine and dogmas are not explicitly stated in the Scriptures. The wording "Holy Trinity" does not even appear in the Bible. We have knowledge of the Holy Trinity because the Holy Spirit guides the church in truth. All Christians benefit from early Ecumenical Councils to establish Christian doctrine; these involved church fathers, bishops, theologians, and final ratification—approval—from the council fathers and Roman pontiff.

13. See *Catechism*, #2034; and Weidenkopf, *Timeless*, chapter 2.

The baptism of Jesus in the Jordan, therefore, opens not only with Jesus's baptism, followed by Jesus's ministry, but the very nature of Jesus's mission: salvation in the name of the Trinitarian God, Father, Son, and Holy Spirit. Jesus's baptism is where Jesus unites himself with humanity: to be one with the suffering people, lost due to sin, and directs them to the Way, the truth, and the life. This salvific mission of baptizing in the name of the Father, the Son, and the Holy Spirit initiates the mission and ministry of Jesus. And similarly, when Matthew ends his Gospel, Jesus commissions his disciples to go out and bless all nations in the name of the Father, Son, and Holy Spirit (Matt 28:19–20).

The Holy Trinity is essentially our identity as Christians. At baptism, by saying the individual's name followed by baptizing—with water—in the name of the Trinitarian God, Father, Son, and Holy Spirit, supernaturally marks the individual as a Christian. The use of any other words or formula means the baptism is not valid and any other words do not identify the individual as a Christian. At baptism, the rebirth of the individual in the name of the Trinitarian God—Father, Son, and Holy Spirit, who creates, redeems, and sanctifies—is cleansed of original sin. This means that the baptismal water poured upon the child (or adult) symbolizes the cleansing of the Jordan, the repentance and conversion from original sin to new life, recreated in the name of the Holy Trinity. John the Baptist's call to repentance and conversion in the Jordan prepares us for baptism in the Holy Spirit.

II—Fruit of this Mystery: Openness to the Holy Spirit

Practical Matters—

Teaching Christian doctrine has been a challenge for the church throughout the centuries. Falsehood opposes truth. We already have indications in the Scriptures of "false" teachers (1 Tim 6:3–5; 2 Pet 2:1–3). So the reality of "false" preaching has been present from the apostolic era. The church dealt with not only "false prophets" but also pseudo-Gospels. Not everything written about Jesus during the lives of the apostles and the post-apostolic era was inspired by God.[14] The church under the authority of the bishop

---

14. Gnostic Gospels written between the second and third centuries already circulated, but also earlier Jewish-Christian "Gospels" such as the Gospel of the Ebionites written in the mid-second century were in existence.

of Rome, the pope, affirmed the inspiration of the books ("canon").[15] The universal jurisdiction of the office of Peter meant what was affirmed as belonging to Christian doctrine applied to the entire church, not just the pope in Rome. "Catholic" means "universal," so the teachings are upheld throughout the church. How could this be possible? Because the Holy Spirit breathes upon and guides the church, the experience of Pentecost—the third glorious mystery.

In the early church the first theological debates concerned the identity of Jesus. Already in the apostolic era the Ebionites rejected the virgin birth and the divinity of Jesus. The truth of Jesus's identity meditated upon in the first joyful mystery of the annunciation reminds us that the one person who could refute the Ebionites was the mother of God herself; the truth of Jesus's identity she communicated herself to the members of her family and the apostles on Mount Zion in Jerusalem where they worshiped in truth: that the Holy Spirit descended upon Mary and she conceived the promised Son of God.

The sect leaders Arius and Nestorius and their derivative sects at the peripheries of the eastern Byzantine Empire, claiming Jesus was created by God, made contact with the Persian and Arab world and beyond the territories of Central Asia. The fundamental error in these heretical movements is that Jesus is a prophet but not the Son of God. Arianism even spread across Western Europe. Only the popes along with their bishops could bring an end to Arianism. The solution to resolving serious religious disputes of the early church was by the office given to Peter, authority granted to him by Jesus to ensure unity in the teaching of morals and doctrine (Matt 16:16–18). The Petrine office draws from both tradition and Scripture; teachings "handed down" are preserved to ensure the continuity with what Christ taught.

We have seen in the first instance where the Holy Spirit descends upon Mary in the first joyful mystery, this encounter between the human creature, the woman chosen to be the mother of the promised Messiah, Son of God, and the Holy Spirit who descends upon Mary and begets the Second Person of Trinity in Mary's womb, the Word of God, God's divine promise made flesh. Mary is the first instance of this radical openness to the Holy Spirit whereby she will conceive and bear the Son of the Most High. The Holy Spirit descends upon Mary even before the Holy Spirit descends upon the church. Clearly, this privileged mission that Mary is given sets her apart, without compromising her freedom to accept or reject this mission; Mary is totally open to the work of the Holy Spirit. We are also called to this openness to the Spirit so God can perform his work in us.

---

15. See *Catechism*, #120

The first luminous mystery reveals the Holy Trinity at the beginning of Jesus's mission. The Holy Spirit is identified with Jesus, descending upon him, with the voice of God the Father revealing he is pleased with his "beloved Son." The Holy Spirit present in both the annunciation and Pentecost is manifested also in this first luminous mystery highlighting the Trinity that belongs to Jesus's mission—the call to salvation. Openness to the Holy Spirit, therefore, is to receive baptism and new life in Christ in the Trinitarian faith.

Second Luminous Mystery—Miracle at Cana

*I—On the third day there was a wedding
in Cana of Galilee.* (John 2:1)

Our Father . . . Hail Mary . . . Glory Be . . .

1. Wedding

A wedding takes place at Cana in Galilee. The journey from Nazareth takes the traveller not far from Tiberius off the western shores of the Sea of Galilee. Recorded only in John's Gospel, the wedding at Cana appears in the second chapter following the theme of light and darkness, the Word made flesh, in the prologue of the first chapter (John 1). Once Jesus is identified as the Lamb of God by John the Baptist, the apostle John records Jesus calling the apostles to follow him (John 1:37-49).[1]

Are we ready for Jesus's first miracle (John 2:1-11)? Or should there be a miracle at such an early stage when his mission has just barely begun. It seems too soon to reveal himself as the Son of God by his divine power; as Jesus stated, "My hour has not yet come" (John 2:4). Nevertheless, Mary plays a fundamental role in interceding in the matter; Jesus concedes on his mother's behalf. At his mother's request, Jesus manifests his divine power and performs his first miracle.

The problem and context is introduced to the audience. The listener is provided with answers to the following questions: What? A wedding.

---

1. At this stage, before the wedding at Cana, John does not mention all the apostles. The list of names includes Andrew, Simon, Philip, Nathaniel, and John the apostle is inferred. The references to John is John the Baptist, the first name to be mentioned in the prologue (John 1).

When? On the third day. Place? Cana in Galilee. Who? Jesus's mother, Jesus, and his disciples. Problem? They ran out of wine.

We are surprised that at the wedding banquet John does not mention the name of the bride and groom, after all, the wedding celebrates their marriage. On the other hand, what stands out is the prominence of Mary: she appears first on the list of invitees; the mother of Jesus is the first person to be mentioned. That Mary appears even before Jesus is surprising, after all, the Gospel focuses on Jesus, not Mary. But John places Mary first. We might ask why she is given this first position in the list of wedding invitees? With Mary placed at the head of the list, John wants to draw our attention to Mary, and so we should keep her in mind as we read the wedding asking ourselves, "Why is Mary central in this feast? The time focus of the opening sentence asserts the "third" day, but in relation to what?

What is a wedding? A celebration of truth, love, and life between a man and a woman that in the truth of their love they will generate life. The love between the man and woman is fruitful because it brings forth life, and life engenders further love as a family. The man, woman, child relationships build on truth and love, the foundation to the family. Therefore, a wedding celebrates the most sublime event between man and woman because of what the marriage "signifies" and what the marriage "promises." Weddings are future-oriented; they look ahead to the celebration of life in procreation and offspring, the celebration of family. The community that witnesses the celebration of truth, love, and life participate in the joy of the couple.

So, when we hear the word "wedding," we associate this feast with the celebration of manhood and womanhood, masculinity and femininity, united to become one flesh that only a man and a woman can experience, express, and celebrate (Gen 1:27–28; 2:24). Wedding celebrations have been expressed across cultures and throughout the ages as the union of a man and a woman who celebrate the joy of life shared by the family and the community. The significance of marriage extends to the society which shows that marriage has societal implications. The wedding celebration binds two individuals who continue to build the family and community; both the personal and the communal dimension create joy. And so, when John speaks to us about a wedding feast we understand the event as a celebration of truth, love, and life. This word "wedding," therefore, is charged with images and symbols, anticipating what lies ahead in a deepening of love while drawing from that which is already experienced. These three spiritual elements remain with us as we read about the wedding of Cana: truth, love, and life. These three elements lead to the joy expressed.

i. The Problem

In the third verse, once John has established the nature of the event and who is present, he raises the problem, "When the wine gave out . . ." (John 2:3). John structures this passage so the problem, the attention is shifted to Mary: "the mother of Jesus said to him, 'They have no wine.'" But we might ask, "Why is running out of wine Mary's problem?" Or, "Why does Mary assume responsibility to find a solution?" John informs us that Mary immediately took the matter of "wine" to her son, also one of the invited guests.

At this stage, within the first three verses, we have the central event, a wedding banquet, two of the invitees are identified, namely, Mary and Jesus, and the problem, running out of wine. We have looked at the significance of "wedding," now, what about the value of "wine"? Why should the lack of wine be such a concern that Mary immediately approaches Jesus? What is the connection between wine and a wedding? How does wine connect Mary to Jesus?

ii. Significance of Wine

Wine at a banquet reflects and expresses a joyful celebration. But wine in this wedding passage signifies more than the "wine to gladden the human heart" (Ps 104:15). The wine, linked to a wedding, and the concern of having run out of wine, with Mary's prominent role, suggests a situation beyond needing more wine for the banquet. Numerous elements that John puts structurally in place at the literal level help us with a spiritual reading.

The book in the Holy Bible that celebrates truth, love, and its life-giving nature is to be found in the Song of Songs. The imagery in Songs celebrates love, anticipating the union of the lover and the beloved. The sensuous imagery of the man and woman celebrates love as a wedding, the anticipated union between the two. The bride expresses her love: "Let him kiss me with the kisses of his mouth! For your love is better than wine" (Song 1:2). The verses relate the kisses of "his mouth" with wine. Wine intoxicates, creating an ecstatic effect, and so, "his mouth" is compared to the effects of wine. While using the sensuous imagery of the lover's kisses suggesting an intoxicating power, the image of kisses compared to wine shows the power of love. So, wine signifies more than to "gladden" the human heart in the wedding scene. John intends to offer us a deeper spiritual layer to understand wine, built on the human experience of lover and beloved in the setting of a wedding banquet. The wedding about love and the life-generating experience it symbolizes physically and spiritually is expressed in wine that heightens the experience of love and transcends love to bring the lover and beloved into a spiritual union. While the erotic presupposes sensory experience as so vividly described in the Song of Songs, the human experience transcends the sensuous to experience the spiritual. A purifying of the senses so that they transcend bodily experience to encounter the spiritual; love purifies, transcends, and transforms the sensuous.

The imagery of wine appears again in the words of the beloved describing her lover, "He brought me to the banqueting house, and his intention toward me was love" (Song 2:4). The "banqueting house" is understood as the "house of wine."[2] The verse immediately makes a connection between wine and love or the "banner of love," a banquet hall, suggesting a celebration of love, namely, a wedding. The wedding feast of Cana appears to echo Songs in terms of love and life. The sensuous language present in Songs is captured by the imagery of "wine" powerfully evocative associated with a "wedding."

iii. Truth in Purity

While the language in Song of Songs has powerful sensuous images, the spiritual depth and transcendence is expressed: "You have ravished my heart, my sister, my bride . . . How sweet is your love, my sister, my bride! How much better is your love than wine" (Song 4:9–10). The language of the lover uses a sibling relationship to describe the truth of his love, expressing that his love for her is not motivated out of lust or passion, but the love he has for his beloved is like the love he has for his sister: truth expressed in purity and innocence without selfish motives or intentions.

"Sister" is repeated in the course of the two verses highlighting the pure nature of a brother's love in the movement towards the beloved: "A garden locked is my sister, my bride, a garden locked, a fountain sealed" (Song 4:12). In this case the virgin metaphors employed highlight the abundance of "life" associated with garden, spring, and fountain. The beloved is untouched, filled with life, and the lover approaches her like a brother and guardian, her protector. The imagery conveys the pre-fallen state where the first man and first woman manifested a truthfulness in their love, a purity of desire and intention between lover and beloved.

The image of "garden" echoes "Eden" where the lover and the beloved desire each other, paralleling the vitality of the garden images; desire that is life-generating. The man and woman generate life at two levels: the spiritual

---

2. *Revised New Jerusalem Bible* Study Edition translates "banqueting house" as "cellar." See note (a) in Study Edition.

in the yearning and presence of each other and the physical directed towards generating life, where their love is fruitful and procreates. Love at the wedding at Cana generates spiritual life.

2. Mary and Jesus

The wedding at Cana in John's Gospel relates to a couple just married, but John ignores their names, as if irrelevant. The relevant names given to us are Mary and Jesus. We know that Paul identifies Jesus as the new Adam (1 Cor 15:45). When we think of the garden imagery alluded to in Song of Songs and also in Genesis, Jesus appears to be identified with his Adamic role, that is, the new Adam. The new Adam was sent to accomplish what the old Adam had failed to accomplish: obedience to God. The garden imagery, then, suggests the first man and first woman before the fall. The new Eve, then, parallels the new Adam: Mary is the new Eve. Adam and Eve collaborated in sin, disobedience, and rupture with God. As with Eve, Mary possesses the freedom to choose, the meditation of the first joyful mystery. Mary, like Eve, is free from original sin. But Mary's response to God radically contrasts that of Eve's. Both women with their knowledge turn to men who have priestly roles: Eve uses her knowledge to justify disobedience, while Adam provides neither guardianship nor leadership and falls with Eve; Mary uses her knowledge of the shortage of wine seeking her Son's intervention, and Jesus listening to his mother performs a miracle to provide wine.

We have the intoxicating love at the wedding of Cana; Mary and Jesus represented as bride and groom, living in the truth of God; the wine signifies the salvific blood of Jesus; Mary intercedes bringing sinners to her Son. The union between Mary and Jesus described in intoxicating love at the wedding of Cana highlights the two central figures in this wedding: Mary's role, as the new Eve, indicates one of collaboration in salvation with Jesus, the New Adam. The wedding's significance—the abundance of wine—points to supernatural life in the blood of Christ. Mary remains present at the cross where Christ sheds his blood for us, and in our lives Mary intercedes for us.

The man/woman configuration, Adam/Eve, lover/beloved, Jesus/Mary unites all three episodes. Adam/Eve introduces sin through a mutual disobedience and radical rupture in their relationship with from God; the lover/beloved represent sensuous love pure and true, assuming the senses but transcending the passionate; and Jesus/Mary reveal an intoxicating love like an abundance of wine, Mary who collaborates in her son's mission—the blood of Jesus that saves. While the love between the lover and beloved reflects the mutual response to love, in the case of Jesus and Mary, they represent the focal point of the wedding, a wedding that is centered on interceding for others. Their roles, Mary as intercessor and Jesus as Savior, water transformed into wine, Jesus fulfills his salvific role by his blood; Mary fulfills her role as mediatrix. The love of Mary and Jesus shares the rich spiritual love of the lover and beloved, raises love to another level: salvation.

We can take this "wine" image further, the theme running through the Wedding of Cana. The first religious allusion we have to wine appears in the book of Genesis with the appearance of Melchizedek: "And King Melchizedek of Salem brought out bread and wine; he was priest of God Most High. He blessed him and said, "Blessed be Abram by God Most High, maker of heaven and earth" (Gen 14:18-19). In the Wedding at Cana, Jesus's first miracle, we have the anticipation or pre-figuring of the wine of the last supper where Jesus, as Melchizedek before him who expresses the priesthood, offers signs of Jesus's priestly ministry. This ministry includes the offering of wine, to lead us in truth, love, and life, in the earthly sense, but leading towards the supernatural level by the Last Supper, the cross, and eternal life. John will also record the profound exchange between Jesus on the cross and his mother standing at the foot of the cross. Mary is the intercessor of this first miracle where a superabundance of wine is miraculously provided; Mary, at the foot of the cross, hears Jesus's last words: "I am thirsty"; Jesus will drink from the chalice in the kingdom of heaven. John writes about these events after the resurrection; he recognizes the co-relating events in terms at a spiritual level, drawing from the Old Testament, revealing how Jesus, Mary, and the wine are prefigured in the old covenant and unveiled in the New Testament. John penetrates the Scriptures with the perspicacious "eye of an eagle." Before his death on the cross, Jesus entrusts his mother to John and John to his mother. As the first miracle, the wedding of Cana finds its source in the cross; John contemplates Jesus, truth, and his saving mission with his blessed mother at his side.

The passion of Christ is centered on wine—his blood. As with the wedding banquet, the celebration of truth, love, and life, the lover and the beloved, are found in the properties of the wine. The wine Jesus miraculously produced leads the chief steward to comment, "But you have kept the good wine until now" (John 2:10). John is leading us to the "true" wine: Jesus—his body offered for us at the cross. The wine at the Last Supper takes on the fulfillment of a "new covenant" because the wine "is" the blood of Jesus: he is truth; he is love; he is life.

The abundance of wine manifested in the miracle of Cana, conveys the abundance of love at the wedding feast where only Jesus and Mary are named; on the cross the superabundance of love pours, the wine that is

Jesus's blood; Jesus offers himself as sacrifice as spouse for the church his bride (Eph 5:32).

3. Wedding Feast of the Lamb

What is this wedding feast of the Lamb? The imagery sounds like mixed metaphors: a lamb is not a person who marries, so how can John speak of "wedding banquet"? What does John convey in Rev 19?

At the end of the Passover Supper Jesus declares, "I tell you, I will never again drink of this fruit of the vine until that day when I drink it new with you in my Father's kingdom" (Matt 26:29). The wine is drunk when Jesus ascends to the Father in heaven as meditated in the second glorious mystery; the wine of the wedding banquet of the Lamb in his Father's kingdom (Rev 19:7–10).

Jesus's body drips with blood from his head pierced with thorns, the lacerations he received from being flagellated so his flesh is ripped, his hands pierced bleeding, his feet nailed, and finally blood dripping from his side. This is the blood to which Jesus refers when he offers wine; this is the blood, his blood of the new covenant. The blood of the paschal Lamb, the wedding banquet celebrated in the Father's kingdom. Jesus offers us an abundance of love at Cana by his mother's intercession. Water transformed into the superabundance of life—eternal life—truth on the cross sacrificed, man slaughtered.

The theme of a wedding feast appears in the Book of Revelation: "Hallelujah! / For the Lord our God / the Almighty reigns. / Let us rejoice and exult / and give him the glory, / for the marriage of the Lamb has come, / and his bride has made herself ready" (Rev 19:6–7). Then, the apostle John continues in the following verse: "And the angel said to me, 'Write this: Blessed are those who are invited to the marriage supper of the Lamb'" (Rev 19:9).

The language of Revelation draws from John's earlier conjugal imagery of lover-beloved, the superabundance of wine, then wine offered as blood sacrificed, the lamb slaughtered. The "lamb" brings us to Passover imagery; the sacrificed lamb or goat, as instructed by Moses at Sinai, with which blood is sprinkled on the people and the altar as a sign of the covenant. However, at Sinai we do not have references to conjugal imagery. We can speak of a "feast" or "banquet" like the Passover where lamb is slaughtered but a wedding feast?

The Lamb takes us to the Last Supper where the disciples make reference to the sacrifice of the Passover Lamb in preparation for the Passover, meditated in the fifth luminous mystery (Mark 14:12; Luke 22:7–8). What is the connection with the wedding at Cana? The life of wine is associated with the life of blood. The Passover ritual requires a lamb to be slaughtered; but the Passover Jesus celebrates with his apostles does not make any reference to the Lamb in any of the Gospels—only in the preparation, while each is consistent with the presence of bread and wine, Jesus's body and blood. The Lamb in fact appears at the crucifixion; Jesus the slaughtered Lamb is the Passover Lamb, sacrificed on the Friday as we meditate in the fifth sorrowful mystery.

We have sensuous conjugal love appear in Song of Songs where the language of love unites lover and beloved; the wedding at Cana highlights the abundance of the "best wine" focusing on Mary's intercession and Jesus's compassionate act, although seemingly apprehensive.

The first luminous mystery, the baptism of Jesus, John introduces Jesus even before his ministry begins as the "Lamb of God" (John 1:29, 36). John the Baptist baptizes in the River Jordan, and when John observes Jesus coming, the following day, John says, "Look, here is the Lamb of God, who takes away the sin of the world!" John the Baptist identifies Jesus as the "Lamb of God" and qualifies his statement, "who takes away the sin of the world." Specific instructions are given to sprinkle the "blood of the lamb" on the doorposts and the lintel of the houses so the first born of Israel will spared when the angel of death kills the first-born of the Egyptians (Exod 12:7), the feast Jesus celebrates with his apostles. Instructions that involve sacrificing a bull as a sin-offering to atone for the sins of the people and make peace with God are also described (Lev 4). The "Lamb of God" who "takes away the sins of the world" expresses the salvific power of Jesus who blots out the sins of all of humanity; this is the man to whom John the Baptist points.

Before Jesus is baptized, before he begins his ministry, he is identified as the "Lamb who takes away the sin of the world." As a prophet, John the Baptist knew the mission of Jesus; he prepared the people for the coming of Jesus by repentance, conversion, and baptism as meditated in the first luminous mystery. Jesus is the Passover Lamb who will be sacrificed, thereby taking away the sins not just of the people of Judah or Israel but "of the world." The wedding feast of Cana in John's Gospel prepares us for the wedding of the Lamb in Revelation.

The Wedding feast of the Lamb requires a spouse—otherwise, why does Revelation make reference to a "wedding"? Who is this spouse? The Lamb offers his blood for the spouse—in the appearance of the life-generating wine as revealed at the wedding of Cana. So, the wedding feast of the Lamb celebrates Jesus who offers himself sacrificed for his spouse, the church—each one of us.

The nuptial language of husband and wife deepened by Paul in his letter to the Ephesians parallels that of Jesus and the church: "Husbands, love your wives, just as Christ loved the church and gave himself up for her to make her holy, cleansing her by the washing with water through the word, and to present her to himself as a radiant church, without stain or wrinkle or any other blemish, but holy and blameless" (Eph 5:26-28). The imagery used to understand the relationship between Christ and his church is compared to that of the conjugal love imagery between the husband and wife.[3] So Christ, offering himself for his church as a sacrificed Lamb; the wedding feast is that of Christ and the church, his bride. The invited members are the martyrs: "They have washed their robes and made them white in the blood of the Lamb" (Rev 17:14) and the community of believers who carried their cross.

The wine associated with Melchizedek, priest and king of Salem, the wine of abundance that Jesus miraculously supplies at the wedding of Cana, the wine of the Last Supper, the blood poured on the cross. The wedding at Cana serves as Jesus's first public act revealing his identity associated with wine, the wedding banquet, and his mother.

4. Mary as Mediatrix

Mary's role at the wedding of Cana cannot be dismissed as a minor detail, especially in John's Gospel who makes deliberate choices in how he organizes his material with a clear focus. Nothing in the life of Jesus should be regarded as merely a piece of information. Mary's role is fundamental in giving flesh to Jesus as we meditated in the first joyful mystery of the annunciation. Mary's encounter with her cousin Elizabeth as we meditated in the second joyful mystery, the visitation, where the two women carry male cousins in their wombs called to prophetic and salvific missions, respectively. In the movement from the old covenant to the new covenant, from John the Baptist to Jesus the Messiah, from conversion to salvation, we have the fulfillment of the Law and Prophets in Jesus, Son of God.

Nor can we ignore Mary at the foot of the cross, meditated in the fifth sorrowful mystery, one of the few people standing, embracing the

---

3. In addition to Christ being a male, this male-female complementary evident in the Old and New Testaments—God and his people (Jerusalem), then Christ/groom and his bride/church made explicit in Ephesians—explains why the Roman Catholic Church allows only males to be ordained priests.

cross of her Son, mourning his death, living with her faith and in the hope of the promise of the annunciation: her Son would sit on the throne of David—a kingdom forever secure. We cannot ignore Mary, either, in the third glorious mystery where she is present when the Holy Spirit descends upon her and the apostles at Pentecost: the mother of our Savior, present at the beginning of the church, where she herself worshiped on Mount Zion. And we cannot ignore the role that Mary played at the wedding of Cana since John highlights the names of two individuals together: Mary and Jesus; the turning of water into wine occurs because of Mary's intervention. The apostle John places Mary in this prominent role at Cana to inform us Mary is mediatrix.

II—Fruit of this Mystery: to Jesus through Mary

Practical Matters—

We are given in the wedding of Cana Mary's role as an intercessor. As we know from Hebrews, there is only one mediator between God and man, the supreme mediator, the high priest, Jesus Christ himself, the only one to reconcile man with God by offering his life as a sacrifice for our sins so that through Christ we are reconciled with God.

But God wants us to be engaged in this salvific act where we become participants not in achieving salvation for ourselves—that many people actually seek—focused on an earthly life of wealth and health, or humanism that has neither salvation nor eternal life as the ultimate end—but we are actively engaged as rational spiritual beings with our intelligence and freedom, to be guided by truth and choose the objective good—to act in accordance with Christ's teachings or not to; to follow the teachings of the church or not to; to follow natural law or not to.[4]

The head servant turns to Mary, informing her they ran out of wine, and after she informs Jesus, Mary tells the servant, "Do whatever he tells you." Mary brings us to Jesus, the message of John's Gospel (2:1-11). This is Mary's mediating role as John shows us in the Scriptures: first Mary leads to Jesus, and second she teaches us to be obedient to Jesus: "Do whatever he

---

4. Pelagius's teachings were condemned in the fourth century, claiming that Jesus represented only a model of Christian living. Trying to explain human freedom, Pelagius denied both original sin and the power of grace. Secular humanism is grounded in the material world, well-being "here and now," and future-oriented concerns do not point to the afterlife but the material world/environment where power shifts from the transcendent God to collective materialism.

tells you." Mary speaks to the chief steward in the imperative act: "do." She teaches us as a mother to be attentive to her Son: "Do whatever he tells you."

The miracle at Cana, therefore, brings out Mary's role in the place of our salvation; her role as mediatrix collaborating with God the Father, Son, and Holy Spirit. From the conception of Jesus to Pentecost, Mary remains present, not as a bystander or passive witness of events; Mary remains silent and "keeps these secrets in her heart." Mary is actively engaged in God's plan for our salvation.

The wedding at Cana shows us that Mary's relationship with Jesus, like Adam and Eve, like the lover and the beloved, is more than a mother and a son attending a wedding. Jesus is moved by his mother's intercession, just as he is moved by her at the foot of the cross. In both instances, Jesus responds with love for his mother: he changes the water into wine, just as he entrusts his mother to his beloved disciple John (John 19:26–27).

History teaches us that devotion to Mary keeps us from falling into heresy. Heresy in the postmodern context politicizes womanhood. For some Christians, Mary no longer serves as model, as mother, spouse, or woman. Womanhood has become a power struggle between male and female, opposition between the sexes, women's rights to have men's jobs. The oppressor-oppressed Marxist dialectic, the battle of the sexes blurs male/female roles at mass creating confusion within the liturgy, and the loss of male/female complementarity. Men and women each have their unique roles, as God created man and woman each in their unique natural state (Gen 2:24). Paul further conveys the complementarity of these roles in the church and their supernatural order (Eph 5:21-28).[5] The loss of Mary as mother and mediatrix means the disappearance of Christian womanhood. With the absence of sexual complementarity, we are left with the gospel of secular Christianity: sexual ideologies rather than the Gospel of salvation. This is equally true for the male where Mary is embraced as the man's spiritual mother to learn the value of womanhood and motherhood, the natural and supernatural.

Christianity without the mother of God is contrary to what Christ instructed. Jesus gave John his mother at the cross, and to each of us he left us his mother. Each act of Jesus signifies far more than a moment contained in time and space. The actions of Jesus transcend the historical

---

5. To put it plainly: the "loss" of mother Mary in Christian communities/denominations has meant the loss of "womanhood," leaving a feminine vacuum in churches as women try find their place and seek to fill spiritual roles assigned to men. This reflects the politicizing of "rights" in the religious sphere. As a result, a "virile" vacuum has been created at holy mass. The fact is, a woman can never fulfil a spiritual role intended for a man and the opposite is also true.

event bringing us into the eternal present and directing us towards eternal life: Jesus gave John his mother not only for John but all his disciples, the entire church. Jesus himself wants the church to have his mother, mother of God to be honored, to be our mother.

The wedding at Cana attests that Mary brings each of us to her Son, Jesus. And Jesus understood how much we need a mother to comfort us and to guide us, to help us grow in virtue. Without Mary's presence of a loving mother, Jesus knew his apostles and believers would fall into error and heresy, into moral relativism and subjectivism, without a trusting mother present to lead each of us to the truth: Jesus, Son of God. This, John reveals to us at the wedding of Cana: Jesus gave us Mary as our mother and mediatrix, and he gives us himself, sacrificed on the cross, as our only Savior.

Third Luminous Mystery—Proclamation of the Kingdom of God

I—*"As you go, proclaim the good news, 'The kingdom of heaven has come.'"* (Matt 10:7)

Our Father . . . Hail Mary . . . Glory Be . . .

Two Kingdoms

"Cure the sick, raise the dead, cleanse the lepers, cast out demons. You received without payment; give without pay" (Matt 10:8). The proclamation of the kingdom is less detailed in Luke's Gospel but is expressed as a command in relation to exorcising demons and healing the sick in general: "Then Jesus called the twelve together and gave them power and authority over all demons and to cure diseases, and he sent them out to proclaim the Kingdom of God and to heal" (Luke 9:2; 10:9).

In Matthew's Gospel, the kingdom is intended for the "lost sheep of the house of Israel" (Matt 10:6). The lost sheep echoes the prophet Jeremiah: "My people have been lost sheep; their shepherds have led them astray, turning them away on the mountains; from mountain to hill they have gone, they have forgotten their fold" (Jer 50:6).

The preaching of the kingdom begins with the house of Israel, the chosen people of God with whom God established his covenant, an alliance to be kept between God and his people. But the Israelites repeatedly proved to be unfaithful. The chosen people are lost and divided, politically and spiritually, due to their fornication with pagan gods. Israel behaves like a harlot, an unfaithful bride (Hos 2:1–5). The prophet Ezekiel echoes the words of Jeremiah, "You have not strengthened the weak, you have not healed the sick, you have not bound up the injured, you have not brought back the strayed, you have not sought the lost, but with force and harshness you have ruled them" (Ezek 34:4). Jesus uses the language of the prophets to appeal to the people, and because God first established his covenant with Abraham and the people of Israel, the message is directed towards Israel, where the "kingdom of heaven is at hand" is proclaimed.

How is one to understand the "kingdom of heaven" that is proclaimed? Is it an earthly kingdom, a heavenly kingdom, or something of both, earth and heaven? Saul, anointed king before David, showed that he lacked fidelity to carry out God's commands (1 Sam 15:10–11). The first king anointed, faithful to God even at the risk of death, was David (1 Sam 16:12–13; 18:11). The ongoing problem of obedience and disobedience to God and carrying out his will remained a recurring theme from Genesis onwards that reflects the tension in the Old Testament between God and his chosen people.

As Jesus preaches, he tells us the "kingdom of heaven is at hand," but at the initial stage the king is not identified. This kingdom is governed by a just and compassionate king as Matthew's Gospel reveals, and Jesus's preaching is intended to reach out to the most vulnerable members of society, those overlooked and forgotten because they are voiceless, or their voices are crushed by the more powerful. Jesus wants his disciples to go out and reach the unheard, ignored, abandoned. The kingdom of Jesus is built on truth and love, mercy, and holiness. The kingdom of Jesus is not shaped by wealth, power, and glory.

Jesus does not state immediately that he is the king of this kingdom which approaches. The kingship of Jesus is fulfilled when he is crowned king sitting on his "throne," the cross, and where he reigns in heaven. In response to Pilate before his crucifixion, Jesus says that his kingdom is not of this world. While Jesus's earthly kingship is misunderstood and ridiculed, the focus of the second sorrowful mystery, the crowning with thorns, his heavenly kingship is in the second glorious mystery, the ascension. In other words, the rosary mysteries reveal that Jesus's kingdom operates at two levels as the Word of God does throughout the Scriptures: literal and spiritual. He is king of a righteous kingdom on earth that we are all called to build, and he is the king in heaven at the right hand of the Father where we will reign with him if we are faithful disciples: "Looking to Jesus the pioneer and perfecter of our faith, who for the sake of the joy that was set before him endured the cross, disregarding its shame, and has taken his seat at the right hand of the throne of God" (Heb 12:2).

Jesus is king in his Father's kingdom prefigured by his proclamation on earth but a kingship rejected by his crucifiers (John 19:21–22). On earth Jesus's kingship signifies peace, mercy, and justice, a salvific kingdom that prepares the believer for the kingdom of heaven. Jesus's celestial kingship, the kingdom, signifies the perfect communion of truth and love—essence of the heavenly kingdom.

The kingdom of God in this third luminous mystery conveys the earthly kingdom that is to be established as God's kingdom on earth and the kingdom of heaven where Christ reigns as king. These two senses of God's kingdom cannot be separated from each other. When the two kingdoms are separated, one falls into an earthly kingdom that is built entirely on humanist principles, losing its God-centered significance and direction, or an eternal kingdom, at the risk of an entirely spiritual kingdom disconnected from God's kingdom on earth ignoring the miseries of the world and Christian responsibility to build a better place on earth—even if only temporary.

The teachings of Jesus tell us he wants his disciples to build a world that is moral, just, and compassionate, but this world is not an end in itself. This call to justice presupposes among the disciples of Jesus a communion of truth and love directed ultimately to eternal life, where Christ is king, worshiped in the eternal banquet, as meditated in the second luminous mystery.

The third luminous mystery teaches us we cannot seek the world as our ultimate end or ignore the misery in the world. Given the characteristics of the kingdom Jesus seeks to establish in this world, and the kingdom he prepares us for eternity, four biblical imperatives are evident in Jesus's teachings, as we find in the Gospels: (i) heal the sick; (ii) raise the dead; (iii) cleanse the lepers; and (iv) cast out demons.

i. Heal the Sick

Healing refers to the apostolic ministry. Jesus did not choose twelve physicians to follow him. Rather, he chose ordinary men, fishermen by trade for the most part. Only Matthew is known to have a trade distinct from the other apostles and loathed by the community—collecting taxes. Jesus chose his disciples not from a "healing" or medicinal background, yet he asks disciples to "heal the sick."[1]

Jesus's disciples cannot be indifferent to the "sick." They need to be attentive and offer assistance. Jesus makes this clear. We cannot claim to preach the Gospel of our Lord and disregard fundamental human needs; the disciples are called to care for others with the love they have for Jesus (Matt 25:31–46). Examples of healing in the New Testament are listed especially in the Gospel of Luke where different social categories of

---

1. Luke "the Physician" is not one of the twelve apostles but a companion of Saint Paul and who is identified with the Gospel bearing his name.

individuals are healed from sicknesses.² These include a man with leprosy (Luke 5:12–16), a paralytic (Luke 5:17–26), a man with a withered hand on the Sabbath (Luke 6:6-11), a centurion's slave (Luke 7:1–10), and a crippled woman (Luke 13:10–17). These miracles highlight the gratuity of love: miracles do not come with monetary or material compensation. Gratuity in healing, acting out of love and goodness, reflect the teachings of Jesus and the value of charity.

Miracles violating the Law of Moses caused the Pharisees to react and served as arguments to arrest Jesus, but Jesus responds by saying, "The sabbath was made for humankind, and not humankind for the sabbath" (Mark 2:27). Healing of the sick becomes integral to the Christian mission where the followers of Jesus, namely the church, develop a structure to ensure the "sick" are taken care of. Men and women will devote themselves for Christ eventually in religious congregations and institutes specifically attached to healing ministries responding to the call of Christ.³ Healing and care for the sick reflects building God's kingdom on earth—in preparation for the kingdom of heaven.⁴

Jesus teaches us that this kingdom to be built on earth begins concretely with the commitment to "healing the sick." Taking the words of Jesus, first the disciples, then the religious institutes with the charism of healing as a primary apostolate, they put the words of Jesus into practice. To ignore the words of Jesus, that is, his instructions to "heal the sick,"

---

2. These details in Luke's Gospel are not surprising since he is the one disciple who is trained as a physician.

3. "Hospital" and "hospice" from the Latin *hospitum* from which the English "host" is derived, conveys this host-guest relationship. The guests were the infirm, homeless, and pilgrims who were "hosted," sheltered, and looked after out of Christian charity. In the mid-sixth century we find the first monastic hospital at the Benedictine monastery of Monte Cassino. The origins of the Fatebenefratelli Hospital in Rome, now an international Catholic hospital, is traced to the first millennium of Benedictine sisters looking after infirm, dying, and homeless, and was refounded by Saint John of God to nurse the ill and provide accommodation for visitors. Knights Hospitallers have their origins in the seventh century when Pope Gregory I commissioned a hospital to be built in Jerusalem to treat the Christian pilgrims, and by the Middle Ages, these "hospitaller knights" in crusader states provided both hospital and military support for the crusaders eventually re-establishing their home base in Malta and renamed the "Knights of Malta."

4. Hospitals have their origins in what Catholicism calls "works of mercy," especially evident today in missionary clinics and Catholic-run hospitals all over the world. The growth of the Catholic Church reflected the concrete witness to the Christian faith "building the kingdom" of Jesus, especially in terms of charitable activities (Matt 25:31–46). For sisters, brothers, and priests, this often involved risking their lives to care for the diseased. Dying for one's neighbor represents the summit of love in Christ's teachings (John 15:13).

is to dismiss what he taught us; we have a responsibility as Christians to make this a better world; a person contributes by their gifts and is called to build this earthly kingdom. Jesus's teaching on the kingdom transforms society to create a world where we care for each other based on Christian principles. We cannot be indifferent to fundamental human needs. A sick person needs to be healed and by using our intelligence and creativity we can discover the meaning of Christian healing as Jesus taught his apostles. Attentiveness to others, to their needs, caring for them with love and compassion, is how we build God's kingdom on earth. But in God's kingdom truth is the foundation grounded in the eternal law of God.

This physical healing of a sick person suggests supernatural intervention that is only possible by the power of the Holy Spirit at work in the lives of apostles and followers of Christ. The church acknowledges this divine presence at work when there have been miraculous healings.[5] When we remember and honor the saints, we acknowledge their radical openness and receptivity to the work of the Holy Spirit. When we ask the saints to intercede for us, we follow the Letter of James to pray for each other (Jas 5:16). Hence, we invoke those who have lived heroic lives of virtue by offering themselves to God, and collaborating with his divine will, to build the earthly kingdom, and to lead us to the eternal kingdom.

Another lesson to be learned from the "healing of the sick": people who sought healing approached Jesus because they had faith in his power to heal them—either directly—or through friends and family who believed in Jesus and his healing power. These people heard about Jesus. "Hearing" the Word directs the apostles to preaching the Word so Jesus can be made known. Only when Jesus is made known can the person respond and seek Jesus. The faith in each situation of the "sick" reveals the concrete efforts made in seeking Jesus and his healing. Faith moves the believer to act.

The physical sense of disease also carries with it a spiritual meaning, and the apostles, as much as they have a duty to build God's kingdom on earth, are also called to the spiritual healing that prepares for the heavenly kingdom where Jesus is king. Physical and spiritual healing are inseparable. Spiritual healing accompanies physical healing. When the paralytic can walk he realizes it is Jesus who has healed him. So, he has both his physical body restored to its natural state, but also his heart, mind, and soul have been opened to the promised one, the Savior sent by God. This

---

5. Supernatural healing—work of the Holy Spirit unexplained by science or medicine—is the condition for the "cause" of beatification and canonization. Divine intervention recognized by Catholic Church means the "cause" is truly supernatural. The person, whether "blessed" or "saint," becomes formally approved as an intercessor worthy of honor/devotion in the Roman Catholic calendar.

acknowledgement is what will give those who are sick eternal life. Healing further serves to witness to others that Jesus is the Messiah, and his followers, those who believe him, may exercise supernatural powers by the intervention of the Holy Spirit.

ii. Raise the Dead

After healing the sick Jesus instructs his apostles to "raise the dead." To take this literally means through supernatural intervention, by Jesus's divine power. Jesus would not have asked the apostles, his followers, to perform acts they could not perform. Jesus knew the power of the Holy Spirit at work in the church would enable his disciples to "raise the dead." Jesus raised his good friend Lazarus from the dead (John 11:1–44) and a young girl, the daughter of Jairus (Luke 8:40–42, 49–56).

We know that a person who is dead cannot be raised back to life unless God's power intervenes directly to raise them from the dead. This is what Jesus and his apostles accomplished in raising from the dead. The Holy Spirit operates in the faithful disciples of Jesus. Raising back to life in this literal sense can only happen by supernatural intervention.

But raising to life can also have a spiritual reading to it as well. A "dead" person due to sin lacks spiritual life; the weight of sin drags the person like a chained prisoner. The chains impede the individual any freedom to move; restricted by chains, one is held and kept back from true life. The darkness in which one lives, a dark dungeon from which there seems to be no escape, spiritual death due to sin. How is the person raised to life? By the teachings of Jesus, by listening to God's Word, by conversion: baptism, confession, the Eucharist. Ultimately, led by Jesus in the company of the angels and saints, we are raised to life.

Jesus teaches his disciples that his mission was given to him by his Father, that he was carrying out his Father's will (John 6:38). He instructs his disciples to "raise the dead to life," which is accomplished by the salvific act of Christ on the cross and the power of the Holy Spirit that breathes divine life into the church. Baptism, confession, the Last Supper that continues on the cross, the resurrection of Jesus, entrusting the apostle Peter with the authority over the church and to feed his sheep, and the descent of the Holy Spirit upon the church, to lead all those who live in the darkness of sin and spiritual death, to the light of Jesus, the truth that leads out of darkness and to life (John 1). To have new life, therefore, to be raised from the dead is the work of the Holy Trinity as we meditated in the second luminous mystery.

In our daily lives we need to be continuously nourished by the Word of God and the body and blood Jesus offers us at the cross in the Eucharist. Our need for grace is ongoing. We depend and rely on Jesus to give us strength throughout our entire lives. And so, the mission of the believing church as Jesus taught his apostles is to raise the dead to life. This is true in our own lives for we are born with sin, and we are brought to life at baptism. This is true for leading others out of darkness and to new life through Jesus Christ, again, by conversion, by baptism and the Eucharist. Our weak condition since the fall means we rely on the body and blood of Christ that he himself offers us and asks us to repeat in "memory" of him: the sacraments of the church raise us to new life and lead us to eternal life.

iii. Cleanse the Lepers

After telling his disciples to "raise the dead," Jesus instructs them to "cleanse lepers." In this case, the verb is not healing but cleansing. Jesus encourages both a caring for lepers like the physical bathing to wash them clean, as well as a supernatural transformation with which they are healed of their leprosy (Luke 5:12–16; 17:11–19). When one thinks of leprosy, a contagious disease comes to mind, and the risks of contracting the same disease.

The well-documented case of the Catholic priest, Father Damien of Molokai, reveals his life was spent working with lepers in Hawaii where he contracted the disease from which he also died. Saint Father Damien applied the teachings of Jesus in a very concrete manner as he not only went to "cleanse" lepers, but he did so, inspired by the truth of the Gospel; he acted with courage, faith, and love and died offering his life for his fellow man by the cleansing of others.[6] The Missionaries of Charity, the congregation that Mother Teresa of Calcutta founded, included in their ministry to "cleanse the lepers": attention is given to them in bathing and cleaning them of their infectious skin disease. Saint Mother Teresa's illustrates the response to Jesus's teachings as Jesus did this himself in his own life by his words and actions.[7]

With Jesus, miracles take place where individuals are cured of their skin disease: "He stretched out his hand and touched him, saying, 'I do choose. Be made clean!' Immediately his leprosy was cleansed" (Matt 8:3). With his divine power performing miraculous acts, Jesus gradually unveiled his divine identity: "Then Jesus said to him, 'See that you say nothing to

---

6. See Bunson and Bunson, *St. Damien of Molokai*, 133–42.

7. See Mother Teresa, *Where There Is Love*, 174–75. My visits to Calcutta, Vancouver, and Rome with the Missionaries of Charity have shown their heroic ministry.

anyone; but go, show yourself to the priest, and offer the gift that Moses commanded, as a testimony to them'" (Matt 8:4).

The spiritual sense of "cleansing lepers" also reflects the cleansing and purification through water at baptism, and the leprosy indicates the sins that have made the person "unclean." Cleansing can be understood as the ministry that leads to conversion of the heart, the mind turned towards Jesus, the healing of the heart and mind caused by accumulated sins, an interior disease impeding spiritual growth.

Even if the care remains entirely physical, as in bathing someone with leprosy, spiritually a kingdom of truth and love is built on compassion. A world of indifference and rejection are incompatible with Christ's teachings. But the acceptance of a person with leprosy means to provide the bathing, the cleansing, simply to love them.

But we are all lepers due to sin. We observe the difference between the old covenant attitude of rejection, segregation, and punishment due to violating the Law and the New Testament in which Christ calls us to reach out to others with the aim to bring healing. But healing is not possible if a person does not first acknowledge their illness or sin. People with leprosy know their condition. Self-awareness means to acknowledge our "disease" so we can seek help and experience the healing power of Christ. We cannot experience Christ's compassion if we first do not acknowledge our disease.

iv. Cast out Demons

The fourth instruction Jesus gives to his disciples is to "cast out demons." Jesus's ministry included the expulsion of demons. The Scriptures give numerous examples of Jesus casting out demons, but two dramatic examples include the two men who were demon-possessed; the demons were sent out and "entered the swine" (Matt 8:28–32), and the man "commanded the unclean spirit to come out" (Luke 8:29).

The expulsions of demons from a possessed person we refer to as "exorcism": Jesus exorcises men possessed by demons. In the Scriptures these demons cause the individuals to act against their will—with incredible violence—and make blasphemous statements. Jesus exorcises these victims and frees them from the diabolical powers possessing them.

The Syrophoenician's daughter (Mark 7:24–30) exemplifies not only the power of Jesus to exorcise demons but also the faith of the individual who approaches Jesus asking for his saving intervention. These demons affect men and women, young and old, Israelites and gentiles. We are told they are "possessed." The gospels highlight first Jesus's power to expel demons but then also the faith of those who are turning to Jesus.

We do not know too much about the Syrophoenician woman, but the emphasis is placed on this woman being a gentile while she exhibits faith in Jesus without knowing the Scriptures. She recognizes Jesus's divinity, and Jesus intervenes. The Syrophoenician's faith in Jesus results in her daughter being freed from a demonic possession.

The two men leaving the tombs and the man in shackles are both described as possessed based on their violent behavior that is uncontrollable. In these physical examples of possession even the people avoided the two men. The possessed man in shackles frightened the people, the reason for him being chained. Jesus exorcises them and frees them from the demons possessing them.

These events involving demons provide an account of liberation from possessions, freedom from chains and shackles, and uncontrollable behavior. To be possessed by a demon reflected fundamentally the loss of one's freedom. Being a prisoner because of an external agent taking over the person's very being. The expelling of a demon involves supernatural intervention—only by divine power can Satan be expelled from a person. When Jesus instructs his disciples to cast out demons, they will expel demons in the name of Jesus, by the blood of Jesus poured at the cross.

We may interpret these events as psychological, suggesting therapeutic and pharmaceutical solutions. The person may suffer from psychosis and so therapy and anti-psychotics are prescribed. Behaviors that need to be "treated." Today when someone appears or claims to be possessed by a demonic spirit, discernment is needed to determine the condition, psychological or diabolical. Therapy and drugs may or may not be the most effective treatment. Jesus teaches us that expulsion from demonic possession requires divine intervention.

A person who is possessed does not choose to be possessed.[8] They are victims of a possession. The help will come from those around them or the witnesses of their behavior like the Syrophoenician woman's daughter. When we speak of someone committing wicked acts, we cannot simply say they must be possessed; that frees them from culpability of their actions. People freely choose evil and commit evil acts. But this is not the case of a possession. Jesus tells his disciples, just as he does with the other three illnesses, to heal, to cleanse, to raise from the dead, also to exorcise.

---

8. On "Exorcism," see *Catechism*, #1673.

v. Beatitudes of the Kingdom

When Jesus gives his teachings on the Beatitudes as recorded by Matthew, the first and eighth Beatitude refers to the kingdom of heaven. Jesus states, "Blessed are the poor in spirit, for theirs is the kingdom of heaven," and he closes pointing out again to the kingdom of heaven: "Blessed are those who are persecuted for righteousness' sake, for theirs is the kingdom of heaven" (Matt 5:3, 8). Jesus teaches us how to live the Beatitudes beginning with humility "poor in spirit" and a willingness to be persecuted for what is true: to build a kingdom here on earth that reflects his teachings in anticipation of his eternal kingdom where he reigns, and which will be our heavenly reward for being his faithful disciples. So our life on earth, our choices, how we live bears fundamentally on how God rewards us with his eternal kingdom.

Jesus teaches us in the Beatitudes the moral responsibility we have towards each other to build an earthly kingdom preparing us for our heavenly kingdom. We cannot separate the two. The reward of the latter kingdom depends entirely on our relationship with Christ: embracing his Gospel of salvation and building the earthly kingdom.

In Paul's Letter to the Colossians, Paul writes that Jesus "has transferred us to the kingdom of his beloved Son, in whom we have redemption, the forgiveness of sin" (Col 1:13). By our rebirth in Christ, the forgiveness us our sins, we belong to the kingdom of Jesus delivered from the "power of darkness" where Satan rules. We strive to live in the truth and carry the light of the Gospel into the world to build God's kingdom in preparation for the eternal kingdom.

II—Fruit of this Mystery: Repentance; Trust in God

Practical Matters—

There is another instance of possession that often comes up today, and that is in terms of addictions in which the individual appears to have lost his freedom. Drugs, alcohol, sexual addictions, and others produce experiences that resemble diabolical possession—or is it? Behavior that is neither desired nor willingly chosen. To live in truth, freedom is sought from the chains of the addiction like the man who lived in "shackles" (Mark 5:1–5). In addiction, the person is a victim because they are unable to overcome these unwanted thoughts and desires that drive their actions, feeling overpowered by them.

Sexual addiction and diabolical possession manifest psychological behaviors of "powerlessness" or "victimhood": (i) loss of control, (ii) unwanted behavior, and (iii) repetition. Catholic men and women striving for holiness find themselves in shackles—addictions—that imprison. The demonic aspect of sexual addiction has a biblical precedent in the story of Tobias and Sarah. Tobias knows that Sarah's seven husbands each died on the wedding night in the bridal chamber, killed by a demon (Tob 6:13–14). This connection between Satan and marriage seems unusual because the Scriptures present marriage in favorable terms, as a blessing, not as a curse. And yet, with these husbands each being killed by a demon on the wedding night, we need to raise the question: why is this the fate of Sarah's seven husbands? Why are these deaths repeated on a wonderful occasion? In the second luminous mystery, we looked at the human and spiritual value of the wedding and the supernatural symbolism associated specifically with the wedding of Cana. Tobias is not yet married; he has good reason to be concerned about marrying Sarah.

Tobias is caught; Sarah cannot be promised to another because according to Mosaic law she is supposed to marry within her clan (Tob 7:11). Tobias is looking for a wife, and he is visiting his own clansmen and has a moral duty to marry Sarah: "Likewise I am not at liberty to give her to any other man than yourself, because you are my nearest relative" (Tob 7:10). So, why is there a demon in these marriages? The angel Raphael reminds Tobias of his father's orders which brings Tobias reassurance. Raphael also gives instruction to perform a ritual which would cause the demon to flee and saying a prayer immediately before sexual intercourse: "Now when you are about to go to bed with her, both of you must first stand up and pray, imploring the Lord of heaven that mercy and safety may be granted to you. Do not be afraid, for she was set apart for you before the world was made. You will save her, and she will go with you" (Tob 6:18).[9] So, before the two can consummate their marriage, the demon needs to be removed, and he is removed through a ritual as instructed by Raphael. But is the ritual enough? The two unite in prayer rather than in sexual union. What is the purpose? Satan has now left but there may be the residual lust that remains with her because Sarah continued to marry out of lust—a demon of lust.

The problem we face today reflects the cycle of death where individuals become victims—victims of the devil—manifested in uncontrollable, unsatiable behavior that is lust-driven. This behavior is reinforced by surroundings where suggestive erotic dress and explicit language in the music,

---

9. The angel Raphael instructs Tobias to produce smoke from the liver and heart of a fish laying them on live ashes. The demons will flee smelling the smoke.

film, and pornographic industries takes hold of the imagination—to possess one's thoughts and very being. We find ourselves at times in front of what we are not seeking—even in the form of advertising. But this sexualized environment begins with the early indoctrination of children in the sex education in public schools that sexualizes the child's perception of the world starting with their own body and that of others. The wide availability, accessibility, and anonymity in consuming internet pornography exacerbates the problem of addiction. The demon of lust—present in the story of Sarah—reflects precisely the diabolical conditions our society creates. The question is whether the person who is sexually out of control—a victim—is the work of Satan, or some deeper psychological disturbance needing to be addressed. Whether therapy or spiritual direction, or both, putting trust in Jesus with hope is where to begin. But this presupposes the person acknowledges their problem. Spiritual healing relies on the truthfulness of the person; the honesty to admit help is needed.

This is why the story of Sarah is one of unwanted lust, and her husbands die as a result, attacked by the devil. She needs someone with the purity and faith of Tobias to help her defeat the devil and overcome her lust. The story then represents both nature involving people's natural desires and unnatural or disordered impulses when they indicate excessive or out of control behavior. Out of control behavior is transformed by the grace of God into spiritual healing. In the diabolical situation of lust, Tobias prays, and as Raphael says of Sarah, Tobias will be her salvation. The holiness of Tobias, his fidelity to God, will liberate Sarah from her lust that is killing her and her spouses. We have then what occurs in a disordered and unnatural way at the physical level, and then, what is radically transformed to bring about a spiritual encounter between the man and the woman and God.

The two go together: we repent of our sins because we believe in Jesus Christ. We trust that Jesus will lead us to eternal life, to his kingdom of heaven. To repent means to acknowledge that Jesus is Lord, Savior, and King, and to confess our sins, the Catholic Church offers us the sacrament of confession. This presupposes we trust that Jesus loves us, that he forgives us, that he saves us, and by the grace of God, we will be coheirs of his kingdom.

The third luminous mystery we can regard as the most eschatological—"end times-oriented"—because in his kingdom Jesus is king for eternity. In the prayer to his Father, Jesus teaches the disciples to pray, "thy kingdom come." This kingdom is where Jesus is king; on earth he sits on the throne of the cross as we meditate in the fifth sorrowful mystery, but in heaven Jesus sits at the right hand of the Father, as we meditate in the second glorious mystery. To put our trust in Jesus and the kingdom

Jesus promises us when we first repent of our sins—this means conversion, new birth, and new life, which opens the first luminous mystery, with the baptism of Jesus. Baptism represents the first step towards the kingdom of heaven.

The proclamation of the kingdom occurs in this world and anticipates what Jesus promises. Based on how we live in the world, the earthly kingdom prepares us for the heavenly kingdom. Our journey begins on earth: if we believe and are baptized, if we are faithful to Christ's teachings, when our journey ends we approach the kingdom of heaven. The kingdom on earth and the kingdom of heaven are inseparable: Jesus teaches us how to live in this world and how we shall be rewarded—or punished—in the next (Matt 25:31–46).

Fourth Luminous Mystery—Transfiguration

I—And he was transfigured before them, and his face shone like the sun, and his clothes became dazzling white. (Matt 17:2)

Our Father . . . Hail Mary . . . Glory Be . . .

1. Mount Tabor

The natural surroundings of cypress trees under the blue Galilean sky and ruins from earlier Byzantine and crusader churches transmit our biblical history and the religious devotion that we experience as pilgrims. Mount Tabor symbolizes the majesty of Christ as we ascend in what feels like stepping into clouds to encounter the transcendent God who sends us his Son.

Mount Tabor stands at 1,886 feet; a sense prevails on the mountain of majesty and mystery.[1] On this mountain, pilgrims celebrate the extraordinary event of the transfigured Christ dazzling white and heavenly. The church marks the transfiguration on the mountain where Jesus is transfigured in the presence of two old covenant figures, Moses and Elijah, and witnessed by the inner core of Jesus's disciples, Peter, James and John.[2] Evidence of a Byzantine church of the fourth to sixth centuries, and a twelfth century crusader church, are traced in the layers of ruins, earlier edifices constructed for the glory of God and visiting pilgrims. The three chapels within the church represent the three huts Peter wished to build—one for Jesus, one for Elijah, and one for Moses.

---

1. In meters, 575 meters.
2. In the Roman Catholic calendar, the solemnity of the Transfiguration is celebrated August 6.

Crusader fortification in 1099 served to protect the pilgrims visiting and praying on Mount Tabor. Three basilicas had been observed by a pilgrim in the sixth century, later destroyed in 1263 by Baybars and his Muslim armies. Four hundred years later the Franciscans were given permission by Fakhr al Din, emir of Mount Lebanon, who had close ties with Tuscany and the De Medici, to live on the mountain. In the early twentieth century the Franciscans commissioned the Italian architect Antonio Barluzzi to design the present Church of the Transfiguration which was completed between 1921 and 1925.

2. Transfiguration

Luke relates the presence of Jesus on Mount Tabor, that he ascended the mountain to pray; Jesus brought with him the "inner core," the disciples whom he chose to be present with him. The same inner core he calls upon in Gethsemane—Peter, James, and John—in his state of agony seeking their companionship as we meditate in the first sorrowful mystery, the agony (Matt 26:36–38). On this mountain Jesus desires the presence of these three apostles to ascend Mount Tabor with him.

Luke provides a highly visual account of what had happened: "And while he was praying, the appearance of his face changed, and his clothes became dazzling white" (Luke 9:29). The face of Jesus is transformed just as his clothing, a "transfiguration," suggestive of Jesus anticipating his glory. Jesus's clothes are compared not just to the brightness but the "flash of lightning" conveying the sense of divinity, the power of God expressed in both the force and flashes.[3] Dazzling, the transfiguration of Jesus looks ahead.[4] Jesus offered his disciples a foretaste of the approaching events, what lay ahead as he often spoke to his disciples about the future to help them understand, to piece together, before his death, his identity, and after his death, his resurrection and ascension to the Father. The transfiguration enables the three apostles to unite these mysteries of the life of Jesus, although this will not be fully understood until Jesus ascends to the Father, witnessed by the apostles, and soon after at Pentecost as the Holy Spirit enlightens the church. On a mountain where the presence of green cypress and the blue sky surrounding Jesus brings together earth and heaven.

With Jesus appear two men: Moses and Elijah, also in glorious splendor. The two figures talking to Jesus are not described with the same divine-like

---

3. "Flash of lightning" in the *New International Version*.

4. As we find in the first and second glorious mysteries following the crucifixion of Jesus.

attributes; rather the luminous presence of Jesus spills onto Moses and Elijah. The two Old Testament figures who converse with Jesus discuss Jesus's departure from Jerusalem without providing details on what was "about to be" fulfilled. The scene suggests a spiritual preparation and anticipation of a prophetic nature as Jesus instructed his apostles to "read the signs" and "look ahead"; Jesus's teachings, his mission, and self-revelation would be fulfilled. The transfiguration anticipates the events to follow in Jerusalem. Until the transfiguration, the ministry of Jesus was associated with Galilee, by many referred to as the "Galilean," or the "Nazarene," who grew up in Nazareth. The city of Judah identified with the birth of Jesus was Bethlehem. From Bethlehem to Nazareth and the transfiguration on Mount Tabor now points to Jerusalem. The words of Jesus highlight his departure towards Jerusalem, the capital of Judah, where the temple stands.

i. Elijah

With the appearance of Elijah, one might ask, "Why the prophet Elijah?" Considered the greatest of the old covenant prophets, Elijah fittingly appears with Jesus on the mountain. The presence of Elijah serves to highlight the parallels with Jesus. The greatest acts associated with Prophet Elijah relate directly to God: Elijah showed the power of the God of Israel over the 450 prophets of Baal. Elijah, the one prophet of the Lord, demonstrated that the God of Israel is the true God and not the false god of the prophets of Baal (1 Kgs 18:17–40). At the end of his ministry, Elijah is taken up to heaven (2 Kgs 2:11).

Reference to Elijah is made when Jesus asks his disciples, "Who do people say that the Son of man is?" The first reply—the claims made by the people—is to identify Jesus with Elijah. When Jesus asks again, Peter understands that Jesus is not Elijah or a great prophet; instead, Peter replies, "You are the Christ, the Son of the living God" (Matt 16:13–18). The prophet Elijah's ascension into heaven anticipates the new covenant resurrection and ascension into heaven of Jesus. Thus, when Jesus speaks of the Scriptures and having come to fulfil the law and the prophets, he is speaking of all prophets signified by the one who embodies all prophets, Elijah. As the Son of God, Jesus is the fulfilment of Elijah's prophetic pronouncements and that of all other prophets (Matt 5:17).

The role of the prophet is to look ahead and offer the people of faith warnings, the call to conversion, and reasons for hope. The exercise of the prophetic ministry provides signs as markers of things to come: the prophet Nathan of a kingdom secure for ever (2 Sam 7:16); Isaiah pointing to the virgin birth of the Messiah (Is 7:14); born in Bethlehem (Mic 5:2); the "Son of Man" (Dan 7: 13–14).[5] Pointing to a figure who will unite Israel—southern and northern tribes—from its division due to sin, this Messiah who brings unity leads the people to victory over the oppressors and will reign as king forever. The twelve tribes of Israel were divided into two kingdoms, Judah (and Benjamin) in the south, and Israel (remaining ten tribes in the north) since the time of Rehoboam, King of Judah and Jeroboam, King of Israel (1 Kgs 11:26–43; 1 Kgs 14:21–31). This division between the south and the north reflects the prophetic language repeatedly calling the north and south to unity. The division can be traced to the death of King Saul and his son, Ish-bosheth who assumed kingship in the north, and King David's reign over Judah in the south (2 Sam 2:8–11).

The significance of oneness in the Scriptures can be traced to the first verse of Genesis where God is the agent of creation (Gen 1:1). God is the sole actor creating over six days. The centrality of oneness as a reflection of the divine appears in the creation of the man and woman when they are united to become one flesh (Gen 2:24). "Oneness" breaks down due to original sin; division results from sin in the world, the rupture with divine order. In spite of division due to sin, God intervenes where one righteous man emerges; the figure Noah and his family whom God spares from a flood (Gen 6:9—9:17). The call of one man, Abraham, through whom the entire world is blessed (Gen 12:1–3) and the covenant established with Abraham and his descendants, one people (Gen 17:1–8). And finally, with the twelve tribes of Israel we have one nation (Gen 49).

Division and corruption manifested themselves as the human condition after the fall; division does not belong to God. We are told how the broken relationship between the man and woman is due to sin (Gen 3:16–17); fratricide when Cain kills his brother follows (Gen 4:3–8); Lemech is the first to practice bigamy also kills a young man for "striking" him (Gen 4:23); the Tower of Babel reflects the division of humanity into different incomprehensible languages, a sign of division due to the sin of pride (Gen 11:1–9); and finally, the divided kingdom of Israel as noted above. These passages express the significance of oneness as God's plan and order for the world in the Old Testament. As we read the original order willed by God, we keep in mind how Christ fulfils the law and the prophets based on his teachings, his life, and who he is.

The prophetic language points to the coming of a king who will unite the people to form one kingdom under one king. This alludes to the second

---

5. See also the first and third joyful mysteries, and the third and fifth sorrowful mysteries.

luminous mystery, the wedding at Cana, of which Jesus is the prophetic fulfillment. To understand the prophets is to grasp how Jesus fulfills the prophecies in terms of the one king and one kingdom. When Jesus speaks of fulfilling the prophecies, he shows that he neither breaks with the old covenant, nor is he rejecting the old covenant, but that he is the "fulfillment" of the old covenant prophecies and the Law. The discourse between Elijah and Jesus on Mount Tabor unveils Jesus talking to Elijah, who represents the greatest of prophets, who intervenes for the one true God of Israel; Jesus, the true God of Israel, stands beside Elijah.

ii. Law of Moses

Jesus is also seen speaking to Moses on Mount Tabor; Moses is identified with the Law. Not only the Ten Commandments of Exodus revealed by God but also the Mosaic significance of the Levitical law regulating the life of the priests and the people, violations of laws and punishment, and the observance of different feasts. The Law divinely revealed, the Law taught by Moses shaped the lives of the Israelites; that which was permitted or forbidden, from food to marriage, from work to worship.

Moses receives and instructs the people of Israel on the Ten Commandments revealed by God (Exod 20:1–18; Deut 5:6–21). When Jesus instructs the Israelites on the commandments, he emphasizes two: "you shall love the Lord your God with all your heart, and with all your soul, and with all your mind, and with all your strength.' The second is this, 'You shall love your neighbor as yourself'" (Mark 12:31). The Passover observance, which was taught and to be observed in perpetuity, Jesus repeats but as a sacred sacrifice "fulfilled" at the cross; a continuation of the Passover meal where wine and bread, Jesus's body and blood, are offered, as meditated in the fifth luminous mystery.

When the Pharisees question Jesus about a man leaving his wife as permitted by the Mosaic teaching allowing a certificate of divorce (Matt 19:8), Jesus returns to God's original plan found in Genesis where the man and woman become one flesh (Gen 2:24) and nobody has the authority to change this reality (Matt 19:6). The fulfillment of the Law, even where Moses permitted a dispensation because of "hardened hearts," Jesus fulfills by "going back to the beginning" to the source, the law of God, and not the dispensation of "man" violating God's law.[6]

---

6. Where Jesus continues and says, "except for unchastity" (v.9), in the *Revised New Jerusalem Bible* Study Edition, "sexual immorality" relates to one of the Levitical prohibitions as in incest (Lev 18:6).

Once again we return to the value of oneness that both the prophets dealt with in a divided Israel as well as the teachings of Moses in divided marriage—division is generated by sin and has an ugly head of ongoing divisions. Jesus underscores the significance of the bond, of being one, as a people governed by common teachings and commandments, laws that serve to unite the people of Israel under one God; the divine order that unites man and woman in marriage to become one reflects God's order for his creation.

The transfiguration scene describes Elijah and Moses in "glorious splendor," both "talking" to Jesus. The two characteristics of the old covenant figures come as a surprise: they appear "glorious," and they are "talking" to Jesus. The scene raises questions of the resurrection where Elijah and Moses appeared along with Jesus in this transfigured state. Jesus in glorious splendor anticipates his resurrection and ascension, but what of the two figures from the Hebrew Scriptures? They gloriously dialogue with Jesus. Elijah and Moses are not "glorious" by their own power, but in the presence of Jesus, they reflect the brightness of the sun, the "dazzle" that also makes Elijah and Moses glowing white.

These two just figures of the old covenant carried out the will of God, faithfully led the people of Israel albeit within their own human limits. And so, they too can anticipate their resurrection by the power of the resurrected Jesus as already suggested by this scene. But neither Elijah nor Moses have yet been resurrected. The resurrection is not possible until Jesus himself has resurrected and ascended to the Father as we meditate in the first and second glorious mysteries.

The transfiguration takes place during Jesus's healing ministry. In Luke's Gospel, Jesus prepares the disciples for his passion, death, and resurrection with discourses before (Luke 9:22) and after the transfiguration (Luke 9:44). The transfiguration serves to convey the anticipated glory of Jesus and the two just figures of the old covenant who will join him after his resurrection and ascension. In Matthew's Gospel, Peter identifies Jesus as the Son of God (Matt 16:16–18), followed by Jesus announcing his passion, death, and resurrection (Matt 16:21); and in Matthew, the transfiguration is followed by the healing of a possessed individual and the second discourse announcing his death (Matt 17:22–23). Matthew and Luke show the same structure with the transfiguration preceded and followed by Jesus announcing his passion, death, and resurrection. The transfiguration serves to instruct the apostles beyond natural death, and to help them understand and prepare for the resurrection and supernatural life.

In Mark's Gospel the transfiguration also appears between the two discourses where Jesus announces his passion, death, and resurrection (Mark

8:31; 9:12). Similarly, Jesus heals a demon-possessed boy and the second reminder of his death. The Gospels of Matthew, Luke, and Mark show the transfiguration where Jesus dazzles in glory dialoguing with old covenant figures, Elijah and Moses, as a tryptic with the transfiguration at the center. Central to the transfiguration, therefore, is the announcement of Jesus's passion, death, and resurrection. Jesus prepared his disciples for his cruel death, but Jesus also points to the resurrection to help them understand what follows. Jesus at the center and Elijah and Moses on the left and right of Jesus, highlights Jesus at the transfiguration showing he is the fullness of the prophets and the laws. But with the two discourses on death, the tryptic can also present Jesus's passion and death that will save humanity from sin and lead those who believe in him to eternal life: this second tryptic would have the way of the cross on the left, at the center the transfiguration, and on the right, the crucifixion, highlighting the resurrection and ascension—in God's salvific plan of the suffering and sacrifice of his Son.

iii "My Beloved Son"

While Jesus was still speaking, a bright cloud covered them, and a voice from the cloud said, "Then from the cloud came a voice that said, 'This is my Son, my Chosen; listen to him!'" (Luke 9:35). The words are heard in the first luminous mystery, the baptism of Jesus, when the ministry of Jesus commences. The Trinitarian presence conveyed on Mount Tabor repeated the words of the Father's approval. With the bright cloud covering all of them, suggestive of a divine presence on the mountain, Jesus is identified as God's beloved, the fulfillment of God's promise, the Law and the Prophets, the Word made flesh.

For the Jews, Jesus may have been another "rabbi," or even a prophet, as they knew many. Jesus may have appeared to represent another such prophet whom the Father sent: three men chosen by God to lead the people of Israel: Moses, Elijah, and Jesus. But Jesus is referred to as "Son," and as "beloved." He is not only a teacher; he is not only a prophet; Jesus is the Son of God, his chosen and his beloved, so he fulfils both the Law and the Prophets as the beloved Son of God who carries out the will of the Father to its fulfillment. This fourth luminous mystery will be completed on the cross, the fifth sorrowful mystery, with Jesus's final words: "it is finished" (John 19:30). The crucifixion brings to completion the final act of Jesus understood in the light of the Law and the Prophets. Mary, the mother of God, grasps these events in her immaculate heart and pierced soul.

The Gospels of Matthew, Mark, and Luke place the transfiguration between Jesus's two accounts, old covenant and new covenant, preparing his disciples for his passion, death, and resurrection. "This is my beloved Son" is a fulfillment of the Law of Moses, the prophecies of Elijah, and this fulfillment is realized by Jesus on the cross before the resurrection and before the ascension. This glorified Jesus the apostles already encounter in dazzling garment. Jesus prepares his apostles, so they know Jesus is the chosen one, the Messiah, the Son of God.

II—Fruit of this Mystery: Desire for Holiness

Practical Matters—

1. Holiness in the Scriptures

The first reference to holiness is found in the book of Leviticus. Besides the Ten Commandments (Exod 20:2–17; Deut 5:6–21), with the Levitical code the people of Israel are directed towards holiness: "For I am the LORD your God; sanctify yourselves therefore, and be holy, for I am holy" (Lev 11:44); and later we find, "Speak to all the congregation of the people of Israel and say to them: 'You shall be holy, for I the LORD your God am holy'" (Lev 19:2). The call to holiness reflects communion with God: because God is holy, we are called to strive for holiness.

Israel is set aside for God, "consecrated," distinct from the surrounding pagan nations. In other words, the standard for holiness is given by God's Laws but also contrasted with pagan nations who have not been set aside for God and so do not have the Laws that lead to—and sustain—communion with God. Israelites falling into pagan practice appear early in their journey out of Egypt across the Sinai. At the foot of Mount Sinai the Israelites, under the leadership of Aaron, carve a golden calf, their "god" (Exod 32:1–6). The setting aside from the pagan peoples as a path towards holiness anticipates the ongoing challenge of the Israelites, the chosen people of God, assimilating to the surrounding paganism.[7]

While holiness clearly identifies the people of God set aside for God, namely, Israel, the New Testament Scriptures show that holiness signifies a change from ignorance to knowledge, the man of passion to the man of obedience; those who put their hope in the grace of Christ seek transformation.

---

7. The problem of pagan assimilation repeats itself throughout the Old Testament. Assimilation to pagan practices prove to be a challenge to Christians today.

Passions of the "old ignorance" reflect the man who does not know Jesus, whereas to know Jesus means to be transformed into the new man not driven by passions but as "obedient" children of God who imitate the holiness of God (1 Peter 1:13–16). Christ's grace means that the "old man" and the life driven by passions in the ignorance of the old man applies to the people of Israel and to all those who seek to follow Jesus, hear his voice, hear the Word of God proclaimed.

The genealogy of Jesus makes references to gentile women: Tamar (possibly Canaanite), Rahab (Canaanite), Ruth (Moabitess), Bathsheba (possibly Hittite), providing evidence of a gentile ancestry in the genealogy of Jesus (Matt 1:3–5). This gentile presence of women anticipates the Gospel intended for "all nations" and not only the people of Israel. The pagan sources in Jesus's matriarchal line provide a clear indication that Jesus is the Messiah for all peoples and that the Gospel offers a universal message of conversion, transformation, and holiness.

2. "Discipline"

When a high school student wants to enter university on a sports scholarship such as football, soccer, or swimming, the student knows very well the kind of gruelling training that is needed. As I learn about my students and I find out about their extracurricular activities, I often find students tell me that they have both early morning practice and weekend practice besides their full load of courses. And in some instances, students also have a part-time job. They know very well if they want to keep their sports scholarship, being an effective player on the team means regular training that requires discipline.

I know that students who do very well in their courses take time each evening to go over their notes, read the assigned text, and write the necessary assignments in a way that is constant and committed. In other words, good students, as with athletes on scholarships, need to be well-disciplined to maintain a good average to remain in their program—and especially if they plan on pursuing graduate studies. So, the minimum—simply passing courses—ruins not only a student's education but becomes detrimental to their future.

Thus, whether in sports, music, drama or any other extracurricular activity, to do well students need to be disciplined. "Discipline" refers to the application of cardinal virtues—namely, prudence, temperance, courage, and justice—and within a Christian framework, faith, hope, and love, the theological virtues also need to be present. Each of these has a role to play in ensuring the individual builds on the virtue that is needed for their studies, activities, and future work.

3. Striving in Virtue[8]

Regardless of how small the act may be, virtue expresses a "heroic" quality of the person who performs the act because virtue is acquired through effort until it becomes a natural disposition. Struggling against our instincts when they show signs of disorder—lust, gluttony, and greed, in particular. Each person knows their weakness and where their battles are fought—and the spiritual equipment needed for combat. Sacred Scriptures, the *Catechism of the Catholic Church*, natural law, serve to teach and even warn us, and in the case of natural law, to order our desires to a good that corresponds to human nature as created by God by concretely exercising virtue. By God's grace we are sanctified through our prayers and actions, we deepen our communion with God, and purify our relations with others.

Integral to growing in virtue is constancy, that is, observing regular prayer habits just as we have regular confession and mass schedule—confession first Friday, or first and third Fridays. Constancy creates virtue-building habits. So, if we know that we put aside a particular day/time for sacraments and prayers, this develops virtue. Without virtue, we cannot grow in sanctity. God provides us with the graces we need through the sacraments and prayers. For this reason, the Catholic Church has traditionally used certain days for prayers, or abstinence or devotions. Friday has traditionally been a day of abstinence from meat; this is a good day of the week to go to confession as Friday is a penitential day, and a way of being constant or regular in observing confession. Saturdays are devoted to the Virgin Mary and the priest may celebrate mass in honor of the blessed Virgin Mary. On Wednesdays we pray our devotions to Saint Joseph including the Litany to Saint Joseph. By keeping these days in mind, we can have a constant prayer life that helps us grow in virtue. Sundays we always keep as the solemn day of the Lord. Catholics who grow in their life of faith and virtue experience the yearning to be one with Christ, to increase the healing experience of confession, the desire to receive Christ in the Eucharist, and to pray in unity with the Catholic community, our fellow brothers and sisters in Christ and the saints of the church interceding for us.

---

8. Aquinas, *ST*, Pt. 2a–2ae, qq. 1-170. All seven virtues are examined: first, the three theological virtues, faith, hope, and charity; second, the four cardinal virtues, prudence, fortitude, justice, and temperance.

The rosary helps us with constancy setting aside the seven days of the week for meditations. As a way of being constant in prayer, the rosary keeps us united daily with the mysteries of the life of our Savior, Jesus, and the prayers of his mother, Mary. These daily meditations, then, help us grow in holiness striving to make concrete each mystery in our lives by building virtue.

Fifth Luminous Mystery—Institution of the Eucharist

I—Then he took a loaf of bread, and when he had given thanks, he broke it and gave it to them, saying, "This is my body, which is given for you. Do this in remembrance of me." And he did the same with the cup after supper, saying, "This cup that is poured out for you is the new covenant in my blood." (Luke 22:19–20)

Our Father . . . Hail Mary . . . Glory Be . . .

1. Last Supper

In Jerusalem, on Mount Zion, the upper room remains where Jesus shared with his disciples his Last Supper. The Passover sacrifice that begins in the upper room finds its fulfillment at Golgotha, on the cross, where the unblemished Lamb, Jesus, is slaughtered. This one salvific event beginning at the Last Supper, then, in Gethsemane, where Jesus sweats blood anticipating his death, is tried by two courts, and ends in his crucifixion. The five sorrowful mysteries connect the salvific passion of our Lord, Jesus Christ. The fifth luminous mystery meditates on the Last Supper, the institution of the Eucharist.

Numerous passages from the New Testament describe this core event that distinguishes the new covenant Passover instituted by Jesus as fulfillment of the Laws and Prophets from the old covenant: "While they were eating, Jesus took a loaf of bread, and after blessing it he broke it, gave it to the disciples, and said, 'Take, eat; this is my body.' Then he took a cup, and after giving thanks he gave it to them, saying, 'Drink from it, all of you; for this is my blood of the covenant, which is poured out for many for the forgiveness of sins'" (Matt 26:26–29). The inseparable connection with the old covenant is identified in the sorrowful mysteries. The "Last Supper" that Jesus observes with his disciples is the Passover. This religious celebration for the people of Israel provides the key to understanding the Eucharist that Jesus institutes coming to fulfil the Laws and the Prophets: Jesus is the promise fulfilled; Jesus is the anointed one.

In Matthew's Gospel, celebrating the Passover, Jesus takes bread and breaks it and invites his disciples to "take, eat" accompanied by the words of fulfilment, "this is my body," and deepened meaning: the bread Jesus breaks and that he shares with his disciples is his body. The objective problem: his disciples see, touch, smell, and taste wine and bread. Yet, Jesus clearly identifies the bread with his body which is to be eaten and the wine with his blood which is to be drunk. While the last supper expresses the context in which the Eucharist is instituted, this context is "unfinished" until Jesus's body is sacrificed and he himself utters the words, "It is finished."

The sorrowful mysteries can be understood as one salvific act that begins with the agony in the garden of the first sorrowful mystery—immediately preceded by the Last Supper—the fifth luminous mystery and ends with the carrying of the cross and crucifixion, the fourth and fifth sorrowful mysteries—Jesus struggles and stumbles carrying his cross to his crucifixion, mocked as king, his flesh is ripped open—one of us—to save us. The Lamb slaughtered, Jesus on the cross, is the transubstantiated bread the disciples eat, following the words of Jesus: "This is my body." The observance of the Passover ritual includes drinking four cups of wine, cups of sanctifying the Passover at the start and after Pss 113–114, followed by the third cup of blessing.[1] Jesus shares the wine with his disciples, giving full meaning and a new reality to the wine: "for this is my blood of the covenant." The disciples are not drinking wine; in Jesus's words, they drink that which Jesus offers them, blood anticipating the cross—"this is my blood"—and "this" refers to the cup of wine that Jesus is holding. He is God, and he has the power to make substantial changes. But the "new covenant" underscored in Luke's Gospel distinguishes clearly from the Old Testament covenant where blood from an unblemished lamb is sprinkled on the altar and on the people as a "peace-offering" made to God (Exod 24:5). Jesus's blood is spilled on the cross as he states in the same verse, "for this is my blood of the covenant, which is poured out for many for the forgiveness of sins." The blood Jesus asks his disciples to drink is that poured on the cross for "many," "for the forgiveness of sins." The new covenant is more than a "peace offering" but is the "forgiveness of sin" that leads to eternal life whereby the body and

---

1. At the time of Jesus, four cups of wine were drunk as part of the Passover supper each according to the Passover ritual. The third cup is the one which Jesus consecrates (Luke 22:20). The fourth cup is not drunk, "for I tell you that from now on I shall not drink of the fruit of the vine until the kingdom of God comes" (Luke 22:18). See Hahn and Mitch, *Catholic Study Bible*, 149.

blood of Jesus washes our sins restoring us in our relationship with God the Father on earth and for eternity. This is accomplished through his sacrificed body, his spilled blood, which we are to receive when we receive bread and wine transubstantiated into his body and blood.

In Mark's Gospel we read, "While they were eating, he took a loaf of bread, and after blessing it he broke it, gave it to them, and said, 'Take; this is my body.'" Then he took a cup, and after giving thanks he gave it to them, and all of them drank from it. He said to them, "This is my blood of the covenant, which is poured out for many'" (Mark 14:22–24). We find in Mark's Gospel the same words present in Matthew's Gospel. Both Matthew's and Mark's Gospels are prefaced with the reference to the Feast of Unleavened Bread when the Passover lamb is sacrificed: "On the first day of Unleavened Bread the disciples came to Jesus, saying, 'Where do you want us to make the preparations for you to eat the Passover?'" (Matt 26:17). We also find, "'On the first day of Unleavened Bread, when the Passover lamb is sacrificed, his disciples said to him, 'Where do you want us to go and make the preparations for you to eat the Passover?'" (Mark 14:12). The preparation is unmistakably identified with the Feast of Unleavened Bread and the Passover lamb that is sacrificed during this observance. A significant wording that is present in Mark's Gospel but absent in Matthew's is the use of the word "sacrifice." The sacrifice in reference to the lamb signals the anticipated sacrifice of Jesus. The Gospel is written after the events took place, and so, in this case, Mark employs words that convey the sacrificial connection between the Passover lamb and Jesus, the Passover Lamb.

"Sacrifice" is the word employed by Mark which creates the sense of offering to God based on the Levitical code of peace offering found in the old covenant. The emphasis on "sacrifice" in this Passover event points to a new sacrifice just as the "new" covenant with fundamental words have deepened their meaning at the Last Supper followed by the crucifixion. The unblemished animal sacrifice finds its fulfillment by an unblemished human sacrifice; Jesus, the Son of God. The lamb sacrificed, slaughtered, sprinkled on doorposts, and eaten (Exod 12:1–27), and slaughtered, blood sprinkled on the people (Exod 24:3–8), is fulfilled by God's Son, sacrificed for all of humanity, on the cross. The sacrifice offered by Jesus reconciles man with God his creator, by the washing away of our sins.

Cleansing begins at baptism by the power of the Holy Spirit; the ongoing, conversion, reconciliation, and renewal is made possible by the institution of the Eucharist where the believer receives Jesus's body and blood as Jesus taught. Reconciliation with God that Jesus makes possible through his sacrifice on the cross and the forgiveness of our sins presupposes repentance of our sins, in particular, mortal sins. Conversion, renewal, rebirth repeat the

FIFTH LUMINOUS MYSTERY—INSTITUTION OF THE EUCHARIST

experience of the River Jordan where John the Baptist first calls believers to repentance and conversion by baptism of water, and following Jesus, baptism of the Holy Spirit. After the rupture caused by original sin, with baptism, communion with God is restored. Because the repetition of sins, especially grave sins, confessing our sins to God's minister, the priest, serves as a necessary move towards purification and communion. Once this sacramental purification has taken place of confessing one's sins to a priest, to the church, and to God, one is disposed to receive the body and blood of Jesus to experience the fullness of communion with God and his church.

In Luke's Gospel, Jesus sits with his apostles for the Passover: "He said to them, 'I have eagerly desired to eat this Passover with you before I suffer; for I tell you, I will not eat it until it is fulfilled in the Kingdom of God.' Then he took a cup, and after giving thanks he said, 'Take this and divide it among yourselves; for I tell you that from now on I will not drink of the fruit of the vine until the Kingdom of God comes.' Then he took a loaf of bread, and when he had given thanks, he broke it and gave it to them, saying, 'This is my body, which is given for you. Do this in remembrance of me.' And he did the same with the cup after supper, saying, 'This cup that is poured out for you is the new covenant in my blood'" (Luke 22:15–20). As in the Gospels of Matthew and Mark, the Last Supper in Luke is prefaced with the day of Unleavened Bread, the day on which the Passover lamb was sacrificed" (Luke 22:7).

Luke's Gospel contains the same fundamental elements as Matthew's and Mark's Gospels, namely, "take . . . bread; eat . . . body; take . . . cup; drink . . . blood." In Luke's Gospel, we encounter the words, "Do this in remembrance of me," and "new covenant in my blood." Luke also makes reference to the kingdom twice, first in relation to "bread" and second in relation to "wine," which precedes the actual eating and drinking of the body and blood of Jesus. Luke makes the distinction between the kingdom that is to come where eating and drinking of the body and blood is fulfilled and the present eating and drinking with his disciples at the Passover, where already they take and eat his body and drink his blood. The language of Luke serves to connect not only the Passover supper with the cross of crucifixion, but also, the kingdom of heaven. Luke shows that the words of Jesus are meant not only for the moment, but they transcend time and move into eternity. In this respect, the "end-times" connections between an earthly kingdom and a heavenly kingdom are felt, which takes us back to the third luminous mystery, preaching of the kingdom, and bears a direct relationship with the third sorrowful mystery, the Crowning with Thorns and Jesus's kingship.

Jesus's last taste of "drink" was in fact wine on the cross that had become vinegar. After this last drink of "wine," Jesus gives up his spirit, saying, "It is finished" (John 19:30). Jesus died as a mocked king wearing a crown of thorns, sitting on his throne of glory. This earthly kingdom where Jesus preaches a kingdom of peace and holiness, mercy and justice, serves to prepare us for the heavenly kingdom where the body and blood of the sacrificed lamb is celebrated at the banquet of the lamb, where Jesus is the eternal king, the second luminous mystery.

The fundamental act that Jesus expresses at the Last Supper connects past-present-future and eternity; through the bread, his body, and wine, his blood, the act begins at the Passover supper, finds its earthly fulfilment on the cross, and serves to prepare us for eternal life. This is why Jesus says, "Do this in remembrance of me." The Passover instructed by Moses, is revealed by God, "This day shall be a day of remembrance for you. You shall celebrate it as a festival to the Lord; throughout your generations you shall observe it as a perpetual ordinance" (Exod 12:14). Jesus observes and fulfils the Passover already known to the apostles. Jesus himself—"Lamb of God"—perfectly fulfills what was already instituted by divine command, his body and blood. Jesus is remembered, not just a thought or sentimental memory, but through concrete acts and gestures where he is truly present as food and drink. Luke includes his Gospel, "Do this in remembrance of me," underscoring that Jesus is the slaughtered lamb to be remembered. Jesus is the Passover Lamb.

Paul, in his letter to the Thessalonians, reflects the teaching of the apostles, what was to be obeyed: "So then, brothers and sisters, stand firm and hold fast to the traditions that you were taught by us, either by word of mouth or by our letter" (2 Thess 2:15). Paul's instructions serve to preserve the teachings of Jesus: "The cup of blessing that we bless, is it not a sharing in the blood of Christ? The bread that we break, is it not a sharing in the body of Christ?" (1 Cor 10:16). "Sharing," in some translations "participating" or "communion" in the body and blood of Christ, conveys the reality that the bread is more than eating bread, and the cup is more than drinking wine as in the Passover remembrance, but an actual communion in the body and blood of Jesus.[2]

Paul writes with this deepened understanding of the Holy Eucharist, "For I received from the Lord what I also delivered to you, that the Lord Jesus on the night when he was betrayed took bread, and when he had given thanks, he broke it, and said, 'This is my body which is for you. Do this in remembrance of me.' In the same way also the cup, after supper, saying, 'This cup is the new covenant in my blood. Do this, as often as you drink it, in remembrance of me'" (1 Cor 11:23–25). Paul employs the words

---

2. *New Revised Standard Version* Catholic Edition employs "participation" and gives "communion" as a variant. *Revised New Jerusalem Bible* Study Edition uses "communion."

retaining the meaning of "remembrance," as Paul clearly states. In both instances, the offering of the bread and offering of the wine, which now, besides the Gospels of Matthew, Mark, and Luke, we also have Paul repeating, the bread is Jesus's body, and the cup, the wine, is Jesus's blood. Paul illuminates, as Luke has done, that this is the "new covenant." There is no doubt that both Luke and Paul wanted to emphasize for the Jews, followers of Christ, the institution of the Eucharist is the "new" covenant that fulfills the "old" Mosaic covenant. Similarly, the gentiles—the pagan non-Jews—will discover how Jesus fulfils the Old Testament Passover. Paul asserts we share in the body and blood of Jesus, what we refer to as "communion" with the Trinitarian God, Father, Son, and Holy Spirit.

This is also how we are in communion with each other as one body, the one mystical body, when the spouse himself, Jesus, unites himself to the church, the bride, the believers, each one of us. So, the language of Paul observes the teaching of Jesus: "For I received from the Lord, what I also delivered to you . . . " (1 Cor 11:23). Paul handed down what he received, which we also refer to as tradition from Latin *trans + dare*—"to give over." Jesus expected of his disciples to "pass down" what he taught them, especially in the upper room, this central salvific act uniting the Last Supper and the crucifixion. The Eucharist is instituted, and we continue to observe this fundamental event integral to our salvation. Jesus does not offer grape juice and crackers. The Eucharistic celebration is not an optional or peripheral observance of our Christian faith. This is not a symbolic act. Everything taking place at a mass is real: Jesus's body is real; Jesus's blood is real. And we are invited to eat his body and drink his blood sacramentally offered, and present. Jesus is teaching us what he wants us to "do."

Paul repeats this; Matthew repeats this; Mark repeats this; Luke repeats this. And even John approaches the Eucharist from its salvific meaning: "Truly, truly, I say to you, unless you eat the flesh of the Son of man and drink his blood, you have no life in you; he who eats my flesh and drinks my blood has eternal life, and I will raise him up at the last day. For my flesh is food indeed, and my blood is drink, indeed. He who eats my flesh and drinks my blood abides in me, and I in him" (John 6:53–56). John retains and teaches that which he received from Jesus, and so he "hands down." The words of John echo the Gospels of Matthew, Mark, Luke, and Paul's letter to the Corinthians. Jesus's body and blood are meant to be eaten and drunk as they are sacrificed on the cross for our salvation: "He who eats my flesh and drinks my blood has eternal life . . ." These words that find their source in the Last Supper where the Eucharist is instituted are fulfilled on the cross; bread and wine means Jesus's body and blood, which he himself offers to all of his followers with this final act on the cross. His body and blood are what saves us. This is why Jesus leaves us the Eucharist; and this is why the apostles continue to observe and teach which Jesus asked them to do in remembrance of him.

In the fourth luminous mystery, the transfiguration, Jesus appears on Mount Tabor with Moses and Elijah; Jesus is the fulfilment of the Prophets; he is the Savior, the Messiah enfleshed in Mary by the power of the Holy Spirit. The fifth sorrowful mystery accentuates that Jesus is king, crucified on his throne of the cross, and anticipates his kingly glory—Jesus sits at the right hand of the Father in the second glorious mystery, the ascension. In the third luminous mystery, Jesus preaches the kingdom where he reigns as eternal king. The fifth luminous mystery, the institution of the Eucharist, reveals the fullness of Jesus's role as priest—sacrifice and sacrificed.

2. Priesthood of Jesus

In the Letter to the Hebrews, describing the priesthood of Jesus, the first priest Melchizedek, king of Salem, pre-figures Jesus (Gen 14:18; Heb 7:3). Melchizedek is associated with origins of an underlying mystery: "has neither beginning of days nor end of life." Jesus does not belong to the priestly tribe of Levi, and neither does Melchizedek (Heb 7:11–14). Yet, both fulfil according to God's plan the priesthood: Melchizedek's offering of bread and wine is perfected by the sacrifice of Jesus's body and blood and his eternal priesthood (Heb 5:5–10). Jesus belongs to the tribe of Judah, and from this tribe, like Melchizedek, assumes the role of priest assigned to him by God himself: "Thou art a priest for ever after the order of Melchizedek" (Heb 7:17). Hebrews tells us that, "For every high priest is appointed to offer gifts and sacrifices; hence it is necessary for this priest also to have something to offer" (Heb 8:3). This priest is Christ who instituted the Eucharist, the "new covenant" in his blood, and so he has perfected the old covenant; otherwise a new covenant would not have been needed (Heb 8:8). Jesus is identified as high priest who offers himself as sacrifice "to put away sin" having appeared "once for all" (Heb 9:26). Jesus's perfect sacrifice as priest was the sacrifice of himself "once for all." And this sacrifice represents one continuous act of self-offering, the sacrificial act which Jesus himself offers as priest for each of us.

This sacrificial act means the divine participation of the faithful in communion—the blood of Christ—as Paul states in his letter to the Corinthians (1 Cor 10:16). This "once for all" sacrifice bears the fruit of redemption; the act serves to save humanity from sins, the act where the Son of God offers himself as priest for our salvation, reaching into the past, the present, and future. It is the present "I Am" (Exod 3:14) that extends across time in an eternal present in terms of its salvific fruit. The act where Jesus's apostles participate in the institution of the Eucharist and the priesthood, they are commissioned to continue this one-time sacrifice of salvation in their ministry of offering his body to be eaten and offering his blood to be drunk; this participation in divine life extends in space and time into the eternal present of Jesus Christ. In his priestly sacrifice of himself, bearing salvific fruit, where we participate in this act of self-giving through his body and blood, through the Eucharist and priesthood Jesus instituted, Jesus's salvific mission continues.

Entering into communion with the eternal presence of the Trinitarian God through the sacrament of the Eucharist, where the apostles and disciples of Jesus, where we enter the divine mystery of Jesus's presence "here with us now." Jesus clearly states in the institution of the Eucharist that his body and blood are offered for the forgiveness of our sins. He is the sacrificed Lamb; he offers the perfect sacrifice of himself, unblemished Lamb, to God. Integral to the sacrifice is the end for which Jesus is sacrificed: forgiveness of our sins; that we may have eternal life.

Forgiveness means our relationship with God is perfectly restored by Jesus's body and blood. Because the Holy Eucharist is fundamental to forgiveness in our relationship with God, but also towards the community, we simply cannot have reconciliation of one without the other. Both ends of reconciliation are needed because offense is always against both commandments, failing to love God and failing to love our neighbor; we cannot love our neighbor in truth if we do not love God, and we cannot love God in truth if we do not love our neighbor (1 John 4:20).

At the resurrection, Jesus's final instruction focuses on forgiveness. Jesus has already preached during his earthly ministry on "forgiveness," but at the resurrection, Jesus gives teachings that pertain to the church. The disciples are locked in a room, afraid of being identified as Jesus's apostles and risk being discovered and executed for blasphemy. But Jesus tells them they were chosen to continue his message of salvation, teaching, evangelizing, shepherding; in other words, the commission relates to that of the church hierarchy. Yet, what is true of the church is also true for each of us; that is, to forgive. But how does apostolic authority and the church forgive? The church forgives through the sacrament of reconciliation as instructed by our Lord, the grace which heals the individual in their rupture with God and with the community (John 20:21–23).[3]

---

3. See, *Catechism*, #980, #1440.

II—Fruit of this Mystery: Eucharistic Adoration; Active Participation at Mass

Practical Matters—

1. Bread and Wine

Not surprisingly, the Jews disputed amongst themselves as John tells us, just as many continue to dispute today about eating and drinking Jesus's body and blood. Since the sixteenth century with the fragmentation of Christianity, the personal appropriation of the Scriptures created confusion, conflict, and wars. From the body and blood of Jesus as taught by Jesus and his disciples we are left with a symbolic act in some denominations of bread or wine, or crackers and juice in others. And the reason for crackers and juice or symbolic wine and bread is the same reason given by the Jews during the time of Jesus: "How can this man give us his flesh to eat?" (John 6:52).

Jesus was already aware of the difficulty his followers had in accepting this teaching. While the apostles, the close followers of Jesus, adhered to his teachings, the disbelieving Jews who resisted and rejected such teachings expressed themselves: "How can this man give us his flesh to eat?" Jesus, as recorded in John's Gospel, prepared us. We cannot ignore or even diminish the centrality of Jesus's teaching in terms of eating his body and drinking his blood if we desire to be in communion with him and have eternal life.

Clearly, if the divine life of Jesus is not within our bodies, then, how do we expect to have eternal life? We cannot by our own efforts obtain eternal life. We cannot simply as an act of faith have eternal life. Faith is manifested by responding to Jesus's instruction to eat and drink his body and blood. So, our faith cannot only be in our head or in our heart. Our faith, as the Scriptures teaches us from Abraham to Jesus, is in our acts. Faith jumps out of the Scriptures through radical deeds. Jesus asks us to receive his body and blood so we may have eternal life. This is why he died. Jesus has accomplished everything for us; it is for us to partake in the Eucharist so our faith is concretely lived in our personal encounter with Christ.

2. Body and Blood of Christ

The act of Jesus offering his life as a sacrifice for us, to reconcile us with God, the Father, invites a three-part response on our part: i.) we accept Jesus as our Savior through baptism; ii.) we seek forgiveness for our sins; and iii.) we receive the body and blood of Jesus. Accepting Jesus as Savior is to recognize he is Lord of our life; he heals us; he saves us. We also need to seek forgiveness. How can Jesus save us if we do not acknowledge our sins and the need for a Savior? How can we say, "Lord, thank you for saving me from my wretched condition" if we do not see the depth of our misery? We need to take ownership of how we have sinned towards God and towards others. This acknowledgement means that we ask God the Father in the name of his Son, Jesus Christ, to forgive us our sins, and pray to the Holy Spirit to help us combat error and sin.

We also sin against the community. And this painful reality means not only turning to God who hears us and answers us, but it also means turning to those whom we have hurt, offended, betrayed, asking them for forgiveness. Asking another in an acknowledgement that we have indeed failed them is humbling, and it takes divine grace to look into another's eyes whom we know we have caused pain by our words or deeds. Seeking forgiveness from those whom we have hurt is the very love Jesus teaches us; to love is the capacity to say, "I am sorry. Please forgive me." Because we know God is merciful and compassionate and loving, we have greater apprehension to turn towards another person, whom we do not know how they will respond after we have offended them. And yet, being a Christian means being able to say, "I am sorry, I have caused you wrong; I have hurt you." How often do our actions not only cause grief to a person, but to a family, or a community? Ironically, a community who shares my values, my faith, journey; and now, I have caused them grief. Hurting one, even if only known to that one person, still affects the entire community. We belong to families, we share with our friends, we are members of a praying community, so the sinful act is not only an offense towards God, and an individual, but to a community. This is why Catholics confess their sins to a priest; he is a minister of the church and acts in *persona Christi*.

3. Doubting Thomas

Saint Thomas the apostle expresses disbelief when he hears the apostles report on the resurrection of Jesus (John 20:24–31). Thomas does not believe the disciples because he refuses to rely on their testimony, and instead, trusts his own sensory experience. He needs to see with his own eyes and touch with his own hands. He desires an encounter with Jesus that relies on two intense sensory experiences: sight and touch, visible and tactile. If the visible presence may be questioned as an illusion, touch is the one sense that marks the "real presence." And so, Jesus gives the skeptic, Thomas, the experience of both so that Thomas may believe. Thomas finally reports to others what he has seen and touched—namely, his encounter with the resurrected Christ.

The many Thomases who will exist after the events of the resurrection, lacking evidence in order to believe, are represented by this one Thomas who signifies the "Thomas" prototype of disbelief. Thomas benefits from the unique privilege of this sensory encounter with Jesus that no one else had. As the apparitions bring Jesus closer and closer to his disciples reaching a highpoint with Thomas, only Thomas will have the sensory experience of our Lord by touching him: "Although the doors were shut, Jesus came and stood among them and said, 'Peace be with you.' Then he said to Thomas, 'Put your finger here and see my hands. Reach out your hand and put it in my side. Do not doubt but believe.' Thomas answered him, 'My Lord and my God!' Jesus said to him, 'Have you believed because you have seen me? Blessed are those who have not seen and yet have come to believe'" (John 20:26–29). Jesus clearly acknowledges that while Thomas believes because he has seen, and touched the presence of the Lord, "blessed are those who have not seen and yet have believed." Jesus reveals the intelligence of faith, knowing that what one believes rests on testimonies, Scriptures, the deposit of faith.

4. Eucharistic Adoration

Both active participation at mass and Eucharistic adoration are the fruit of worship: the desire to receive the body and blood of Christ. Receiving the Eucharist followed by an extended period of worship through adoration reflects the relationship between communion and adoration. To receive someone means wanting to be with the person; adoration is not only communion but a personal union. When we speak of an encounter with Jesus, when we have this personal relationship, we experience this union with our Lord in adoration. Prolonging the presence of the beloved, extending the time spent loving God in adoration, represents the supernatural reflex of receiving communion and extending this encounter of truth and love.

Because the two sacraments are inseparable, communion and confession, circumstances may require that while the person cannot receive sacramental communion, they may participate in a spiritual communion both during mass, and extended into adoration. Eucharistic adoration is the most sublime act a human being can perform: because we love God, we desire to remain in his divine presence, to adore. Only humans can engage in such an awesome act encompassing the intelligence and the will, the mind and the heart.

While the Catholic Church teaches that Sunday is a day of obligation for mass, a spiritually mature believer attends Sunday Mass not out of obligation but out of love.[4] Visiting someone because you love them and paying a visit out of duty makes two different statements about the relationship: communion out of obligation vs. communion out of love. While the dutiful act certainly carries with it merit because the individual fulfills the obligation as opposed to neglecting or ignoring it, but from a spiritual standpoint, love transcends duty and the law. Love prompted by truth seeks fulfillment in the presence of the other—the beloved. Our ultimate desire as humans is union with God—nothing is greater than this communion of love.

Because God sent his Son to us so we can have a personal communion and encounter with Christ in the Eucharist, and at mass, Jesus is at the center glorified by his saints, all present as one body; we fulfill this desire of communion when we speak of "going to mass." Disciples of Christ who discover the fulfilling richness of the mass where one worships in communion with others as a community of believers, they soon find themselves seeking to repeat the Sunday experience, just as one repeats any experience of great fulfillment and delight, and so, weekday masses become part of the mass participation. Love is a desire that seeks fulfillment; human love only finds its perfect fulfillment in Christ. The lover seeks the beloved, and the beloved rests in the lover. This restlessness is like an endless search, a deep thirst that needs to be quenched; only Christ can do this; only the Eucharist can offer supernatural consolation that is most sublime: finding rest in the lover—our God.

Sin has the adverse effect of turning away from the lover, creating a separation, a rupture, and so long as that rupture remains, the risk increases of exacerbating the chasm caused by sin—repeated, serious sins. With sin, one slides into the slippery slope into the abyss not knowing how to recover from this profound darkness, this deep interior swamp that causes death in one's spiritual life, death because sanctifying grace is lost with serious sins. Darkness is felt with the "distance" between man and God, man and the church, man and himself. Our reassurance is that if the person seeks repentance and conversion, Christ receives the sinner with open arms, but the desire to return to God must be there: repentance means to acknowledge sin and return to God by living according to his teachings, his commands, his precept of truth and love.[5] And so, the church makes the two sacraments available to us on a regular basis and encourages us to benefit from both confession and the Holy Eucharist as frequently as possible so as to remain in God's grace.

The summit of our spiritual life on earth is the Holy Eucharist; in the Eucharist we encounter our Lord; we receive our Lord who offered his life

---

4. See, the *Catechism*, #2180, #2181.

5. The penitential season of Lent is meant for believers, non-practicing believers, and non-believers. God calls all of us to conversion and deeper conversion (Joel 2:12–13; Mark 1:15).

for us because he loves us, and so we may have eternal life. Communion is a personal encounter with Jesus. Communion recognizes only one true and absolute lover exists: God. Each of us, created by God, is the beloved whom God seeks, so we may live in truth and happiness for all eternity. We are God's beloved. Jesus's sacrifice is our way back to God.[6]

God is the lover who seeks us and waits for us, who prompts us, provokes us, and anticipates our reply, our "yes," to Eucharistic communion, to the personal encounter in adoration, to the purification Jesus offers to heal our rupture, our sins that cause separation. In confession, Jesus himself waits to make himself fully present to us sacramentally; in Eucharistic adoration, Jesus, fully present sacramentally, body and blood, soul and divinity, waits for us.

Our daily struggles, our ongoing battles, are overcome by removing the clutter caused by noise, distractions, temptation, so we can hear the voice of God and overcome sin. Jesus knocks on the door of our heart; he waits for us so we can let him in (Rev 3:20). Jesus also teaches us that we have the responsibility to share this good news that enriches and offers us supernatural life. We are called to bring the good news of salvation to others, so the sinners, lukewarm, the indifferent, the ignorant, the confused, and the zealous may each hear the riches that God seeks to offer us in his Son, in his church and sacraments, and his saints.

Participation at mass and adoration implies inviting others to bring the good news of salvation; the promised Messiah has come to all those who accept him, giving us eternal life. Jesus offered his body and blood on the cross so that those who believe will eat and drink his body and blood and have eternal life. This sacrifice of himself that he offers, the Paschal Lamb crucified, is for our salvation. Our hearts and minds are moved by his teachings, his healings, and the sacrifice of himself because he loves us. Love is offering of ourselves as a sacrifice for the good of others. Jesus offers himself for our salvation; there is no higher good than our salvation because this means eternity with God, eternal communion with God in an eternal banquet where the wedding feast of the Lamb is celebrated (Rev 19:7–9). Jesus wants us all to share in this banquet. And we already prepare ourselves on this pilgrim journey with confession, through participation at the Holy Eucharist, and adoration as we approach eternal life.

---

6. Aquinas's *Summa Theologiae* is structured (and planned) to lead us back to God. The focus of Pt. 2 and Pt. 3, from the Incarnation to the sacraments, is to direct man, in his fallen condition of sin, back to God, through Christ, grace, the sacraments, and a life of virtue.

SORROWFUL MYSTERIES

First Sorrowful Mystery—Agony in the Garden

I—"Father, if you are willing, remove this cup from me; yet, not my will but yours be done." (Luke 22:42)

Our Father . . . Hail Mary . . . Glory Be . . .

1. Gethsemane

When we stand at the Church of All Nations in eastern Jerusalem facing the Temple Mount with the Kedron Valley separating the church from the city of Jerusalem, we find ourselves in the vicinity of the olive orchard of Gethsemane. The present neo-Byzantine church designed by Antonio Barluzzi, built in 1924, preserves the site where Jesus prayed in his state of anguish.

Sorrow and distress caused Jesus to sweat drops of blood. The rock in the church where Jesus prayed remains; pilgrims touch the rock knowing at this site Jesus knelt, asking his Father to "remove this cup from me," and then, "not my will but yours" (Luke 22:42).

With about thirty pilgrims present, I celebrated mass, the rock in front of us, between the altar and the pilgrims. It was 8 a.m., the first mass of the day in Gethsemane. The atmosphere intense, experiencing the embrace of our Savior praying with him, one with him, in his agony as we carry our crosses especially in times of sorrow and distress. And yet, in front of this rock, our crosses are lifted as we recognize the love of Jesus for us, love that heals, that saves, his agony began by sweating blood for us, blood that leads to eternal life.

2. Prophesy

The prophecies of Jesus's passion go back to the prophet Isaiah who writes around the sixth century BC and gives the vivid description, "He was despised and rejected by others; a man of suffering . . ." (Isa 53:3). An appearance broken, points to Jesus already in the Garden of Gethsemane. Jesus's condition results from carrying out the Father's will, carrying his cross for us, carrying our sins. Jesus knows Isaiah and he understands his mission: to carry the sins of humanity to the cross, nailed to the cross. Jesus's sweat, dripping blood, signifies the fear of anticipating that which awaits him, that to which he will be subjected. But worse than the physical pain, he suffers for our fallen condition, our brokenness, our sins.

Blood drops in the garden, blood spilled on the cross, blood that saves us. God the Father, the creator God, loves the human beings he created. Jesus knows this, and the mission of Jesus is to restore this rupture affecting the very metaphysical structure of the person, sin whose consequences no man can reconcile, redeem, or restore except the Son of God. To reconcile us with God, Jesus must undo that rupture caused by the first sin of the man and woman, the sin causing personal fragmentation and a shattered relation with God, fragility in human relations, and even brokenness with nature. Isaiah prophesies Christ's mission: ". . . yet we accounted him stricken, struck down by God, and afflicted. But he was wounded for our transgressions" (Isa 53:4–5). Jesus already bore our sins sweating blood in Gethsemane, the agony in the garden, in this first sorrowful mystery.

From the flagellation, the crowning with thorns, and finally the crucifixion that awaits Jesus, the passion that begins in Gethsemane continues that very same night to stand before Caiaphas, at the high priest's residence. With his own blood poured out for us, Jesus destroys sin, original sin against God creating separation between God and man, God's goodness and human sinfulness. Jesus heals and restores this deep-seated brokenness with his body and blood on the cross.

We sense Paul's frustration with the Jews (Rom 10:1–4). Why don't the Jews believe? After all, Jesus was a Jew born into the house of David, and the Jews, scribes, Pharisees, and elders knew the Scriptures. Why do they not recognize in Jesus the fulfillment of the Law and Prophets? Yet, many Jews believed in Jesus and his teachings: the twelve apostles of Jesus were made up of Jews. But the ones who knew neither the Law nor the Prophets also embraced the teachings of Jesus; as Paul states, "They show what the law requires is written on their hearts . . ." (Rom 2:15). Natural reason can lead us to God, and grace raises our intellect to believe in Jesus, Son of the ever living God.

Non-believers may even receive the grace to desire baptism when they seek the truth and finally grasp truth's fulfillment in Jesus Christ.

Isaiah speaks of this derision on our part: "He was despised and rejected by men," and this same man, Isaiah tells us, "But he was wounded for our transgressions, he was bruised for our iniquities" (Isa 53:3, 5). Isaiah tells us in the following verses, "All we like sheep have gone astray; we have turned every one to his own way" (Isa 53:6). Jesus seeks to unite a scattered flock—"his own way" means division; each stubbornly goes his own way. The words of Isaiah echoes the chaotic period of Judges: "every man did what was right in his own eyes" (Judg 21:25). Pride results in division and a scattered flock when we fail to listen to religious authority, but instead listen to ourselves and go our own way.[1] While Isaiah spoke over two and a half millennia ago, Jesus came to unite us, as one people, baptized in one faith, no longer stubbornly scattered. But even today, people turn away from their shepherd, and each listens to his own opinions of what is true and false, what is right and wrong. We call this relativism.[2]

Pope Benedict XVI, in addressing the conclave before the papal elections in April 2004, spoke of the "dictatorship of relativism." The paradox of everyone deciding what is true and false, right and wrong. By contrast, Jesus was completely committed to the will of God the Father: he utters, "if this cup may pass," but then Jesus continues, "not my will, Father, but yours." We understand that Jesus reverses the disobedience, the self-determination of the first humans. The man and woman in the garden of Eden, in their desire to be like God through their own power under the influence of the serpent, refused the will of God. Saint Augustine of Hippo refers to this as the *perversio imitatio Dei*—"perversion of the image of God" which signifies the *perversio voluntatis Dei* "perversion of the will of God."[3] Jesus manifests only one desire: to carry out the will of the Father.

Isaiah writes, "He was oppressed, and he was afflicted, yet he opened not his mouth" (Isa 53:7). This silence will bring Jesus to his trial: a lamb to be slaughtered. The contrast is evident: the refusal of the first man to obey, who with the woman brings sin into the world, while the total obedience of God's Son restoring our relationship with God the Father, bringing about our salvation.

---

1. "Obedience" represents a core virtue in Catholic spirituality, one of the three evangelical councils, the other two being chastity and poverty. Obedience is meditated in the fourth joyful mystery, the presentation.

2. Since the sixteenth century, relativism has also crept into Christianity, subjectivizing the Christian experience at the expense of doctrine and morality.

3. Augustine of Hippo, *Confessions*, Book VIII, ch. 16, par. 22.

3. Agony

Jesus calls upon the inner core of the apostles, Peter, James, and John, the same three who were present with Jesus at the transfiguration (Luke 9:28–36), the fourth luminous mystery, and appear with Jesus in Gethsemane. We read, "And taking with him Peter and the two sons of Zebedee, he began to be sorrowful and troubled" (Matt 26:37). And Jesus tells them, "My soul is very sorrowful, even to death; remain here, and watch with me" (v. 38). The language of Matthew clearly expresses the humanity of Jesus, "sorrowful," to convey the intensity of Jesus's agony, "sorrowful, even to death." Jesus also captures our own humanity when we are confronted with the reality of pain and suffering.

During our sharing session on the last evening of our pilgrimage in Jerusalem, the agony of Jesus resonated in particular with a pilgrim who was dealing with cancer, and he felt the anguish of what lay ahead. His wife, sitting beside her husband, appeared to experience the same anguish as her husband. But this pilgrim's wife suffered in another way: knowing her husband's condition, she embraced the suffering of Mary at the foot of the cross. We hear in these personal testimonies that Jesus takes on our humanity, complete humanity, with the exception of sin, so he shares in our suffering. The greatest suffering he experienced in Gethsemane is our sin. The fragility and brokenness of our nature—our human condition after the fall.

And in this state, Jesus turns to his closest disciples—Peter, John, and James—and exhorts them, "remain here, and watch with me" and returns to the disciples and asks, "So, could you not watch with me one hour?" (Matt 26:38, 40). The three apostles are overcome with fatigue; they cannot "watch" with Jesus for even one hour. We discover the weakness of the disciples. Jesus's closest apostles are fragile—like us. Even though Peter, James, and John do not know what lies ahead, they fail to keep Jesus company for just one hour. We discover in this scene the limits of the human condition. How much we are in need of God's grace to help us, to overcome our limits even if our weaknesses are not serious sins, they can keep us from the zeal that is needed to live and communicate our faith. Jesus even acknowledges "the spirit indeed is willing, but the flesh is weak" (Matt 26:41).

The Roman Catholic tradition of one hour of Eucharistic adoration, fruit of the fifth luminous mystery, is associated with keeping Jesus company for that one hour. Jesus asked his three apostles for their company, but they fell asleep. Did the apostles understand what was taking place at that Last Supper with the words to the Passover being fulfilled? Did they not question the strange behavior of Judas abruptly leaving a sacred banquet? And now Jesus praying on the Mount of Olives seeking their company anticipating his passion, in agony at his very core, his disciples appear distant, physically, emotionally, and spiritually. We are confronted with the reality of the human condition: Jesus in his solitude and agony, the apostles in the weakness of their fatigue. Jesus sought at least one hour from his three closest disciples to keep that night watch with him, to be on "guard" so as to stay awake with him, to "keep watch" against our own human limits, whether it's fear or fatigue.

4. Betrayal

We come across another weakness, in this case one that represents sin. What makes betrayal a sin? Because the act reflects the falsehood of the person committing the act; "false" because the individual behaves as if a trustworthy friend, in this case an apostle chosen by Jesus himself to be one of the Twelve. And so, Judas, like all the apostles, knows all about the life of the apostles as a community led by Jesus. And in this community, Judas had a very specific task: he "had the money box"—Judas served as the treasurer for the twelve apostles. Judas, therefore, found himself in a privileged position to know the finances of the community, and also believed he exercised influence on the others in how to use their funds. Such a position as an apostle and treasurer meant he was trusted. Judas allowed himself to be trusted, misleading others to think he believed in Jesus, his teachings, his mission. Judas exercised his apostolic role under false pretenses.

Much can be said about Judas and the motivation of his betrayal. No doubt, Judas experienced disappointment: disillusioned about Jesus and his messianic kingdom shrouded in spiritual language, and the prominent place reserved Judas in the king's court appeared increasingly uncertain. But a new, "surer" opportunity arose: handing the Messiah over to Caiaphas and his men. Whatever the exact motives, Judas finally betrayed Jesus. One of the Twelve who ate with Jesus and the others, who prayed with them, knew where they gathered. Judas had enough information to fulfil his role as disciple and betrayer.

And his role as betrayer Judas performed very well. Promised to be paid if he informed the Jewish religious authorities where to find Jesus, Judas's utilitarian disposition meant he exhausted his use for Jesus though he believed he benefited from the relationship at the start. But by the end, Judas realized he could still benefit as an apostle by making a small profit—handing Jesus over to the temple guards since the Jewish religious authorities wanted Jesus executed. Not disturbed in any way by his conscience, Judas approached Jesus with the chief priests' soldiers and disclosed Jesus's identity,

"The one I will kiss is the man; arrest him" (Matt 26:48). The kiss expressed a sign of brotherhood, loyalty, and trust; Judas uses it to betray Jesus and make his profit. And so, the entire betrayal reflects a relationship built not on love or trust but on personal gain and falsehood.

Is it then the self-focused attachment to money that leads to the sin of betraying Jesus? Why does Judas claim to be concerned about the poor when money is spent on perfume to bathe Jesus? Or was Judas "virtue-signaling," expressing concern for the poor when it really did not cost him anything, and meant nothing to him, but made him appear "righteous"? Praying in the garden of Gethsemane, only Jesus foresaw the course of events. A radical contrast emerges between Jesus's divine mission in obedience to the Father's will and Judas's betrayal succumbing to his own greed, his personal mission. Jesus is turned over to the high priest's soldiers by his apostle; Judas, motivated by a "payment," appears gratified to rid himself of Jesus.

Judas is frustrated with Jesus's apparent passivism; Jesus, meek and gentle like a lamb, detached from the world in his poverty, preaching a baptism of conversion and rebirth, Jesus asserts himself to be the truth, to love our enemies, focused on God's kingdom, communion with the Father, and eternal life. Jesus re-educates Judas in the meaning of the expected Messiah: to reconcile man with God. Jesus did not fit the description of a political liberator or national unifier.

Jesus was not a militant warrior seeking political liberation of Israel. We can consider the second century BC Maccabean revolt led by the powerful figure Maccabaeus who combated against Seleucid armies, the remnants of the Greek Empire (2 Macc 8). A messianic figure—a military leader—was expected: to revolt against the Roman armies. Jesus did not fit this earthly picture, the militant expectations and political aspirations. Jesus's kingdom is not made of combating soldiers and warring armies. The God of truth and love does not send his Son to provoke hatred, violence, and bloodshed. The message of Jesus was not intended for armies seeking earthly glory in the killing fields by spreading the divine message by the sword. When Peter took his sword and struck the ear of the high priest's servant, Malchus, we are told, "Jesus said to Peter, 'Put your sword back into its sheath. Am I not to drink the cup that the Father has given me?'" (John 18:11). Jesus is king of an everlasting kingdom that transcends this world and also includes building God's kingdom here on earth with Christ as its cornerstone. That Judas did not understand Jesus's teachings does not come as a surprise when the other apostles also grappled with the teachings of Jesus. But lack of understanding should not lead to betrayal.

We notice that the agony in the garden represents three perspectives of human nature: (i) where the apostle's temptation deals with the world and material possession, the sin of greed takes over and betrayal results; (ii) the three apostles, overcome with fatigue, unable to keep watch with Jesus, succumb to the fragility of the flesh and fall asleep; and (iii) Jesus in his agony expressed grief and sorrow, but faithfully fulfills the Father's will: "yet, not my will but yours be done." (Luke 22:42).[4] Three possibilities emerge in how our response is shaped carrying out the Father's will: by our sinful inclinations, by our human condition, or by total trust in God.

5. Father's Will

In Jesus, we do not have the opposition of two conflicting wills, one human and one divine; Jesus's will is completely in conformity to his Father's will. Nevertheless, Jesus experiences suffering as he anticipates torture and death, enough to cause him to sweat blood: "and his sweat became like great drops of blood falling down on the ground" (Luke 22:44). Jesus conformed his will to the Father's plan for our salvation, but the reality of human sin in all its forms also reflected his agony: humanity suffering in the obstinacy of sin mortifies Jesus. He suffered in the garden because he loves us.

Jesus sweats blood; he is fearful. He knows his mission: to save man. Salvation depends on him. His sacrifice; the cross awaits him. He is the Passover Lamb to be offered. Jesus is the Word of God. The sweating of blood marks the first drops that will continue to spill until his death on the cross. In the garden, Jesus finds himself with his apostles who provide no comfort. In the presence of Peter, James, and John, Jesus remains alone. The Son of God in this moment of agony cannot count on the comfort or relief of his closest disciples.

Jesus's knowledge creates a state of anguish that profoundly torments him to the very core of his being. The nature of Jesus, absolute truth and goodness, are contrasted to a sinful humanity that needs a Savior, though many will reject him. Even those who accept him will straddle between apathy and cowardice. And some will show courage and faith to the point of martyrdom. Apostolic and missionary zeal while characterizing Christianity will reflect the radical few who follow Jesus. The members of the church, the most faithful to follow Jesus to the point of offering up their lives for the truth, will be the ones to build Christ's church, shepherded by Peter and his confession of faith (Matt 16:16–18; John 21:15–17). Jesus knows the rejection that awaits him from "his own," the Jews, and from his followers, immediate and future. The lack of faith to transform minds and hearts, the

---

4. Jesus's human will conforms to his divine will as there is no opposition between the human and the divine natures in Jesus; he is one divine person. See, *Catechism*, #475.

lack of courage that impedes conversion, the lack of truth leading to errors in doctrine and morals, sad realities since the apostolic era. Jesus knows; he agonizes. The greatest suffering for Jesus is human sin. Jesus suffers at the failure to recognize his mission of salvation.

The events of Gethsemane deal with human nature. Jesus, truly human, suffers as humans do; his human nature is fully present in each stage of his suffering.[5] Jesus has no sins of his own, but he does know the human condition offending God, breaking God's laws, violating the law of human nature. Had Jesus not suffered, he could not have shown his love for us. At Gethsemane Jesus offered himself according to the Father's will, for all of humanity so that all might be saved; nobody was excluded in the Father's plan of salvation: "For God so loved the world that he gave his only Son, so that everyone who believes in him may not perish but may have eternal life" (John 3:16). And yet, many reject God's Son, and his salvific message. We can never underestimate or diminish the humanity of Jesus, and with that, his suffering intensely present in the garden of Gethsemane, prophesied by Isaiah centuries earlier (Isa 53:3–5). The cup Jesus is called to drink agonizes him, but he conforms himself to the will of his Father: "yet not what I want but what you want" (Matt 26:39).

Gethsemane anticipates man's reconciliation with God through the Son of God, Jesus Christ. The garden "undoes" what the first man had done in the garden of Eden, pursuing his own will, satisfying his instincts: ". . . and he ate" (Gen 3:6). The two gardens teach us about disobedience and obedience, Eden and Gethsemane, respectively: in Eden, man falls in disobedience; in Gethsemane man triumphs in obedience.

---

5. Saint Thomas Aquinas asks the question, "Was it fitting for Christ to die on the cross?" and provides seven reasons that it was fitting for Jesus to die on the cross: 1.) As an example of virtue of courage, not fearing death; 2.) sin entered by the fruit of a tree, Jesus atoned by being nailed to a tree; 3.) that nature might be purified by the blood of Jesus; 4.) by dying on the cross, Jesus prepares us for our ascent to heaven; 5.) with his arms outstretched, Jesus reaches out to the entire world; 6.) on the cross, Jesus teaches the breadth, height, length, and depth of virtue; 7.) the ark/rod in salvation history are like steps to the cross. Aquinas, *ST*, Pt. 3, q. 46, art. 4, rep.

II—Fruit of this Mystery: Virtue of Contrition; Conformity to the Will of God

Practical Matters—

We know by human experience we are moved by the smallest and simplest gestures of kindness and love shown towards us: a bouquet of red roses, a box of select chocolates, an Italian red wine, homemade lasagna for dinner. We feel gratitude when someone goes out of their way for us. We are moved when goodness is shown. The reassurance we need that we are appreciated and loved is expressed in concrete acts. Jesus takes this act of love as far as offering his life on the cross for us.

The first sorrowful mystery itself teaches us why the fruit of this mystery expresses conformity to the will of God. The mystery of Jesus's agony, asking, "let this cup pass," and then adding, "yet, not what I want but you want," conveys the interior tension of the human desire to collaborate with God's divine will and the agony of what lies ahead. Perhaps illness, persecution, or death, possibly sharing in another person's suffering, the aches experienced with the demands of purity, and even fidelity implies long-term marital monogamy. Fundamentally, God's will for his church, and thereby, for each of us is "sanctification" (1 Thess 4:3). Christ's journey shows us the path to holiness, so as to fulfil the Father's will. Gethsemane expresses the depth and breadth of holiness whereby it seeks the very being of the person.

This first sorrowful mystery is associated with the virtue of being "contrite." We know from the noun "contrition" how the human soul ought to be when receiving the sacrament of confession: "contrite." Contriteness of heart represents the condition for a valid confession and is reflected in the Act of Contrition:

> O my God, I am heartily sorry for having offended you, and I detest all my sins because of your just punishments, but most of all because they offend you, my God, who are all-good and deserving of all my love. I firmly resolve, with the help of your grace, to sin no more and to avoid the near occasion of sin.

Contriteness is expressed in the first four words where the penitent identifies their sorrow: "I am heartily sorry . . ." The prayer addressed to God continues to express this state of sorrow. The expression of a contrite heart is not only the person's disposition of the heart, manifested kneeling before the priest confessing their sins, but also the detachment from sin: "to sin no more and to avoid the near occasion of sin . . ." The radical holiness

Jesus calls us to live is reflected in Catholic morality and its source, not only in the Bible but also the natural law participation in the eternal law of God. Detachment from sin remains the disposition of the contrite heart, avoiding occasions that lead to sin, "to sin no more . . ."

If we think of our personal struggles, whether obvious weaknesses, or our sins that surprise us, contrition recognizes and acknowledges our offense against God and others. The repetition of the same sin becomes a character defect or "vice": pride, greed, envy, anger, hate, lust, sloth . . . making it difficult to overcome. A contrite heart is one where we regret our sins, desirous to be one with the will of God. Seeking a life of holiness does not permit falling into any sin, whether grave or venial. A contrite heart leads to sorrow and regret, a holy desire that tells us we must combat our weaknesses. Falling into serious sin leads to betraying the one who loves us, his will for us, his plan for us, to be in communion with God the Father in his kingdom for eternity. When we submit to our will rather than God's, reflecting the temptation and path of self-interest, we re-enact the "pride" experienced in the garden of Eden. Contrition teaches us to return to God, God's path, the road of holiness, the purity of the garden of Gethsemane, which is the "will of God" for us, "that you abstain from immorality" (1 Thess 4:3).

One might wonder, then, what is the opposite of contrition? When does the heart lack "contriteness"? Can a person confess their sins, whether to a priest or to God and still lack contrition? Confessing sins to a priest itself requires both courage and humility and marks the beginning of the purification process. When the same priest, the regular confessor, absolves the penitent, this creates a relationship of accountability which is especially helpful to grow in sanctity. Confessing directly to God, one can easily fall into an attitude of "God knows me, and God forgives me for my sins," and therefore makes little effort to make changes reflecting true contrition. And while this is true at the supernatural level, where God forgives us when we confess directly to him, at a natural level the person may make less of an effort to overcome sin by falling into a spiritual sloth, lacking the personal contact with a priest. The willingness to seek forgiveness begins with the act of courage and humility as the penitent seeks the mercy of God and reconciliation with his church offered by the priest who acts in *persona Christi,* the "person of Christ."

Grave sins, oftentimes of a sexual nature but not limited to sins driven by lust, as many can fall into grave sins of unchecked fixated thoughts caused by pride, hatred, anger, envy, greed, sloth, besides lust. Sins fermenting in the heart and mind suggest gravity because these sins poison the person's mind and heart, and the relationship with others and God. If these sins are unchecked and without frequent confession, they become vices turning into personality traits like a spiritual hardening of the arteries. A contrite heart will seek continuous purification through frequent confession and acts that battle against these sins. The lack of contrition by owning up to sin, failing to confess sins, and taking steps to overcome sins with the grace of God, means the individual fails to recognize the offensive nature of the sins they commit.[6] The wounded condition of humans, as Saint Thomas puts it, has clear repercussions on the individual's capacity to be contrite. A spouse who is accustomed to lying will not see the gravity of lying. So, what is being done to stop lying after confession? A person driven by repeated lustful acts fails to recognize the gravity of these acts, unchecked by individual confession. What steps are being taken to deal with the lust-driven acts? Contrition is both seeking forgiveness and steps taken to make changes.

Jesus treats sexual sins seriously not only because they violate the laws of man, but, sexual sins violate human nature and God's eternal order. Jesus preaches conversion, as in the case of the adulteress, Mary Magdalene: "Neither do I condemn you. Go your way, and from now on do not sin again" (John 8:11). Even though Jesus repeatedly shows compassion in his ministry teaching, healing, and exorcising, with matters pertaining to human sexuality Jesus appeals to divine order finding its source in the eternal law of God. When Jesus is questioned on divorce by the Pharisees who remind him of the certificate of divorce permitted by Moses, Jesus goes back to the beginning, to God's order: "Have you not read that the one who made them at the beginning 'made them male and female,' and said, 'For this reason a man shall leave his father and mother and be joined to his wife, and the two shall become one flesh?'" (Gen 1:27; 2:24; Matt 19:3–9). But the disciples respond, "If such is the case of a man and his wife, it is not expedient to marry" (Matt 19:10). Jesus does not water down the divine teaching; instead, he connects the Pharisees and his disciples to the reality of God's creation. Jesus also looks ahead, and his teaching is directed to its ultimate end: chastity is exercised for the kingdom of heaven (Matt 19:10). The church teaches us, as Christ taught, to strive for holiness. Holiness is God's way, not man's way. Bible-based moral errors express personal interpretations and nothing more. On issues of sexual morality the Scriptures remain clear: we benefit from tradition, the church magisterium, for moral coherency, and from natural law that participates in the eternal law of God. The emergence of neopagan sexual morality among Christian communities betrays the teachings of Christ.[7] In more traditional cultures, both Christian

---

6. Aquinas, *ST*, Pt. 1a-2ae, q. 85, art. 3.

7. See the 1968 prophetic encyclical of Saint Paul VI, *Humanae Vitae;* and by Saint John Paul II, based on his Wednesday audiences delivered in Rome from 1979-1984, writings published as the *Theology of the Body*. Both pontiffs appeal to the Bible and

and non-Christian, the natural sense of marriage and the traditional family prevails. Unfortunately, and somewhat paradoxically, some Christian denominations are creating a disservice in this regard by justifying a morality that violates both natural law and the Scriptures.

In spite of the biblical sexual ethics that has its source in the natural law that participates in the eternal law of God, a sexual ethics that Jesus teaches based on Genesis, we need to ask whether a contrite heart is possible under our present circumstances: family, education, mainstream and social media, where the path to holiness is dismissed and communion with God ignored. Without a contrite heart how can the individual follow the will of God or claim to? What is the catechesis offered by the Catholic Church to bring clarity in the midst of confusion? We need saints more than we need postmodern moral theologians. Oftentimes, we hear the need for "change" because times have changed, and so, rather than a conversion of heart, Christ's teachings are changed and replaced with man's teachings. Underlying a contrite heart is the hard reality of faith.

Sin that is serious and repetitive sin is referred to as "obstinacy." This may not reflect the moral problem of a vice or addiction that the person is battling against, but rather, a person who refuses the path of holiness and has replaced truth with personal opinion. Is this not what Satan did in the garden of Eden? Replace God's truth with the serpent's cunning claims as if true? God created humans with both intelligence and freedom and their natural capacity to know right from wrong. And so, the person remains capable of seeking to know what is true if the truth is sought and not simply justify their own self-focused desires. Obstinacy is to be found in refusal—a hardened heart. Rather than conversion, obstinacy rationalizes and justifies sin, so the individual no longer appears to sin.[8] Obstinacy reveals a refusal to combat sins because they are no longer regarded as sin, falsely reasoned as acceptable and permissible, but not sinful. We can identify a slippery slope. The church as a prophetic institution points to what lies ahead, even teaching us that certain sins lead to the "wrath of God." The church has a prophetic mission in its teachings: namely, to uphold Christ's moral teachings as found in the Scriptures and the eternal law of God.

Without a contrite heart, how does one recognize their need for a Savior and salvation? Only those who acknowledge their sins and sinfulness understand we need Jesus to reconcile us with God. The revealed promise that God will send us a Savior fulfilled in his Son Jesus Christ is because we are sinners and sinners know they need the Savior; we know we are called

---

natural law to explain Christian sexual ethics.

8. Aquinas, *ST*, Pt. 1a-2ae, q. 85, art. 3

to conversion, not to celebrate the triumph and parading of sin. The act that saves us, Jesus accomplished by giving up his life for us. But, Jesus also waits for our response; to choose him, Jesus, Son of the ever-living God, the way, the truth, and the life—the path to holiness and eternal life.

If people are confused today, especially about moral truths, it reflects the competing voices seeking to draw adherents, members, and followers. Not because these dominant voices in our world claim to teach or offer what is true, but because they package their message to appeal to the masses. The politically-motivated influences in mainstream media are geared to elect leaders with the agendas to satisfy a materialist, consumerist, and hedonist vision of the person. Fundamentally, a vision and utopia that is godless.

The powerful voices applauded and worshiped as gods and goddesses in the movie and music industries attract viewers and manipulate consumers. These industries do not produce values based on truth but bowing to power, wealth, and lust: the reward is status, gold, and sex, not God. The golden calf has become the object of praise, and the youth are led to believe this is all good: rebellion, blasphemy, and perversion. Satan continues to actively seek to subvert the goodness of God and the truth taught to us by Jesus Christ.

But relying on the human intelligence and will with which God created us, we know we also encounter individuals who discern, reflect, appeal to common sense and their conscience, who seek God's Word in the Scriptures, and what has been handed down and preserved in the church since the apostolic era. And those who have kept and preserved God's Word through prayer and the sacraments shape their lives and daily choices, seeking the will of God, knowing that contrition for one's sins is the path to sanctification.

Second Sorrowful Mystery—Scourging at the Pillar

I—*Then Pilate took Jesus and scourged him.* (John 19:1)
Our Father . . . Hail Mary . . . Glory Be . . .

1. Judas Betrays Jesus

Judas arrived with a mob holding clubs and swords sent by the chief priests, scribes, and elders while Jesus was speaking to his disciples (Matt 26:49; Mark 14:44). Kissed by Judas, the sign used to identify Jesus, signals the act of betrayal.

The nighttime occurrence of Jesus's arrest shrouds the act in mystery; only the apostles knew where Jesus withdrew to pray. Soldiers with clubs and swords arrived in the dark to seize a man praying. Not surprisingly, Jesus, consistent with his language of peace, did not show or express any kind of resistance. When Peter used his sword to cut the right ear off of the high priest's slave, Malchus, Jesus immediately reacted: "No more of this!" (Luke 22:51). Jesus healed the severed ear and demonstrated in his words and actions that the followers of Christ were to be men of peace, not men of revenge, bloodshed, and death (John 18:10–11). Jesus set the example from the moment of being taken prisoner that the Christian message was built on truth, love, forgiveness, and mercy. Jesus, the only light in the darkness, was paradoxically taken prisoner from a silent location of prayer in the dark of night. Jesus rhetorically states, "Have you come out as against a robber, with swords and clubs to capture me?" (Matt 26:55; Mark 14:48). Jesus points out, "But this is your hour, and the power of darkness" (Luke 22:53).

Betraying Jesus by a "kiss," Jesus questions the apostle: "Judas, would you betray the Son of Man with a kiss?" (Luke 22:48). The kiss as a sign of brotherhood, love, and peace, a practice widespread across Mediterranean and Semitic cultures to this very day between men expressing something akin to a family bond. What is employed as a sign of truth in these male relations, Judas perverts the meaning of the kiss using the gesture of affection to betray Jesus. What motivated Judas's act of betrayal? Greed? Disillusionment and weakness for money. A preoccupation with counting coins. "Is Jesus worth it?" "Is he worth expensive perfume?" (John 12:5). Not for Judas. In Judas's mind, Jesus did not prove to be the temporally powerful Messiah he had anticipated. Pride? Judas was expecting, like other followers of Jesus, a kingdom of worldly glory, power, and wealth (Matt 20:20–22). Jesus gradually unveils his identity and his kingdom: "My kingdom is not of this world" (John 18:36).

Judas was one of the apostles stuck in a worldly vision of a "king" and "kingdom" to do more with power and glory than peace and self-giving love. If Jesus fulfilled the prophesies of the Davidic Messiah, then he should resemble, if not exceed, the royal power and temporal authority demonstrated by King David. While Judas was not alone in grappling with the kingdom of Jesus, Judas's understanding was restricted to a literal reading of Scriptures, failing to grasp the spiritual language intended by Jesus; that is, the eschatological understanding of Jesus's Kingdom: Jesus made clear at his trial, "My kingdom is not of this world."[1] A correct understanding of the teachings of Jesus has profound implications in recognizing him as the only-begotten Son of God. The fulfillment of Jesus's teachings at the resurrection affirms or corrects the apostles' understanding of Jesus's teachings. And this is why at Pentecost, the third glorious mystery, the Holy Spirit descends upon the church, leading the community of believers to the "complete" truth: "When the Spirit of truth comes, he will guide you into all the truth" (John 16:13).

Present-day faithful believers often comment, "Judas had no choice in the matter; he had to betray Jesus in order for the crucifixion to be carried out, necessary for the redemption of man." Even Jesus acknowledges in the context of the betrayal, "But how then would the scriptures be fulfilled, which say it must happen in this way?" (Matt 26:54; Mark 14:49). In John's Gospel, Jesus raises the question, "Am I not to drink the cup that the Father has given me?" (John 18:11). Nevertheless, Judas did have a choice. He was not forced by God to betray Jesus. Had Judas been forced to act, he could not exercise freedom, and he could not have been culpable of his crime. Culpability or guilt requires freedom for an act to be evaluated as moral or immoral. God knew Judas's temperament, his weaknesses, and

---

1. The levels of reading Scripture: 1.) literal; 2.) symbolic; 3.) moral; 4.) mystical. See, *Catechism*, #115-#117; Aquinas, *ST*, Pt. 1, q. 1, art. 10, rep. 1; and Hahn and Mitch, *Catholic Study Bible*, x–xi.

how he would treat Jesus in the midst of temptation. After all, Judas did not stand alone in failing to makes sense of Jesus's kingdom, but only Judas reported to the chief priests and handed Jesus over to them and their soldiers. Had Judas chosen differently, God would have foreknowledge. God knew the heart and disposition of Judas, the betrayal of Jesus, and the unleashing of events that followed.

The people of Israel with whom God had made his covenant, Mary and Joseph, deeply religious and descendants from the house of David, Mary spiritually prepared by God by her immaculate conception to bring his Son undefiled by human flesh into the world, the widespread philosophical influences of Greek culture, the Roman Empire's network of roads and centralized political system: God knew the course of events. In darkness, Judas surrenders himself to darkness; he fits perfectly into God's plan for our salvation.

2. Caiphas's House

Jesus was brought across the Kidron Valley to the house of the chief priest, Caiphas (Matt 26:57). The site today is marked by the Church of Gallicantu.[2] Within the vicinity of the church, we find the stone steps where Jesus walked leading to the sight of the trial. Only John's Gospel relates the account that they took Jesus prisoner and proceeded first to Annas's house, the father-in-law of Caiphas, and for some, still the legitimate high priest (John 18:13). With these events taking place in the evening after Gethsemane, we must conclude, it must have been late at night before they walked to Caiphas's palace from Annas's residence.

Jesus was scorned during the night while he was waiting for Caiphas; the chief priests, the elders, and the scribes anticipated his trial, "Now the men who were holding Jesus mocked him and beat him; they also blindfolded him and kept asking him, 'Prophesy! Who is it that struck you?'" (Luke 22:63). We are then informed in Luke's Gospel, "When day came . . ." (Luke 22:66).

Situated in the lower part of the Church of Gallicantu, we find the pit calling to memory where Jesus was kept prisoner, now a place visited for prayerful reflection and meditation. Mocked throughout the night, and held captive until the morning of his trial, the insults and physical mistreatment began during the same night. All Gospel accounts indicate Jesus was sought out by a mob with clubs and swords, men of the chief priests, meaning that

---

2. Literally church of the "cock-crow." The church is administered by the Resurrectionist Fathers.

even before his trial, Jesus was treated as though guilty and suffered at the hands of soldiers treating Jesus as a criminal. The crime Jesus was accused of, and being tried for at Caiaphas's residence, was blasphemy. Jesus does not deny the charges; instead, the words of Jesus confirm the accusations when he is finally sentenced to death by the religious court.

3. Peter's Threefold Denial

The Gospels inform us that the evening when Jesus was imprisoned by Caiaphas's soldiers, Peter found his way to the high-priest's courtyard hoping to observe the trial and wait for Jesus. With the high priest's soldiers present, Peter stood at a distance, not knowing how the events would unfold. Warming his hands at the fire, a woman recognized Peter; but he denied any association with Jesus. Peter is identified in three separate instances as having been seen with the "Galilean," but Peter, a Galilean himself, three times denied any connection with him, as Jesus prophesied.

As Jesus is tried, Peter's denial or failure to acknowledge any connection with Jesus could not change the course of events that followed. Peter acted entirely out of cowardice and self-interest. While certainly not as compromising as the betrayal of Judas, still, Peter belonged to Jesus's inner core, one of the closest of the apostles, and the very apostle to whom Jesus had entrusted his church. What does this act of cowardice reveal? Jesus already knew Peter's weakness as Jesus also knew Judas's?

Although a man of authority and faith, in his three-fold denial of Jesus, Peter showed a lack of strength. Nevertheless, Jesus offers Peter the possibility to reaffirm his love for Jesus with the threefold question at the resurrection, asking Peter, "Do you love me?" (John 21:15–16). Peter's repeated three-fold affirmation of his love to the point where he feels offended reveals that Jesus continued to entrust Peter to lead his flock, the flock whom Jesus is asking Peter to feed. Not only will Peter have a place of primacy and universal authority over the church, Peter will sacrifice his life for Christ when executed in Rome.

But human frailty remains. Jesus suffers not only physically at the hands of the mobs who mistreat him, but Jesus also suffers, aware of the weakness of the human condition that leads to sin, betrayal, and denial. Jesus builds his church on this reality of this human fragility. Jesus chose twelve apostles who followed him but who also manifested human weakness. Peter being questioned parallels that of Jesus. One can speak of "Peter's trial" where Peter is "accused" of being a companion of Jesus. Peter saves his life through denying any connection with Jesus. Peter manifests the human condition that applies to each of us, and Jesus knows this. Peter stood outside while Jesus was being questioned, and he did not have the courage to identify himself as a disciple of Jesus, afraid of the consequences. But we know Peter's fear is transformed into courage because Peter eventually not only defends the faith, he assumes the role of the first Pope entrusted to him by Christ, and he dies a martyr's death in Rome.

Jesus's trial reveals why God sent his Son into the world; we cannot enter the kingdom of heaven on our own efforts; we cannot even be in communion with God on our own strength because our human condition weakens us—even enslaves us. We need Jesus to free us, to lead us, and to strengthen us. Only Jesus can save us. He came to raise our human condition by grace through his body and blood so we may become children of God, live as children of light, and inherit eternal life.[3]

4. Divinity and Kingship

At Caiaphas's house, the Sanhedrin accused Jesus of blasphemy and intended to bring him to Pilate for execution (Matt 26:64–66; Mark 14:60–64). The questions Pilate asked Jesus, however, did not relate to blasphemy, but to Jesus's kingship: "Are you the King of the Jews?" (Matt 27:12; Mark 15:2; Luke 23:3). Pilate's questioning dealt with the political issue of kingship, not the religious matter of Jesus's divinity, the latter being a concern for the religious court. In fact, Jesus is tried for two distinct offenses, claiming divinity, the other, claiming kingship.

Jesus's trial was seen as a religious matter—condemned for blasphemy by the high priests and their court. According to the Mosaic Law, Jesus's crime, a religious offense, was to be punished by execution (Lev 24:15–16). But, as a religious matter, carrying out a religious execution was not the responsibility of Pilate. The Roman prefect dealt with matters of a political nature such as uprisings and revolts; the prefect's job was to crush whatever created instability in the empire. The trial, therefore, moved down the stone road from Caiaphas's residence to the Praetorium where Pilate arrived for the Jewish Passover to keep any uprisings in check, questioning Jesus on his kingship: "So you are a king?" (John 18:33).[4] When the charges shifted from "blasphemy," a religious matter dealt in the Jewish court, to

---

3. See *Catechism*, #421; Rom 5:20–21.

4. The capital of the Roman province of Judea was the coastal town of Caesarea Maritima. The Praetorium refers to the fortress built by Herod the Great to protect the Second Temple. The location places Jesus at the center between the Praetorium and the Temple.

"kingship," to a political charge, handled in the Roman court, Pilate questions Jesus whether he was the king of the Jews.

Pilate, we know from the Scriptures, expresses apprehension to condemn Jesus because he finds no guilt in him (Luke 23:4). Pilate understood the accusations were motivated out of jealousy and hatred that turned Jesus over to Pilate: "For he realized that it was out of jealousy that the chief priests had handed him over" (Mark 15:10). Even Pilate's wife, though a Roman pagan, sensed that something was not right and tells her husband, "Have nothing to do with that innocent man, for today I have suffered a great deal because of a dream about him" (Matt 27:19).

Ultimately, the sins of humanity—our sins—led to the condemnation of Jesus. The recurring sins at the root of evil are evident: lust, pride, greed. Pilate is subject to Roman law which means he must acknowledge when evidence is lacking to condemn and execute an accused—namely, assure a just trial. What could Pilate do? A logical Roman, having grown up in a stoic environment that taught to restrain emotions and prize virtue, Pilate could not break Roman law, nor did he want to provoke a charged rebellious crowd and create an uprising.

The recorded events as presented in the Gospels of Matthew, Mark, and Luke highlight the innocence of Jesus, shuffled between two courts, failing to find evidence to condemn him. Nevertheless, the determined religious court comprised of chief priests, scribes, and elders, sought a pretext to have Jesus executed. The religious evidence for the charge of blasphemy was not lacking; Jesus explicitly acknowledges his divine power and his divine nature, precisely the reason why the religious counsel wants him executed. So, if the chief priests adhered to their religious laws which included execution for blasphemy, why should Pilate make the claim these religious leaders were motivated out of envy rather than religious observance? Because Jesus attracted many followers; they understood he was the Christ, the anointed one, that he was the Son of God, and that Jesus led his followers to the eternal kingdom. The religious authorities who rejected Jesus's claim while they knew the Scriptures failed to recognize in Jesus the fulfillment of the promised Messiah. The apostles make Jesus's messianic and divine identity their mission after the resurrection when the spirit of truth brings clarity: to show by the Scriptures how Jesus brings to completion the biblical promise of a Savior and that the religious authorities who wanted Jesus executed, in fact, failed to understand the Scriptures: that Jesus, the promised Messiah, is the Son of God.

Pilate's job is not to find evidence against Jesus on religious grounds, or to prove the chief priests and the religious counsel that their charges of blasphemy are well-founded. Pilate's concern remains political, and this includes preventing rebellions. The trial's move to accuse Jesus of asserting his kingship certainly concerns Pilate as Roman prefect. But even this accusation of being "king" represents a weak argument to have Jesus executed; Jesus admits his kingdom is not of a political nature—his kingdom "is not from this world" (John 18:36). An understanding of kingship that even his disciples did not fully grasp. John's Gospel makes it clear that the Jews in the Roman Province of Judea could not put a man to death by their religious law (John 18:31), but they could justify Jesus's execution under Roman law.

In Luke's Gospel we have three trials: because Jesus is a Galilean, Pilate sends Jesus to Herod, the ruler over Galilee. Herod's trial repeats the earlier trials: the chief priests and scribes relentlessly push their accusations seeking Jesus's condemnation. Herod ridicules Jesus, putting a rich cloak on him, mocking Jesus's kingship (Luke 23:8–12). Jesus remains throughout, silent as a lamb.

5. Pilate's Dilemma

Pilate needs to appease the crowds who were getting louder. Pilate found a solution: to give the people the option of choosing between releasing Jesus reminding them he was their king, or to release the condemned criminal, Barabbas (Matt 27:20–26; Mark 15:11; Luke 23:18–19; John 18:39–40). Was there a way out of executing an innocent man and avoiding a rebellion? The religious authorities clearly wanted Jesus executed for blasphemy. To Pilate's surprise, the people preferred to have a criminal released and an innocent man executed. The mindless mob repeatedly shouted, "Crucify him!" Although Jesus was not found guilty of any crime, other than speaking the truth. And so Pilate, "washing his hands," responds, "I am innocent of this man's blood" (Matt 27:24). The innocence of Jesus is conveyed more forcefully in Luke's Gospel: "Why, what evil has he done? I have found in him no ground for the sentence of death" (Luke 23:22). Pilate wishes to set Jesus free, but the mob, in an excited frenzy, insist a third time: "Crucify him! Crucify him!" Pilate speaks like a logical Roman governor who is prepared to apply the law to punish a criminal, but he must be a criminal to suffer the force of the Roman law. But Pilate, observing the hateful mob, instigated by the Jewish religious authorities, insists, "I have found no case against him that deserves death, so I shall have him flogged and then let him go."

In response to Pilate, voices grew louder with political threats insisting on the crucifixion of Jesus. In John's Gospel Pilate asks, "Are you the king of the Jews?" And Jesus replies, "My kingdom is not of this world." John's Gospel focuses on "truth" and Jesus came to bear witness to the truth (John 18:37). In response, Pilate echoes Roman stoicism: "What is truth?" We need to consider whether truth lies on the side of force, power, and coercion. Or whether truth is on the side of the most passionate, vocal, and militant. Pilate's philosophical question proved crucial, knowing he stood before a mob that had no interest in truth but demonstrated to be passionate about crushing the person who claimed to be a witness of truth. Indeed, central to the teachings of Jesus: "I am the way, the truth, and the life" (John 14:6).

Pilate submits to the mob by satisfying their irrational demands: the murderer and insurrectionist Barabbas is released, and Jesus—teacher, healer, and exorcist, Messiah, King, and Son of God—was handed over "as they wished" (Luke 23:25).

6. Flagellation

From the Church of the Condemnation where we have Pilate's words, "Here is the man," *Ecce Homo* (John 19:5), and from below the arch on the Via Dolorosa in Jerusalem that marks the first station of the cross, the Church of the Condemnation, pilgrims proceed to the Church of Flagellation. Thus, the agony in the garden, first sorrowful mystery, to the flagellation, second sorrowful mystery, highlight the physical and spiritual suffering of Jesus—man guilty, condemning man innocent—but the innocence of Jesus will save man from his guilt.

We know that the mockery and lashing had already begun the night Jesus was imprisoned on the grounds of Caiaphas's palace, kept in a pit, as the excavations show at the Church of the Gallicantu. Jesus now is scourged as part of his passion remembered in this second sorrowful mystery, gradually leading up to his crucifixion; scourging occurs between the first and third sorrowful mysteries, the condemnation and crowning of thorns of Jesus. Since the Roman authorities had been entrusted with the civil trial of Jesus, the punishment that followed Jesus's condemnation was immediately implemented; the religious authorities and the mobs they controlled delivered Jesus to the Roman soldiers for the anticipated crucifixion (Matt 27:20, 26).

Scourging means to whip or lash with the intent of producing severe pain, another way of speaking of torture. The second sorrowful mystery can be called the "torture of Jesus." Flogging involved a short whip that had several either single or braided leather pieces of various lengths. Small iron balls or sharp pieces of sheep bones were tied. Jesus was stripped of his clothing with his hands tied to an upright post. The flogging served to weaken Jesus, almost to the point of death. The iron balls, leather thongs, and sheep bones would cut into his skin as the soldiers repeatedly whipped his back, cutting into the skin of Jesus. The whipping continued so it would cut deep into the Jesus's tissues. With the ongoing whipping, tearing into the skeletal muscles led to Jesus's profuse bleeding. Pain and blood loss, the meaning of "passion," precisely what Jesus had undergone, finally halting in circulatory shock. Given the amount of blood Jesus lost throughout his body, he could not have survived long on the cross.

Who caused this? Judas? The Jewish religious authorities? The Roman soldiers? The cause is all of us. Certainly, this second sorrowful mystery shows how far people can go to condemning someone innocent out of pride, envy, hatred. But, ultimately the cause of Jesus's death is sin, our sin. And for this reason, Jesus suffered not only physical torture but the spiritual suffering knowing that the very people God created and loved justified punishing and executing an innocent man. Only Jesus, the Son of God, restores us to communion with God. For this reason, Jesus was sent into the world: to save us from our sins, to reconcile us with God, so we may have eternal life (John 3:16).

Thus, we move physically from the garden of Gethsemane to the Church of Gallicantu situated over Caiphas's palace (John 18:28); and from the Church of Gallicantu to the Church of the Condemnation, associated with Pilate or the Praetorium. With the condemnation, Jesus is handed over to the Roman soldiers to be crucified (John 19:16).

II—Fruit of this Mystery: Virtue of Purity; Mortification

Practical Matters—

Peter was frightened by the presence of the mob of soldiers who arrested Jesus. Being interrogated, Peter, too, might have the same fate—he could be next. Shocked by the arrest of an innocent man, his own teacher and Lord, darkness seemed to prevail. We know mobs exert power; when emotions escalate the force of the masses defy reason. Peter knew Jesus was innocent; acknowledging his ties with Jesus was the "right thing to do." Being frightened speaks to us of human nature: how we are intimidated or coerced into doing something we are against out of fear. Like Peter, this reflects our lack of courage to follow what we know to be true. Peter witnessed how a collective mob acts and reacts, not thinking, but stirred up by others, shouting, "crucify him." Where would we be in this scene? Like the suspicious woman? Frightened like Peter? Like a yelling mob?

Does this not in many respects reflect our society that refuses to think and simply repeats what they read in news feeds, social networks, mainstream media, with the TV screen in the sitting room or games room where one stops thinking and relies on instant electronic sources for what is true and false, how to feel, what to believe and not believe. The relaxing ritual of putting our brains on "pause" so we do not have to work at making connections, checking out sources, appealing to common sense, to determine whether something is true or false. Thinking requires effort, but in an age of immediate digital information, "thinking" is done for us. We become like the mobs stirred up by what we read, repeating what we hear; our emotions keep us from reflecting because feelings drive our emotive reactions. We should not be surprised that Peter reacted as he did aware of the consequences if he were identified as an associate of Jesus. Whether it's the apostolic era or the twenty-first century, whether imposed by coercive government policies or fueled by militant mobs, danger sets in when people stop thinking. We depend on truth whereby God illuminates our minds and hearts. And the followers of Christ are taught to be a lampstand of truth (Matt 5:15–16).

We cannot think when we are governed by emotions. Whether mobs shout or news shocks, we are made to feel angry, revolted, and so like a mob we demand justice—"crucify him" to a man who is perfectly innocent. We must distinguish "truth" from "falsehood." God created humans in his divine image and likeness: with intelligence and freedom to know what is true and pursue what is good (Gen 1:27).

Our emotions can mislead us and direct us to envy, anger, hate and in our present social context we can certainly add lust to the list; we fail to think with clarity. How do we make proper judgments and decisions? We need God's grace, his Word, to enlighten our minds; but our minds must also be purified along with our hearts. This is why Jesus tells us in the Beatitudes, "Blessed are the pure in heart, for they will see God" (Matt 5:8).

We cannot even imagine the infliction to which Jesus was subjected and endured with the lashing followed by a crown with thorns, the third sorrowful mystery, or the weight of the cross, the fourth sorrowful mystery, or the physical agony of being nailed to the cross, the fifth sorrowful mystery. Jesus's sheer physical pain, experienced by the tearing of his flesh that caused extensive bleeding all over his body, filled the night and day with horrific suffering and pain. The torturous lashes began at Caiaphas's palace where Jesus was abused throughout the night like a criminal to be made a spectacle of at the religious court.

How does this mystery, the virtue of purity, connect with the flagellation? How can mortification be fruitful?

Our bodies need to be cleansed from vices, especially the vice of lust, since one of the primary effects of the fall is concupiscence—disordered desires of the flesh.[5] While Jesus fully experienced human desires, they were not disordered. Being fully human, his desires were that of a man; one could compare them to the innocence and holiness of Adam before the fall, keeping in mind the fundamental difference that unlike Adam who is created by God, Jesus is "begotten, not made, one in being with the Father."[6] The fullness of Jesus's humanity meant he experienced natural desires. Jesus's love was selfless, true, focusing on the good of the other, knowing that his giving of himself for the other was the truest way to love humanity. Jesus offered himself for our sins, and because one of the greatest effects of the fall was the sin of concupiscence, Jesus, nailed to the cross, immovable, exhausted, bleeding, and thirsty, the offering of his pure flesh purifies us of our sinful flesh. Jesus experienced enormous suffering, a body that was repeatedly whipped to purify us of our impurities.

The sins of the flesh are associated with sexual sins, whether in thoughts or in actions. How often have these sins of husbands and wives caused children to suffer innocently because of parents separated due to marital infidelity? How often have sins of the flesh hurt vulnerable individuals, trusting those in positions of responsibility and authority? How have the sins of the flesh created a society demanding more and more "flesh," more sexual freedom, introducing laws protecting unnatural and unholy sexual appetites? How has lust been marketed, endorsed, and promoted in the movie, music, and pornographic industries where God's gift of human sexuality has become a tool of Satan? In sexual addiction, sexual trafficking, sexual violence, and the hypocrisy of societies that show sexual permissiveness violating the laws of God, while punishment for sexual crimes violating the incoherent laws of man.[7] Sins of the flesh have been dismissed as sins and replaced with people's rights. Sexual rights. The sins of the flesh have resulted in an unnatural contraceptive mentality extending to aborting a fully developed preborn human being; rights to same-sex "marriage" for adults, and then, imposed on school curricula indoctrinating children. And pornography, the "machinery" that

---

5. See, *Catechism*, #405; and #2351-#2359.

6. Words prayed in the Nicene Creed. See, *Catechism*, #465.

7. Abortion and gender affirming therapies are legal for minors—even without the knowledge of the parents—while conversion therapy has become illegal for adults. (It is beyond the scope of this work to go into the details concerning countries/states/provinces and legislation.)

both triggers and gratifies sexual impulses only to create extreme forms of pornography and further addiction.[8]

Products are sold with subliminal sexual language and images. Perfumes, clothing, automobiles, alcohol—sexually suggestive. We live in a world today that is the antithesis of purity. Societies have fallen victim to worshiping the golden calf, turning sexual activity into idol worship. Human sexuality, distorted, corrupted, self-interested sex, is marketed. In spite of the wreckage disordered sex causes to individuals, relationships, families, and societies, the sex industry creates demands, and increases consumption, especially in the advent of digital technology. In the midst of this moral rot, we are called to purity.

The second sorrowful mystery teaches the disciple of Christ that the only way to be purified of disordered sexual impulses is by seeking the grace Christ offers through his body and blood, the sacrament of reconciliation and communion, the means we may be equipped and strengthened, so our bodies and souls are oriented towards the worship of God. While God's grace is preached, we also believe that divine grace leads to interior conversion and personal transformation. Catholics believe in the work of grace, and we are called to live by grace. Human sexuality unites men and women in marriage open to procreation, but human sexuality is also the offering of ourselves to God exercised in chastity, and in a holy life of self-giving celibacy.[9]

Steps towards Purity

1. Choosing: following Christ means making choices daily between greater holiness, lesser holiness, and unholiness. These choices shape our relationship with God, with others, and with ourselves. Virtue-building (not virtue-signaling) should be part of the daily Christian regimen. The good that is to be pursued and the evil that is to be avoided—the very basis of the natural law finds its way into our daily choices as disciples of Christ.

2. Strengthening: We belong to a church that supports us and strengthens us on our pilgrim journey as we strive for holiness. By the power of the Holy Spirit received at baptism we enter into communion with God the Father through his Son. Those whom God sends us, Saints Michael, Gabriel, and Raphael, our guardian angel, the blessed Virgin Mary, Saint

---

8. Pope Paul VI warned of the moral breakdown of society and the exploitative effects upon women once artificial contraception becomes morally acceptable. Pornography exacerbates this moral degeneration. See *Humanae Vitae*, #22.

9. See, *Catechism*, #2348-#2350.

Joseph, God's Saints and Blesseds, and those whom God puts on our path to pray for us, offering us their intercession. We also have each other to pray as members of Christ's church.

3. Sacraments: The church offers us the sacraments of reconciliation and communion to both strengthen us in purity but also to increase the grace we need to combat sins of impurity. The Catholic Church teaches what Christ taught: "Blessed be the pure in heart, for they will see God" (Matt 5:8). The vision of God is not possible without a life that is grace-filled. Christ's teachings are life-giving and lead to eternal life but they require choices, effort, and sacrifices on our part. Jesus opened the door to paradise for us: our sins are forgiven, our relationship with God has been restored, but we must desire this for ourselves—forgiveness of sin, relationship with God, and paradise. Jesus does not impose on us something we do not want. Jesus forces nothing upon us. Freedom has always been fundamental to Catholic ethics because our reward and punishment are based on the freedom we exercise. To accept what Jesus offers us and to live by what he teaches or to reject this. Many have accepted the gift of salvation; many have rejected this gift. Following Christ is neither a cerebral nor a memory exercise; nor is being Christ's disciple about "feelings." Following Christ is reflected concretely in our day-to-day activities, our purity in heart, mind, and actions. The sacraments offer us the graces we need to be faithful, courageous, and coherent in our daily life as Christians.

4. Spiritual Reading: Prayer and grace, seeking the guidance of trustworthy individuals, living by the sacraments; perhaps we do not even have any issue with purity because impure thoughts never cross our mind. But then what about building on the present state of purity, becoming "purer"? Ridding the mind of cluttering thoughts of people, places, plans, activities, can be filled with spiritual thoughts through the daily reading of Scriptures or the lives of the saints. This cleansing process of the mind serves to purify it from the clutter taken up by mainstream media, social media, and the noise of the world. Does our mind really need all this "clutter"? No, of course not. And so, we can use the valuable space available in our heads and make proper use of the spiritual faculty of the soul by exercising its intelligence and freedom to grow in sanctity with the material we read—or even movies we watch—that serve to spiritually nourish the soul to increase our purity of mind and heart.

5. Confessor: Whether serious sins persist, or one desires to strengthen their state of purity and grow in sanctity, a regular confessor is advisable. The confessor gets to know his penitent over time and can provide the counsel

needed with the sacrament of confession to strengthen the penitent in spiritual warfare (Eph 6) which fundamentally involves the ongoing spiritual combat confronting the Christian. The grace of the sacrament of reconciliation and the counsel of the confessor serve to spiritually build the penitent who seeks to grow in purity and sanctity and engage in spiritual combat.

Third Sorrowful Mystery—Crowning with Thorns

I—And the soldiers wove a crown of thorns and put it on his head . . . (John 19:2)

Our Father . . . Hail Mary . . . Glory be . . .

1. Handed over to the Romans

The Scriptures tell us quite distinctly they stripped Jesus ". . . and put a scarlet robe on him, and after twisting some thorns into a crown, they put it on his head. They put a reed in his right hand and knelt before him and mocked him, saying, 'Hail, King of the Jews!'" (Matt 27:28–29).

The Jews had already mocked Jesus as a prophet at the palace of Caiaphas, the high priest who ordered Jesus to be arrested by his soldiers as recorded in Luke's Gospel (Luke 22:63–65). The mockery of a prophet reflects the religious nature of Jesus's crime and punishment. The charges laid against Jesus related to blasphemy; the accusations of the religious authorities were directed not against any prophetic claims but Jesus's identification with the divine. The political charge laid against Jesus enabled the Jewish religious authorities to hand him over to the Romans so as to be punished according to Roman law. At this stage, the mockery and insults striking Jesus do not reflect any religious controversy since being punished in the Roman civil court concerns civil or political matters: in the Roman court the charge against Jesus was claiming to be king, the charge pressed by the Jewish authorities and the mob inciting to have Jesus crucified.

The crown represents kingship, authority, and royalty. But a crown of thorns ridicules Jesus's identity as king. Judas and others like him were expecting a crown made of precious metal, studded with precious gems, the characteristics of an earthly king. Certainly, such a crown was fitting for the king of the universe. But paradoxically, the greatest king who lived had thorns twisted into his head. And yet we know "Jesus is King!" Jesus identifies himself as king, not an earthly king as understood by Pilate, and probably Judas and other disciples, but king of a heavenly kingdom. And so the mockery of his kingship, casting insults at Jesus, physically enforced by thorns piercing his head, served to ridicule his claims.

Although the chief priests, the scribes, and the elders studied the Scriptures, the ones who charged Jesus with blasphemy failed to see any connection between the Law of Moses, or the Prophets, and the teachings of Jesus who came to fulfil the Law and the Prophets. For the religious leaders, Jesus was neither king nor Messiah, only an offensive blasphemer, some fraud drawing thousands of followers. Nevertheless, Pilate sensed the jealousy and hatred of the high priests manifested towards Jesus.

2. Throne of His Ancestor David

If we reflect on the first joyful mystery, the annunciation, and re-examine the words of the angel Gabriel speaking to Mary, the angel informs Mary, "And now, you will conceive in your womb and bear a son, and you will name him Jesus. He will be great, and will be called the Son of the Most High, and the Lord God will give to him the throne of his ancestor David. He will reign over the house of Jacob forever, and of his kingdom there will be no end" (Luke 1:31–33). So, God gives to Mary's son, Son of the Most High, the "throne of his ancestor David." The angel's announcement to identify this child to whom Mary gives birth is placed within a supernatural framework, "Son of the Most High," namely, "Son of God," revealing the divine personhood of Mary's Son; but at the same time, the child receives Mary's flesh and is placed in a family lineage, that of the house of Judah. The kingdom of his "ancestor David" is fitting because Mary comes from the Davidic house besides Jesus's spiritual father Joseph. Moreover, and of particular significance, the house of David is associated with messianic kingship, starting with the reign of King David (2 Sam 5:1–5).

This Davidic lineage confers kingship upon Jesus but also the messianic nature of Jesus's mission as Son of the Most High. The angel could have identified any of the numerous kings within the house of Judah; the kingdom had reigned for centuries and the "father is David." Nathan's prophesy and the angel's message that fulfills the prophecy with the birth of Jesus is found in the words of Nathan addressing King David: "Your house and your kingdom shall be made sure forever before me; "your throne shall be established forever" (2 Sam 7:16).

David represents the first king to exercise royal authority faithful to God to the point where David is identified with priestly qualities (2 Sam 6:12–15). David also represents human nature that falls but turns to God with a contrite heart seeking God's forgiveness (2 Sam 12:1–15).[1] These royal, priestly, and human characteristics underscore David as a king faithful to God, a king who places the will and glory of God above any human ambitions, while acknowledging his sinfulness. David has a sense of the awesome nature of the transcendent God as conveyed powerfully in his psalms. Since David is anointed king from the start of the reign of Judah, David embodies the entire history of the people of Judah. The privileged position of the tribe of Judah can be traced to the words of Jacob addressing and blessing his fourth son Judah on his deathbed: "Judah is a lion's whelp . . . The sceptre shall not depart from Judah, / nor the ruler's staff from between his feet . . ." (Gen 49:9–10).

David was anointed during the reign of Israel's first king, Saul. Because God disapproved of Saul's conduct, the prophet Samuel anointed David, chosen by God, as king. Saul's son Ishbosheth reigned over the tribes outside of Judah in northern Israel, while David ruled over Judah and Benjamin in the south (2 Sam 2:8–11). The significance at this stage shows division in house of Israel. This tribal division of the people led by God marks the political but also spiritual language of the Old Testament. The division of tribes is not God's will; rather, establishing unity among the tribes of Israel, north and south, one people divided by sin, sets the groundwork for the Messiah's mission to restore unity.

The political division carries into a spiritual brokenness; sin is not willed by God. The oneness of God is reflected in the oneness of a people, of God and his people, symbolically expressed in the one-flesh of husband and wife (Gen 2:24). This carries over into the New Testament with the oneness of the Christian faith, one baptism, one Lord (Eph 4:5–6). But ultimately, the union is Christ and his bride, the church (Eph 5:31–32). The Catholic Church has been especially emphatic over the centuries in preserving the oneness of the church; the language of "one" appears in the creed. The challenge has been to preserve the "oneness" of the church in the midst of heresies, and in modern times, moral errors spreading across Christian denominations. Furthermore, tradition that has been a sign of apostolicity and apostolic continuity serves to preserve the "oneness" of the church with the Church of the apostles, specifically, the apostles Peter and Paul martyred in Rome. The divided church resembles the divided people of Israel, the broken

---

1. Psalm 51 (50), also known as the *Miserere*, expresses the depth of David's contrition in the language of a heart that seeks cleansing. This psalm is used in the Roman Catholic breviary at Lauds (Morning Prayer) on Fridays.

marriages, the broken relationships between God and the individual. This is not God's plan. The house of Jacob is a united people; Jesus leaves us one church under the authority of Peter, guided by the Holy Spirit.

3. The House of Jacob Forever

"He will reign over the house of Jacob forever, and of his Kingdom there will be no end" (Luke 1:33). The house of Jacob that includes both the people of Israel who were faithful but also those who were unfaithful because the twelve tribes were divided and scattered like sheep, each going their own way. The emphatic nature of "oneness" in John's Gospel transmits a message of unity among the apostles and the believers reflecting the oneness of the Father and the Son, "that they may all be one" (Jn 17: 21). Oneness is a fundamental constituent of the church that Christ founded as the tribes of Israel were originally one, but sin creates division.

When a king rules, he rules one people; he serves to preserve the unity of the people and not to create division. The skill of the Roman emperors from which the early church benefited was to create ecclesial structures uniting the people across the empire and the church. A "shepherd" who scatters and loses his flock instead of keeping them together can hardly be called a "shepherd." We may look at the history of division in a kingdom and realize that the kingdom never represented one people but a forced union of peoples due to territorial expansion. This explains local rebellions and insurrections where languages and cultures of distinct peoples are forced into a kingdom. The unifying principle, the foundation of "oneness," is ultimately Christ and his church.

But Israel has its source in one father, Jacob, son of Isaac, and Isaac, son of Abraham. The unity of Israel, therefore, means twelve tribes. From the time of King David the messianic language conveyed the reign of a king "for ever" (2 Sam 7:16). At the annunciation, first joyful mystery, the angels speak of the reign of Mary's child over, the "house of Jacob," the original twelve tribes, not just south or north, but a king who sits on the throne of Jacob, a united Israel. The messianic language taken literally is understood in political terms. And many expected the messiah to reunite Israel; a messiah from the house of David to restore unity to the divided tribes.

So, the kingship of Jesus is associated with a history of a divided people to whom Jesus brings unity if we understand these events in political terms—at the temporal level. Yet, Jesus's Kingdom "was not of this world." In the garden of Gethsemane, Jesus clearly does not want violence, weapons, and killing. This sort of passive king appears absurd, and he is mocked as king because he does not appear to exercise any military power over his people. If he were king of the Jews, then, why did the Jews hand him over for execution?

When we hear that Jesus will rule over the house of Jacob, the language of "oneness" is the essence of the angel Gabriel's message. Oneness has its source in the one God; oneness is the property of the divine; oneness reflects the work of the Spirit. The kingdom of Jacob over which Jesus rules is essentially "one" kingdom, including all those who have been faithful to the God of Abraham, God of Isaac, and God of Jacob, and Jesus, Son of God.

Northerners, such as the Galileans, remained faithful to their Jewish religion and never assimilated to the Samaritan culture and practices. So, while Jesus has his origins in the house of David, he grew up in Galilee where Mary and Joseph lived. In this sense, Jesus grew up in a divided world, a divided Israel. He witnessed division, the rejection of the Samaritans and Syro-Phonecians. His mission was to bring forgiveness, unity, and salvation through his cross.

The oneness Jesus brings to the people of Israel is not the political unity of a temporal king, a Messiah who restricts himself to the people of Israel. As the anointed one, Jesus will unite all people, Jews and gentiles, northerners and southerners, all the known peoples across the Mediterranean, North Africa, the lands of the East, the languages we hear about at Pentecost, the third glorious mystery. This supernatural unity of languages, peoples, and cultures, one baptism to acknowledge Jesus, Son of the ever-living God, constitutes the "one people"—the kingdom that Jesus unites of the twelve tribes of Israel, in a spiritual kingdom on earth but also the eternal kingdom where Christ reigns as king.

4. His Reign Will Have No End

The nature of Jesus's kingdom is expressed in the angel's announcement to Mary, ". . . and of his Kingdom there will be no end"—what does this mean? It might appear clear enough that an "eternal" kingdom is ruled only by a divine being, a divine king. Why did the Jewish scribes drawing from the prophets not seize the sense of Scriptures to identify an eternal kingdom as the messianic fulfillment in Jesus Christ? A supernatural kingdom conveyed by the angel where we are united eternally as one family, in one kingdom, where Jesus reigns as king?

During the time of Jesus's ministry, the Judaism we know had different schools of biblical interpretation simply based on the fundamental differences between the Sadducees, Pharisees, Samaritans, and Essenes. We might call the Sadducees materialists since they did not believe in a spiritual world outside of a transcendent God. The Pharisees, instead, believed in a spiritual world retained in Christianity, besides the transcendent God, angels and resurrection of the body. The Pharisees clearly acknowledged both a spiritual world and a material world. The Essenes emphasized spiritual purity and detachment from the material world. For the Samaritans their holy mountain was Mount Gerizim and not Jerusalem. These sects reflected fundamental differences in their interpretation of the Scriptures. While Paul persecuted the Christians, he also belonged to the sect of Pharisees; this meant he already possessed some understanding and belief in the resurrection. Divine intervention led Paul not only to the road of Damascus but also to Christianity.[2]

With such differences in interpreting the Scriptures, it should not come as a surprise that Christ was reasonably understood by some, poorly understood by others, and probably misunderstood by many. We still have the problem today in terms of how to interpret Scriptures and most evident in the rapid fragmentation of Christianity since the sixteenth-century *Sola Scriptura*—"Bible only"—movements.

In Jesus's own lifetime the presence of the Jewish sect of Essenes demonstrates the radical differences in interpreting the Hebrew Scriptures. The Essenes read the Scriptures, forming an ascetic community of celibate vegetarians who lived outside of the towns. Marriage existed as an exception. This tells us that already in the lifetime of Jesus communities were taking celibacy as a path to radical detachment from the world. In the case of the Essenes, even the site of their communities in Qumran, near the Dead Sea, feels like prohibitive dwellings in the dry desert. John the Baptist may possibly have been associated with this sect because of his radical asceticism and that he never married. We find parallels in the desert fathers and monasticism as Christianity began to emerge and spread as a distinct and radical way of life from Judaism. After the resurrection, early Christians understood the supernatural message of Christ's teachings, and with

---

2. Given that "oneness" is a hallmark of Catholicism the disagreement over inspired books of the Old Testament and the apocryphal books of the New Testament, Pope Damasus affirmed the inspired books at the Council of Rome in 382 AD, the books of the Old and New Testaments. This ensured that Catholics were reading the same books across Christendom and avoided disputes over questions of inspiration. So from 382 AD the Old Testament had forty-six books settling controversies stemming from Jewish sects; then, with the New Testament containing twenty-seven books. The disputes over the "deutero-canonical" books of the Septuagint surfaces during the sixteenth century although the deutero-canonical books had always been part of Catholic and Orthodox Bibles, and historically, used by the Greek-speaking Jewish communities. (See, Bergsma and Pitre, *Old Testament*, p. 24.)

Pentecost their faith and courage offered the strength to be persecuted and die for Christ their Savior and his eternal kingdom where his holy followers would live with him forever.[3]

Pilate's hearing showed the kingship of Jesus was not understood; Jesus tried to instruct Pilate and Jewish religious authorities and the mob that his kingdom "is not of this world." Instead, Jesus was charged and accused for claiming to be king as the Jews had intended and then transferred to the Roman soldiers where he is mocked, whipped, crowned, and nailed. But the crowning of thorns in the midst of derision emphatically highlights that Jesus's kingdom is not of this world. So, which world is this? The world that awaits each of us, the kingdom of God where Jesus reigns as king, where we shall all be one in this kingdom with those who faithfully followed or lived by the teachings of Jesus.

An eternal kingdom, a kingdom that will last forever, cannot be a kingdom on earth because all kingdoms come and go, rise and fall. Even the longest reigning monarch comes to terms with the reality of death followed by divine judgment. The question is not what a person leaves behind, but whether they are prepared for what lies ahead. Only Jesus, who is king, reigns forever; his kingdom has no end. Only Mary, the mother of the king, is the celestial queen in this kingdom that has no end: Mary queen of the universe whom we meditate in the fifth glorious mystery.

What other signs do we have of kingship fulfilled by Christ? As we have seen, God instructs Nathan to tell David, "Your house and your kingdom shall be made sure forever before me; your throne shall be established forever" (2 Sam 7:16). So, we have already in 2 Samuel the understanding of a Davidic Kingdom whose lineage, whose descendant will secure this kingdom "forever." But if we think about this, how can people, a man who is mortal and dies, establish a throne "forever"? Or are we to understand this differently? The only one to secure an eternal kingdom is the Son of God, as the angel tells Mary. Only the divine is forever, only a divine king can secure a kingdom "forever." Nathan's messianic prophecy points unmistakably to the divine; the language of the prophet Nathan does not convey an earthly kingdom or a mortal king exhausted by time and space and consumed by death. Nathan points to "everlasting" and a divine king to fulfil this mission.

---

3. In terms of "Scriptures" during the life of Christ this means what we call today, "Old Testament." Biblical scrolls found at the site of Qumran known as the "Dead Sea Scrolls" in the 1940s revealed the sacred texts of the Essenes (see Bergsma and Pitre, *Old Testament*, 35-39.) The Sacred Scriptures of the Pharisees contained more books than the Samaritans and Sadducees while the Essenes had more books than the Pharisees. The Sacred Scriptures of the Essenes correspond largely to the Deuterocanonical/Septuagint Books found in Roman Catholic Bibles.

When Jesus states that his "kingdom is not of this world," he wants us to know that he is the fulfillment of the messianic promise, the kingdom that God's people had been waiting for, the Messiah sent to unite the people into one kingdom, to unite and save all of humanity from that which causes division, for nations, peoples, families, and marriages: sin. Jesus the king saves his people from sin and unites us into one kingdom to be secure for ever.

5. Your Kingdom Come

In the prayer that Jesus himself teaches the apostles—and us—the "Our Father," Jesus directly invokes God's kingdom: "Your kingdom come" (Matt 6:10). The entire prayer is directed to the Father, and the structure of the prayer makes it easy to learn, to remember, and to repeat. Jesus does not refuse the humble request of his apostles: "teach us to pray." He could tell them pray whatever comes to their mind and heart. Or to let the Spirit lead them in prayer. These, too, spontaneous or charismatic, reflect possible forms of prayer. But Jesus replies giving the apostles a specific prayer to pray. Now Jesus does not instruct them when to pray the "Our Father," once a day, once a week . . . so as to avoid "repetition." Jesus does not say any such thing. He recognizes the significance of their request: his apostles want to pray and Jesus teaches them a prayer and leaves it at that.

Catholicism has followed Jesus's format by using formalized prayers, and the Catholic Church offers a rich tradition of prayers relating to the Trinitarian God, to the mother of God, to the angels and saints, and to each one of us. This ensures that the people pray, as Jesus taught us, reflecting the format of the Our Father: 1.) the prayer as worship directed to the Persons of the Trinity, in this case the Father: "hallowed be your name"; 2.) prayer as an act of supernatural hope: "your kingdom come"; 3.) prayer as communion with the will of the Father: "your will be done"; 4.) prayer as petition directed to the Father in the name of Jesus: "Give us this day our daily bread"; and 5.) prayer as reconciliation directed to the Father and others, "forgive us our debts / as we also have forgiven our debtors" (Matt 6:9–12). Formalized prayers in Catholicism convey these five elements; the Our Father represents one of the daily prayers as part of the liturgy of the hours or the rosary. The fifth element, "forgiveness," central to the teachings of Jesus, the Catholic Church makes available the sacrament of reconciliation.

While the prayer Jesus taught us to pray contained only a few verses, Jesus does not give indications on how long a prayer must be. Pastors in some Christian denominations may find a need to assemble many words and long sentences to convey their spontaneous prayer to God. Catholics do not criticize such prayers: prayer is prayer. If this is how the Holy Spirit leads a believer to pray, a Catholic recognizes the value of prayer, rather than being critical and divisive over prayer. In the Catholic tradition, formalized rhythmic prayer as Christ taught us reflects the desire to pray, to unite ourselves with Christ, his mother, the saints, to the church, in our the pilgrim journey towards eternal life. We find rhythmic prayers as a litany in the books of Ecclesiastes (Eccl 3:1–9), Daniel (3:52–90), and the Gospel of Luke (1:46–55, 68–79). Prayer is always good. Only the evil one questions the value of prayer offered to God.

So, when Jesus teaches us "your kingdom come," this means God the Father's kingdom, yet to be realized; "may your kingdom come" exhorts an act to be done or completed—hence, a future act. We know on earth Jesus is the king of his kingdom built on truth and love, a kingdom of peace; but this kingdom may not be completely realized on earth; the future kingdom, "may you kingdom come," conveys the kingdom "without end," where Jesus reigns forever. As Jesus tells Pilate, his kingdom is not of this world. So, in the exhortation, "May your kingdom come," each day we draw closer to the kingdom of God being realized, both, in the temporal order, but also the spiritual or eschatological order.

II—Fruit of this Mystery: Virtue of Moral Courage

Practical Matters—

When the soldiers mock Jesus as "king," putting a purple robe on him to make fun of his majesty, a reed to signify his authority which is ridiculed, and the crown of thorns to make him bleed from his head—as if he is not already bleeding enough—they act out of ignorance. How often are human actions the result of not having all the information, or that the only information we have draws from mainstream media, social media, and nothing more. What information did the Roman soldiers have on Jesus other than being the "king of the Jews," and since Jesus was handed over to them by the Jews to be crucified, how did the Romans respond? The Romans treated Jesus accordingly, as to what was expected of them.

To act morally and responsibly we need to be informed. We put the crown of thorns on Jesus each time we sin. After all, his suffering was the result of our sins, past, present, and future. When we do not know the truth about something, we have the responsibility to be informed. We should assess the reliability of the information presented to us. We should exercise our intelligence—to do our homework—and not simply rely on news sources without critical reflection. We have a responsibility to grasp what is true, so we can do what is right. We can put pieces of information together and determine if this harmonizes with Christ's teachings. A natural order exists in the world that God created. When this order is violated, we can be sure a rational being has erred. This reference to God's order is referred to as natural law which participates in the eternal law of God. No authority on earth is above God's eternal law but rather participates in God's eternal law by the use of reason and of the will.[4] God is the source of truth and goodness. Jesus is the fullness of truth; Jesus is the absolute love of God.

The question concerning the Romans insulting and putting a crown of thorns into the head of Jesus, we need to be vigilant and ask ourselves how often we do the same. Or perhaps we do not even act with the same ignorance as the Roman soldiers when we are coerced into behaving in ways that do not correspond to our actual beliefs. But social pressure leads individuals to violate their principles. So one may act sinfully out of poor information leading to ignorance, though the veracity of claims can be verified, or one may act sinfully out of coercion due to social pressure, though one still remains free. Would it not be interesting to talk to these Roman soldiers and ask them, "Why are you doing this to Jesus?" "Why are you insulting him?" "Have you actually thought about who this man is?" These soldiers, like all humans, can think, reflect; they have hearts and minds. I wonder if they actually understood what they were doing. Just before dying on the cross, Jesus addresses his Father: "Father, forgive them; for they do not know what they are doing" (Luke 23:34).

Accepting and promoting sin reflects the social norm created by the movie and music industries, followed by the mainstream media, then, further endorsed through government legislation. As one priest boldly declared in a homily in northern Italy, "We now parade and celebrate the triumph of sin." How do we recognize a need for a Savior if we fail to acknowledge our sins? Generations of youth now adapt to laws that permit—and society promotes—perverse sexual behavior, "perverse" because it violates natural law, not only the teachings of Jesus. Some parents collaborate in the rapid disappearance of Christian morality, while other parents are denied their rights to ensure their children receive a Christian education. Inadequate, confusing, ambiguous catechesis on the part of the church does not help matters; if anything, this exacerbates the problem of moral erosion in our society. We continue to put thorns into the sacred

---

4. See, Aquinas, *ST*, Pt. 1a-2ae, q. 91, arts. 1, and 2.

head of Jesus so long as we continue to violate his teachings. Yes, the soldiers acted out of ignorance, and how often do we perpetuate ignorance ourselves by failing to bring the truth of the Gospel, the radicality of the Christian life to others as Christ taught his apostles? Freedom is in the truth of the Gospel, not the lust, pride, and greed of the world.

This is our king, "King of the Universe!" King forever—mocked and ridiculed, rejected and tortured. Jesus suffered for our sins, because of our sins. Clearly, Jesus's kingdom is not of this world because his kingdom does not represent human glory and power, but the glory and power of God.

From the first martyr, Saint Stephen, who was stoned to death by the Jews as the religious authorities sought to eradicate the Christian presence, Christians were subjected to persecution and execution (Acts 7:54–60).[5] The repeated waves and especially cruel attacks against Christians commanded by Roman emperors throughout the centuries; the saints endured persecution and accepted martyrdom. Christians have stood for their faith since the beginning of Christianity. Martyrs in all continents where Christians professed their faith were slaughtered by the hundreds in Vietnam, Korea, and Japan often due to government suspicion viewing them as agents of a "foreign" religion. And Christians who survived a precarious existence in Muslim countries, subjected to discriminatory laws even though these Christians inhabited the Arab world for centuries before the existence of Islam.[6] Christian communities have been eradicated in North Africa and Asia Minor/Byzantium. And in Africa today, Christians, students, priests, and seminarians, religious and churchgoers, are targeted by Muslim radicals. Bombings by Islamic terrorists of churches often occur on solemn Christian celebrations. In Iraq on Christmas Day (2009, 2013), in Nigeria on Christmas Day (2011) and Pentecost Sunday (2022), in Sri Lanka on Easter Sunday (2019). In spite of threats, the very real risk of death by simply going to worship in their churches, something taken for granted in Western societies, these Christians continue to adhere to their faith which they witness concretely with courage.[7] Being a Christian is not a matter of repeating Bible verses but rather concrete actions of courage. And for the person who truly knows Jesus, this means the Gospel radically lived.[8]

5. In the Roman Catholic calendar the feast of Saint Stephen is observed December 26.

6. Destro, "Genocide, Statecraft," 59–92.

7. More recently, these attacks against Roman Catholics are being experienced in France where both priests and lay people have been killed during worship services by "radical" Muslims.

8. I find it ironic when I hear Christian denominations proselytizing to win converts among Christians in the Greek Orthodox and Egyptian Coptic churches in parts

But courage is not possible if faith is lacking. A person does not suffer or certainly does not die for something they are unsure about. Nor does a person die for opinions. Christians die because we know what we believe is true. By the grace of God, Christians die for their beliefs as a testimony of their faith. This has been true throughout the two thousand years Christianity has existed; the very survival of Christianity and Christian communities bears radical witness to the Gospel message. We follow Jesus Christ, Son of the ever-living God who is the fullness of truth. Jesus is the truth we live and die for.

So, courage is built on faith, and courage testifies a person's faith. This may not be a bloody martyrdom or horrific persecution. Courage can also be the day-to-day struggles of carrying our cross, bearing our cross patiently as one seeks to be faithful to the teachings of our Savior. Mary, our blessed mother, serves as the best example as a person who faithfully follows Jesus, not always knowing the suffering she may encounter, or even fully understand, but she remains a woman of faith and puts her complete trust in God knowing that he seeks only what is good. Mary faithfully receives the Holy Spirit to bring Christ into her womb, and she remains faithfully present at the crucifixion of her Son. Mary embodies courage. If we understand courage to be a sign of our faith, then, we recognize this virtue in Mary and the saints. Similarly, we recognize the courage of Joseph, husband of Mary and spiritual father of Jesus. Assuming the responsibility of both Mary and Jesus, not always knowing where this would take him, Joseph, as a man of faith, demonstrated his courage repeatedly in ensuring the protection of Mary and of Jesus.

If we lack faith, then, we will lack courage. How often do occasions arise where we can be witnesses of our faith, but we withdraw, hidden. We do not have to state our beliefs, but at least our beliefs may be reflected in how we live, the choices we make: simply making the sign of the cross at a meal, or letting friends know we have mass to go to on Sunday, or that we are having a meeting with a parish prayer group, or we belong to a Bible study, or it is Friday, and we suggest seafood or vegetarian so as to abstain from meat, or simply wearing a sacramental, the crucifix, the Virgin Mary, or Saint Michael the Archangel. Perhaps we might even go a step further by inviting family or friends to mass or one of these sanctifying activities. Yes, our small acts of courage witnesses what we believe.

When it comes to bearing the cross in marital commitments because at times, perhaps too often, one experiences more frustration than joy, or

---

of the Middle East and North Africa where Christians have struggled for centuries to preserve their Christian faith in the midst of persecution and martyrdom.

at least the harmony and peace expected in married life is lacking. The responsibility of parenthood and marital fidelity even when a husband or wife is left alone. Yes, courage is needed to bear the difficulties and to carry the cross. Commitment to one's spouse and children demands patience, hope, and grace. Courage, determination, force, perseverance express the same virtue; these synonyms convey shades of differences but they all relate to the virtue of courage, the cardinal virtue that underlies Christian holiness perfected by grace.

We can think of the many daily crosses, situations that frustrate us, discourage us, what we hear going on in our society, and we think, "Can it get worse?" The teachings of Jesus are either ignored, distorted, or rejected. When we think of our society, the neopagan beliefs and attitudes that are pushed, we need to remember what the early Christians experienced: they too were in a pagan culture, in pagan surroundings, and they were persecuted if discovered and executed. We can persevere, and we can ask for greater courage.

Christian courage, built on faith and moved by the Spirit, explains why our Christian religion has spread across continents throughout the centuries. Evidence of the horrific executions of Christians in the Roman Colosseum built in the 80s during the reign of Vespasian is evidence of this courage.[9] The Catholic Church possesses records documenting evidence of these brutal executions. The cardinal virtue that witnesses the Christian faith: courage. Although Christians are not subjected to public executions as in the Colosseum, we may still be threatened indirectly for our beliefs in terms of job loss, not getting hired, not getting a promotion, the risk of being charged and fined for expressing or adhering to our Catholic beliefs, that is, following our conscience.

Within our own Catholic communities, when we are hurt by the actions of others whom we trust, or disturbed by the misleading claims of prominent theologians, we feel betrayed, slapped in the face; these are concrete experiences where we need courage to persevere in our faith and stand up for what is true.

In our families we may come across religious indifference, or even worse, individuals who do not even believe in God. Those who do not bother with mass, and people who live sinful lives, yes, we can judge a person's actions as right or wrong in the light of the Gospel—and even natural law. God created us with intelligence; we are expected to use it.

---

9. In the Roman Catholic calendar the memorial of the Roman Martyrs is observed on June 30.

We have the coherency of truth that strengthens us. A Christian without courage will not advance in the spiritual life.

In a conversation with a student of mine, I told him, "Catholicism is not for wimps." He thought for a moment and asked, "Well, what about my grandmother who is at home baking cookies?" I replied, "Do not underestimate grandmothers, the strength and courage of grandmothers who continue to practice and transmit their Catholic faith after all their life experiences with spouse, children, grandchildren, siblings, community, social transformation, and changes within the church they grew up in. Grandmothers certainly serve as an example of courage." To grow in courage requires our willingness to cooperate with God's grace.

Jesus is crowned with thorns as king. Only in Christianity! Our religion serves us on earth, but prepares us for eternity, where Jesus is king forever. Mary, his mother, our mother and our queen, remains present to strengthen us, protect us, and to armor us with courage in our battles.

Fourth Sorrowful Mystery—Jesus Carries His Cross

I—*So they took Jesus; and carrying the cross by himself . . .* (John 19:17)

Our Father . . . Hail Mary . . . Glory Be . . .

1. Via Dolorosa

We associate Jesus carrying his cross with the tradition of the stations of the cross that dates back to the middle ages, well-known as the *Via Dolorosa* in the Holy Land, from which the fourteen stations of the cross derive. Both the fourth sorrowful mystery and the fourteen stations repeat biblical events along with oral traditions.

The second and third sorrowful mysteries—the flagellation and the crowning with thorns—and the first station—Jesus is condemned to death of the *Via Dolorosa*—render present the passion of Jesus. Similarly, the fourth sorrowful mystery and the second station—Jesus takes up his cross—reflect one biblical and spiritual reality of Jesus's passion. Throughout the centuries Christian pilgrims who wanted to go to the Holy Land to physically follow Jesus's journey from his trial to his burial in the tomb could rarely accomplish this journey physically. The *Via Dolorosa* was brought to Italy in the form of the fourteen stations by the Franciscans who had become custodians of the Holy Land in the early thirteenth century.

Travelling by foot, on horseback, or by boat across Europe to the Middle East proved to be a dangerous journey. In many ways, still today, security remains tight, with undercover and armed police often travelling with pilgrims on buses, hotel security equipped with firearms, churches guarded by soldiers holding machine guns. Such scenes depict the security needed in the Holy Land when tourists and pilgrims visit. So, we can imagine what it must have been like in the eleventh to thirteenth centuries when Christianity was finally defeated in the Holy Land by the Muslim armies under Baybars.[1]

The crusaders departing from Europe were regarded as holy warriors who "took the cross" for Christ and Christendom. The Christian pilgrims were easy targets for raids, ambushes, and threats given their vulnerability travelling great distances.

The medieval period produced Catholic religious and intellectual culture that created Europe's monastic libraries, majestic cathedrals, and outstanding universities from Italy to France to England to Sweden expressing their faith in God, their devotion to Mary, and their honor to the many saints. To give one's life for Christ and for Christendom whether in the monastic tradition or a religious order, or to "take the cross" on a crusade, did not seem as "extreme" as it does today in our secular world where God tends to be eclipsed or relegated to one hour of Sunday worship or quoting a verse or two from the Bible.

Because of the high risks involved and the desire to make the pilgrimage, the stations of the cross in local churches served this purpose from the thirteenth century onwards. What are the events that the New Testament records when Jesus carries his cross? The stations are biblical or inferred by the Scriptures but also found in oral traditions.

First Station: Jesus is Condemned to Death
(Matt 27:26; Mark 15:15; Luke 23:25; John 19:16)

Between the first sorrowful mystery—the agony—and second sorrowful mystery—the flagellation—we encounter "the condemnation" as the first station of the cross. The biblical basis for the first station, the Church of the Condemnation is conveyed by the *Ecce Homo*, "Here is the man" (John 19:5) with the arch visible above the station.

Second Station: Jesus Takes Up His Cross
(Matt 27:32; Mark 15:21; Luke 23:26; John 19:17)

This fourth sorrowful mystery and the second station draws from four biblical references. And so the tradition of the *Via Dolorosa* emerges from these passages. The Gospel of John states, "carrying his own Cross" (John 16:19). The emphasis on carrying his cross represents the moment of exaltation for

---

1. Weidenkopf, *Timeless*, 216–61 on the Crusades; 259–61 on Baybars.

Jesus: the cross is his glory, Jesus exalted truly as king on the throne of his cross. What can we say, then, about the spiritual significance of carrying the cross? Jesus states quite plainly addressing his disciples, "If any man will come after me, let him deny himself, and take up his cross, and follow me. For whosoever will save his life shall lose it: and whosoever will lose his life for my sake shall find it" (Matt 16:24–25).

Jesus teaches us with his words: "take up your cross." Golgotha, the crucifixion, precedes Tabor, the resurrection. The path to eternal life does not exclude suffering; on the contrary, suffering to some degree, Jesus informs us, is part of the journey. In some Christian circles people have issues with the crucifix—the body of Jesus nailed to the cross—because they prefer to focus on the resurrected Christ, but clearly, we are told and shown by Jesus, the way of the cross is the way to eternal life, "take up your Cross," integral to the Christian journey—words that cannot be ignored. We cannot hide Jesus on the cross.

Third Station: Jesus Falls the First Time (Oral Tradition)

Given the weight of his cross, the slabs of heavy solid wood, solid enough to support his weight, his overall physical condition after lashings resulting in profuse bleeding that he fell does not surprise anyone or even raise the question why this is "not in the Bible." Oral traditions serve to fill in gaps based on human experience and reality itself. Jesus fell: exhausted in the afternoon sun, the first fall reflects his condition, both weak and fragile.

Fourth Station: Jesus is Met by His Blessed Mother (Luke 23:27–28, 31/oral tradition)

The women wept. How does a mother respond to the accusation made against her innocent son? Mary who received the angel's message herself knew the child she carried in her womb was the Son of God. Holy. Sinless. Spotless. Members of her family knew Mary represented the most reliable source of information for the apostles since Mary conceived Jesus and she knew fully of his humanity and divinity. Only Mary could have provided the reliable information needed for Luke to write his Gospel as he gives us the most detailed account of the conception of Jesus in the first joyful mystery. Mary grappled with the trial in relation to God's plan for our salvation. A courageous woman; a mother who suffered with her beloved Son. From the conception of Jesus, Mary offered her Son to God's plan for our salvation.

Mary tried to make sense of the events taking place before her, a religious woman, familiar with the Scriptures, the dangers Jesus endured from the time she gave birth to him. Mary possessed the angel's message, and she kept all these things in her heart (Luke 2:51).

This encounter between Jesus and his mother in Mel Gibson's movie *Passion of the Christ* depicted the intensity of emotions between mother and son. The most powerful scene in the entire film where a mutilated man, crowned in mockery, meets his distressed mother in a state of anguish—how would a mother react seeing her son in such condition? How would a son feel in the presence of his mother, with a crown of thorns on his head, bleeding, marks of lashing, carrying his cross? The eyes of Jesus and Mary met, and they spoke to each other in the silence of suffering. Mother and son, their hearts united.

Fifth Station: Simon of Cyrene Helps Jesus Carry His Cross (Matt: 27:32; Mark 15:21)

In Luke's Gospel we are directly brought to Simon of Cyrene, fifth station. The place name refers to a North African town in present day Libya: "As they led him away, they seized a man, Simon of Cyrene, who was coming from the country, and they laid the cross on him, and made him carry it behind Jesus" (Luke 23:26). The presence of Simon of Cyrene suggests that Jesus does not carry his cross alone. Exhausted, dripping with blood under the afternoon sun, an observer, a passer-by, is given the opportunity to help Jesus, and Simon of Cyrene is present and consents.

The fact that the Cyrenean appears in the Gospels of Matthew, Mark, and Luke creates a relational dimension to the cross and suffering itself. Jesus is not alone in carrying his cross; neither are we. The Cyrenean's presence proves providential. At the moment, where Jesus endured so much under the weight of the cross, out of nowhere, Simon of Cyrene appears—not one of Jesus's disciples or a family member but a stranger. Like Peter's denial, we can imagine that most people expressed fear observing what happened to Jesus and hesitated to be associated with him—his mother an exception. Others must have been in total shock feeling powerless to do anything to help, caught between the authority of the Jewish Sanhedrin and the application of Roman law. But the horizontal dimension of the Cyrenean's presence emphasizes the role of the other, our fellow man, who is there to support us on our journey, especially at times when our cross feels too heavy to bear. Did God send his Son help? Is this not what God offers us when we are in most need? Help?

Mark's Gospel provides the most details: Simon of Cyrene was coming in from the country, simply a "passerby," which meant he did not observe the events taking place but arrived on the scene. We are even told the names of his sons, so he must have been known in the community: "father of Alexander and Rufus." A man with two sons now helps Jesus carry his cross, an ordinary man from the country on a visit to Jerusalem. The ordinariness of the Cyrenean as he stumbles on an extraordinary scene; he has no idea that he is carrying the cross of the Savior of the world. The Gospels of Matthew, Mark, and Luke highlight the fraternal support of Simon of Cyrene. On our journey we are not alone when we suffer, although our suffering may be great. And so, the humanity of Jesus is emphasized where he is helped by someone who stumbles upon the scene.

John's Gospel provides another perspective where he states that Jesus was "carrying the cross by himself" (John 19:18). A vertical dimension of "carrying" is conveyed in John's perspective because the focus shifts to Jesus and his throne of glory which is what the cross is meant to be. Jesus carries his cross as king, and he will be enthroned upon it. The perspective given by John suggests Jesus rules as king as he carries the cross to his enthronement.

Sixth Station: The Face of Jesus Is Wiped by Veronica (Oral Tradition)

A woman bold enough, strong enough, upon this road that Jesus walked brings Jesus a cloth to wipe his bloody face. We know the name of this woman given to us by tradition: "true image"—*Veronica* because tradition maintains that the cloth she used to wipe the face of Jesus left the mark, the imprint of Jesus's face.

We can ask ourselves if we respond like Veronica, ready and swift to reach out—to Jesus, to others. Or do we withdraw in fear? Veronica moves forward; she acts. She presents a cloth to wipe the face of Jesus. As we follow Christ on our journey carrying our cross, we may think we need help. But like Veronica, do we see the help others need, and far greater than our own needs? The sixth station resembles the fifth station where Simon of Cyrene appears: the journey Jesus walked, the journey we walk; God places people on our path, but that also means God calls us to reach out to others and wipe their tears, their blood, to help them carry their cross.

Seventh Station: Jesus Falls a Second Time (Oral Tradition)

As disciples of Christ, following him on the road to eternity, approaching the sufferings of Golgotha, as he instructs us to take up our cross and follow him, we know that we, too, fall. The weight of our cross, however, unlike Jesus who carries our sins, relates to the effects of our own sins, and our failure to grow in virtue. Vulnerable to the weight of our weaknesses, we risk falling under the weight of our cross. Lack of patience? Quick to get angry? Tendency towards envy? Pride? Greed? Persistent lustful thoughts? Hateful feelings? Unless we practice virtue, seek the sacraments of reconciliation and the Eucharist, the weight of our "defects," our vices that go unchecked, will not only cause us to act sinfully but develop sinful habits.

Eighth Station: Jesus Consoles the Women of Jerusalem (Luke 23:27–31)

Followers of Jesus included Jews who were caught between the religious authorities whose objective was to have Jesus executed for blasphemy and the Roman authorities carrying out the execution for Jesus claiming to be "king." The execution served as a public event to teach people not to repeat the same crime. A lesson to be taught in the Roman case, for claiming to be king, and in the Jewish court, the punishment for blasphemy. While the position of the religious authorities must have been respected by their fellow Jews since they had the authority to pronounce decisions on such matters, the difficulty in the case of Jesus was that everyone who listened to him or observed him knew his innocence, and so he could not be justly condemned as a criminal of any sort. Precisely the message that Pilate, a Roman pagan, tried to get across to the collective mob shouting in a frenzy to have Jesus crucified: "I find no basis for an accusation against this man" (Luke 23:4).

Luke's Gospel tells us, "A great number of the people followed him, and among them were women who were beating their breasts and wailing for him. But Jesus turned to them and said, 'Daughters of Jerusalem, do not weep for me, but weep for yourselves and for your children'" (Luke 23:27). Jesus speaks prophetically as he knows if this represents the treatment of an innocent man, how are the guilty to be treated? What awaits the women of Jerusalem and their children in the years ahead?

The women express their anguish, the confusion of a punishment inflicted on an innocent person. These women stood and wept, powerless to do anything about the unjust matter. They only conveyed their own pain in the presence of Jesus. We find that the fourth and eighth stations are directly linked, Mary being among the women of Jerusalem, and detaches herself from them in order to be with her son.

Ninth Station: Jesus Falls the Third Time (Oral Tradition)

In this station where Jesus falls for the third time, we imagine the heaviness of the cross that he carries, the heavy burden on his shoulders. Jesus, innocent of any crime—even the slightest transgression—is harshly treated and severely punished as a criminal. The cause: our sins. The road Jesus stumbles only to liberate us from Satan's hold on us, broken in our relationship with God, with others, with ourselves. The *Via Dolorosa* Jesus walks brings healing—meant for us.

In this ninth station we can also understand that our own sins cause us to fall repeatedly, reflecting the weight of our cross. But another side to our cross also exists, striving for holiness: as we seek to follow Jesus and the grace he gives us to strengthen us in our combat against Satan, the battles may be heavy, temptations increase; Satan has his tactics. Seeking an easy solution, a "quick fix," to rid ourselves of our cross—we think we cannot bear it—but the cross is the path to sanctity.

Tenth Station: Jesus Is Stripped of His Garments (Fifth Sorrowful Mystery)

This tenth station is treated with the crucifixion at the end of Jesus carrying his cross. The five remaining stations at the end of the *Via Dolorosa* all take place at the site of crucifixion, Golgotha, where today stands the Basilica of the Holy Sepulchre. Although defeated at the Battle of Satim with the fall of the crusader kingdom of Jerusalem, the crusaders reached an agreement that kept the site of the crucifixion and its basilica of the Holy Sepulchre in Christian hands. The significance of the basilica as a center of the Christian faith allows Christians to worship Jesus where he was crucified and buried and rose from the dead. The basilica's crusader architecture remains visible as it represents the second layer of pillars and building structure solidifying in crusader style over the earlier Byzantine basilica dating to the reign of Saint Helena of Constantinople.

Eleventh Station: Jesus is crucified (fifth sorrowful mystery); twelfth station: Jesus dies on the cross (fifth sorrowful mystery); thirteenth station: Jesus is taken down from the cross (fifth sorrowful mystery); fourteenth station: Jesus is laid in the tomb (fifth sorrowful mystery).

II—Fruit of this Mystery: Virtue of Patience

Practical Matters—

What is the connection between the fourth sorrowful mystery, "Jesus Carries His Cross," associated with the *Via Dolorosa,* and "patience"? Is the virtue of patience that important in the spiritual life to grow in holiness? Patience is fundamental for sanctity. We shall see why.

What Is Patience?

Time and patience go hand in hand. We want things done immediately. The sooner the better. The longer an act takes the more impatient we become. This applies to everything in our daily life: whether it's standing in a queue or waiting for a service. When it comes to being patient with ourselves in the spiritual life, it means we will not be saints tomorrow. We will need to curb our anger, to be vigilant about envy, to overcome our greed, to refrain from lustful intentions, to rid ourselves of laziness, not to have recurring hateful thoughts, and especially to deal with our pride. All of these vices, different ones for each of us, some more serious and more difficult to eradicate than others, like different weeds rooted in the ground, we have to uproot them. We need patience. Sins that repeat themselves prove to be especially frustrating because we think we have overcome this sin, then we fall again. Patience is needed. Someone may believe if they confess their sins to a priest they will never repeat the same sin again. Well, this should be true for mortal sins, but for venial sins often associated with personality traits or defects, such sins are far more difficult to eradicate. Any persistent sin requires patience.

A sinner dealing with specific issues will benefit from a regular confessor—not just going to confession: to identify the root cause of the recurring sin and to find practical strategies of battling the sin. By the grace of God, one is strengthened to overcome sin, including repetitive sins. Christ has redeemed us by his blood. With his divine help, we are purified of our sins and sinful tendencies. Patience is needed. The spiritual life and growth in sanctity rarely happens overnight.

Jesus shows us the road to eternal life; he leads the way. We have our journey here on earth, with high moments and low ones, we fall down and we get up, as we take our cross and follow our Savior. Four points to keep in mind:

1. Patience with Ourselves—

We can speak of our resurrection in Christ at baptism, freed from death and original sin, but we still experience the effects of original sin. We know this from our unholy inclinations. Our life on earth means falling, repeatedly. Our sinful falls, even our weaknesses and defects, mean we need continuous recourse to the sacraments of reconciliation and the Eucharist, so we are built-up to carry our cross. Grace received through the sacraments strengthen us in our patience. We sin, but we want to be holy. We are not patient with God because he will not "make" us holy fast enough. We are not patient with ourselves because we repeat the same sins. But God knows this helps us grow in sanctity: bearing our cross over time, patiently.

Suffering refers not just to physical suffering; we may experience emotional and psychological conditions that cause suffering due to loneliness, feeling disconnected, unloved, and rejected. We may have good health; we feel we are fragmented psychologically. We need patience that God heals us with his love even in our solitude, our loneliness, our depressed state.

Lack of patience; think of the kind of vices the lack of patience generates: anger, which can lead to hatred, lack of forgiveness towards others, as well as not forgiving oneself, perhaps even lacking patience with God, which leads to distancing oneself from God due to anger. In the case of addictions, one needs to especially exercise patience. Addictions are dealt with over months and years through spiritual and psychological healing and support. This requires especially patience with oneself.

2. Patience with Others—

Our interaction with others begins in our home from the time we are children, with our parents, with our siblings, and extended family. We experience our relations in the school setting for many years where we acquire friendships. In the workplace with our colleagues, we develop professional relationships that may become friendships or remain as acquaintances. Finally, when we marry, we discover the value of intimacy but also the demands of long-term commitment. Similarly, in religious life we learn the value of sharing our responsibilities with individuals whom we have not chosen but whom God has put on our path to form a community. Or in the priesthood, in friendships with fellow priests; even here patience is exercised.

Relationships, in some instances, are chosen, as in friendships and marriage, but in most instances, relationships represent those individuals we do not choose, as in family, work colleagues, religious life, priesthood.

The kind of patience we exercise depends on the nature of our relationship. Parents require patience with children, but this patience differs from the patience needed with a spouse. Children are still learning; often they do not understand. And as children grow, they experience the effects of different stages of growth. A spouse is expected to be a mature adult, but patience is needed to work through personality differences, misunderstandings, and expectations. Work colleagues are not spouses but as mature adults they still manifest weaknesses—even defects; they can get quickly frustrated, become rather demanding, or sound "bossy." The work setting requires patience. In religious life men or women of different family and cultural backgrounds learn to share a common life together, fundamentally, by being patient with each other. The same applies to the priesthood; patience is needed with both parishioners and fellow priests.

Patience, like any virtue, is acquired; we are not born with virtues. Although some people are more disposed to certain virtues than others, nevertheless, we still acquire virtue. This means that concrete situations that we find ourselves in that demand our patience is how we grow in patience. Virtue's concreteness means we grow in virtue through real life situations. We need to learn to accept the time that is needed for our own personal growth in being patient with others. We cannot control the behavior or change the temperament of others. We need to grow in patience. We can pray for the grace of patience each day, and especially in moments where we think we might lose patience. We can pray to focus on the goodness of the person that God has put on our path. We can refocus our thoughts from what is causing our impatience by simply allowing time to pass.

In matters of addiction, we especially need patience with others. We pray that Christ and his saints intervene and intercede in the life of persons afflicted with addictions and experience healing. This remains true for any sinful lifestyle of repeated "bad" sinful habits; we pray that these individuals may amend their ways—ourselves included. This requires patience.

An engaged couple whom I helped prepare for their marriage needed to resolve a conflict causing a tension in their relationship: one of the two always appeared predictably late for their dates with the other, and one was always waiting, predictably impatient. The solution for the couple meant changes for both: one needed to learn punctuality, the other, patience. What happens in these cases where an impatient friend waits for a very tardy friend—repeatedly—a couple who are about to marry? Sadly enough, their meeting starts off with a disagreement, whether in their car or while walking, on the way to church or to a restaurant; the date begins with tension. Irritating habits of a spouse, children, parents, siblings, relatives, in-laws, colleagues, parishioners—even after we politely point them out, they repeat them. We need patience. We must not forget, others need to be patient with us—we may not see it, but others do. And does God not lose patience with us? Well, God is always willing to forgive us, so he must be very patient. We grow in patience as we grow in strength to bear our cross: with ourselves, with others, even with God.

3. Patience with God—

This may sound strange: how can we have patience with God? Knowing that God is absolute truth and goodness, how can we think of being patient with him? In fact, this is where patience is most lacking and yet, most needed, our patience with God. We are a people of prayer, and one form of prayer is that of petition. We have requests. Daily petitions for different needs. How long are we willing to wait for God to respond? The fact is, not very long. We want answers—and fast. God does not function this way; the fact that I have put in a request one day does not mean I get a response from God the next.

God is not our candy machine that whenever we insert a coin, a candy comes out. A candy machine does not require patience; it requires a coin. But God wants us to grow in faith, in hope, and in love. Spiritual growth occurs over time and time is built in the very word: "patience." Patience with God is needed precisely because he wants us to grow in sanctity. So when we have petitions we make, we cannot expect the response to be either immediate or even what we want. God answers in his own time and what is best for us. The purifying and didactic function of patience appears in the Scriptures when the Israelites spent two generations, forty years, wandering in the desert to the promised land. The Israelites grew impatient—but God wanted to prepare them spiritually for the land which he promised them (Num 32:13; Josh 5:6). As the Israelites bitterly complained, God wanted them to learn to trust him, and as they journeyed ahead towards the promised land, God wanted them to truly be a people of faith, a people of hope, a people of purified hearts. These virtues the Israelites acquired over two generations. We can see, then, from the book of Numbers how time is integral to spiritual growth because of the patience that is implied. Patience, therefore, builds up virtues.

With patience God wants us to continue to trust in him and ultimately to love him in our encounter with Jesus. This reminds me of one morning in Rome where I had ministry at one of the basilicas, and two women came to talk to me, one after the other. The first woman arrived, middle-aged and unmarried, apparently in good health; she held a good position and with stable employment. She complained that God did not answer her prayers: she prayed a novena for a husband to one of the Saints without any results. She did not meet a man suitable for marriage. The woman seemed entirely focused on this unanswered prayer that she expressed in her clear frustration and disappointment with God. She sounded unhappy and ungrateful. Immediately after her came another woman. Much older, perhaps in her nineties. She dragged herself into the basilica on crutches, approaching me so she could finally talk to me. She began by telling me she thanked God for the beautiful day. Then, she thanked God for giving her the strength to reach the basilica because with her poor health and her bad legs she felt apprehensive about walking, but she thanked God that she reached the basilica. This woman amazed me; she expressed her thanksgiving repeatedly. I had not even noticed the sun that morning until she brought it to my attention.

The contrast between the two women seems rather obvious. But the real point concerns patience. The middle-aged woman lost her patience with God; as a result, she failed to find any goodness in her life, not even that morning. She had plenty of good things to thank God for, but she failed to recognize them because of her lack of patience. The elderly woman walking with crutches clearly showed patience with the cross she carried—her fragile condition, her weakness—but nevertheless, she thanked God; that day she had the strength to reach the basilica and praise God for the beautiful sunny morning.

4. Patience in Spiritual Battle

Patience clearly has implications in our spiritual life: the joy or sadness that we experience within ourselves, how we communicate this joy or sadness to others, and our relationship with God, whether it reflects one of gratitude and thanksgiving or thanklessness and dissatisfaction.

The fourth station where Jesus carries his cross is associated with the fruit of the virtue of patience. We can see the significance of patience in our spiritual life by how we carry our cross. We cannot escape the cross; if we try to reject our cross we are not worthy of the name "Christian." As disciples of Christ, we bear our cross whatever it may be, and we do so patiently because patience signifies spiritual growth and sanctity. God gives us the grace we need to bear our cross patiently.

We know we have recurring situations, repeating sins, difficult relationships, character defects that make us susceptible to losing patience. And yet, in these areas of weakness and fragility, of defects and sin, this is precisely where we ask God for the grace to strengthen us, to provide us with the armor we need for spiritual battle. We know Satan can take advantage of our weaknesses and so we need patience to put on our armor, and to march into the battlefield like soldiers, courageously engaged to win the battle, and not lose patience and retreat (Eph 6).

Patience equips us for spiritual warfare. Spiritual battles cannot be fought and won in a day. Spiritual battle is ongoing, engaging lifelong combat. Battles fought against temptation, against Satan's tactics. We fall, and we may fall repeatedly caused by the same sin, even grievous ones, while we find ourselves also working on personality traits and weaknesses leading to venial sins. Only with patience, prayer, and God's grace do we win these battles.

Fifth Sorrowful Mystery—Crucifixion and Death of Our Lord

I—*There they crucified him* . . . (John 19:18)
Our Father . . . Hail Mary . . . Glory Be . . .

1. Our Lives Forever Changed

We recall that in the fourth sorrowful mystery, Jesus carries his cross, where we find the *Via Dolorosa* in Jerusalem. The eleventh to fourteenth stations all occurred at the Basilica of the Holy Sepulchre where Jesus was crucified on Golgotha. We can draw from these five stations and their biblical sources to help us enter into the mystery of Christ's crucifixion.[1] These include (eleventh) the crucifixion; (twelfth) the death of Jesus; (thirteenth) Jesus is taken down from the cross; and (fourteenth) Jesus is buried in the tomb.

We can understand that with the five stations occurring on site at the Basilica of the Holy Sepulchre, each biblical event as recorded in the Scriptures, pilgrims desire to unite themselves with Christ and to follow him—and still do on the *Via Dolorosa* and in Catholic Churches around the world—Jesus's way to the cross. These remaining four stations provide a biblical breakdown of what is contained in the fifth sorrowful mystery.

Eleventh Station: Jesus is Nailed to the Cross (Matt 27:35; Mark 15:24; Luke 23:33; John 19:23)

How do we grasp Jesus nailed to the cross? Too painful to even imagine—the nails driven through his hands and feet. Already Jesus was bleeding

---

1. Starting with the stripping of Jesus (tenth station) at the end of the fourth mystery.

profusely from the lashings he received and the crown of thorns pierced into his head. Now, nails are hammered into his flesh. The body of an innocent man, loved by his mother standing at the cross of her Son. Undoubtedly, Jesus was a controversial teacher and healer because of the claims he made and the religious laws the Pharisees claimed he broke. Jesus was not understood or believed by all; nevertheless, he spoke only the truth, he acted only to love. And he is now nailed on the cross. A sacrifice of himself that he offers to save us.

Twelfth Station: Jesus Dies on the Cross (John 19:33)

The agonizing bleeding caused by the nails and the force of his weight, held by nails on a cross, leads to Jesus's asphyxiation, besides his massive blood loss. An excruciating death is the outcome. Jesus dies naked. Jesus dies nailed on the cross. Jesus dies for us. "Instead, one of the soldiers pierced his side with a spear, and at once blood and water came out" (John 19:34). The "side" is associated with the "sacred heart" of Jesus; and indeed, he spilled his blood for us, the heart that loves us, that saves us. And water that came out of his side. We meditate on the pouring blood and water of Jesus and the new life the Son of God offers us.

Thirteenth Station: Jesus is Taken Down from the Cross (Luke 23:53; John 19:38)

Jesus died on the Friday he is crucified. But early morning of the Sabbath, the "Day of Preparation," Joseph of Arimathea, having spoken to Pilate, was granted permission to take down the body of Jesus. While Joseph belonged to the Jewish Council, he also believed in Jesus and did not support the decisions and acts of the council (Luke 23:51). Joseph provides an example of one of many Jews who in silence were either sympathetic to the message of Jesus or believed in his message; Joseph "was looking for the kingdom of God." The value of searching, seeking what is true; God will guide us and lead us to the fullness of truth as evident with Joseph of Arimathea. We find in Joseph's case that he does not support the actions of the council, which means he followed his conscience; he does not submit or succumb to any kind of pressure by expressing consent or agreement with the condemnation of Jesus.

Fourteenth Station: Jesus Is Laid in the Tomb
(Luke 23:53; John 19:40-42)

Luke's Gospel tells us that they "laid it in a rock-hewn tomb where no one had ever been laid." The generosity of Joseph of Arimathea is shown towards the man he believes in, though in secret (John 19:38). Nicodemus, the Pharisee who visited Jesus by night (John 19:39), also assisted Joseph. Both men seeking the kingdom of God found the kingdom in Jesus's teachings. The fact that the men used a new tomb in a garden not far from the crucifixion is evident in the Basilica of the Holy Sepulchre as a place of crucifixion and the original tomb site.

A visit to the holy tomb in the Church of the Holy Sepulchre contains the slab identified with the body of Jesus when he was taken down from the cross. Once removed from the cross and placed on a slab, they brought the body of Jesus to the tomb where it was prepared for burial (Luke 23:55-56).

2. Death of Jesus

The fifth sorrowful mystery focuses on the reality of Jesus's crucifixion and death. As a man Jesus suffered on the cross; as a man Jesus also died. The stress on Jesus's humanity which is underscored with his death in this fifth sorrowful mystery answers the ongoing heresies right into the medieval period, minimizing or even rejecting the humanity of Jesus. These movements of Manichean and Gnostic origins held "anti-materialist" views: the followers identified the material world as evil or corrupt because the body was associated with sin and suffering; the body constitutes matter. So, Jesus could not truly have suffered if he did not have a body; his body reflected some kind of illusion. The anti-material view of the world prevails in Christianity knowing that Christian denominations reject both sacraments and sacramentals as they did in the medieval period. In fact, the Dominicans preaching the mysteries of the rosary emphasize the humanity of Jesus in response to the Manichean heresies among Cathari adherents, widespread in southern France—the reason Saint Dominic started his preaching mission in southern France.[2]

We still know today of Christians who refuse to wear or display crucifixes because they have difficulty acknowledging a crucified Christ, the body, the Savior on a cross. But the resurrection does not occur without the crucifixion. Again, we see the emphasis on divinity while diminishing the humanity of Jesus—a gnostic spirituality denying the bodily-sensory

---

2. Dorcy, *Saint Dominic*, 25–35; Vost, *Hounds of the Lord*, 22–23.

reality of the incarnation. Jesus suffered for us. Jesus saves us through his flesh. This was God's plan for our salvation: the Son of God suffered for our sins and died on the cross for us. This means God saw the crucifixion as the most fitting means to save us and for God to show his love for us. This is why Catholics continue to wear, display, and venerate crucifixes. The Passion Friday (Good Friday) liturgy includes the rite of the veneration of the cross where the faithful kiss, touch, or bow before the crucifix, a powerful part of the liturgy where young and old, mothers, fathers, and children all come forward to venerate the crucifix.

3. Salvific Act

The crucifixion is the salvific act in the life of Christ—the "power of the cross" that conquers sin and death and restores God's human creation with the Father. The crucifixion cannot be separated from the religious context of the Passover as the fulfillment of the Law and Prophets.

The five stations of the *Via Dolorosa* observed at the Holy Sepulchre in relation to the crucifixion are themselves acts which derive their meaning from the one central act of Christ, his sacrifice on the cross. The sacrifice of Jesus is understood within its biblical context to make sense of who Jesus is and what he accomplished or more precisely "fulfilled." Only then do we understand the crucifixion in time and space—an event that occurred around 33 AD and whose effects of divine saving power continue past-present-future—an eternal present.

Jesus, human and divine, Son of God, produces the "effects" of the crucifixion in the temporal order and the eternal; Jesus unites humanity with the eternal, God the Father. The crucifixion restores humanity's rupture caused by original sin of the first man and the first woman with God—the removal of sin obtained through the sacrament of baptism.[3] An individual enters eternal life because of Christ's salvific act but also the individual's response to God's gift of his Son. We participate in divine life offered by Christ already while on earth in preparation for eternal life—the participation in divine life through the sacraments of the church.[4]

At the crucifixion the body and blood of Jesus were visibly real, his suffering audible, for those who stood by and witnessed his agony on the

---

3. "Baptism, by imparting the life of Christ's grace, erases original sin and turns a man back toward God . . ." *Catechism*, #405.

4. "By his death and Resurrection, Jesus Christ 'opened' heaven to us. The life of the blessed consists in the full and perfect possession of the fruit of the redemption accomplished by Christ." *Catechism*, #1026.

cross. The Gospel of John records Jesus's last words. Amongst the early Christians, gnostics refused to believe that Jesus was truly human, but only divine, because the body was corrupt and evil. The Ebionites, another early "Jewish-Christian" heretical group did not accept the divinity of Jesus, but only his humanity. Only the mother of Jesus, mother of God, could provide an accurate account of the exchange between her and the angel Gabriel at the annunciation—first joyful mystery.

Jesus repeatedly told the Pharisees they knew and taught the Scriptures, but they failed to understand. The Scriptures need to be correctly interpreted, otherwise people can teach and preach errors. Jesus chose Peter as the first pope from whom we receive authoritative teaching and who ensures the unity of what our faith and morals consists of; in other words, preserving and transmitting the teachings Christ left us.

Although Jesus is sacrificed on the cross, body and blood, Jesus first offers his body and blood at the Last Supper: "While they were eating, Jesus took a loaf of bread, and after blessing it he broke it, gave it to the disciples, and said, 'Take, eat; this is my body.' Then he took a cup, and after giving thanks he gave it to them, saying, 'Drink from it, all of you; for this is my blood of the covenant, which is poured out for many for the forgiveness of sins'" (Matt 26:26-28). We observe and celebrate the Passover as instituted by Jesus himself at every Catholic Mass but in a particular way, we refer to the Last Supper on Holy Thursday the same evening that Jesus suffered in the garden of Gethsemane after the Passover supper, first sorrowful mystery. These two events, the Last Supper and what follows shortly after, the crucifixion, cannot be separated.

4. Law and Prophets

"The Law and the Prophets," Jesus repeats in his teachings: "Do not think that I have come to abolish the law or the prophets; I have come not to abolish but to fulfill" (Matt 5:17). The teachings of Jesus, his ministry, his miracles, the Last Supper, the crucifixion, starting with his birth, are meant to be understood in the light of the Scriptures pre-figuring his birth, that is, God's promise. Jesus enlightens us on how to interpret the Scriptures: old covenant figures, places, and events, serve to point to Jesus as the fulfillment of these figures, places, and events found in the new covenant. Jesus reveals to us that besides reading the Scriptures at a literal level, Scriptures have a spiritual sense in conjunction with his life and his salvific mission.[5] To understand the crucifixion in connection with—"fulfilling"—the Law

---

5. For the senses of Scripture, see second sorrowful mystery fn. 1.

and Prophets, we will limit ourselves to passages from Exodus, the Psalms, and Isaiah, and in the New Testament, elements of the transfiguration—the fourth luminous mystery.

i. Exodus

The drama of Exodus, where the Israelites are led out of Egypt, establishes the central religious event of "liberation": the Passover. Once the Israelites have crossed the Sea of Reeds, another key event is expressed: the ratification of the covenant at the foot of Mount Sinai. These two events belong to salvation history, finding their fulfillment in Christ.

Instructions are given concerning the Passover feast also to be observed by subsequent generations. The blood of the unblemished lamb: "Your lamb shall be without blemish, a year-old male; you may take it from the sheep or from the goats . . . some of the blood and put it on the two doorposts and the lintel of the houses in which they eat it" (Exod 12:5–7). The blood on doorposts and lintel spares the first-born males of those homes while the angel of death proceeds to strike the first-born, both boys, girls, and livestock where such blood is not present on the doorposts. Moreover, specific instructions are given concerning how the Passover meal is to be eaten including unleavened bread (Exod 12:8).

After the Ten Commandments have been revealed, the people of Israel acclaim, "All the words that the LORD has spoken we will do" (Exod 24:3). In ratifying the covenant, the book of Exodus provides details on the ritual: "Moses took half of the blood and put it in basins, and half of the blood he dashed against the altar . . . Moses took the blood and dashed it on the people, and said, 'See the blood of the covenant that the LORD has made with you in accordance with all these word'" (Exod 24:6, 8).

Jesus celebrated the Passover with his apostles according to the Law prescribed by Moses: "You shall observe this rite as a perpetual ordinance for you and your children. When you come to the land that the LORD will give you, as he has promised, you shall keep this observance. And when your children ask you, 'What do you mean by this observance?' you shall say, 'It is the passover sacrifice to the LORD' . . ." (Exod 12:24–27). We recognize converging elements that identify Jesus with the Passover Lamb: he is male, and he is without blemish; while the Passover words are repeated, Jesus equates the "bread" he holds with his body. This sounds strange to the apostles because the words Jesus uses do not fit in the ritual. Rituals have a formalized structure, and any change, even one word, becomes immediately obvious and can cause controversy.

But this is not the case; when Jesus holds the bread saying, "This is my body," even if the meaning was not yet clear, there is no indication that the apostles react. Jesus continues with the Passover wine, using the ritual language (Exod 24:8), holding the chalice, but fulfilling the covenantal language: "the new covenant in my blood" (Luke 22:20). In Luke's Gospel, Jesus introduces the word conveying fulfilment not found in the Exodus Passover: "new." But the apostles do not appear to react to the words "*my* body" or to "*my* blood." My italics. In the language and gestures, Jesus fulfills the binding laws of Exodus where the Passover is observed over generations, and with his apostles, Jesus offers and "fulfills" the Passover ritual. But, the "fulfilled" aspect of the Passover is not yet complete. This fulfillment takes place on the cross where Jesus offers his body as sacrifice and spills his blood, and only when completed on the cross, Jesus says, "It is finished" (John 19:30). The sacrifice on the cross is the paschal Lamb that Jesus fulfills: the blood of the lamb that saves the first-born from the angel of death is now the blood of Jesus that saves us from death and gives us eternal life.

The two events, the Last Supper and the crucifixion, cannot be separated and need to be understood as one act: the Passover Supper on Holy Thursday that is fulfilled on Friday at the crucifixion. In the very words that Jesus himself utters, "It is finished" (John 19:30).

ii. Psalms

In David's psalms we read, ". . . they pierce my hands and my feet. All my bones are on display; people stare and gloat over me" (Ps 22:16–17). The details that David gives in this Psalm, applied to Jesus almost a millennium later, shows remarkable details that bears signs of the suffering Messiah pointing to Jesus. We know David prefigures Jesus as a prophetic and priestly figure, but especially as king. The details of Jesus's kingship we meditate in the second sorrowful mystery. David represents the king who submits himself to God's will; he establishes Jerusalem as the capital of Judah, and in his religious fervor dances around the ark of the covenant as it is brought to Jerusalem. Conveying a divine message, Samuel tells David that his son will be God's son, and God will be his Father, and the throne of David "will be established forever" (2 Sam 7:14, 16). When David writes these words, "they pierce my hands and my feet," their prophetic tone find their fulfillment in Jesus, a descendant of David, "Son of David," as we know from events recorded in the Gospels.

iii. Isaiah

Verses from the prophet Isaiah who writes about half a millennium before the birth of Jesus also identifies a figure in language strikingly connected to Jesus: "But he was wounded for our transgressions, crushed for our iniquities; upon him was the punishment that made us whole, and by his bruises we are healed" (Isa 53:5). The elements in Isaiah's prophesy that identifies Jesus: first, "the bruising for our iniquities," and second, "upon him was the chastisement that made us whole." The language of Isaiah points to an innocent person wounded and crushed not because this victim committed any offense, but rather through his suffering, the people were "healed" and made "whole." The contrasts are vivid: bruised/wounded and transgressions/iniquities, and finally becoming whole/healed by this victim. The passion of Jesus's "stripes," his suffering, reflects what Jesus "undergoes"; he is the one who is acted upon; the one to receive the wounds and bruises as we have seen in the previous sorrowful mysteries.

iv. Transfiguration (Also Fourth Luminous Mystery)

One of the central elements of the transfiguration is the presence of Elijah and Moses with Jesus on Mount Tabor. Why specifically Moses and Elijah, two Old Testament figures? The transfiguration serves to show the connection between the Old Testament and the New; Moses, Elijah, and Jesus. Moses who represents the Law, and Elijah the greatest of Prophets, fulfilled in the person of Jesus.[6]

These passages from the Law of Moses and Prophets as well as their representation in the New Testament, are indicative of how the Old Testament Laws and Prophets point to Jesus Christ. The central event in salvation history is the crucifixion of the Son of God, the Paschal Lamb, the promised Messiah. We have looked at a few passages from Exodus, the Psalms, and the Prophet Isaiah to identify how the events of the crucifixion are hidden in the Old Testament.

v. Mary at the Cross

One of the most surprising aspects of the crucifixion was the very few people present at the cross. The miraculous powers of Jesus witnessed by thousands. Who was at the cross with our Lord? Humiliated, naked, nailed, bleeding,

---

6. Details on the transfiguration are given in the first luminous mystery.

in agonizing pain, Jesus was left almost alone to die. In John's Gospel, the beloved disciple, Saint John; Mary Magdalene, who had a radical conversion experience; Mary, the wife of Clopas; and Mary, the mother of Jesus remain (John 19:25). Jesus speaks first to his mother in reference to John—"Woman, here is your son"—then Jesus tells John in reference to Mary, "Here is your mother. And from that hour the disciple took her into his home" (John 19:27). As he dies on the cross, Jesus ensures that his last words included his mother and his beloved disciple. But, in speaking to John, Jesus addresses all of us. And Jesus asks each of us to take his mother into our homes. "This is your mother." In turn, we are children of Mary; she intercedes for us as our mother as she intervened at Cana for the chief steward. Jesus wants us to receive his mother as our mother because he knows that through Mary's intercession, we are led to Jesus, and we grow in sanctity.

II—Fruit of this Mystery: Virtue of Self-Denial

Self-denial is our own participation in the cross of Christ. Self-denial is like ongoing training, the reason we have elements of self-denial, especially in the last three mysteries, courage—crowning with thorns, patience—carrying the cross, and self-denial—crucifixion. Each of these mysteries requires our willingness to offer up something of ourselves.

Practical Matters—

It seems strange that the non-apostolic denominations create an opposition between Jesus and Mary.[7] But Jesus does not compete with his mother, nor does Mary compete with her Son. These either/or arguments reflect human squabbles, people projecting their own divisive nature on the Scriptures, their own pride that gets in the way. This "choose me or my mom" hardly reflects the relationship between Jesus and his mother. When we stick to the Bible, we see how much Jesus loves his mother, entrusting her to John, and in turn, Jesus places John in the hands of his mother. These final words of Jesus as he dies on the cross transcend the moment of crucifixion. Jesus's words are meant for John, the "beloved disciple," and all the disciples who follow Jesus: "Here is your mother" (John 19:27). Jesus leaves with us his

---

7. "Non-apostolic" refers to those denominations that are traced to the sixteenth century Reformation with the Bible as their "authority." Apostolic churches trace their origins to the apostles: the Roman Catholic Church derives its apostolic authority clearly from the Scriptures (Matt 16:16–19) and the martyrdom of Peter (and Paul) in Rome.

mother to intercede for us, to be our model of holiness, to contemplate the Son of God just as she contemplated him.

The life of the believer and the moral life cannot be separated. A separation of the faith and acts is simply non-biblical. As Scriptures reveals to us in the Old Testament and New Testament, the person who believes demonstrates their faith by works without dividing the person into two: the one who believes and the one who acts. It is the same person who believes and acts (Jas 2:14–26). Jesus clearly reproaches those who claim to believe and fail to act according to their beliefs, calling out to him, "Lord! Lord!" (Matt 7:21). A person who does not strive to live by the teachings of Christ and professes to be a Christian should ask honest questions: "Whom do I believe? What do I believe? How does that change how I live?" Christ's sacrifice on the cross is a testimony of love for all those who want to follow him.

The fundamental moral problem is sin. The challenge for the disciple of Christ reflects this incoherence that continues to affect us: the persistent reality of inclinations, temptations, and sin. We continue this thorny battle by the grace of God to strive for holiness and combat sin; this is spiritual warfare and growth. Sanctity without spiritual battles is not possible, just as sanctity without grace is not possible. We know the core of our faith is the crucifixion, death, and resurrection of Jesus, Son of God. The spiritual richness and beauty of Roman Catholicism is that the crucifix is visibly central to our faith: the body of Jesus is crucified—the one whom we encounter in our churches. We wear the crucifix around our necks to signify that we are followers of Christ who sacrificed his body and blood for our salvation. With all the decorations hanging from people's necks, we should be faithfully wearing this most beautiful sign of our salvation, or images of the blessed Virgin Mary who brings Jesus into our world, or of the saints who offered themselves by the power of the Holy Spirit as witnesses of the Gospel.

As disciples of Christ we are a people of the cross and resurrection. We cannot have the resurrection without the cross, as we saw in the fourth sorrowful mystery, we carry our cross as Christ himself taught: "If anyone desires to come after Me, let him deny himself, and take up his cross, and follow Me" (Matt 16:24). I have been in many churches in different parts of the world. I have always found the entry procession with the crucifix a powerful witness of our Catholic faith: we are a people of the cross. One mass that stands out in my mind was in Kapiri Mposhi, Zambia, on Palm Sunday. Hundreds of people gathered outside the church for the procession. At first silence. Then the drums began to beat, and the singing immediately followed. Then, the altar boy raised the crucifix, and everyone's eyes were focused on the crucifix as the procession moved down the dust road. Visibly Jesus, Son of God, brought us all together—his sacrifice on the cross. Our thanksgiving for God's gift of salvation, our need for a Savior, explained our celebration in one Catholic faith. This is why the mysteries of the rosary serve not only as a didactic tool and daily reminder of the life of Jesus but a meditative exercise that helps us enter the mysteries of the life of Jesus, where we are not observers but participants following him in thanksgiving and asking Mary for her intercession so we may grow in truth and sanctity.

As spiritual training exercises, the church gives us Advent, Lent, and Fridays to deny something of ourselves to grow in our spiritual life or even offer these acts of self-denial for a person or particular intention. Self-denial is concrete training, to grow in virtue and the spiritual life. Acts connected to our instincts represent the ones most difficult to deny, and therefore, the most challenging, but also spiritually purifying. People know their weaknesses and their inclinations towards sin. Self-denial in areas where we struggle with sin provides good training and discipline to help us combat sin. Nobody dies from acts of self-denial. Catholics are meant to be warriors in the spiritual life.

Whenever the occasion arises to engage in sensuous pleasures, related to instincts, food, or sex, or even entertainment as in movies, music, and social media, a sense of self-restraint, or even abstinence, can be exercised. Discernment is needed: How excessive are these acts? Is sin involved? Limits to control, to discipline pleasure-inducing habits, helps us to grow in sanctity. Anytime is a good time to start self-discipline. When I teach philosophy in Goa, India, my students are young men in their late teens and early twenties; their diet consists primarily of vegetarian meals with occasional meat on Catholic feasts. They are healthy and joyful men of prayer. Self-denial can include vegetarianism and keeping the Catholic tradition of abstaining from meat on Fridays. The wisdom of Catholicism has been to observe Friday abstinence from meat, so we do not just succumb to our appetites and indulge; instead, the Friday crucifixion of Jesus on our minds, we offer penitential acts of self-denial.

A lack of self-denial is connected to spiritual sloth—or overindulgence. We have opportunities for spiritual training to build us up spiritually, but we find excuses not to. Wake up early in the morning! This is good discipline for the spiritual life and will help us combat sloth. The quiet morning is the best time to pray, when the mind is fresh and body rested. We can always go to bed early or deny ourselves a half hour of sleep. The early morning time can also be used for spiritual reading and meditation.

Truth, we know today, is in crisis. Opinions are treated as facts. We are exposed to fake news. Entertainment sells sex. People treat movie and music celebrities as if they are gods and goddesses. Where is the truth in all this? We are exposed to lives of sinful indulgence. Pleasure without limits. How does this all influence us?

The price of truth, even in our own society to defend what is true, let alone teach what is true, is threatened. Our society endorses and promotes abortion, same-sex marriages, transsexual story hours, gender reassignment rights for children, Marxist-driven postmodern ideologies directed towards power. We cannot even walk across a sidewalk that should be restricted to pedestrian stripes without ideology being pushed our way. The dominant "approved" narrative we find reinforced in the mainstream media. Parents and teachers are silenced when they defend pro-life values and traditional marriage; standing up for womanhood or manhood is now questioned. Truth is not being heard, only the rights people demand and impose, fueled by the media, yelling like the mob "crucify him" when the truth is spoken. Truth found in God's laws; truth found in the eternal law of God.

Has our society become like the Israelites who after receiving the Ten Commandments carved and worshiped a golden calf of power, glory, and lust, assimilating to their pagan surroundings? Moses was disgusted.

Our salvation is the cross. Our response is to the Person of Jesus Christ; he is the way, the truth, and the life. Everything that needed to be done to save us has been fulfilled; Jesus says, "It is finished." But we still need to do our part. God does not save us by zapping us. We have freedom to accept and to refuse his gift, to receive Jesus and live by his teachings, or distort his teachings and ignore what is true. We have freedom based on our capacity to think and to make choices. So our salvation accomplished by Christ on the cross waits for our response: "Yes Lord, I believe! Yes, Lord, I will follow you! I will take up my cross and be your disciple because I know you love me—and I love you."

GLORIOUS MYSTERIES

First Glorious Mystery—Resurrection of Our Lord

I—*"I have seen the Lord!"* (John 20:18)
Our Father . . . Hail Mary . . . Glory Be . . .

1. Basilica of the Holy Sepulcher

The Basilica of the Holy Sepulcher in Jerusalem contains the tomb of Jesus as its focal point. In the holy tomb where we offer the holy mass and worship our Savior, probably the most spiritually intense experience on a pilgrimage to the Holy Land.

Candles, the smell of frankincense and of myrrh, two of the gifts offered to Jesus at his birth, representing his death and divinity—the other being gold which decorates the tomb, symbolizing Jesus's kingship.

The final destination for pilgrims is Jesus Christ, Son of God, true God and true man. The holy tomb offers pilgrims the occasion to experience something of the divine and human. Pilgrims risked their lives on journeys, whether by boat sailing across the sea, or on foot, horseback, or caravan across the Balkans, the Byzantine Empire, Syria, and finally to Jerusalem. A perilous journey motivated out of thanksgiving or to obtain graces or indulgences.

Arab Muslims—warriors—conquered this region of western Asia, followed by Turkish Muslims who brought an end to the Christian crusades. Motivated by their faith, arriving from Europe, the crusaders "took up the cross" with the hope that if they died in battle, God would have mercy on their souls for their past sins, anticipating to be finally received in paradise by God.[1]

---

1. See Weidenkopf, *Timeless*, 219–23.

On July 15, 1099, conquering Jerusalem and wresting it from Muslim control, the crusaders entered the basilica. Practically destroyed under the Fatimad dynasty, the basilica's tomb paradoxically was left intact, and by divine providence, the tomb became the mark of identification.

Only the atrium and the rotunda remained of what the eastern emperor Michael IV Paphlagon (1034-41) had rebuilt. The basilica as it stands today contains chapels dedicated in 1149, the work of the crusader period. The Romanesque church was built over the courtyard during the time of Constantine, where we see the present-day basilica linked to the rotunda; building projects of the crusader period from 1163–70 included the belltower that remains visible today. On entering through the main doors, the calvary chapels were built immediately to the right.[2] Providence has worked through history so Christians can visit the site where our Savior was buried and from where he resurrected. God wanted to strengthen our faith so we have not only a historical and geographic center, but also a physical, tangible point of reference to encounter Jesus—in a faith grounded on witnesses. The basilica testifies to these truths of Scriptures—the basilica protects—and has even kept hidden—these truths we find in the New Testament surrounding the death of Jesus.

i. Holy Tomb

Jesus was placed into the tomb of Joseph of Arimathea, who went to Pilate asking for Jesus's body, "Then Joseph bought a linen cloth, and taking down the body, wrapped it in the linen cloth, and laid it in a tomb that had been hewn out of the rock. He then rolled a stone against the door of the tomb" (Mark 15:46).

During the time of Jesus, tombs were opened and closed because of subsequent family members buried in the tombs. The tombs were sealed by a round heavy stone—cut like a wheel—requiring several people to roll away the stone from the entrance of the tomb. The women going to the tomb ask, "Who will roll away the stone for us from the entrance to the tomb?" (Mark 16:3).

Visiting the Basilica of the Holy Sepulcher, the tomb of Jesus was built behind the Syrian chapel. The *Aedicula,* "small structure," refers to the top of the tomb where Jesus was laid; over this tomb is where Jesus rose from the dead.[3] The smell of frankincense and candle flames fill the

2. Murphy-O'Connor, *Holy Land,* 52–54.

3. The altar itself over the tomb provides enough space for the priest to preside and one or two people to join in prayer and circulate through the tomb while he presides

senses as one enters this mystery of our Lord's death and resurrection. Archaeological findings in 2016 reveal the actual slab on which Jesus's body was laid was placed under the altar.[4] The experience of the holy tomb produces a glimpse of paradise.

If we keep in mind that the tombs during Jesus's day required several people to roll the stone, if the tomb were to be visited, these visits were directly related to the perfuming of the body. Bodies were not in closed coffins, and not in buried walls, nor even in the ground, but wrapped in linen and placed on benches or shelves within the tomb. When these bodies were completely decomposed, leaving nothing but bones, the bones were crushed and placed into jars—a common jar with other family members.

When we follow the stations of the cross, third sorrowful mystery, in the fourteenth station, Jesus is placed in the tomb, precisely the location where Jesus was anointed, wrapped in linen cloths, and sealed in the tomb: the sight of the tomb is also where the resurrection occurs.

During the time that Jesus was dead, what we call Holy Saturday, or the Day of the Tomb, the body of Jesus lay between the Friday and Sunday, the crucifixion and the resurrection. Before the resurrection of Jesus, Saint Thomas Aquinas explains Jesus descended to hell to lead all the souls of the just, including the patriarchs, to heaven: "Christ's descent into hell," to deliver all those who were detained before the crucifixion of Jesus and were liberated by him. We pray this in the Nicene Creed: "he descended into hell."[5]

ii. Women at the Tomb

If we continue with Saint Mark's Gospel, we read, "When they looked up, they saw that the stone, which was very large, had already been rolled back" (Mark 16:4). The first sign that we have an unusual situation is the stone was rolled away; it takes several people to roll away tombstones. The immediate question: Who moved the stone? Here the event would be witnessed and transmitted by the women who reached the tomb.

1. Mary Magdalene and the other Mary (Matt 28:1);

---

since the time to visit is limited; the mass and visit totals 20–30 minutes maximum because of pilgrims lined up waiting outside. The Catholic pilgrim company, 206 Tours, arranged for us to have mass first thing in the morning to allow the pilgrims to participate at mass. My pilgrimage to Jerusalem in 2019 was in thanksgiving for ten years of ordination to the priesthood.

4. This is the same altar where Holy Mass is celebrated. See also, Murphy-O'Connor, *Holy Land*, 218–19.

5. Aquinas, *ST*, Pt. 3, q. 52.

2. Mary Magdalene, and Mary mother of James, and Salome (Mark 16:1);

3. Mary Magdalene, Joanna, and Mary mother of James (and other women) (Luke 24:10);

4. Mary Magdalene (John 20:1)

All four Gospel accounts express the inexplicable removal of the stone. In the case of Matthew, an angel descended, followed by a violent earthquake, and rolled away the stone. Clearly, Matthew wants to offer an explanation to the fact that when the women reached the tomb, the stone was removed, as we find in the three remaining Gospels. Whether it's three women or two women or just one, in each case the evidence is coherent: there is no stone. The devoted women present at the crucifixion certainly went to the tomb.

Mark's Gospel indicates the women "bought spices, so they might go and anoint him. And very early on the first day of the week, when the sun had risen, they went to the tomb" (Mark 16:1–2). The women set out for the tomb to anoint Jesus. And they waited for the day after the Sabbath respecting Mosaic teaching, what is now our Sunday.

iii. Dark/Light

What do the Scriptures tell us about the tomb? The Day of Preparation approached, the Sabbath, sunset on the Friday, ". . . and the tomb was nearby, they laid Jesus there" (John 19:42). Joseph of Arimathea, a member of the Jewish Council, or Sanhedrin (Mark 15:43), asked Pilate for the body of Jesus (Matt 27:58). We also know that the tomb was guarded, given the Pharisees' ongoing preoccupation with Jesus—an "imposter"—and familiar with the words of Jesus that on the third day, "I will rise from the dead," the Pharisees ensured the tomb was guarded so the disciples of Jesus could not remove him (Matt 27:62–66). The tomb was new, hewn from rock; Jesus was bound in linen cloths once he was anointed with herbs and spices, placed on a rock shelf, then, once everyone left, the tomb entrance was covered with a tombstone, sealed, and guarded.

John's Gospel informs us that it was "still dark" (John 20:1). John highlights the dark/light contrast which he focuses on just as we read in the prologue of John's Gospel. Mary Magdalene represents a dramatic story of "turning around"; she faithfully follows Christ to the cross, representing the human experience of conversion. This radical shift from adultery to sanctity, having met Jesus, Mary Magdalene's life is transformed (John 8).

Mary Magdalene, a disciple of Christ, lived in darkness until Christ led her to the light; she embodies the truth of Jesus and love purified by truth. Mary Magdalene is filled with desire to meet our Lord in a rock-hewn tomb (Luke 23:53). John presents Mary Magdalene with this propelling force of love that cannot wait. We might ask whether Mary Magdalene represented one of the few followers of Jesus who seized the message of Jesus—that he would rise from the dead. Did Mary Magdalene visit the tomb with this anticipation? Perhaps she joined the other women or anticipated their presence to anoint Jesus once the stone was removed. But the encounter between Mary Magdalene and Jesus reflects the power of radical love when it has been purified by the truth of Jesus's teachings. Love dominates, but for Mary Magdalene she discovered that love is purified by truth.

First Appearance—Jerusalem: Jesus Greets Mary Magdalene

Mary Magdalene returns to the tomb, anxiously seeking her Savior, repeating the words to herself that he would rise, the person who changed her life. She arrived at the tomb in the dark of the morning. John tells us that Mary Magdalene goes to the tomb on the first day of the week early, "while it was still dark" (John 20:1). Mary Magdalene immediately notices the stone removed from the tomb. And that the tomb is empty. Mary Magdalene runs to tell the disciples, Peter and John, "we do not know where they have laid him" (John 20:2).

So, they all run back to the tomb—Mary Magdalene, Peter, John. Reaching the tomb, John stoops to look, and though he does not go in, he notices the linen cloths lying there. Peter enters the tomb, and apart from seeing the linen cloths which had wrapped Jesus, he also sees "the cloth that had been on Jesus's head, not lying with the linen wrappings but rolled up in a place by itself" (John 20:7). At this stage, John enters the tomb, the empty tomb, "he saw and believed" (John 20:8).

A vivid account is provided: a napkin on the head of Jesus, now rolled, not with the linen cloths but separate. We have a sense of movement that is conveyed by Peter's observation and that John records: the napkin that is separate from the linen cloth and rolled; movement in a sealed and guarded tomb relating to Jesus; he is no longer lying on a slab as he had been positioned at his burial.

The first experience recorded of the apostles is Peter and John. Though John outran Peter in his youthful enthusiasm, he did not go into the tomb. Peter, to whom authority was entrusted by Jesus, enters first; John acknowledges Peter's authority. Only afterwards does John who reached the tomb first go into the tomb (John 20:4–8). What is the experience of both? An empty tomb, or specifically, a linen shroud and removed cloth.

We are told they "saw and believed; for as yet they did not understand the scripture, that he must rise from the dead" (John 20:8–9). But now with the tomb empty, the connections are made: Prophets, Law, and Jesus; they believed. An understanding with the empty tomb that they previously did not experience. Peter and John previously acquired knowledge without fully grasping; now they have knowledge with understanding. The Pharisees too "knew" the Scriptures, and yet they "did not know" the Scriptures because they did not understand how the Prophets and the Law veiled Jesus who was unveiled with the incarnation, death, and resurrection.

Mary Magdalene remains confused about the empty tomb. She wants to know where Jesus's body is. Why did she not leave with Peter and John? Mary Magdalene's words when she reports to Peter and John: "we do not know where they have laid him" (John 20:2). How was the stone removed? Mary Magdalene made two inferences: the stone was rolled away, the body of Jesus removed. But Peter and John witnessed the shroud and napkin, and Jesus missing from the tomb. Peter and John believed because at that point they understood the Scriptures. Mary Magdalene stood outside of the tomb waiting, wondering who removed the body of Jesus from the tomb, and why this was done.

We can imagine this state of confusion. Mary Magdalene at this stage did not enter the tomb, nor was she thinking about the Scriptures like Peter and John who entered the tomb. Mary Magdalene's thoughts remained focused on her Savior, who was first crucified, and then, his body removed from the tomb. Why? What more injustice? Who could do this? Love desires the presence of the other. These are two faith experiences: the apostles whose knowledge of the Scriptures allows them to grasp the meaning of the empty tomb, but Mary Magdalene, prompted by her love for the Lord, has the human need of his tangible presence. Mary Magdalene's heart burns with love. She does not see Jesus. They have taken her Savior away.

"But Mary stood weeping outside the tomb" (John 20:11). So, she finally enters the tomb herself once Peter and John left. She observes where Jesus's body was lain. Hearing the question, "Why are you weeping?" Mary Magdalene replies, "Because they have taken away my Lord and I do not know where they have laid him" (John 20:13). From the start, Mary Magdalene expressed the same concern: "Where did they put our Lord?"

Now in the tomb, as Mary Magdalene turns around, still convinced Jesus was taken away, she notices someone. During this whole time Mary Magdalene wept, and she was asked, "Why do you weep?" We sense the emotional intensity of these events following the crucifixion, a series of inexplicable occurrences. Believing to be speaking to the gardener, Mary Magdalene asks him to tell her where Jesus has been laid (John 20:15).

She wants to know where Jesus is because he is not in the tomb. So, where is he? What have they done with him? "Just tell me where he is." Are these not the words of love? The fidelity of a woman to the one who transformed her. Now, Mary Magdalene expresses her love for Jesus by being present to him—truth responds with love.

I wonder how Mary Magdalene felt at that moment. The resurrection of Jesus is the greatest event in the history of humanity. This woman who grieves and is confused looks to see where her executed Savior has been laid. If only someone could tell her. An empty tomb, linen wrappings, and cloth on the ground, angels where Jesus should have been lying, and now apparently, the gardener. The first day of the week, sunrise, and these dramatic events take place in a tomb.

Still looking in the tomb where Jesus was supposed to be, she hears "Mary" and turns to the voice. Upon hearing her name, she recognized Jesus's voice. Each person has their own way of articulating sounds even if they are the same sounds. Jesus calling her name, unique to his voice, "Mary" (John 20:16). The sonority, the pitch, the intonation, unique to Jesus calling Mary's name. Only then, only upon hearing her name, uttered by her Savior, does Mary Magdalene turn around and recognize him.

The voice of the shepherd. Is this not where Saint John leads us, focusing on the voice of Jesus when Jesus calls her "Mary"? "My sheep hear my voice. I know them, and they follow me" (John 10:27). And Mary Magdalene clearly knows his voice. What is in the voice? Distinct person, words made up of sounds identifying the person. Calling the person's name, knowing the individual, like being called one by one as we enter into the kingdom of heaven. Jesus calls each of us by name, the shepherd who knows his sheep, and each passes through the gate. In the voice we hear, we find knowledge of the other, to recognize the voice means to know the other. In the voice we have the first word, our name, by which God calls us. We have God who speaks his word of truth. We have in the Word of God, the incarnation, Jesus Christ himself who is incarnated in the flesh of Mary. The word that draws us to truth, to Christ, to his healing love—as we all need healing, just as Mary Magdalene did.

And so, Mary replies, "Rabouni," "teacher of the Word," "teacher of truth," "Word that saves." Jesus speaks to Mary Magdalene of his ascension and to tell the disciples that he will be going to his Father and their—*your*—Father, to his God, and their—*your*—God (John 20:17). The words express unity: one God, one Father by whom Jesus was sent and to whom Jesus will return. While distinguishing that we are the adopted children of the Father, we are one with the Father, and Jesus teaches us we will return to the Father.

And what are Mary Magdalene's words returning to the disciples: "I have seen the Lord!" (John 20:18). Mary Magdalene announces the resurrection.[6] The disciples believed and understood upon seeing an empty tomb, but Mary Magdalene proclaims the resurrection having seen Jesus and receiving instructions from him, "Go and tell, say to the disciples . . ." (John 20:17). An affirmation of Jesus's oneness with the Father; to believe in Jesus means to follow him and to return to the same God, the Father who sent him. One could imagine the excitement and joy of Mary Magdalene. She wept believing that Jesus was taken away, not knowing where he was placed. And now, she not only sees him in front of her, but he speaks to her first by calling her name: "Mary."

Jesus first appears to Mary Magdalene, and she spreads the news of having seen the Lord. Proclaiming and spreading the good news of the resurrection is amplified by the further appearances made by Jesus.

Second Appearance—Emmaus: Jesus Breaking Bread

In Luke's Gospel we have the details of two men going to Emmaus, a village about seven miles from Jerusalem (Luke 24:13–35).[7] They were walking together "talking with each about all these things that happened" (Luke 24:14). Jesus joins them—not uncommon walking between villages joining others on the journey even if the individuals are unknown. But they do not recognize him, focused on the conversation and the road ahead. When Jesus asked what the men were discussing, Cleopas answered, "Are you the only stranger in Jerusalem who does not know the things that have happened there in these days?" (Luke 24:18). This suggests that the people in Jerusalem were speaking of the events surrounding the crucifixion. When Jesus replied, "What things?" Not recognizing, Jesus they were surprised the companion was oblivious to the news (Luke 24:19). Cleopas replies, "The things about Jesus of Nazareth, who was a prophet mighty in deed and word before God and all the people, and how our chief priests and leaders handed him over to be condemned to death and crucified him. But we had hoped that he was the one to redeem Israel" (Luke 24:19–21).

---

6. For this reason, Mary Magdalene is considered the Patroness of the Order of Preachers. Pope Francis raised the memorial of Saint Mary Magdalene to a feast day, observed July 22.

7. Approximately 11.25 kilometers.

Cleopas summarizes the events that occurred and the identity of Jesus, then gives a time frame: "It is now the third day since these things took place" (Luke 24:21); in other words, the morning of the resurrection. The core event circulating proved to be consistent: the tomb of Jesus was empty. But since the men repeated that Jesus's body was not seen, Jesus intervenes, saying, "Was it not necessary that the Messiah should suffer these things and then enter into his glory? Then beginning with Moses and all the prophets . . ." (Luke 24:26–27). Jesus points to the Scriptures to show that the one crucified was the Christ—the "anointed one"—the Law and Prophets fulfilled.

Now, the men at Emmaus, themselves without recognizing Jesus, requested, "stay with us" (Luke 24:29). And Jesus shares their meal with them, he blesses the bread, breaks the bread, and gives the bread to them, familiar gestures and words. Their eyes opened, they recognize Jesus, and Jesus vanishes (Luke 24:30–32). At that moment, the men ask each other, "Were not our hearts burning within us while he was talking to us on the road, while he was opening the scriptures to us?" (Luke 24:32). When they returned to Jerusalem the resurrection was confirmed, and they related the events on the way to Emmaus to the apostles: "he had been known to them in the breaking of the bread" (Luke 24:35).

Their hearts burned; the Scriptures were opened to them. They recognized Jesus in the breaking of the bread. Jesus opens the Scriptures by revealing he is the fulfillment of the Law and the Prophets just as he interpreted Moses and the Prophets for them. These events taking place from Jerusalem to Emmaus; after Emmaus the men return to Jerusalem to join the apostles. The resurrection of Jesus continues to spread like a wildfire, witnesses present and the presence of Jesus confirming these stories.

Third Appearance: Jesus Shows Thomas His Wounds

Jesus's appearances continue as the drama unfolds with more people believing. Still on the first day of the week, namely, Sunday evening, we hear, "Jesus came and stood among them and said, 'Peace be with you.' After he said this, he showed them his hands and his side" (John 20:19–20). Jesus appears to the ten disciples. First, it was his voice, now we have his wounds: "his hands and his side." These are the marks of the crucifixion of Jesus, evidence of the man who on the day before the Sabbath had been crucified. Now he is resurrected from the dead.

When the disciples tell Thomas they had seen the Lord, Thomas replies with skepticism: "Unless I see the mark of the nails in his hands, and put my finger in the mark of the nails and my hand in his side, I will not believe" (John 20:25). Thomas represents the classic skeptic. The doubtful person who needs more than just a witness account to believe—even if there were ten witnesses. Some people are skeptics by trait, others by profession. Seeding doubts is victory for the skeptic. The skeptic may even doubt his own existence.

Thomas demands empirical evidence that he can touch Jesus; sight does not persuade Thomas into believing; he needs the tangible experience of physical contact. And we are told that eight days later the disciples of Jesus were gathered and Thomas was among them, "Put your finger here, and see my hands. Reach out your hand and put it in my side. Do not doubt but believe" (John 20:27). Thomas replies at this stage, "My Lord and my God!" (John 20:28). Thomas believes, as Jesus tells him, because he had seen, but, "Blessed are those who have not seen and yet believe" (John 20:29). Jesus knows that the belief of his followers for generations to come will be the eyewitness testimony of his own apostles. This means that the faith of those who have not seen relies on the witness accounts of those who were present and experienced the resurrection of Jesus. Our faith rests on their testimony, so what we believe is historically grounded and documented.

Fourth Appearance—Tiberius: Jesus Eats Breakfast with His Apostles

I remember one of our pilgrimages began on Easter Sunday in Jordan, then continued into Israel and Palestine, extending across biblical lands with our Easter liturgical readings. We read about more and more witnesses of Jesus's resurrection recorded in the Scriptures; we visited and prayed on the biblical sites in our Scripture readings following the Roman Catholic Easter readings. Our pilgrimage continued. We stood at the same locations where Jesus appeared in Galilee. We felt so close to these events recorded in the Bible. On the shores of the Sea of Galilee, John's Gospel spoke to us: "After these things Jesus showed himself again to the disciples by the Sea of Tiberias; and he showed himself in this way" (John 21:1). A detailed account relates the events. Simon Peter, Thomas, Nathanael, James, and John, and two others join Simon Peter fishing. The seven went fishing but they caught nothing. As day breaks, Jesus stands on the beach, but he was unrecognizable; and then, Jesus asks for fish, so he must have yelled from some distance, then he tells them to "cast the net on the right side of the boat" because they had not caught anything. They followed Jesus's instructions. They soon discovered they could not haul in the net because of all the fish. Until that moment, they wondered who this person might be. John finally recognizes him and tells Peter, "It is the Lord!" (John 21:2–7). And so, Simon Peter dove into the water and swam to the shore.

John describes the event with details including measurement; the boat was about a hundred yards from the beach (John 21:8).[8] Jesus instructs them to bring fish so they can put it on the charcoal fire and Jesus invites them to have breakfast (John 21:10, 12). Jesus took the bread and gave it to them, as he does the same with the fish (John 21:13). Jesus "takes" and "gives"; he "feeds." In this passage Jesus reveals more of himself than the previous appearances: he shares with the disciples bread and fish. This event of Jesus having breakfast with his apostles is remembered and celebrated in the Holy Land in the town of Tabgha at the Church of the Primacy of Peter.[9] The church faces the Sea of Galilee, and the rock-cut steps are also mentioned by Egeria who travelled to the Holy Land in 380 AD.[10]

These events we hear about in John's Gospel show similarities with the events in Luke's Gospel (Luke 24:36-43), where Jesus appears to the disciples behind locked doors eating fish in front of them; they thought they were seeing a ghost. The resurrection of Jesus was not entirely understood, even though Jesus told his disciples during his ministry that he would rise on the third day. Moreover, Jesus makes clear that this resurrection is the fulfillment of the Scriptures. Jesus's increasingly physical presence extends to eating breakfast with his disciples. Jesus reveals in these related events he is truly risen.

II—Fruit of this Mystery: Virtue of Faith

Practical Matters—

Our faith in the resurrection of Jesus rests on what evidence? The empty tomb followed by witness accounts of the resurrection of Jesus; the apostles and others offered testimonies of the physical presence of Jesus: Jerusalem, Emmaus, Lake Tiberius.[11]

The recorded events of the resurrection by eyewitnesses are fundamental to our Christian faith; it means that what we believe rests on the testimony of the apostles, followers of Jesus, and others who experienced

---

8. About 91.5 meters.
9. Since the crusader period known as *Mensa Christi*, "Table of Christ."
10. Murphy-O'Connor, *Holy Land*, 319. The chapel, built in 1933, identifies the location where Jesus ate breakfast with his disciples after his resurrection.
11. Egeria, *Egeria's Travels*, 97; see also Kilgallen, *New Testament Guide*, 48.

the presence of the risen Lord physically in different contexts. Mary Magdalene, a faithful follower of Jesus, hearing his voice and seeing him, was the first to announce the risen Lord. The disciples at Emmaus, who recognized Jesus in the breaking of the bread, realized their hearts burned in his presence. The appearance of Jesus to the ten visibly, and then the tactile presence of Jesus to Thomas, when the latter touched the wounds of Jesus. Finally, in Galilee at Lake Tiberius, Jesus eats breakfast with his disciples, eating broiled fish with them.

Our faith rests on these testimonies. Now, we have faith because we believe that Jesus rose from the dead even if we did not witness this ourselves. We believe the apostles who witnessed the resurrection of Jesus. We have faith because God helps us with his grace to believe. We know Jesus is true God and true man, so he has the power to save us and to give us eternal life.

Dealing with Doubt

When we believe, like Mary Magdalene, we are transformed; our lives necessarily change. To encounter Jesus means to be forever changed. An encounter with Jesus is truly personal.

The lack of faith is evident in how people live their lives. Already present in the book of Genesis, the serpent leads the man and the woman to doubt God. Doubts about God's truthfulness and goodness; Satan instills in the person's mind and heart doubt. Faith begins in the home with parents who teach their children the commandments, to love God and to love each other. In the rite of baptism, in the "reception of the child," addressing the parents, the priest or deacon states, "You have asked to have your children baptized. In doing so, you are accepting the responsibility of training them in the practice of the faith. It will be your duty to bring them up to keep God's commandments as Christ taught us, by loving God and our neighbor."[12] Catholic schools exist to nourish the faith of the child: to teach what is true and good as found in the Scriptures and the magisterium of the Catholic Church and in natural law. Catholic schools serve this purpose: to help build the faith of the child with a Catholic spiritual and moral formation.[13] The child is baptized in the faith of the parents, but this faith to be lived out concretely needs to be nourished and sustained if we are to overcome the poisonous effects of doubt when we lose trust.

---

12. Roman ritual, "Rite of Baptism for Children."

13. Catholic schools fulfil their mission only when they provide the child/adolescent—besides academics—with a spiritual and moral formation that reflect Catholic teaching—biblical, magisterial, and natural law.

At one time, we could count on the Christian values of society to transmit some degree of religious awareness. But the subjectivism that prevails in our once-Christian societies where each person decides what is true and good, and militant groups campaign to change laws in conflict not only with Christian values but even violate the natural law, has transformed Western societies to look increasingly and aggressively pagan, even imposing and exporting their neopagan culture abroad.

In Christianity we find two extremes that have emerged since the sixteenth century: one extreme is "fideistic," where the truth of biblical faith is limited to a literal level without exercising reason to deepen this faith by probing the layers of meaning in the Scriptures; and the other extreme is "rationalism," where truth is limited to scientific evidence, while dismissing matters of faith. We should seek to harmonize faith and reason, Scriptures and science, rather than opposing them. The same Holy Spirit, the source of one truth, gives us both revelation and science.[14]

Our faith is manifested in our works; our works manifest our faith. Our faith draws upon grace, and grace provides us with the strength we need to carry out works. Catholicism is a grace-filled spirituality. We see evidence of this Catholic spirituality in the history of our cathedrals, shrines, monasteries, and medieval universities. These spiritual structures that serve as religious, moral, and intellectual pillars of societies throughout two thousand years and across the world reflect the Catholic faith and mission that believes and preaches the resurrected Christ.

---

14. John Paul II issued the encyclical *Fides et Ratio* in 1998 on this very discussion; the relationship between faith and reason.

Second Glorious Mystery—Ascension of Our Lord

I—So then, when the Lord Jesus had spoken to them, He was received up into heaven and sat down at the right hand of God. (Mark 16:19)

Our Father ... Hail Mary ... Glory Be ...

1. Ascension

We are told in Mark's Gospel, "... he is going ahead of you to Galilee; there you will see him, just as he told you" (Mark 16:7). The disciples encounter Jesus in Galilee; he appears to them at the shores of Tiberius where he has breakfast with them (John 21:12–13).

After appearing to them in Galilee, Jesus ascends into heaven: "taken up into heaven" (Mark 16:19). Before ascending, Jesus leaves his disciples one final command: "Go into all the world and proclaim the good news to the whole creation. The one who believes and is baptized will be saved; but the one who does not believe will be condemned" (Mark 16:14–16).

Just before his ascension, Jesus leaves a command to proclaim the Gospel and baptize; the end goal is to save humanity—Jesus conveys his message of salvation with exactness. Whether this means parents bringing their children to be baptized, or someone who asks to be baptized, the objective remains the same: salvation through Christ. Neither children nor adults are excluded. Samaritans are not excluded, nor are Greek and Roman gentiles excluded. We discover at Pentecost that the Gospel of salvation is truly for all people. While the invitation is intended for all, not everyone is disposed to receive the body and blood, either because they do not yet believe or their moral behavior violates Christ's teachings. Parents have an instrumental role to play in their child's faith journey starting at baptism:

the removal of original sin, transmitting new life in Christ, belonging to the Christian community, and instructing their children to follow the commandments of God. And so baptism in the Holy Spirit cleanses, recreates their child in Christ, and reconciles the child to our Father in heaven. The child belongs to the Trinitarian community of faith.

An adult, after reflection and prayer, and conforming himself to the teachings of Jesus called "conversion," signifies not only an act of faith but a radical act of conforming one's life to Jesus Christ and his teachings. Baptism is not lip service, but radical living according to what Christ taught us: pursuing the Way, the truth, and the life—Jesus himself—to love God, and to love our neighbor as ourselves. This is what the disciples are called to preach, and this is what we are taught to live.

In Mark's Gospel we have explicit reference made to the ascension of Jesus witnessed by the apostles; Jesus was "taken up into heaven" and similarly we find in Luke's Gospel, "While he was blessing them, he withdrew from them and was carried up into heaven" (Luke 24:51).

Events from the resurrection to the ascension in Mark's Gospel shift from Jerusalem to Galilee, so the latter may be where the ascension took place. However, the geographic information provided in Mark's Gospel does not identify the ascension specifically with Galilee. The events between the resurrection and ascension constitute a series of appearances, increasingly physical with the presence of Jesus and increasingly numerous in terms of witnesses. Unlike the resurrection, the ascension is not a series of events, but rather one ascension into heaven—Jesus returns to his Father.

The apostles are reminded that everything written about Jesus in the Law of Moses, in the Prophets, and in the Psalms has been fulfilled (Luke 24:44). And at this stage, Jesus speaks of their minds being opened so they may understand, adding that his disciples are "witnesses to this": his suffering, rising from the dead, and repentance for the forgiveness of sins will be preached to all (Luke 24:47).

Jesus brings his disciples "as far as Bethany" and blesses them. As he withdrew, Jesus "was carried up into heaven" (Luke 24:50–51). Jesus appeared outside of Bethany, and we know that Bethany is where Jesus visited his close friends, Mary, Martha, and Lazarus.

Unlike the resurrection that occurred over many days—weeks—after forty days in fact, the ascension occurred as a singular event. The ascension takes place in the presence of his disciples, speaking to his disciples, and blessing his disciples. Jesus's final words, "go into all the world"—the great commission—was followed by Jesus being taken up to heaven. Before Jesus ascends, therefore, he reaffirms his teachings, making clear his identity in relation to the Law and Prophets; he instructs his disciples to bless and baptize to save humanity.

If we now look at the opening passage from the Acts of the Apostles, again reference is made to Jesus's ascension into heaven: "When he had said this, as they were watching, he was lifted up, and a cloud took him out of their sight" (Acts 1:9).

The ascension is not the extended event as the resurrection. In all references to the ascension, Jesus is taken up to heaven in a cloud, and this occurs only after Jesus gives his final instructions to the disciples. Reference is made to John's baptism in water, and now already with the anticipation of the Holy Spirit, Jesus tells his disciples, "... but you will be baptized with the Holy Spirit not many days from now" (Acts 1:5). This is the reference to the outpouring of the Holy Spirit at Pentecost.

After the forty days, once Jesus ascended to heaven, he is enthroned at the right of the Father. When Jesus was questioned by the high priest, "Are you the Messiah, the Son of the Blessed One?" (Mark 14:61), Jesus replies, "'I am'; and 'you will see the Son of Man seated at the right hand of the Power,' and 'coming with the clouds of heaven'" (Mark 14:62). So, allusion is made to both "sitting on the right hand of God" and being "taken up into heaven" (Acts 1:9).

We might think of Jesus's ascension in terms of being raised up to heaven, leaving the earth, an ongoing action without any rest. But, we also need to ask, when he is taken up, and when he ascends, where does he go? And this is what Jesus states in Mark's Gospel: "at the right hand of the Father." So, the ascension cannot be separated from Jesus returning to the Father and sitting on the Father's right hand, expressing this eternal union between Father and Son. Jesus not only spends his ministry preaching the oneness between God the Father and God the Son, but he also teaches before his departure from the world, his return to the Father, the Spirit of truth will be sent (John 14:12–17).

Because the ascension is the fulfillment of what Jesus reveals of himself as the Messiah and the Son of Man (Dan 7:13), we need to ask how else Jesus is the fulfillment of messianic prophecies. We examine the expression Jesus uses in Mark "the Son of Man" (Mark 14:62).

Jesus employs the eschatological language foretold by the prophets using the expression Son of Man which we find for the first time used by the prophet Daniel. The image of the cloud suggests a divine presence as recorded in the Acts of the Apostles. When Jesus says that he has come to fulfil the law and the prophets (Matt 5:17), this has been realized at the Last Supper and consummated on the cross marking the new covenant as we meditated in the fifth sorrowful mystery. These prophecies of a messianic nature indicate that the Messiah will come to save the people of Israel. Jesus, the Messiah, teaches he has not only come for the people of Israel, but all of humanity. Restoring the kingdom of David is part of the messianic prophecies: the fulfillment of the prophecies begins with the angel announcing to Mary that God has chosen her to give birth to the Messiah as we meditate in the first and third joyful mysteries.

2. Son of Man

In this second glorious mystery, we can look more closely at the ascension by the use of the prophetic expression, "Son of Man." This phrase appears in Luke's Gospel with an eschatological reference of "last days," as Jesus states: "The days are coming when you will long to see one of the days of the Son of Man, and you will not see it" (Luke 17:22). In Matthew's Gospel before the Sanhedrin and just before his execution, Jesus responds to the high priest, "From now on you will see the Son of Man seated at the right hand of Power and coming on the clouds of heaven" (Matt 26:64); the image alludes to the writings of the prophet Daniel. But the reference also alludes to Psalms of David: "The LORD says to my lord, 'Sit at my right hand . . .'" (Ps 110:1). Jesus is regarded as a blasphemer by the high priest because Jesus equates himself with the messianic figure in Daniel, the "Son of Man," a glorious messianic personage. In fact, the association with the Son of Man sitting at the "right hand of Power" places Jesus in a religious court where he is accused and tried for blasphemy. But his trial shifts into a political direction to justify Jesus's execution as meditated in the second and third sorrowful mysteries, flagellation, and Jesus takes up his cross, respectively.

The prophet Daniel writes at the time of the desecration of Jerusalem during the Babylonian captivity in the sixth century BC. The allusion to the "Son of Man" is built up as a climax after Daniel describes four beasts, each more terrifying than the previous (Dan 7:1–12; 13–14, 21–22). The beasts symbolize cruel and wicked kings, but the fourth beast was "making war on the holy ones" until the "Ancient One came." A shift from earth to heaven where we encounter in a royal courtroom an individual, "one like a human being coming with the clouds of heaven" (Dan 7:13).[1] Daniel further prophesies that, "To him was given dominion and glory and kingship, that all peoples, nations, and languages should serve him. His dominion is an everlasting dominion that shall not pass away. . ." (Dan 7:14). The eschatological language from the mouth of Daniel characterizes

---

1. "One like a human being," translated from Aramaic. NRSVCE, note: Dan 7:13, "one like a son of man."

the "Son of Man" with his universal kingship over "all people" and eternal, his reign will "never pass away."

The "clouds" also described in the Acts of the Apostles are associated with Jesus's ascension followed by a cloud. The Son of Man in Daniel's prophetic vision is to be judged worthy by the court and given a kingdom incomparable in size and affluence to any other kingdom. The Son of Man is crowned and the court also pronounces upon the fourth most wicked beast, a verdict of condemnation. The wicked beast becomes powerless; his dominion is transferred to the "Son of Man" and the "holy ones, the saints of God" (Dan 7:27). The "Son of Man" takes on a divine meaning with eschatological associations: his kingship "shall never be destroyed."

Even before the prophet Daniel, the eighth-century prophet Isaiah provides a sign (Isa 7:14): "Look, the young woman is with child and shall bear a son, and shall name him Immanuel."[2] The annunciation, first joyful mystery, fulfils Isaiah's prophesy when the angel Gabriel appears to the Virgin Mary, telling her, "He will be great, and will be called the Son of the Most High, and the Lord God will give to him the throne of his ancestor David. He will reign over the house of Jacob forever, and of his kingdom there will be no end" (Luke 1:32–33). The messianic language associated with the house of David appears in Nathan's prophecy: "and I will establish the throne of his kingdom forever" (2 Sam 7:13); also in the Psalms, "I will establish your descendant forever" (Ps 89:4), and "their sons also, forevermore, shall sit on your throne" (Ps 132:12). The angel's message to Mary at the annunciation draws from the Word of God to reveal the source of her conception; the child is born of the Holy Spirit. With the Scriptures familiar to Mary, we hear her response to what God has planned for her, the Word she is called to conceive.

The language of the annunciation is linked to the language of the ascension; the words of the angel's message to Mary, and her consent, find their fulfillment as promise in the ascension. Jesus was crucified and died, he resurrected, but now, in the ascension we see the fulfillment of the old covenant in Jesus Christ: now the new covenant.

3. Jesus's Kingship

Meditating the sorrowful mysteries and luminous mystery, a dominant theme in the Scriptures is "kingship" integral to the identity of Jesus: he is king. The ascension is the prophetic fulfillment of his kingship; Jesus sits at the "right hand of the Most High." The prophet Isaiah continues, "For

---

2. NRSVCE note: "young woman" in Greek, "virgin."

a child has been born for us, / a son given to us; / authority rests upon his shoulders; / and he is named / Wonderful Counselor, Mighty God, / Everlasting Father, Prince of Peace. / His authority shall grow continually, / and there shall be endless peace / for the throne of David and his kingdom. / He will establish and uphold it / with justice and with righteousness / from this time onward and forevermore" (Isa 9:6–7). Words used to identify the messianic figure signaling salvation, "Mighty God," "Prince of Peace," who will sit "upon the throne of David" and his kingdom lasts "forevermore." At the annunciation, the words used by the angel to address Mary conveys her mediating role as chosen mother of the Messiah; humanity depends on Mary's "yes," her *fiat:* "Let it be with me according to me your word," meditated in the first joyful mystery. The Davidic lineage of this son to be born, child of the house of Jacob, is made explicit in Isaiah, and repeated in Luke's Gospel, "the Lord God will give to him the throne of his ancestor David." The throne belongs to the king of Judah; David, born in Bethlehem, anointed king of Judah by the prophet Samuel.

God, addressing the prophet Nathan, says, "go and tell David, my servant." Nathan relates the words of God to David, telling him, "I will establish the throne of his kingdom forever. I will be a father to him, and he shall be a son to me ... Your house and your kingdom shall be made sure forever before me; your throne shall be established forever" (2 Sam 7:13–14, 16).

We have in these verses reference to the Davidic dynasty which comes from God: the messianic kingdom. We hear that David's kingship unites Judah and Israel; David captures Jerusalem which he makes his new capital (2 Sam 5:6); and David brings the ark of the covenant to Jerusalem: "David danced before the LORD with all his might; David was girded with a linen ephod" (2 Sam 6:14). But Nathan's prophetic language takes on especially personal elements expressed in the relationship between God and the Son of David: "I will be a father to him, and he shall be a son to me" (2 Sam 7:14). This language denotes a personal relationship between God and this Davidic king: he is Son of David.[3]

Now David is the father of a dynasty that will be secure forever. We are not simply told the kingdom will be powerful, which means capable of defending itself if under threat; the expression of "sure forever" transcends temporal space and time. Here, the prophecy conveys something of the eternal, a kingdom that has properties of the divine presence. Only God can be the source of a kingdom that moves beyond the earthly kingdom and into eternity. Nathan's prophecy expresses the Davidic kingdom

---

3. Bergsma and Pitre maintain, "this is the first time in the Old Testament that an individual person (as opposed to a group; is referred to as the "son of God" (cf. Gen 6:1–4; Exod 4:22). *Old Testament*, 364.

announced by the angel Gabriel to the Virgin Mary. Jesus fulfills the prophetic announcements by his very life where he now reigns forever at the right hand of the Most High, God the Father.[4]

But when the angel announces to Mary that she has been chosen by God to give birth to his Son whom she will call Jesus, the angel speaks to Mary of their ancestor Jacob: he will sit on the throne of his father David, and he will rule over the house of Jacob. We have looked at David as king of Judah and Israel, and the Davidic covenant when Nathan tells David his kingdom will be forever secure. The angel informs Mary that this child called "Jesus" "will reign over the house of Jacob forever" (Luke 1:33). How do we understand this reference to Jacob?

4. House of Jacob

The first book of the Bible informs us of Jacob's blessings (Gen 49). Addressed to Jacob's twelve sons, the blessings are expressed as prophecies and foretell what will fall upon his sons. After Reuben, Simeon, and Levi, Judah is then addressed: "Judah is a lion's whelp; from the prey, my son, you have gone up . . . The sceptre shall not depart from Judah, nor the ruler's staff from between his feet . . ." (Gen 49:9–10).

Judah is the fourth son of Jacob which makes this blessing a surprise. What about the first three sons, in particular, the first born son, Reuben? Reuben fornicated with his father's concubine (Gen 35:22). Simeon and Levi conspire together and act unjustly towards the Shechemites having slaughtered them while they were recovering from circumcision (Gen 34:24–25). Unlike the first three sons, Judah receives a blessing of power and authority: Jacob blesses Judah with kingship; "The sceptre shall not depart from Judah."

Jacob, father of the twelve tribes of Israel, blesses Judah before his death, bestowing upon him a unique place amongst brothers: "Judah, your brothers shall praise you . . . your father's sons shall bow down before you" (Gen 49:8). A sign of uninterrupted kingship is further expressed: "the sceptre shall not depart from Judah" (Gen 49:10). The language of Jacob singles out Judah as the son who justly deserves the blessing bestowed upon him amongst all twelve sons.

The message the angel transmits to the Virgin Mary is directly linked to Jacob's blessing traced to the words of Genesis: Jacob, Judah, David and finally Jesus. Mary certainly understood these biblical relations being a religious woman; she knew the significance of the promised Messiah for

---

4. See, Pss 89:3–4; 132:11–12.

whom the faithful people of God were waiting. The son of Mary, Son of the Most High whom she will name Jesus, will sit at the right of the power (Matt 26:64), at the right of God (Mark 16:9).

The second glorious mystery, the ascension, finds its source in earlier prophets, from Nathan, to Isaiah to Daniel showing the second glorious mystery is a fulfillment of prophecy: the angel Gabriel appearing to Mary reveals the fulfillment of God's promise through the incarnation of God's Word. This chosen woman responds freely with her yes: "Let it be with me according to your word"; the Word of God is enfleshed, the Second Person of the Trinity, God's wisdom—the law, the prophets.

The ascension fulfills the Law and Prophets. As we have seen this mystery is inseparable from the first joyful mystery, the annunciation. Just as Mary says in her freedom and with her faith, "Let it be with me according to your word," the ascension is precisely this fulfillment of God's promise transmitted from the time of Abraham with whom a personal covenant is first established (Gen 17:1–8), and in the words of the angel, the fulfillment of this promise rests on Mary's "yes." Her favorable response means the Son of God will be born in Mary's immaculate flesh, and Jesus will carry out his mission to save humanity by his flesh and blood and divinity, leading us to eternal life. Through his resurrection from the dead and ascension to the Father where he sits at the right hand, Jesus offers us a place in his eternal kingdom.

II—Fruit of this Mystery: Virtue of Hope; Desire for Heaven

Practical Matters—

The virtue associated with the second glorious mystery is "hope," and we can understand why: in following Jesus Christ we hope to enter the kingdom of heaven where we shall have eternal life. We hope to experience the peace and joy that Jesus has promised us: to be with him for all of eternity. Jesus sits at the right hand of the Father, as he had told us he has come to fulfil the Law and the Prophets. We can hope to live with him and share eternal happiness with him.

This "desire for heaven" associated with this mystery means that our hope is directed towards something far greater than we could possibly know or even imagine here on earth. But our hope rests on those experiences where we have tasted peace and joy, truth and purity, this sublime state, and to remain in this state of ecstasy forever.

A promise is something that looks ahead. And what God promises, he promises out of his love for us; he asks that we remain in communion with him by following his commandments, and so these promises may be fulfilled—not as a condition—but by our burning desire to be one with God. This desire finds its fulfillment through his Son, Jesus Christ, who unites us with God through the body and blood of his Son, thereby leading us to eternal life with the Triune God.

But to hope in something for which we wait, and not only wait while living on earth, but to wait until after our death, requires God's grace. We cannot hope in the promises of God by natural reason alone. We have evidence to believe in Jesus, the Scriptures and church tradition, but hoping for eternal life in the kingdom of heaven, something that is unknown to us except in faith, requires that we put our trust in God, and therefore, we need his grace to nourish and strengthen our hope that presupposes faith. Saint Thomas tells us faith precedes hope in the order of virtues that are acquired, just as hope leads to love. Each virtue builds on the previous.[5]

The challenge to hope is related to how we live our lives. We can live each day and express our hope for eternal salvation, or we can live each day, indifferent to sin, focused on the pleasures of this world, and what these pleasures offer, so that, hope for heaven is eclipsed by the material world. Who wants to think about the afterlife when we become attached to the seductions of this world? And who really wants to think about death? Life becomes simply what we live here and now. As one of my atheist philosophy professors told our undergraduate class, "At death, that's the end, folks." But even many Christians live their life as if there is neither judgement nor eternal life to think about—as if only our material existence on earth matters. The creed is professed but the profession of faith is not followed by interior conversion.

Our soul matters and our body matters, and how we prepare ourselves substantially united, body and soul, in the inevitability of death, and what happens after death matters. How do I live my life? To whom have I surrendered my life? To Christ or the golden calf?

Without faith, hope is not possible. We need to have faith in the resurrection and the ascension of Jesus in order for us to have hope that I, too, will join Jesus for eternity in his kingdom promised in the old covenant and Jesus fulfills in the new covenant—to be one with Jesus for all of eternity.

---

5. Aquinas, *ST*, Pt. 1a-2ae, q. 62., art. 3.

What is the reason for this hope? What if God had not sent his Son to save us? And what if our life simply ended, decomposing after death in our graves, as atheists and materialists believe? This is what exists without hope. Nothing. Nothingness. But God, who is the Creator, is a God who creates in truth and love. "Nothingness" cannot be the end of the story. By affirming the existence of something, the knowledge of our existence, that depends on the existence of a first being greater and more powerful than I, the source of my existence, of my very being, the being upon whom I depend for my very my existence: God the Creator.

God created us to be in communion with him. God created us for life. That's why death frightens us. Death is not part of nature. Life means to exist as a living being, a corporeal and spiritual being. God creates life, he sustains life, and he gives us new life through baptism, and eternal life through Jesus Christ. We are just beneath the angels in the hierarchy of being because we are spiritual beings with intelligence and freewill; we can pursue truth and choose good. Thus, we are embodied sensory beings with a spiritual soul above brute animals. The composite of body and soul lead us to be one with God forever. God brings us back to him with our freedom, as he gently draws us in different ways. Or we can refuse; the gift of salvation can be accepted or rejected. We exercise our freedom. And hope means that we will be guided by truth, choose what is good, and by God's grace persevere in virtue so we may be one with him in heaven. God sent us his Son to bring us back to him. God is a God of truth and love and wants us to be eternally in communion with him which is why he created us.

This is our hope: eternal life. This reflects the second glorious mystery, why we meditate on this mystery and pray, uniting ourselves with the mother of our Savior. So we may be saved and share in the eternal kingdom promised to us. This hope, believing, knowing, and anticipating something far greater than what we could possibly explain in our earthly life, this hope transforms how we live, the choices we make each day.

Hope is reflected in our detachments; what we are willing to let go, whatever those possessions may be, knowing we shall not be taking them or needing them after we die. Well, we will not be taking anything with us except our soul. Do we live each day in a spirit of freedom and detachment, knowing that our earthly goods remain with us for a period of time? And when the time comes, whatever those possessions—we need to let go—people, things, places? In this spirit of detachment, the willingness to let go means we can fix ourselves, thoughts, heart, soul, and body on God. Yes, even our body that moves us to pray, that leads us to act in our prayerful gestures, going to church, kneeling in adoration, joining a pilgrimage, or caring for a dying person.

The exercise of the virtue of hope continues to our last breath for the ultimate hope of our salvation, which we obtain by the grace of God, through the body and blood of Christ, and our repentance for all our past sins. After a journey of forty years following the voice of God from slavery to freedom, Moses led the Israelites out of Egypt through the wilderness to the promised land. Moses ascends Mount Nebo where God shows Moses the land promised to the people of Israel, but God tells Moses, "I have shown it to you with your own eyes; however, you will not cross over into it" (Deut 34:4). The end of Moses's mission was not to be experienced by Moses; he will die in the hope that the Israelites will take possession of this land. To die in faith. This is what it means to have hope; what we hope for may never be realized in our lifetime, but we can still die in hope that is sustained by faith—that our promised land awaits us.

Mary, the mother of our Savior, at the foot of the cross, experienced the torment of a mother, her pierced soul, united with the passion of her son. Her son, the promised Messiah, king, crucified on the cross, a slaughtered Lamb, Mary immaculate grasped in the depth of her soul the teaching of Jesus; her intelligence was not clouded in any way. The purity of her mind enabled Mary to see God's redemptive work. Mary recognized in front of her the crucified Lord, but the secrets she kept in her heart allowed Mary to hope beyond the cross of her Son: for eternal life.

The lack of hope, or its absence, is what leads to despair. A person who has nothing to hope for at the spiritual level falls into despair as life itself loses meaning. With the sense of purpose being lost, fundamental questions persist: "Why am I here?" "Where am I going?" "What purpose does my existence have?" A Christian believer may be attacked, even ambushed, but their faith leads to hope in the midst of persecution. We only need to think of the persecuted Christians and Christian martyrs of the past and present who drew from their faith, and hoped in eternal life where they are united with Christ, his blessed mother, and the angels and saints of heaven.

The lack of faith pulls at hope because hope has nothing to anchor into. This lack becomes filled with hopelessness and despair. This lack can be traced to the fall. The man and the woman created by God, after the fall transmit their sin, that rupture with God caused by disobedience. It becomes evident that man prefers his own gods, gods he creates for himself, turning towards his own disordered condition by the gods who direct him.

Yet, we discover, from the start of Genesis onwards, signs of hope. We have a state of original grace followed by original sin. God gives reason for hope found in the words of the *Proto-Evangelium*: "I will put contempt between you and the woman, / and between your offspring and hers. /

He will strike your head, / and you will strike his heel" (Gen 3:15).[6] Hope that the woman's seed—"he"—will bruise the head of the serpent. While the serpent continues to attack those who put their faith and hope in Christ, the serpent proves troublesome but powerless (1 Cor 15:54-55). So, God does not abandon the man and woman in their state of sin. In the *Proto-Evangelium*, in spite of the fallen condition, God gives the man reason to hope. And this hope comes through the woman's seed. What at first appeared cause for despair, God leaves room for hope. In their fallen condition, the man and the woman still have faith: God is Creator. God is just. He punishes and he gives signs of hope. Signs of hope after the fall in the book of Genesis include Seth and his descendants (Gen 4), God spared Noah and his family (Gen 9), priesthood of Melchizedek (Gen 14), covenants with Abraham (Gen 22), Isaac (Gen 26), and Jacob (Gen 35), "Go to Joseph," *Ite ad Joseph*, (Gen 44), blessings of Judah (Gen 49).

We can also consider the contrasting figures from the New Testament in relation to hope and despair. Even among the closest of Jesus's followers we can find infidelity. In the first instance there is Judas who betrays Jesus for money. As meditated in the first sorrowful mystery, the agony in the garden, Judas shows signs of being preoccupied with money, giving the pretext of his concern for the poor when an expensive perfume is used to anoint the feet of Jesus. Judas claims that the money could have served for a better cause (John 12:6). Judas kept the "money bag" (John 13:29). After the betrayal, even if the weakest of the apostles handed Jesus over for money, there was no turning back for Judas. Indeed, Judas, having recognized his sin, could have asked for forgiveness at any point from the time Jesus picked up his cross, all the way to the crucifixion. Instead, he expressed his regret to the chief priests who used Judas for their own ends. Indeed, this hopelessness led Judas to despair. The money he received from them was meaningless, and he threw it into the temple. Now was the time to look for Jesus. He could have said, "Lord I sinned against you, forgive me." Judas in a state of despair, believing his acts were too grave to be forgiven, was led to suicide by hanging himself (Matt 27:6-7).

The other example given to us in the Scriptures is that of Peter. The disciple to whom Jesus entrusted his church and belonged to the inner circle of three, Peter, James, John, with Peter always listed first. Peter responded to the questioning in Caiaphas's courtyard as Jesus had foreseen. The cock crowed a third time precisely as Jesus told him; Peter remembered

---

6. Genesis 3:15 has gone through a series of translations with the male and female pronouns, in reference to the offspring and the woman. Re-translation of these pronouns include she, he, and it. For a theological explanation of the "Proto-Evangelium," and commentary, see Bergsma and Pitre, *Old Testament*, 122–23.

the words of Jesus (Mark 14:66–72). Peter had every reason to despair in his lack of courage due to fear. Authority was entrusted to him; he belonged to the inner circle. During Jesus's trial Peter denied knowing the very one whom he previously recognized as the Son of the living God. Peter acknowledges his weakness, but he does not give up—he has hope in the love of Jesus. Peter remains committed to Jesus whom he followed during the years of Jesus's ministry. Peter remains hopeful. But in order to be hopeful he needs to recognize his weakness: he sinned; he depends on the love of Jesus to forgive him and strengthen him.

In the intimate, moving, and powerful exchange between Peter and Jesus at Lake Tiberius just before Jesus's ascension, Jesus asks Peter, "Do you love me?" (John 21:15–16). The question, repeated three times, permits Peter to "undo" his threefold denial. In his loyalty, in spite of weakness, Peter reaffirms his love for Jesus, while Jesus reasserts Peter's duty to feed the sheep of the Lord; that is, Peter will assume the responsibility of shepherding Jesus's sheep. Peter, instead of falling into despair, expresses his love for Jesus. Peter has faith; he is a man of hope. The second glorious mystery teaches us that our hope derives from our faith anchored in Christ.

Third Glorious Mystery—Descent of the Holy Spirit upon the Apostles and the Blessed Virgin Mary

> I—*Divided tongues, as of fire, appeared among them, and a tongue rested on each of them. All of them were filled with the Holy Spirit and began to speak in other languages, as the Spirit gave them ability . . .* (Acts 2:3–4)
>
> Our Father . . . Hail Mary . . . Glory Be . . .

1. Language

Language is the human property we possess to communicate with others; our thoughts, our feelings, our beliefs. Only humans have language, reflecting the spiritual powers of the rational soul. When someone speaks only a few words in another person's language, the effect is a delightful smile. Why is that? Language creates connection—a human bond.

Listening to someone so they feel understood is fundamental to human relations. Imagine if we are speaking to someone, and the other person has no idea what we are talking about, and they look at us with that expression of "Huh?" or "What?" A feeling of a barrier or division exists. The frown on the face, wrinkled forehead, are physical signs of not being understood. Such signs make us feel uneasy because communicative barriers emerge. We rely on communication to ensure we understand and are understood; language serves this connective purpose.

People do not have to be from different linguistic communities to experience the effects of division. It can happen in our relationships, in our homes, at work: we speak the same language and yet misunderstandings surface.

Language enables us not only to create and nurture human bonds, but at the rational level, language transmits truth. When language is manipulated and misused, it conveys ideologies and falsehoods, forming divisions. Was it not through the deceptive words of a serpent that the man and woman fell from grace to original sin (Gen 3)? And the builders of Babel, did they not use a common language to "surpass" God (Gen 11)?

2. Holy Spirit

If language reflects the spiritual capacities of our soul in the different stages of life, then God sends his Spirit, the Third Person of the Trinity, as Jesus had promised, so that our spiritual potential may be perfected. Even in silent prayer before God, we communicate our interior disposition towards the divine. By the power of the Holy Spirit, we are transformed from natural beings to supernatural beings. We are not just born of flesh; with the Holy Spirit we are reborn of the Spirit (John 3:5–6).

The radical transformation of the person makes an impact on the community of believers. The Catholic faithful do not congregate like a cultural institute or sports club, but we experience a supernatural bond that unites each of us, not by our individual strength, but by the power of the Holy Spirit, and through the unifying power of the body and blood of Christ that we receive at communion or spiritual communion.[1] Similarly, when that communal bond has been ruptured due to sin, the sacrament of confession, with God's minister, the priest, acting in *persona Christi*, restores that rupture with both God and his church. The supernatural life relies on our cooperation, our freedom to accept or reject the invitation of God's Spirit.

The descent of the Holy Spirit on the day of Pentecost marks the beginning of the Christian church: the apostles along with Mary, mother of Jesus, are gathered together, waiting (Acts 1:13–14). The first sign of God's Spirit is the violent wind and tongues of fire resting on each of them.

The dramatic signs of Pentecost, audible and visible, reveal God's presence; then, the powerful effects of the Spirit: filled with God's Spirit they began to speak in other languages signaling God's Spirit at work, Spirit of unity breaking down barriers.

Language makes us rational, relational, spiritual beings; language invites us to think and reflect; language directs our relationships with others and with God; language enables the individual to pray and worship, seek

---

1. If a person is not in a state of grace, or is not disposed to receive communion, they can make a spiritual communion reflecting their desire to be united with the body and blood of Christ. See, *Catechism*, #1380, #1415.

forgiveness. God's Spirit gives us the grace we need so language builds our community and creates supernatural bonds. The power of God's Spirit is to unify, to build, to construct. The Holy Spirit's presence continues Christ's mission of preaching one Lord, one faith, one baptism (Eph 4:5). Fragmentation, division, splintering denominations, cults, and sects cannot be signs of the Holy Spirit but rather the divisiveness and sinfulness of man, the arrogant and proud creating divisions in the body of Christ.

The language of love is expressed in gestures and acts. And in the presence of God, we remain in contemplative silence. Yet, whether action or silence, these still presuppose thoughts and desires embedded with words. Humans cannot get away from language. The first effects of God's Spirit is the removal of barriers creating unity, the desire to praise, to worship, to reach out to others as one family—God's children united in one salvific message.

Unity is the sign of God's Spirit at work in his church. God's church is inseparable from the message of salvation: Jesus Christ, Son of the living God, is our Savior. God the Father sends his Son for one purpose: that we may have eternal life. The Spirit promised by Jesus descends upon the apostles and Mary; and the same Spirit upon each one of us. This is the Catholic Church that Christ left us. One church. Transcending all language barriers and cultural divisions because God's Spirit breathes upon the church and gives the church life. Pentecost teaches us the oneness of the church and the one body of believers that we are called to be.

We are called to be receptive to God's Spirit which guides us in all truth. Truth does not belong to us. Truth finds its source in God. But guided by the Holy Spirit we come to know who truth is, namely, Jesus Christ. To be receptive to truth means to live by the truth and to correct errors in the light of the same truth. This is the difficult part. We need to pray for the virtue of courage to proclaim the truth.

God's Spirit fills us with this divine power to strengthen and embolden us. We have received gifts, as Saint Paul says, and these gifts serve to strengthen the body of Christ, they are the signs of God's Spirit at work. This is the language of Pentecost, the descent of the Holy Spirit uniting us through our common baptism in Christ, and with a common mission, to bring the truth of the Gospel to the world that hungers and thirsts.

With the Trinitarian language that is used, Jesus unveils the Holy Trinity on Pentecost Sunday; Holy Trinity Sunday is celebrated the Sunday after Pentecost: "When he had said this, he breathed on them and said to them, 'Receive the Holy Spirit'" (John 20:22).

The language of John's Gospel transmits missionary zeal: the disciples are sent on a mission to evangelize having received God's Spirit. This is true for all those who receive God's Spirit in baptism: the missionary responsibility with which each one of us is empowered—to evangelize. We also have a sign of the church's salvific mission entrusted in a specific way to the apostles and their successors; they are granted authority to forgive or to retain sins: "If you forgive the sins of any, they are forgiven them; if you retain the sins of any, they are retained" (John 20:23). Authority was conferred to Peter by Christ himself, and then transmitted to the apostles (Matt 16:18).[2] When the moral law is violated, truth cannot be modified to accommodate people's sinful ways or behavior. While God's love and mercy are infinite, they are coherent with his laws, natural and divine. God sent us his Son and gives us his Spirit so we can live in truth and grow in holiness. Holiness is fundamentally where we conform ourselves to the way Jesus set out for us, not the way humans set out for themselves eating from the forbidden fruit, building a tower to make themselves great name, or engaging in perverse sexual activity where man repeatedly defies God (Gen 3; 11; 19).

In our "post-truth era," we are at a crossroads: the Way of Jesus, Son of God, who is truth and love, and all other ways. The novena to the Holy Spirit, which is regarded as the first and official novena of the church, corresponds to Jesus telling his disciples, just before the ascension, to wait for the Holy Spirit in Jerusalem.

Jesus, resurrected from the dead, ascends to the Father. But even before his ascension to assure his apostles they were not left alone, Jesus promised to send them the Paraclete, the Spirit that descends upon them (John 14:16, 26). We have this ascending and descending motion: Jesus, Second Person of the Trinity ascends; the Holy Spirit, Third Person of the Trinity, descends.

3. Upper Room

They waited together in the upper room, also known as the room of the Last Supper, which can still be visited in Jerusalem today. This room, restored by the crusaders to preserve the original sacred space, was considerably altered by the Muslim occupants. The location where Jesus met with his apostles for the Last Supper is where the Holy Spirit descended upon the apostles while in prayer with the Virgin Mary.[3]

---

2. In Roman Catholicism the apostolic penitentiary is the congregation that deals with "internal forum" or "conscience." The apostolic penitentiary is not limited to sacramental confession but includes indulgences.

3. The Pentecost novena begins nine days before Pentecost—placed between the Ascension and Pentecost.

3RD GLORIOUS MYSTERY—DESCENT OF THE HOLY SPIRIT

The upper room can be visited in Jerusalem near the Tomb of David just adjacent to Dormition Abbey on Mount Zion. We speak of "upper church" where the Holy Spirit descended upon the apostles, also known as the Church of the Apostles. The upper room, referred to as the Cenacle, represents two major biblical events: the Last Supper and the descent of the Holy Spirit.

The Last Supper occurred in the upper room: "He will show you a large room upstairs, furnished and ready. Make preparations for us there" (Mark 14:15). The Last Supper is clearly associated with the first sorrowful mystery, the agony in the garden. The Last Supper in the upper room refers the location designated by Jesus for the Passover preparation—the anticipation of eating the sacrificed lamb, sharing bread, drinking wine—to offer his body and blood. In the upper room, the apostles look forward to Jesus's presence, "While staying with them, he ordered them not to leave Jerusalem, but to wait there for the promise of the Father. 'This,' he said, 'is what you have heard from me; for John baptized with water, but you will be baptized with the Holy Spirit not many days from now'" (Acts 1:4–5). We have the instructions given by Jesus telling his disciples to wait in Jerusalem for the Holy Spirit. The distinction at this stage is made clear: John baptized with water, but now the disciples are baptized in the Holy Spirit. The fundamental distinction is made between John's baptism, water, and the baptism of Jesus, Spirit.

They proceed to Jerusalem: "When they had entered the city, they went to the room upstairs where they were staying, Peter, and John, and James, and Andrew, Philip and Thomas, Bartholomew and Matthew, James, son of Alphaeus, and Simon the Zealot, and Judas, son of James. All these were constantly devoting themselves to prayer, together with certain women, including Mary the mother of Jesus, as well as his brothers" (Acts 1: 13–14). "Together" while in prayer, Acts continues, "When the day of Pentecost had come, they were all together in one place" (Acts 2:1). Waiting with faith and hope, the apostles are united in prayer at a holy site in Jerusalem. So, the southwestern hill of Mount Zion is associated with both the upper room of the Last Supper and the upper room of Pentecost.

But what are those fifty days of Pentecost before the coming of the Holy Spirit? The harvest festival of fifty days known as "Pentecost" begins immediately after Passover. The male Israelites dedicated their first loaves of bread from the first fruit of their spring crop (Lev 23:15–17). The apostles were waiting with Mary, the mother of Jesus, when ". . . suddenly from heaven there came a sound like the rush of a violent wind, and it filled the entire house where they were sitting" (Acts 2:2). In addition to this powerful wind that enveloped the house, "Divided tongues, as of fire, appeared among them, and a tongue rested on each of them" (Acts 2:3). On Mount Sinai they received the tablets of the old covenant; on Mount Zion they received the Word made flesh in the Eucharist. The Holy Spirit descends in this mighty wind echoing God's loud, fiery theophany on Mount Sinai (Exod 19:16–19). The verse that expresses divine activity, being blessed by God's Spirit, is given to us: "All of them were filled with the Holy Spirit and began to speak in other languages, as the Spirit gave them ability" (Acts 2:4).

We are told specifically that the mother of Jesus prayed with them. Mary experienced the presence of the Holy Spirit "descend upon her" in a unique way at the annunciation, first joyful mystery, when the Son of God is made flesh in her womb. Mary accepted the Holy Spirit to act upon her as the angel announced her role in salvation and the fulfillment of God's promise. Throughout her life, Mary exercised her freedom in perfect conformity with God's will. She never sinned. Nor did Mary know original sin. Yes, like all humans Mary needed a Savior, and Jesus saved her on the cross—in anticipation—preserving Mary from original sin. At the annunciation, Mary received the angel's message and the Holy Spirit into her womb, at Pentecost, Mary is praying with apostles when the Holy Spirit gives birth to the church. Mary's presence signifies her maternal wisdom, love, and guidance. And so, at Pentecost, with all the other apostles present, we refer to Mary as the mother of the church, for she is the mother of us all. Like Eve, she is mother to humanity, but unlike Eve, Mary is mother to humanity reborn. Mary, at Pentecost, is identifiably mother of the church where she waits with the apostles for the Holy Spirit as instructed by Jesus: "wait in Jerusalem" (Acts 1:4–5).[4]

4. Speaking Other Tongues

We have the cause-effect relationship: first, the powerful descent of the Holy Spirit at Pentecost; second, the effect which is speaking in other "tongues" (Acts 2:4). The Spirit marks the beginning of the new covenant community, the body of believers who waited in faith and hope, who listened to the teachings of Jesus, observed his acts, grasped Jesus is the Son of God, the promised Messiah. Jesus sends the Holy Spirit, the Paraclete; God's Spirit is the gift that breathes divine life upon the covenant believers; that same Spirit that animates the community with truth, love, and life. The "tongues" convey a relational value for the church in the context of Pentecost and the many different

---

4. Mary, Mother of the Church, is celebrated on the first Monday after Pentecost Sunday. The memorial was put into to the Roman calendar by Pope Francis in 2018.

language speakers. Pentecost signals the beginning of the Great Commission as instructed by Jesus: "go out and bless all the nations."

"To speak other tongues" reminds us of the earlier divine intervention that was divisive rather than unifying. Humanity spoke one language until a tower under construction pierced the skies with the intent to "make a name for ourselves" (Gen 11:4). A common language served to unite humanity and worship God the creator. The tower-builders served to dishonor God, seeking to surpass God and honor themselves, "make a name for ourselves." Original sin was brought into the world by the deceptive use of language, distorting words to tempt and seduce the woman and the man. Man continues to pervert the image of God in which he is created, striving to fulfil his ambitious accomplishments to overthrow God, to dethrone God, and make a "name" for himself. The name of God is holy; when man's name is treated as holier and more laudable than God's, God intervenes. Due to sin, the scheme to dethrone God instead of worshiping God as creator leads to punishment: "'And this is only the beginning of what they will do; nothing that they propose to do will now be impossible for them. Come, let us go down, and confuse their language there, so that they will not understand one another's speech.' So the LORD scattered them abroad from there over the face of all the earth, and they left off building the city" (Gen 11:6–8).

At Pentecost, the disciples of Jesus, Aramaic-speaking Galileans, were heard speaking other languages (Acts 2:7–8). The list associated with regions across the Mediterranean from east to west and north to south. Parthinians, whose territory stretched from the northern Euphrates into what is today eastern Iran. Medes, the inhabitants of northern and northwestern Iran. The Elamites inhabited southwestern Iran. Mesopotamia stretching across the region between the Tigris and Euphrates Rivers. Cappadocia refers to the central region of Anatolia, modern-day Turkey, and Pontus, a strip of land across the southeastern Black Sea. Speakers of Phyrigian, the language of central Anatolia, modern Turkey, Egypt, part of Libya, and Rome, are all included on the list. Also, from the Mediterranean are Cretan-spakers south of Greece, and from the Arabian peninsula, those who spoke Arabic. Jews and Jewish converts in Jerusalem for Pentecost heard these Galilean disciples of Jesus speak to them.[5]

---

5. It should be noted that in these lands of the Bible, some ancient Christian communities have survived centuries of war, persecution, and discrimination, and in some cases, the complete genocide of Christians. Apart from these ancient communities struggling to survive across Palestine, Lebanon, Syria, Jordan, and Iraq, Pontus along the Black Sea in modern Turkey still has pockets of Christians. Pope Francis referred to a "genocide" of Christians in the Middle East in July, 2015. Only one city in the Pentecost list, namely Rome, after centuries of persecution targeting Christians, became a spiritual power center of Christian missionary activity by which the entire world would be evangelized.

From as far west as Rome where Latin was spoken, stretching to the northeastern regions where Parthinian-speakers lived, extending to the southern Arabian peninsula where Arabic-speaking inhabitants were found, we discover from this passage in the Acts of the Apostles the power of the Holy Spirit acting upon the people present, reaching out to the speakers of the known world. This dramatic spiritual event occurred in Jerusalem where Christ was crucified, resurrected, ascended, and where the Holy Spirit descends upon the apostles and the nascent church.[6] The Christian message breaks down all barriers. By the power of the Holy Spirit the impulse was to reach out to others—complete strangers of diverse languages and cultural backgrounds. From the time the Holy Spirit descended upon the apostles, the missionary language of the church was to proclaim the message of salvation, the move outward towards blessing peoples in the name of the Father, the Son, and the Holy Spirit. This reference to Acts serves as a historical document to demonstrate how early Christianity interacted and evangelized all known peoples and nations from the Arab peninsula to northeastern Iran, across the Euphrates and Tigris, modern day Turkey across to Rome in the Italian peninsula. The apostles moved by the Spirit did not keep Christ for themselves; they spoke and shared with all others the hope and joy of the Christian message: Jesus is the way, the truth, and the life.

Christianity as a missionary religion started two thousand years ago with its origins in Jerusalem, in the upper room, on Pentecost. The spread of Christianity moved from Jerusalem across to the neighboring countries by the Jews who first heard and received the message proclaimed by the apostles: that Jesus, the Messiah, Son of God, has come, fulfilling the Law and the Prophets. Taking this same message to Asia Minor, today modern Turkey and Greece, and to Rome, the capital of the Roman Empire in the West, the same message was further transmitted southeast of Judea to parts of Arabia and northeast to Parthinia, and across the Euphrates and Tigris modern day Iraq. From the early church, Christianity was driven by "mission"—to save all people.

---

6. In the eastern periphery of Christianity, Nestorianism, a heretical sect, circulated based on a defective understanding of the "Person" of Jesus. The Nestorians denied that Mary is the Theotokos or "God-bearer" and claimed Mary is Christokos or "Christ-bearer." The Council of Ephesus affirmed in 431 AD that Mary is "God-bearer." The Nestorian claims emptied Jesus of his divine personhood. This heresy which circulated in the Eastern periphery of Christianity into Persia, Arabia, and central Asia, facilitated the advance of Islam among heretical pockets of Nestorian Christians. A central authority assures a universal—"catholic"—doctrine is taught, preserved, and defended, namely by the Church of Rome using the centralized Roman imperial model of government to correct and prevent the spread of doctrinal errors evident in the Eastern peripheries of Christianity. See Weidenkopf, *Timeless*, 131–33, 173.

5. Paraclete—"Counselor"

At the Last Supper, Jesus prepares the apostles for his passion, death, and resurrection, drawing their attention to the "counselor" whom the Father will send (John 14:16). The "counselor"—or *parakletos* in Greek—means "helper" or "advocate." The Paraclete is sent to strengthen the disciples once Jesus is resurrected, to instruct the apostles in the truth (John 14:26). The Holy Spirit acts in Christ's church. Scriptures tell us, "When the Spirit of truth comes, he will guide you into all the truth; for he will not speak on his own authority, but whatever he hears he will speak, and he will declare to you the things that are to come" (John 16:13). Since the Spirit guides the disciples of Jesus into the fullness of the Gospel, the Spirit counteracts the work of Satan, who from the start set out to confuse, deceive, and distort leading believers away from God, his Son, his church. The Spirit continues the teaching mission of Jesus bearing witness to the truth.

Again, prophetic fulfillment is recognizable when we read Isaiah. The reference to Mount Zion immediately situates these events south of Jerusalem where Mount Zion stands (Isa 2:3). The upper room is associated with both the Last Supper and the descent of the Holy Spirit. The prophecy, "for out of Zion shall go forth the law," is fulfilled in Christ sending his disciples, "Go therefore and make disciples of all nations, baptizing them in the name of the Father, and of the Son, and of the Holy Spirit, teaching them to obey everything that I have commanded you" (Matt 28:19–20). We have reference to "law" in Isaiah's prophecy "going forth," as we have in this apostolic commission in Matthew's Gospel, "Go therefore..." Christianity's mission is to go out, "baptize" and "teach" all of humanity following Christ's command in the name of the Holy Trinity.

6. Gifts and Fruit of the Spirit

We associate the Holy Spirit with baptism when we first received the Trinitarian God, whom we celebrate the Sunday after Pentecost. The God in whom we are reborn and recreated, we are given new life filled with God's grace and supernatural life. We again associate the Holy Spirit with confirmation when we are sealed by the Holy Spirit whom we received at baptism; the fullness of the Holy Spirit is received in terms of the gifts present and at work in our lives.

The gifts are seven: Wisdom, Understanding, Counsel, Fortitude, Knowledge, Piety, and Fear of the Lord (Isa 11:2–3). Three of these gifts are strengthened by praying three mysteries of the rosary:

Table 1: Gift and Mystery

GIFT	DECADE	MYSTERY
Piety	First Joyful	Finding in the Temple
Fortitude	Second Sorrowful	Crowning with Thorns
Wisdom	Third Glorious	Descent of the Holy Spirit

The rosary, therefore, not only contains the meditative mysteries that find their source in the Scriptures, but further strengthen three of the gifts of the Spirit. In the rosary, each of these gifts appears in one of the decades, Joyful, Sorrowful, and Glorious: piety, fortitude, wisdom. This reflects the journey of the Christian: we grow in piety through what we learned at home, beginning with respect for one's parents, the love of God, holy practices; fortitude is needed in our Christian journey both in living out our faith in the midst of obstacles and temptation. And finally, over the years we grow in wisdom, which presupposes a spiritual foundation and like the other virtues is strengthened and perfected by the Holy Spirit at confirmation.

When we live according to the seven gifts of the Spirit, they produce fruit. Saint Paul lists nine gifts of the Holy Spirit: "love, joy, peace, patience, kindness, goodness, faithfulness, gentleness, self-control" (Gal 5:22–23). In Jerome's Latin Vulgate, three other fruit are indicated: "modesty, continence, and chastity," so altogether, twelve.[7] Many of these fruit are associated with the virtuous life, and not unique to Christianity. We find characteristics of these fruit already present in Graeco-Roman philosophy, where the four cardinal virtues—intellectual and moral, prudence, temperance, courage, and justice—are associated with personal integrity. The three remaining fruit of the Spirit, indicated by the Saint Jerome Vulgate—modesty, continence, and chastity—continue from the biblical nine. The three are interrelated; Saint Paul's extensive preaching on the subject of purity reflects an elaboration of what Jesus taught in relation to living by the Spirit. Saint Jerome identified in these nine fruit of the Spirit the "hidden" three relating to Saint Paul's nine. Beginning with "modesty," as shown visibly in dress, an external sign of one's interior disposition, "continence" follows, expressing self-restraint from pleasure-inducing sexual acts. The disposition of modesty and continence prepare for the virtue of

---

7. Modesty, continence, chastity are found in the Douay-Rheims translation (1899, American Edition) based on Saint Jerome's Vulgate. As a result, Catholics refer to the twelve fruit of the Holy Spirit.

"chastity." Acquiring a natural disposition, whether celibate or married, expressed in the manner of dress, conversation, reading, and visual material, self-denial, affecting one's thoughts and acts whereby the disposition of chastity ultimately has been cultivated.

These fruit are also attached to mysteries of the rosary so that while praying individual mysteries, we can be strengthened in the fruit of the Holy Spirit:

Table 2: Fruit and Mystery

FRUIT	DECADE	MYSTERY
Charity	Second Joyful	The Visitation
Chastity	Second Sorrowful	Scourging at the Pillar
Patience	Fourth Sorrowful	Carrying the Cross
Faith	First Glorious	The Resurrection

Charitable acts are central to the teachings of Jesus Christ. In Galatians, Paul speaks extensively of distinguishing the life of the flesh and the life of the Spirit, and the person who is born in Christ lives by the Spirit of God, which makes "chastity" one of these twelve fruit reflected in how we allow God's grace to work in our lives so that we live truly by the Spirit. Similarly, patience is needed in our spiritual life and for growth as meditated in the fourth sorrowful mystery. Faith is meditated in the first glorious mystery. Faith in the resurrection shapes how we live our lives. The crisis today when people are preoccupied only with life on earth, the rights to satisfy disordered desires and unnatural whims, corrupt supernatural faith.

The rosary, therefore, serves as a prayerful instrument as we pray this third glorious mystery where the Holy Spirit descends upon the church at Pentecost and pours upon the church these gifts from which the fruit of the Christian life grows: the power of God's Spirit that moves the church and breathes divine life into her members. God strengthens us by the power of the Holy Spirit. It depends on our willingness to receive, to cooperate, to conform ourselves to the will of God which is our holiness (1 Thess 4:3–5).

II—Fruit of this Mystery: Wisdom; Love of God

Practical Matters—

The Holy Spirit descends upon the church and upon each one of us through baptism and confirmation to help us grow in the gift of wisdom. But we know how often we succumb to errors. We exercise our intelligence by making judgement—what is true and what is false, what is good and what is evil, whether in human relations, society, or politics. News networks, mainstream media, social media, internet searches, instead of helping us find answers and clarity, create more confusion with ideologically driven reporting and data. Difference between factual knowledge that leads to judgments of good and evil based on what is true and false should be in harmony with Christ's teachings and natural law principles. This is why God has created us with intelligence: so we can use our God-given intelligence to make judgments. So, when we act against truth and succumb to the lies of the deceiver, then we sin just as when we sin against the Ten Commandments (Exod 20: 2–17), or the eight Beatitudes taught by the Son of God (Matt 5:3–12).

1. Ten Commandments (Exod 20: 2–17)

1. Worship God alone—and no other. 2. Keep the Sabbath holy. 3. Do not blaspheme. 4. Honor your father and mother. 5. Do not kill. 6. Do not commit adultery.[8] 7. Do not steal. 8. Do not lie. 9. Do not covet your neighbor's wife.[9] 10. Do not covet your neighbor's goods.

So, we are taught these commands, we know them, and when we violate them we sin. Nobody can change the natural law or the divine law, not even human laws that violate divine truth.

2. Eight Beatitudes (Matt 5:3–12)

Christ gives us eight Beatitudes, as we find in Mathew's Gospel, which focus on how we should conduct ourselves leading to holiness:

---

8. The sixth commandment covers all forms of disordered sexual activity: masturbation, pornography, fornication, adultery, homosexual acts, pornography, artificial contraceptives, abortion, and other disordered acts. See, *Catechism*, #2351-#2359.

9. The ninth commandment corresponds to the sin of "lust." Pornography pertains to the sixth commandment because the visual material instrumentalizes, degrades, and exploits humans with a self-focused sexual end. See, *Catechism*, #2354.

1. Blessed are the poor in spirit, for theirs is the kingdom of heaven.
2. Blessed are those who mourn, for they will be comforted.
3. Blessed are the meek, for they will inherit the Earth.
4. Blessed are those who hunger and thirst for righteousness, for they will be filled.
5. Blessed are the merciful, for they will be shown mercy.
6. Blessed are the pure in heart, for they will see God.
7. Blessed are the peacemakers, for they will be called children of God.
8. Blessed are those who are persecuted because of righteousness, for theirs is the kingdom of heaven.

Christ teaches us that if someone wishes to follow him, the Beatitudes are the path that lead to eternal life. Christ teaches the value of each: poverty, mourning, being meek, seeking justice, exercising mercy, being pure, peace-making, being persecuted for what is right. Ultimately we exercise the Beatitudes in the name of our Lord, Jesus, who teaches us the truest good (Matt 5:12).

Beatitudes are fundamental to the Christian life, but they are not easily put into practice. Christ does not teach us, "eye for eye; tooth for tooth . . ." (Exod 21:24), which reflects human justice. Jesus wants us to live by the grace he offers us. The supernatural life transcends human categories although rooted in that very human nature God created in us. Our fallen state, however, inclines us towards concupiscence making the perfection of the Beatitudes beyond our reach. Jesus sends us the Holy Spirit, the Paraclete, at work in the sacraments of the church, so the Beatitudes as taught by Jesus are attainable.[10]

Wisdom leads us to the perfection of truth which is God himself, not only to the knowledge of God but an even deeper love of God. God has created us with intelligence—to know him—and the purpose to know him is to love him. Even though our knowledge of God is incomplete and limited due to our finite intelligence, we love God our Father and Creator, his Son whom he sent to save us so we may have eternal life, and the Holy Spirit who teaches us truth and fills us with love. Knowledge informs us so we can choose, and our will can be directed towards loving God and others in truth. Wisdom is inseparable from the knowledge and love of God.

We receive the gift of wisdom at confirmation from the Holy Spirit to assist us on the path of truth. We know due to concupiscence that the

---

10. See, *Catechism*, #1264.

intelligence is prone to error.[11] To help us, besides providing us with the natural capacity to reason, God has revealed himself through his Word made flesh, his Son, Jesus Christ. With our intelligence we can come to know naturally what is proper to "human nature"; with the Holy Spirit we have Scriptures and the magisterium to lead us to a fuller understanding of divine truth. The spiritual life is not "hit and miss." God assists us with both natural and supernatural knowledge. God seeks our love because he loves us and knows that true happiness is to be in communion with God the Father, the Son, and the Holy Spirit. We need the Holy Spirit to lead us in truth and to reach out to share the good news of salvation with all the nations.

In the third glorious mystery, we meditate the descent of the Holy Spirit descending upon the church. The Holy Spirit is actively at work in the church from Pentecost. The community of believers is governed by the Pope with his bishops, and this magisterial authority is guided by the Holy Spirit. The canon of Scriptures recognized by the Catholic Church reflects the work of the Holy Spirit; the sacraments that confer graces upon the individual beginning with baptism, then, confession, communion, confirmation, anointing of the sick, and in some cases, matrimony or holy orders, finds their source in the Holy Spirit at work in the church.

---

11. See, *Catechism*, #2515.

Fourth Glorious Mystery—Assumption of the Blessed Virgin Mary Body and Soul into Heaven

I—You are the exaltation of Jerusalem, you are the great glory of Israel, you are the great pride of our nation! (Judith 15:9)

Our Father . . . Hail Mary . . . Glory Be . . .

1. Mount Zion

Photos of Jerusalem often show Mount Zion with the magnificent Basilica of the Dormition. The basilica is one of the highlights visiting Jerusalem and usually last on the pilgrim's itinerary, taking into account the chronology of events and geography. At Dormition Abbey, pilgrims experience the deepened mystery of the salvific power of Jesus first experienced by his mother and the first of God's creation to go directly to heaven.

Biblical references to the Old Testament indicate Mount Zion referred to as the "eastern hill," the Jebusite stronghold that had been captured by King David and became known as the "City of David" (2 Sam 5:7). The prophet Micah refers to both in a parallelism, Zion and Jerusalem: "Therefore because of you / Zion shall be ploughed as a field; / Jerusalem shall become a heap of ruins, / and the mountain of the house a wooded height" (Mic 3:12). Based on such passages as Micah's reinterpretation of the two hills, Mount Zion was understood to be the western hill, and the city of David, the eastern hill.[1]

The Basilica on Mount Zion was dedicated in 1910, *Dormitio Mariae*. The tradition of associating Mount Zion with the dormition of Mary is reflected in the archaeological layers of the Basilica and written records. With

---

1. Samson, *Come and See*, 172.

excavations taking place, foundations were discovered of the well-known Byzantine Basilica of Hagia Sofia dating to the fourth century. This basilica had been visited in 670 by Arculf, the Frankish bishop who reported the northwest of the Basilica was visited by pilgrims as Mary's "resting place."[2] Further excavations firmly established that the site of the Basilica was identified with the earliest Christian community.[3] When the church fell into ruins, the crusaders erected a church dedicated to the dormition of Mary.

Zion is associated with Mary's resting place where the mother of our Savior was assumed into heaven. Zion's Dormition Abbey is also identified with the Christian community at Pentecost, the third glorious mystery. We gradually piece together the spiritual connections between these mysteries.

Veneration to Mary and her assumption into heaven are inseparable from the earliest Christian community whose faith in the resurrection of Jesus meant to be rewarded with eternal life. Literary and archaeological sources indicate that Mary lived in Zion and her dormition took place there.[4] Witness accounts in the third glorious mystery indicate that Mary, the mother of Jesus, was present with the apostles at Pentecost (Acts 1:13–14). Christianity taught since its origins that the resurrection from the dead was followed by judgment; then, either eternal reward or eternal punishment. Therefore, the most beautiful image of truth and love that we have of our faith beyond the crucifixion reveals Jesus rising into the clouds into heaven—the ascension, the second glorious mystery, and Jesus's ascent into heaven prepares us for the fourth glorious mystery.

We know that Jesus entrusted his mother to John from John's Gospel: "'Here is your mother.' And from that hour the disciple took her into his own home" (John 19:27). This indicates that Mary lived with the beloved disciple, to whom Jesus entrusted his mother. This historical recording of events provides the basis to our spiritual reading: we receive Mary in our homes as our mother because Jesus entrusts his mother to us, as his disciples, and Mary embraces us as our mother.

2. Ebionite Heresy

We know from the Scriptures the tension that existed in the early church: "Who is this Jesus?" The disputed question of Jewish followers of Christ concerned keeping Jewish religious observances, an ongoing issue dealt with by Peter and Paul (Acts 15:7–11), and in terms of heresy, the failure to recognize

2. Pixner, *Paths of the Messiah*, 398-99.
3. Pixner, *Paths of the Messiah*, 399.
4. Pixner, *Paths of the Messiah*, 402–03.

that the Christ has come in the flesh. Instead, false doctrines were taught regarded as the work of antichrist (1 John 4:1–3). We have evidence in the apostolic era of Ebionite teachings rejecting the virgin birth of Jesus Christ. This supernatural birth coming from the Holy Spirit, only Mary could shed light on these matters. Were it not for the mother of God intervening in these early errors, Christianity would have emerged as an Ebionite sect—or disappeared altogether. Here we acknowledge once again the role of the Virgin Mary both to cooperate with the Holy Spirit incarnating God's Son, but also in preserving the truth of Jesus's supernatural and divine birth.

We find in the early church Mary at the center of controversy, and only she could set matters straight. But, the Ebionites had no reason to believe in a supernatural birth. In Mary's own lifetime, in the church after Pentecost, Mary dealt with errors and falsehoods. Only Mary could correct the heresies, but the heretics could also ignore Mary. Instead, the Ebionites, and other heretics like the gnostics, continued to perpetuate the most serious error in the apostolic church: the denial of the virgin birth of Jesus. The implications of these errors will plague Christianity for centuries and resurface in derivative forms of Gnosticism.

The apostles, including the pillars of the church, Peter, James and John, were in Jerusalem around 50 AD. Paul was also there, looking for a collection for the poor in Jerusalem. Before Mary was taken up to heaven, she was surrounded by the apostles.[5] The Haggada, written in Hebrew, stemming from Jesus's family, is Mary's response to Ebionite claims and provided Luke with material as a basis for the first two chapters of his own Gospel. And we know the intimate details that Luke relates to the conception of Jesus.[6]

The Ebionites, meaning "poor ones" from Hebrew, were a Jewish-Christian heretical movement that did not accept the divinity of Jesus or the virgin birth. Though the Ebionites considered Jesus the Messiah, they continued to observe Jewish laws and rites to be saved, relying on a Hebrew Gospel of Matthew.[7] Disputes involving the Jewish Christians before and after Pentecost relate to the teachings of Jesus and his divinity.[8] Conflict continued on interpreting Scriptures, the Person of Jesus, and Jewish observances. Mary's claims were subjected to Ebionite criticism. Mary suffered not only at the cross as the mother of the crucified Jesus, but even after the church of Pentecost when skeptics and heretics refused to accept Mary's account of

---

5. Pixner, *Paths of the Messiah*, 404.

6. Pixner, *Paths of the Messiah*, 405.

7. Somewhat similar to Islam where respect is shown towards Jesus as "prophet," but not Jesus as "Son of God."

8. At this time in biblical history, the church cannot point to the New Testament because the New Testament was still being written.

supernatural events. Thebutis, a former Essene priest, probably founded the Ebionite sect; he denied both the virgin birth and the pre-existence of the Second Person of the Trinity, co-eternal with God. Jesus suffered the derision of those who did not believe him; Mary suffered knowing her testimony of her Son's conception was rejected among the heretical Jewish Christians.[9] These heresies will be repeated throughout the centuries.[10]

3. Council of Ephesus

The issues concerning Mary related to the nature of Jesus were debated in the early church. At the Council of Ephesus (431 AD) the title "Mother of God" or Greek, *Theotokos*, was formulated in opposition to the heretical usage of mother of Jesus, *Xristokos*. The profound theological significance of the title "Mother of Christ," although it appeared true, failed to address the substance of the person of Jesus leaving us with the nature of a man without any divinity. Such errors manifested themselves in relation to Mary; as with the Ebionite claims, that Mary was the mother of the incarnate Christ but nothing more. When the philosophical principles of "substance," "nature," and "person," with the benefit of the Greek lexicon, were refined by the Council of Ephesus, Mary is understood to be the mother of a divine Person—the Second Person of the Trinity whose nature is both human and divine.

The Holy Spirit worked in the lives of individuals, faithful disciples of Jesus, honored since the early church, and a particular filial devotion to Mary, while divine worship was reserved for Jesus, Son of God. The Catholic faith allows for mystery that avoids a polarization between fideism and rationalism, a disposition of receptivity towards the truth revealed in the Scriptures and the magisterium, and our capacity to exercise natural reason.

Jesus himself preaches repeatedly to the disciples that we find in John's Gospel "that they may all be one. As you, Father, are in me and I am in you, may they also be in us" (John 17:21). Catholicism has strived to keep these words of Jesus alive, uniting the Catholic world with "universal"—*catholic*—teaching. A common faith articulated in the Nicene Creed and an objective morality that unites all Catholics. Oneness is fundamental to Catholicism because the church is the spouse of Jesus, and she is One. Mary reflects this

---

9. Pixner, *Paths of the Messiah*, 405.

10. In one of my Scripture courses, a Pentecostal student refused to use the title "Mother of God" in reference to Mary. A Greek Orthodox student wrote with conviction, "Mother of God." The Roman and Greek churches tracing their origins to the apostles share the same reverence for Mary and appreciate the theological significance of the title, *Theotokos*.

oneness, striving for unity of doctrine, uniting her children as Christ united his disciples so they may be one as Jesus and the Father are One.

4. Devotion to Mary

The biblical verse associated with the assumption of Mary is taken from Judith, who prefigures Mary: "You are the exaltation of Jerusalem, you are the great glory of Israel, you are the great pride of our nation!" (Jdt 15:9). By killing Holofernes, the Assyrian commander, Judith liberates the people of Israel. Mary, by giving birth to the Son of God, brings the liberator of humanity and conqueror of the evil one.

One year, on a pilgrimage to the Holy Land, as we knelt praying around the Virgin Mary in her *Dormitio*, pink rose petals slowly fell from the ceiling of the basilica. We looked at each other wondering where the rose petals came from as they fell gently like feathers to the mosaic floor. It seemed as if Mary sent them as she looked upon us from heaven where she was assumed showering us with rose petals.

Devotion to Mary is supported by the archaeological evidence from Nazareth, the town of Mary's birth, and her conception of Jesus. In the synagogue church in Nazareth, the graffiti on the column of the fourth century reads "Greetings Mary."[11] The Church of the Dormition marks the Jerusalem skyline as it stands on Mount Zion. The bell tower, four corner turrets; the church is designed in a neo-Romanesque style, the site where Mary "fell into an eternal sleep." In the crypt the wood and ivory sculpture represents Mary's *Dormitio*.

With this background we can understand the centrality of Mary in the early Christian community not only as the mother of the Messiah, whom Jesus entrusts to John, and to each of us to take into our home, but Mary is the living God-bearer, proclaimed at the Council of Ephesus in 431 AD. The *Theotokos* resolves the controversy over the person of Jesus; the role of Mary and her divine motherhood is fundamental to combat heresy.

Mary's presence represents a woman at the heart of the church, a mother uniting her children, a prayerful intercessor, and a personal testimony of events in the life of Jesus. Mary's body received the Son of God, her body gave flesh to the Son of God, and she remains with us. This woman chosen by God to bring his Son into the world, Mary is at the center of this first Christian community that finds its life, its nourishment, its salvific mission in Jesus Christ.

---

11. See, E. Alliata, OFM, in Pixner, *Paths of the Messiah*, 407. Also, Luke 1:28.

Mary cannot be separated from the birth of the church any more than she can be separated from the birth of her Son. She fulfilled and continues her role as mother, as the New Eve, mother of the living; Mary collaborated perfectly with God's plan. She gave birth to the New Adam who crushed the sin of the first Adam by perfect obedience. Eve died because she sinned. Eve refused to obey. Eve experienced the rupture with God and rupture with the man God created. Now a disordered world. Mary, the New Eve, by her obedience to God, "undoes" the disorder and brings salvation to the world: Jesus, Son of God. Eve was born from the flesh of Adam; Jesus was born of the flesh of Mary.

Because she is chosen by God to give birth to his Son, Mary is prepared in advance. She needs a Savior like all of humanity, but her Savior anticipates her cleansing from original sin by preserving Mary from original sin. Mary does not contract nor is she contaminated by original sin. By Jesus's anticipated salvific power on the cross, what we receive at baptism, removal of original sin, Mary received at her conception, preserved from the stain of original sin.

Yes, we work our way back to Mary's birth, her condition at her birth: immaculate. Mary, like Eve, remained free to choose good or evil, to obey or to disobey. We find many parallels between Mary and Eve, but the fundamental difference between Mary and Eve reflects obedience and disobedience, respectively. If we compare these two women, we understand the fundamental difference of "doing what I want because it pleases me" and "doing what God wants because it pleases God."

We know from Genesis that sin brought death into the world. Sin and death go together: both spiritual death and physical death. The first man and woman sinned gravely against God in their act of disobedience, and so they suffered the consequences of punishment as God told them would happen if they disobeyed.

Even though both were created without sin, unlike Eve, Mary did not sin; she fully collaborated with God's plan. Her immaculate conception was part of God's plan, but she still remained free to obey or disobey. Mary stood at the cross with her Son experiencing her Son's suffering like any mother although her immaculate soul enabled Mary to see beyond the crucifixion with faith and hope. Mary prayed with the apostles at the church on Pentecost; Mary is an integral part of the nascent Christian church, the community of believers receiving the Holy Spirit.

5. Assumption of Mary

With all this, we need to ask the question: If Mary died, why did she die? Death is the result of sin (Gen 2:17; 3:3). The teaching of the Assumption is based on Mary not having sinned. Thus, Mary could not have died. But her earthly journey did end. And upon that end, she was taken up into heaven.

Mary is free from sin, and so Roman Catholics do not say that Mary died, but rather, "Finally the Immaculate Virgin, preserved from all stain of original sin, when the course of her earthly life was finished, was taken up body and soul into heaven glory . . ."[12] Logically, if death is the result of sin, and Mary never sinned, then, how could she have died? And so, we speak of her "assumption" into heaven or "dormition," but not death. This is why the Abbey in Jerusalem commemorating Mary's Assumption is called "Dormition Abbey"—where Mary fell asleep and was taken into heaven. Whereas Jesus died because he was executed—crucified and bled to death.

Now why do we say that Mary was "assumed" into heaven, and not resurrected into heaven or simply speak of the resurrection of Mary? With Jesus, we have biblical details of both his resurrection and his ascension. Jesus is the Son of God, one in substance with the Father; this co-eternal union that exists between Father and Son results in Jesus's resurrection, and ascension to the Father as meditated in the first and second glorious mysteries. Mary, however, created by God, is a creature and not divine; Mary is not resurrected because she does not die, so we speak of "assumption" because it conveys being "taken up" to heaven by God's power without knowing death. Jesus died because he was killed. Jesus first resurrected from the dead and after forty days ascended into heaven. Neither of these applies to Mary; she did not resurrect from the dead, nor did she ascend after forty days. To keep this real distinction, we use another word to describe Mary at the end of her earthly life: she was "assumed" into heaven. Mary was assumed—"taken up"—into heaven by God. Now, this is fitting because Mary is without sin.

We know that by God's grace, if we persevere in our faith, and live by that faith we profess, we will experience death and resurrection—of the soul and of the body. With death we experience the separation of the soul from the body because the spiritual soul is not present to animate the material body. Our soul is separated, and we are judged immediately after death whether we will be rewarded with eternal life with Mary, Joseph, the angels, and saints, or with eternal damnation with Satan and his fallen angels.[13]

---

12. See, *Catechism*, #966.
13. See, *Catechism*, #1021, #1024, #1035, #1038.

If we are rewarded with eternal life, then, we need to be cleansed of the remaining impurities that have not been accounted for while on earth, what we refer to as the remission of temporal punishment due to sin.[14] Purgatory serves this purpose as we read in 2 Maccabees: "Then, under the tunic of every one of the dead they found sacred tokens of the idols of Jamnia, which the law forbids the Jews to wear. And it became clear to all that this was why these men had fallen. So they all blessed the ways of the Lord, the righteous Judge, who reveals the things that are hidden; and they turned to prayer, beseeching that the sin which had been committed might be wholly blotted out" (2 Macc 12:40–42). This beautifully sensitive passage of desiring to see the sin of fellow soldiers blotted out explains how the soldiers intervened for their fellow combatants through prayer. We find in this passage of Maccabees both the sense of purgation due to sin and indulgence that is offered through prayer. We also find in Paul's writings the expression of purgatory: "If what has been built on the foundation survives, the builder will receive a reward. If the work is burned up, the builder will suffer loss; the builder will be saved, but only as through fire" (1 Cor 3:14–15). Purgation presupposes salvation: "he himself will be saved, but only as through fire." This reflects the condition of the person's soul before death. And once our soul has been cleansed, we will be one with God in the company of the angels and saints.

The physical rising from the dead takes place with the second coming of Jesus: the resurrection of the bodies, living and the dead, body and soul, will be transformed into our resurrected state because the body and soul belong together. Although human or spiritual souls can exist without bodies as they are self-subsistent (can exist on their own), our bodies belong to the spiritual-material composite of who we are as human beings—body and soul—and constitute our human nature. In other words, the resurrection includes our bodily nature but transformed as "spiritual bodies."[15]

6. Assumption of Mary and Immaculate Conception

The Assumption of Mary, this fourth glorious mystery, is directly linked to the Immaculate Conception.[16] These solemnities remind us of Mary's role in our salvation: God chooses Mary to bring his Son into the world. Mary's response in the first joyful mystery invites our contemplation: in her womb the Word is made flesh. The Marian solemnities are inseparable because it's

---

14. See, *Catechism*, #1031.

15. See, *Catechism*, #997-#1001.

16. The Roman Catholic calendar celebrates the Immaculate Conception, December 8, and the Assumption of Mary, August 15, as solemnities.

not only Mary's unstained conception that makes her immaculate, anticipating the intervention of her Son at the cross, but her fidelity throughout her life. Mary's immaculate state in her own lifetime hinges upon her fidelity to God. She was always free, like Eve, to refuse the will of God, or to obey God. But Mary remained perfectly faithful even in the midst of suffering. We can remain faithful when everything is going well, when we have earthly blessings and rewards. But Mary watches her innocent son slaughtered like a lamb. A pious mother, a religious woman, whose guiltless son ends his life on the cross. As we unite ourselves with Mary, we become one with Jesus.

We noted in the fifth joyful mystery that Mary and Joseph, after finding Jesus in the temple and returning to Nazareth, "His mother treasured all these things in her heart" (Luke 2:51). What things? When Mary and Joseph finally find Jesus, Mary says, "Look your father and I have been searching for you in great anxiety" (Luke 2:48). And this is only the beginning because Mary will be with Jesus at the cross. Mary's heart, immaculate, as she is preserved from original sin, her suffering is bound to that of her Son. When the Prophet Simeon tells Mary, "a sword will pierce your soul too" (Luke 2:35), his words are represented by the image of the immaculate heart pieced by a sword.[17] Mary prayed with the apostles in the upper room when the Holy Spirit descended upon the church as we meditate in the third glorious mystery.

And so, following Pentecost, we have this image and devotion to the immaculate heart of Mary again; Mary's suffering is directly linked to Jesus Christ. We celebrate these two days dedicated to Jesus and Mary, one day following the other, the sacred heart of Jesus on the Friday, followed by the immaculate heart of Mary, on the Saturday.

We might ask ourselves what sources outside of the Scriptures speak of "devotion" to Mary. We rely not only on Scriptures but also archaeology and the church fathers to help us put together a proper understanding of Mary, the woman Jesus entrusted to John and to us. We encounter in Luke's Gospel Mary, greeting her cousin Elizabeth, and telling her, "Surely, from now on all generations will call me blessed." But why does Mary even say this? Mary rejoices with her cousin Elizabeth, "for the Mighty One has done great things for me" (Luke 1:49). Mary points to Jesus, the child she carries in her womb; God's greatness, Mary's Magnificat, is Jesus in her womb, God's Son.[18] Mary immediately acknowledges the greatness of God, his

---

17. In the Roman Catholic calendar, we celebrate the Immaculate Heart of Mary on the Saturday after Corpus Christi, and the Sacred Heart of Jesus, the Friday after Corpus Christi.

18. The words spoken by Mary in Luke's Gospel are included in the Roman Catholic Breviary, Mary's Magnificat, prayed in the evening—Vespers.

omnipotence, in contrast to her "littleness." Chosen to bear the Christ child, Mary acknowledges her blessedness and that she will be called blessed for all ages to come as we meditated in the second joyful mystery.

Our salvation hinges on this initial fundamental event: the incarnation of the Second Person of the Trinity. This means that Mary is honored in her unique role as the chosen woman to be mother by the power of the Third Person of the Trinity. Mary is the mother of our Savior. She is the sorrowful mother. She is the mother of the church. She is the woman chosen by God to intercede for us, the mediatrix. And when Mary is taken up into heaven body and soul, she is the first to experience the reward of salvation because of her mission and total fidelity to that mission. On Mount Zion, in the upper room, where the Christians had their first synagogue-church, a place of prayer was built to remember her, to honor her, to continue to ask for her intercession as she joined her Son, Son of God, in heaven. The saints reunited with Jesus as he promised those who believed in him and followed his teachings would inherit eternal life; the saints in the presence of God intercede even more effectively than they had on earth. The Virgin Mary is remembered and honored in Nazareth where she was born, and in Jerusalem where she spent her last days before she was taken up to heaven.

The apostles slowly grasped Jesus's message of his resurrection and ascension; and that his mission was not a political one. Mary who kept the events in the life of Jesus quietly in her heart, her purity helped her grasp divine truths with faith and hope, "blessed are the pure in heart for they will see God" (Matt 5:8). Many know the Scriptures but lack understanding. Mary, chosen mother of the divine child, her purity, her trust, her faithfulness, reflects her fundamental role in our salvation. The first Christian community of apostles, limited in their understanding, relied on Mary's testimonies and gave Mary a place of honor beyond all others as mother. A hierarchy is naturally formed in terms of intercession, reverence, honor, and finally worship of the Trinitarian God.[19] Mary remained constant throughout her life in her fidelity to God's plan.

II—Fruit of this Mystery: Devotion to Mary

Practical Matters—

Devotion to Mary reflects our filial response to Christ's teachings. Mary's mission in collaborating with God's plan by bringing his Son into the world for

---

19. Devotion proper to the blessed Virgin Mary is referred to as *hyperdulia*.

our salvation, the child to whom Mary gives birth, results in our awe and thanksgiving. Devotion to Mary is inseparable from our worship of Christ. Everything about Mary points to Jesus; our filial love for her directs us to Jesus, Son of God. The Son of God is the cause of our devotion to Mary.

So, devotion to Mary reflects what the Scriptures tell us about her, and the events in her life not recorded in the Scriptures, especially where she played a central role dispelling early heresies. Devotion to Mary has been fundamental in the preservation of the Christian faith; this devotion has meant for followers of Christ not to fall into errors relating to the identity of Jesus. To be devoted to Mary means to worship Jesus Christ, true God and true man; devotion to Mary points to her Son. And Mary knows this. In our misery, our uncertainty, our sinfulness, our fears, our battles against Satan, Mary gets us through them with her prayers, her presence, her protection. And Mary leads us to the one whom she knows, the only one who can save us, Jesus. Mary knows; she received the message from the angel: "'The Holy Spirit will come upon you, and the power of the Most High will overshadow you...'" (Luke 1:35).

We have many Marian feasts, and many countries and cities have national and local Marian shrines. Where the Catholic Church has planted the seeds of Christ, his mother is present—"this is your mother"—and so Mary is honored in shrines, basilicas, and cathedrals all over the world. Even countries in Europe that abandoned their Catholic religious roots can trace their Christian origins by their cathedrals—and Mary, who is mother of the church. In Finland, the city of Turku has an "M" for Mary on their city flag in a Marian blue background dating to the medieval period. The Cathedral of Turku (consecrated in 1300) was dedicated to the blessed Virgin Mary and Saint Henry. Catholicism displays a great love for Mary; she is the mother of our Savior.

Speaking to a family from Sri Lanka, I was told Sri Lanka's proselytizing "Bible Christians" lead Catholics away from the Catholic Church because they claim "Catholics focus too much on Mary and the saints." The Catholic Church traces its beliefs and practices to the apostolic era that already expresses honor, reverence, and love for the Virgin Mary and the martyrs, the saints. Sadly, these attacks create divisions, the ongoing splintering of Christ's church. The Holy Spirit is at work in our lives, through prayer, through the sacraments, through grace, and finally the holy choices we make. The work of the Holy Spirit manifested in someone who has lived their Christian faith radically and heroically is worthy of not only love, reverence, and honor, but even asking for their intercession in our lives. We take saints as models of how to live our own life. Their sanctity is celebrated acknowledging the work of the Holy Spirit. If we celebrate births, anniversaries, graduations, promotions for ourselves and others, why not celebrate the lives of the saints? If I am asked to pray for fellow believers, why should I not turn to the mother of God for her intercession? Satan employs many tactics to undermine the church Christ founded; division is Satan's best strategy. Mary continues to unite her children as mother of the church and mother of our Savior.

The youth, looking for models and mentors in their life, have replaced Mary and the saints because of the profanation and bashing that goes on with movie and music celebrities. Glossy magazine covers appropriate Catholic figures only to dishonor them. If we do not have Mary and the saints as models of holiness and as intercessors, the young and old will create their own gods. Music that rebels, movies selling sex, the ongoing blasphemy in these industries, and paradoxically, we have Christians who go about attacking Mary and the saints. Iron spears, elephant tusks, and crystals . . . become fashionable replacements. Tattoos to the point of making faces unrecognizable. The Christian identity has been replaced with the pagan.

Yet, we have signs of hope. Sitting in the basilica, Santa Maria Maggiore in Rome, three college-age men apprehensively walked up to me. They spoke to me in English with a Spanish accent. I found out they were from Spain, so I spoke to them in Spanish. The three stood together with their hands opened. They asked, "Could you bless our rosaries?"

Devotion to Mary has significant implications, spiritual and human. While Satan waits to devour the presence of Christ (Rev 12:1), devotion to Mary serves to carry out the mission of the Holy Spirit: accept Jesus, the Son of God, into our lives and proclaim Him to the world.

Table 3: Rosary Schedule

MYSTERY	Days			
JOYFUL	Monday			
LUMINOUS		Thursday		
SORROWFUL	Tuesday		Friday	
GLORIOUS	Wednesday		Saturday	Sunday

Cycle 1: Monday-Tuesday-Wednesday: JOYFUL-SORROWFUL-GLORIOUS
Cycle 2: Thursday-Friday-Saturday: LUMINOUS-SORROWFUL-GLORIOUS
Cycle 3: Sunday   GLORIOUS

Fifth Glorious Mystery—The Coronation of the Blessed Virgin Mary

I—*And a great portent appeared in heaven, a woman clothed with the sun, with the moon under her feet, and on her head a crown of twelve stars.* (Rev 12:1)

Our Father . . . Hail Mary . . . Glory Be . . .

1. Catholic Queens and Saints

The Catholic Church contains a history of outstanding women who represent major figures in their fidelity to Christ and his church. Among these Catholic queens and royal figures include canonized saints demonstrating courage in the radicality of their choices, exercising charity, going out to battle, obedience to truth, and putting their trust in God. Without these queens, not only would Christian religious culture have been impoverished, but Christendom itself would have experienced a different trajectory. The Catholic church treasures the natural vocation of women to marriage and motherhood, but Catholicism has always promoted the supernatural vocation of spiritual marriage to Jesus and supernatural motherhood as consecrated virgins, lay religious, and even widows entering a cloister. The blessed Virgin Mary, queen of heaven, serves as the model of charity, courage, and fidelity. Our queen of heaven intercedes for all of us.

i. Saint Helen: Empress of the Roman Empire (246/50–330 AD)

Born in the Eastern Provinces of the Roman Empire, Helen was the mother of the emperor Constantine the Great.[1] Once Constantine was crowned emperor and Helen made empress, she converted to Christianity. Helen was then given by her son, Constantine, access to his treasury which she used to locate the relics of Christianity. Helen was responsible for the building of the Church of the Nativity in Bethlehem and the Church of the Disciples in Jerusalem.[2] Having visited the biblical lands stretching from Syria to Palestine and finally Jerusalem, Helen became associated with having found the true cross. When Constantine dreamed of the sign "Chi-rho"—XP—the first two initials of "Christ," before entering battle, Constantine ordered to have the sign painted on his soldiers' shields. In 312 AD Constanine's army won the battle of Milivian Bridge. On his deathbed, Constantine was the first Roman Emperor to convert to Christianity, and his mother became the first Roman empress and saint.

ii. Saint Clotilda: Queen of France (474–545)

The second wife of King Clovis I who reigned from 481–509, Clotilda was conferred the title of queen of all Franks.[3] As a Christian, Queen Clotilde played a key role in her husband's conversion to Christianity from paganism. Clovis was baptized by Remigius of Reims in 493 on Christmas Day. Unlike most of the Germanic tribes who followed the Arian heresy, Clotilde's Christian observances belonged to the Roman Catholic faith. Under the leadership of Clovis who embraced the Christianity of his wife, Catholicism, the people of Western Europe also adhered to Catholicism. The threat of Arianism gradually disappeared.[4] After Clovis died, Clotilde invested money in building churches and monasteries. Her tomb is beside that of Clovis in the church of Saint Géneviève in Paris.

---

1. Weidenkopf, *Timeless*, 90, 108.

2. Also known as the Church of Eleona, "Olive Grove." Egeria also makes reference to the church. The Olive Grove Church was destroyed by the Persians in the seventh century. The ruins of the original Eleona Church stands beside the Pater Noster Church, the site where Jesus taught the "Our Father" to his apostles. By the crusader period, the Olive Grove Church was associated with the Our Father. The Pater Noster Church now has a Carmelite convent built to the adjacent church.

3. The country name "France" comes from the "land of 'Franks'"; in Latin, *Francia* in German, *Frankreich*.

4. Arianism resembles the early Ebionite heresy.

iii. Saint Margaret: Queen of Scotland (1045-1093)

Daughter of English parents, King Edward the Exile and his wife Agatha, Margaret was born and grew up in the religious surroundings of the Hungarian court.[5] Margaret's father, Edward, represented the closest successor to the kings in England and was called back. But soon after they landed in England, Edward died under suspicious circumstances. From the Hungarian court and still a child, Margaret was brought up in the English court, with her brother, Edgar, a possible contender to the English throne. In 1066, the English were defeated by the Normans under the leadership of William the Conqueror at the Battle of Hastings. The family fled north to Northumbria, but due to their shipwreck off Scotland, Margaret and her Anglo-Saxon royal family were offered refuge by King Malcolm III. Margaret married King Malcolm III when she was about twenty-five years old; he was a widower with two sons.

Queen Margaret and King Malcolm had eight children, six sons and two daughters. Edgar, Alexander, and David all reigned as kings of Scotland. Edward the first-born died in battle with his father, King Malcolm, against the English in 1093. Margaret was known to read the Bible to her husband that served to "Christianize" his moral character.[6] Under the inspiration of Lanfranc, future archbishop of Canterbury, and her experiences at the Hungarian court, Margaret brought Scottish Catholicism in line with the Church of Rome. With such an influence over her children, especially her last-born, King David I of Scotland, they acquired a sense of being just and holy rulers themselves. By Margaret's initiative, the Benedictines established a monastery at Dunfermline, Fife, in 1072, and the restoration of the ancient Iona Abbey. Pope Pius IV canonized Margaret in 1250.

iv. Saint Jadwiga: Queen of Poland (1373/4-1399)

Well into the modern era, Poland demonstrated its loyalty to its Catholic faith, to Jesus and his blessed mother. Despite attempts to suppress Catholicism in Poland by the Swedish Lutheran monarchy, the threat of Ottoman Muslims, Russian Bolsheviks, German Nazis, and again Russian Marxists, Poland stood firm in its Catholic faith. Poland did not experience the religious rupture as in other parts of northern and western Europe. This oneness and religious continuity of Roman Catholicism in Poland ensured a united voice defending Poland's Catholic identity and moral values.

---

5. Graham, *Margaret Queen of Scotland*, 18.
6. Graham, *Margaret Queen of Scotland*, 36.

Jadwiga is the first female queen of Poland, born in the capital of the kingdom of Hungary, Buda. Jadwiga was the youngest daughter of Louis the Great of Poland and Hungary and Elizabeth of Bosnia, a family known for their devout Catholic faith and religious observance. Growing up in a religious environment, Jadwiga was devoted to the Virgin Mary and attended mass every day. She was crowned queen in Krakow, the capital of Poland, in 1386 when she was fourteen years old. Jadwiga married the grand duke of Lithuania, Jogaila, a pagan who converted to Catholicism before their marriage. Jogaila was baptized into the Catholic faith; Jadwiga married Jogaila in Wawel Cathedral, February 15, 1386, and he was crowned king of Poland. The marriage led to the union of Poland and Lithuania. Political rebels who did not accept Jogaila as king murdered Jadwiga's mother, Elizabeth. Jadwiga, then, led the Polish army into Ruthenia where the majority of the governors accepted her royal authority. Queen Jadwiga was known for her charitable works, establishing and restoring churches, hospitals, and schools. She also ensured the restoration and funding of the University of Krakow. She died on July 17, 1399, four days after the death of her baby girl. "Saint Jadwiga's Cross" where Christ had spoken to her can still be seen at Wawel Cathedral above her relics. She is considered a medieval mystic. She was canonized in 1997 by John Paul II.

v. Saint Bridget of Sweden (1303-1373)

Saint Bridget reflects the spiritual richness of Swedish Catholicism that reached its summit in the medieval era.[7] Bridget married at the age of fourteen Ulf Gudmarsson, with whom she had eight children. Her mother, Ingeborg, belonged to Swedish royalty, and through her mother's lineage, Bridget was related to Swedish kings. Their second daughter is venerated as Catherine of Sweden. The religious depth of Bridget and Ulf and the Catholic culture of Sweden generated a religious climate rich in sculpture, painting, and architecture.

Ulf died in 1344 shortly after Bridget returned from a pilgrimage in Compostela, Spain. She then joined the Third Order of Franciscans, became engaged in helping the poor, and lived a prayerful life. She founded the Order of the Most Holy Savior with the principal monastery located in Vadstena, Sweden. The foundation of the order included both monks and nuns with separate cloisters. While they lived a life of poverty, a reflection of the

---

7. *Revelations of St. Bridget of Sweden*, vii-ix.

intellectual tradition of Catholicism associated with the religious orders was their freedom to keep as many books as they wished.[8]

Bridget went on a pilgrimage to Rome in 1350, a Jubilee Year, with her daughter Catherine including priests and her followers to obtain authorization of her newly founded order. In the order, the abbess who signified the Virgin Mary presided over nuns and monks. The approval came in 1370 three years before her death when Pope Urban V approved of the order. Bridget became well-known while living in the city of Rome for over twenty years until she died, apart from her pilgrimages to Jerusalem and Bethlehem.

The Council of Basel in 1436 confirmed the orthodoxy of her revelations. Bridget had visions of Jesus since she was ten years old and the center of her spirituality was the Passion of Christ. The specific revelations Bridget received was to honor the passion of Jesus: he received 5480 blows, and so fifteen Our Fathers and fifteen Hail Marys are to be said with a prayer—*oratio*—for an entire year. Once the year is over the wounds of Jesus will have been honored. Bridget died on July 23, 1373. She was canonized in 1391 by Pope Boniface IX. On October 1st, 1999, Pope John Paul II named Saint Bridget of Sweden co-patroness of Europe. Her relics are found in both the Bridgettine Church in Rome and at Vadstena Abbey in Sweden.[9]

---

8. These monasteries were built by nuns and monks with the support of the faithful and whatever lands the bishop or generous landowners might offer. The Protestant Revolution began in Germany in 1519 by Martin Luther, an Augustinian monk, who was eventually excommunicated by Pope Leo X. Protestant "reformers," both moderate and radical, were actively agitating for change, hence, "revolution": John Calvin, Andreas Karlstadt, John Knox, and Ulrich Zwingli were among the leading reformers. Moderate Protestants such as Luther considered followers of Calvin to be radical—and heretical—which explains the bloody wars between Lutherans and Calvinists. Monarchs in northern Europe, and England and Scotland, under the influence of landowners, rejected the authority of the Roman pontiff also in the name of *Sola Scriptura* (only the Bible has authority, not the pope nor the magisterium). The Protestant monarchs and the influential nobility (landowners) benefitted from the wealth and prestige of Roman Catholic lands. The cathedrals, monasteries, and churches that took centuries to construct commissioned by Catholic monarchs and bishops with the labor and support of the Catholic faithful, including monks and nuns, were appropriated, sold, or designated as national churches. Catholics were devoted to the saints: the cathedrals and churches "housed" the relics of the saints and also gave the Virgin Mary an honorable place of veneration, all pointing to Christ and the Trinitarian God who is at the center of the Christian faith. See, Logan, *Middle Ages*, 225–252. The intellectual-religious setting became increasingly tense as well. At the start of the reform, movements which led up to the Protestant Revolution, Sweden's University of Uppsala proved to be a stronghold of Catholic sympathizers who resisted the Lutheran reforms.

9. After its suppression by Lutheran monarchs along with the suppression of the Catholic Church in northern Europe, the Bridgettine Order was "refounded." Saint Elizabeth Hasselblad, a convert from Lutheranism, received papal approval for the

vi. Venerable Isabel of Castile: Queen of Spain [1451-1504]

Isabel of Castile has been one of the most influential—and controversial—queens in shaping Christian civilization.[10] With her husband, King Ferdinand II of Aragon, Isabel of Castile unified Spain; they became known as the "Catholic Monarchs," a title granted by Pope Alexander VI. She was declared "Servant of God" in March, 1974.[11]

Isabel was the daughter of John II of Castile and Elizabeth of Portugal.[12] By the instruction of her deeply religious mother, Isabel learned, at an early age, the value of religion and piety. Isabel reflected a woman of determination who stood her ground. Given the number of suitors who proposed to her in order to forge political alliances with Europe's monarchies, Isabel refused, preferring to honor her childhood betrothal to Ferdinand. Isabel was only six years old when the marriage had been arranged. Although they were second cousins, violating the degrees of sanguinity for marriage, a papal dispensation was obtained so they could marry.

Only Grenada remained for the Reconquista of Spain after the Spanish rulers reclaimed the Iberian lands. Military advances reached their summit by 1492 when the Catholic monarchs, Isabel and Ferdinand, defeated the last remaining bastion of Islam on the peninsula: the Emirate of Granada. The principal mosque was converted to a church.

With the return of Grenada to Spain and Christianity, the Catholic monarchs were in a position to finance Columbus's maritime exploration, reaching the East Indies by sailing West. Christopher Columbus (Italian: Cristofero Colombo) was technically sponsored by Queen Isabella. Columbus sailed from Palos de la Frontera, August 3, 1492, and reached the Bahamas, October 12, at a location he named in honor of the "Holy Savior," San Salvador.[13]

---

refounded Bridgettine Order in 1940.

10. See Weidenkopf, *Timeless*, 314–16.

11. Queen Isabel received the title "Servant of God" when her canonization process was approved in 1974. After the process was stopped in 1991 due to issues concerning her expulsion of the Jews, Pope Francis asked the Spanish bishops to reopen the cause of canonization in 2020.

12. Queen Elizabeth of Portugal appears in the Catholic calendar as "Saint Elizabeth of Portugal." Her memorial day is July 4.

13. In thanksgiving for their safe voyage and the lands they came to possess, it was common practice for Catholic explorers (Spanish, Portuguese, French) to name cities, towns, even countries after Saints or the liturgical feast at the time of landing or exploration. Many cities in the State of California are named after Franciscan saints or devotions: Ventura (Saint Bonaventure), San Francisco (Saint Francis), Los Angeles

Isabel's youngest daughter, Catherine of Aragon, married England's Arthur, Prince of Wales. With Arthur's premature death, Catherine married Arthur's younger brother, King Henry VIII of England. From a devout Catholic mother and father, Catherine of Aragon upheld her strong Catholic faith and fidelity to her marriage. King Henry VIII, a capricious king known for his marital infidelity, and seeking a male heir, was determined to divorce Catherine of Aragon to marry Anne Boleyn. The English king broke with the Church of Rome to create his own Church of England. King Henry VIII obtained the divorce he demanded through his newly created Church of England and state-sponsored executions to enforce the recognition of his new marriage, formalized in the Oath of Supremacy and Oath of Succession, respectively. Catherine, his legitimate wife and Queen of England, loved by the English people, was removed from the English throne and from public sight.

2. Biblical Queens

Both the Old and New Testament Scriptures convey the roles of queens in biblical history culminating with the queen depicted in the book of Revelation. Mary's Queenship finds its source in her Son, Jesus, King of Kings.

i. Queen of Sheba

We are told in the Scriptures that the queen of Sheba heard about the wisdom of Solomon. She visited Solomon arriving with a retinue, with camels and spices, gold and precious stones (1 Kgs 10:1–3). The queen spoke to Solomon of what she had on her mind and tested him with hard questions (2 Chr 9:1–2). The queen understood that Solomon's wisdom reached the lives of his wives and servants because they heard Solomon's wisdom (1 Kgs 10:8; 2 Chr 9:7). The queen realized that the God of Israel took delight in Solomon, setting him on the throne as king, and because God loved Israel,

---

(Our Lady of the Angels). The city name, "Corpus Christi," Texas, comes from Latin, "Body of Christ," reflecting the liturgical date of exploration. Or a city might be named after the patron saint in honor of the monarch: St. Louis (in honor of King Louis XIV). The "Dominican Republic" and the capital "Santo Domingo" are both named after Saint Dominic, the Spanish founder of the Order of Preachers. In Montreal, Canada, the streets are named primarily after saints and so are many towns. Mont Royal, the hilltop overlooking Montreal, glows from the Christian cross lit up at night. The use of crosses and statues are indicative of the Catholic culture and the visible presence of Christianity. This is especially evident in Rio de Janeiro, Brazil, with the iconic statue of Christ the Redeemer who overlooks the city with outstretched arms.

would establish them "forever." Solomon was made king to ensure justice and righteousness would be executed.

The language of the queen of Sheba is prophetic: though Solomon does not last forever, nor does the kingdom of Israel, the queen's language anticipates a descendent of Solomon and a kingdom that will last forever, namely Jesus and his eternal kingdom. The language of the queen is echoed by the angel Gabriel who speaks of David and Jacob to Mary at the annunciation; David, who is Solomon's father; and Jacob, who is the father of the twelve tribes of Israel. This explains the queen of Sheba's use of the plural reference, "them," relating to the twelve tribes. This signifies the throne on which Jesus will sit as the angel tells Mary. And by royal lineage, Mary's Son, who is king, also makes Mary the queen mother.

ii. Song of Songs 4:7, 12

In mystical theology, the bride in the Song of Songs is reference to the Virgin Mary. The language of Song of Songs provides sensuous details, clearly life-giving with the vibrant colors, the taste of fruit, language of a "closed" garden that awaits the spouse: "You are altogether beautiful, my love; / there is no flaw in you . . . A garden locked is my sister, my bride, / a garden locked, a fountain sealed." The language of life created by these verses is precisely the life that Mary gives to us through Christ. The garden symbolizes something sensuous and because the garden is "enclosed," making it virginal, this garden is life-generating. We cannot ignore the purity in this exchange: the lover refers to his bride as his "sister" to show that the love can only be understood at the purest levels possible. The best resemblance of the lover's pure intent corresponds to the man and the woman in the garden of Eden before the fall, where both humans were governed by the purity of nature, of life, reflecting the goodness of God's creation.

Song of Songs is associated with King Solomon, and therefore, one needs to consider the rich images in the development of the canticle intended for a queen. One of the interpretations in the mystical tradition finds its source in Saint Bernard of Clairvaux, to apply the pure and chaste life-giving relations conveyed in the powerful images as the lover addresses his beloved, Jesus addressing his mother.

Mystical theology provides a layer of meaning that is not explicit in the Scriptures but may be inferred on the basis of connecting different books and passages with Christ clearly at the center.[14] The layers of meaning that apply

---

14. While teaching Sacred Scripture, I discovered that Catholic students employed fewer parallel verses in their assignments, but with a sense of layers of interpretation

to Jesus are also associated with the central human figure in the life of Jesus: his mother. Mary is the one whom the angel approaches; Mary is the one who consents to the message; Mary is the one who receives the Holy Spirit; and Mary is the one who incarnates the Son of God.

The mystical interpretation of Saint Bernard attributes the lover and the beloved to Jesus and Mary, suggested by the enigmatic wedding couple at the wedding at Cana whose names are unknown. Instead, at Cana, John's Gospel only provides the names of Jesus and Mary at the Galilean wedding. Mary intercedes for the chief steward by going to Jesus; her Son appears to hesitate because "my time has not yet come" (John 7:6). Nevertheless, Jesus heeds to his mother's request as we meditate in the second luminous mystery.

The love between Jesus and his mother is what the Song of Songs conveys, and what we find fulfilled in the wedding at Cana. The hearts of Jesus and Mary are one both in their love, cooperation, and their suffering.

iii. Psalms of David

The Psalm directed towards a king includes the later presence of a princess. References to "king" in the Old Testament without a specific name, but in this case a divine king, point to Jesus Christ: "Your throne, O God, endures forever and ever. / Your royal scepter is a scepter of equity; / you love righteousness and hate wickedness. Therefore God, your God, has anointed you / with the oil of gladness beyond your companions . . ." (Ps 45:6-7). The explicit divine references especially with allusion to "forever and ever" can only mean a divine presence.

A few verses further, the Psalm introduces us to a female figure, "at your right hand stands the queen in gold of Ophir" (Ps 45:9). The female royal figure expresses her queenship in relation to the king, "Hear, O daughter, consider and / incline your ear; / forget your people and your father's house; / and the king will desire your beauty. Since he is your lord, bow to him" (Ps 45 10–12). The female figure is identified with Mary because the king is divine and Mary's relationship with her Son from conception is bowing to a divine king. The Psalm prefigures a woman who has a regal function in relation to the king.

The beauty of Mary reflects her innocence, her purity, her virginity. Mary's virginity before and after conceiving, and after giving birth to Jesus,

---

compared to the non-Catholic students, who provided more biblical parallels without expressing a deeper level of interpretation other than the literal (Alliance, Baptist, Evangelical, Nazarene, Pentecostal, Reformed . . .).

represents a fundamental quality of who Mary is and her role in our salvation, mother of the Messiah. The woman's beauty and virginity are highlighted in the following verses: "The princess is decked in her chamber with the gold-woven robes; / in many colored robes she is led to the king; / behind her the virgins, her companions follow" (Ps 45:13–14). To emphasize the beauty of the princess, one of the characteristics is found in the quality of the robes she wears; a train follows her, "gold-woven robes" and "many-colored," which falls behind her, conveying the elegance of the princess. Colors and quality of fabric, the richness of layers creates a sense of royalty; besides, beauty and such qualities fit Mary because she is the chosen woman to be the mother of God's Son. The regal language describes not only Mary, although she is described with exceptional beauty in regal attire, but the "cause" of Mary's presence, her role, and as a result her virginal beauty is directly related to Jesus Christ, the king.

The princess is all about the king—"she is led to the king," and in the following verse, "With joy and gladness they are led along as they enter that palace of the king" (Ps 45:15). So, the movement is towards the king: he is the goal, he is the reason for this virginal beauty; the princess has prepared herself for the king.

Given the language of this Psalm identifying the divine king, and then the woman who is both virginal and beautiful and seeks this king with "joy and gladness," the verses are regarded as prefiguring Mary as queen, just as her Son is king. The queen in gold who stands at the right of the king embodies and perfects the qualities of the princess. And so she receives the title, "Mary, Queen of Heaven."

iv. Queen Mother of the Davidic Kingdom

King David's wife, Bathsheba, approaching King Solomon, her son, is treated with reverence as the queen mother. The passage from 1 Kings, which the Catholic Church has traditionally used in application to Mary, shows this relationship of deference towards the queen mother: "So Bathsheba went to King Solomon, to speak to him on behalf of Adonijah. The king rose to meet her, and bowed down to her; then he sat on his throne, and had a throne brought for the king's mother, and she sat on his right" (1 Kgs 2:19).

The relationship between the king and his mother reflects the filial respect that is owed to a mother. We hear King Solomon express his willingness to hear his mother and reassures her that her request will be fulfilled: "I will not refuse you." The exchange between mother and son, queen and king, creates a remarkable parallel with the wedding at Cana where Mary makes a request to her Son, Jesus, and he carries out the request. The difference, however, being that Jesus is apprehensive at first, and then concedes to his mother's request, while Solomon immediately agrees to the request but does not carry it out.

In the New Testament, the Davidic role of king as messianic promise is fulfilled by Jesus. The prophecy of Nathan and the announcement of the angel Gabriel are realized in Christ. Jesus belongs to the house of David. He is anointed king by his Father who sent him. Mary shows a parallel role as found in Kings (1 Kgs 2:19–20): Mary is regarded as the queen mother; Mary turns to her Son at Cana, and her Son responds. The wedding at Cana expresses this fundamental bond between Jesus and his mother, as king and queen mother, respectively.

v. Queen Esther

Esther was a Jewish queen married to a Persian pagan, King Artaxerxes. Because the king found Esther to be the most beautiful among virgins, finding "favor and devotion" in his sight, King Artaxerxes placed the royal crown on Esther's head (Esth 2:17). The king later promoted Haman to the position of the chief officer, but Haman hated the Jews and intended to eliminate them by falsely claiming that the Jews were planning an insurrection against the king. As a result of Haman's rumor, Artaxerxes wanted all the Jews executed. Esther found out about the edict of putting the Jews to death from her uncle Mordecai, who turned to Queen Esther for her intercession. But in Artaxerxes' court, nobody was permitted to communicate with the king unless summoned by the king himself. But if Esther did not approach the king on this matter, the Jews would be put to death. So, Esther risked her life and interceded on behalf of the Jewish people. Artaxerxes told Esther that the law of summoning applied to the people, not to the queen. And having heard the news of Haman's plot, Artaxerxes ordered Haman's execution, and the Jews were saved (Esth 7:10).

We have three elements associated with Queen Esther that serve to pre-figure the Virgin Mary: first, Esther's queenship; second, Esther's intercessory role; and third, saving the people from death. The second and third, the intercessory and salvific roles, are central in Esther pre-figuring Mary as queen: Mary serves as an intercessor not just at the wedding at Cana but as a mediatrix to defeat death by giving birth to Christ who will destroy death and the works of Satan. In Queen Esther's story, slaughter is represented by the diabolical figure Haman. We already have the enmity between the woman and the serpent, the devil, in the *Proto-Evangelium* (Gen 3:15) and as conveyed in the first joyful mystery. Satan's devouring presence appears immediately after the woman adorned with twelve stars indicative of Mary (Rev 12:1; 4–5). The woman's battle against Satan is further conveyed when the woman in labor pains, ready to give birth, is threatened by the dragon, waiting to devour the child. Both Genesis (3) and Revelation (12) point to Mary—her offspring—and the devil waiting to "devour."

vi. New Testament: Virgin Mary, Queen of Heaven

The central female figure in the New Testament is Mary. The mother of our Savior cannot be ignored, dismissed, or put in brackets. Mary is the chosen mother of God's Son; Mary is "blessed among all women" (Luke 1:42); to bear the Son of God Jesus receives Mary's flesh. Mary carries out God's will from conception to when she stands below the cross. Mary occupies a unique place in salvation history, given her faithful and collaborative role in the incarnation and at the crucifixion, where she remains united with God's plan for our salvation as Jesus, in agony, breathes his last breath.

Saint Luke, chapter 1

The words in Luke's Gospel present the unfolding drama of God's plan: "and the Lord God will give to him the throne of his ancestor David. He will reign over the house of Jacob forever, and of his kingdom there will be no end" (Luke 1:32–33). The verses state the Son of Mary will be king, "throne of his father David," and to reign over the house of Jacob means the unified nation of Israel, king of one people. Finally, "the kingdom will have no end" indicates this kingdom is forever. The declaration of the angel's announcement expresses kingship and divinity, both of which Jesus possesses. By extension, since Mary is the mother, just as Bathsheba was the mother of Solomon, Mary's role represents that of queen mother. When the fifth glorious mystery speaks of Mary as queen of heaven, this reflects Jesus, who is king of heaven—an eternal kingdom. Mary, as the king's mother, shares in this kingdom as queen. The coronation of Mary follows her assumption into heaven as we meditate in the fourth glorious mystery. Mary is crowned because she fulfils her role as mother of the king just as Jesus fulfils his role as king, and both reign as king and queen, forever secure in God's eternal kingdom.

The passage offered to us in Luke's Gospel reflects the centrality of the Davidic kingdom which Jesus inherits as the anointed messianic king, a kingdom that is forever and a kingdom that is united. Jesus will repeat this in his teachings to the apostles in John's Gospel; Jesus instructs his apostles that unity reflects the oneness between him and his Father (John 17:11). Mary is queen of one kingdom: she is queen of heaven.

Revelation, chapter 12

Revelation uses many symbols which have layers of meanings. Some of the figures display recognizable characteristics even though the cryptic language makes Revelation complex to "decipher." In Catholicism, the woman (Rev 12) has been traditionally identified as Mary because of the regal features of the woman and the context of her giving birth—both royalty and maternity point to Mary.

The key verse from Revelation associated with Mary: "And a great portent appeared in heaven, a woman clothed with the sun, with the moon under her feet, and on her head a crown of twelve stars" (Rev 12:1). Why should this woman be interpreted as Mary? The fact that the woman was "with child"; the central event of the New Testament is the incarnation. Once we establish the woman to be Mary, then the crown of twelve stars involves attributing to Mary the role of queen. Jesus is king, the fulfillment of the Davidic kingdom, and Mary is queen; this correctly serves to give the title of the fifth glorious mystery of the rosary, "crowning of Mary, queen of heaven."

We can speculate on the significance of the twelve stars as part of the crown; we know this may be the twelve tribes of Israel or twelve apostles. But when re-reading Luke's annunciation message, the house of Jacob constitutes twelve tribes, and the emphasis, therefore, is one people as opposed to the divisions existing between the north and south of Israel. Similarly, if we take the twelve stars to refer to the twelve apostles, the stars reflect the language of Saint John's Gospel when Jesus emphasizes the oneness of his apostles: "that they may be one as we are one" (John 17:11). The symbolism of the twelve stars strongly suggests that of unity. This further corresponds to a mother who wants to bring her children together as one family without divisions. A queen strives to unite warring factions in her realm while crushing the advances of the enemy.

This oneness brings us to the church: the language of the angel Gabriel at the annunciation, just as the language of Jesus in John's Gospel, focuses on "one." The church of which Mary is mother continues the teachings of Christ and his mandate to his apostles to bless all nations (Matt 28:19); this requires a unified message in doctrine and morals.

II—Fruit of this Mystery: Eternal Happiness

Practical Matters—

Confusion and error has been a serious problem in the history of the church, both in doctrine and morals. Oneness in doctrine is indicative of whether we are Christians or a sect; oneness in morals teaches us whether we are Christians purified by Christ or worshipers of the golden calf. And so Mary, crowned as Queen, unites her children into one church: "One Lord, one faith, one baptism, one God and Father of all" (Eph 4:4–6).

The desire for happiness is not something learned but is inherent to all humans. We make decisions in the hope of attaining some degree of happiness or greater happiness. To be happy is the engine of human existence. We also know that in the effort to be happy, bad decisions can be made: choosing poorly, choosing sin instead of sanctity, making choices that gradually lead down a slippery slope of sin, sliding one's way down to hell. Immediate changes need to be made in one's life if the choices seeking happiness are not made in the light of truth. In other words, happiness entails conversion. Happiness without truth can never be happiness. Truth is found in the Person of Jesus Christ.

"Happiness" may sound like a mundane or trite term; perhaps too worldly for the Christian. But happiness is also translated as "blessed," Latin, *beatus* and Greek, *makarios* as in the Beatitudes, "Happy . . ." in some Bible translations, "Blessed . . ." in other translations (Matt 5.1–12). Blessedness conveys the spiritual depth of happiness on earth and the summit of happiness in heaven.

Jesus enters the world precisely to bring us blessedness, true happiness. His teachings focus on living a happy life. But Jesus does not teach us that blessedness excludes pain and suffering. Blessedness means carrying our cross and following Christ, whatever that cross may be. If we deny our cross, we can never be truly blessed. Our human existence will be superficial, living on the surface, a kind of epicurean ethos that is self-interested or a hedonistic ethos that is pleasure-seeking. A superficial happiness, a self-focused existence, is neither taking up one's cross nor the language of Christ.

We can attain some happiness on earth to be relatively happy, but complete happiness we shall not have because of our inclination towards sin with the propensity towards pride, or greed, or lust; then, our weaknesses and defects create relational difficulties and interior fragmentation. But if we follow Christ's teachings, we can certainly have happiness on earth, but it will not be complete.[15]

---

15. Saint Thomas Aquinas makes this very clear: perfect happiness can only be in heaven. See, *ST*, Pt. 1a-2ae, q. 3, art. 3.

The eternal happiness associated with the fifth glorious mystery awaits each of us if we are faithful to the Gospel, to the teachings of Christ. Catholic moral teaching draws from natural law, tradition, and the Bible. To be Catholic means to belong to a universal church; local or particular churches participate in the one universal church founded by Christ, governed by his Vicar, the Pope, along with the local bishops of the church. We need to keep in mind that Satan is the prince of deception. Catholicism avoids doctrinal fragmentation and moral relativism by its universal teaching intended to be objectively rooted; this universality ensures we are one in faith and morals as Christ taught (John 17:11).

Our eternal blessedness then is perfectly realized in heaven, where happiness is complete. We shall have reached our heavenly reward after our years of fidelity on earth, living by the grace of God, the sacraments of the church, in prayer, receptive to the needs of others, whether in our family, in our church, or community we live in.

The way to eternal happiness means following Christ and carrying our cross as we follow him. We shall be, by God's grace, perfectly one with Christ, his blessed mother, the angels and saints, our family and friends—all who have been faithful to their baptism, to the Word of God, and faithful to Christ's church. Fidelity to Jesus brings us to eternal life: the kingdom of heaven where Jesus is the eternal king. We have Mary to intercede for us, the mother whom Jesus gives to us as our queen, to keep her children united, one family of faith. We are on our way, armored with the rosary and the Bible. Amen.

Holy Mary, Mother of God
[Luke 1:26-38; Council of Ephesus, 431 AD]

Pray for us sinners
[John 2:1–12]

Now and at the hour of our death. Amen.
[Matthew 25:1–13]

Conclusion

The rosary and the Bible provide the spiritual armor we need as Christians to engage in the spiritual warfare that Saint Paul warns us about (Eph 6). The meditative prayers of the rosary rooted in the events of the Old and New Testament provide the powerful foundation to our biblical faith as Catholics; not just what we believe but how we are called to live, from contemplation to action, from action back to contemplation.

Our vocation is to grow in truth and love and to teach others to do the same so as to make Catholic living concrete. Parents and teachers of Catholic schools play a fundamental role in providing a Catholic formation for schoolchildren, adolescents, and the youth. The need for Catholic formation does not diminish for college or university students either; in fact, the young adult can discover the truth of Catholicism in its rich biblical history and Christ-centered spirituality. And we should be prepared to answer questions about our beliefs and practices as Catholics.

Our spiritual life begins with our parents who teach us prayers—to love God and each other. Family life is spiritually anchored in the parish with the reception of the sacraments that provide us with the graces we need to live our Christ-centered faith. Our parish provides an ongoing support to enrich our prayer life and the space we need for Christian fellowship. Sometimes we feel blocked by attitudes such as "I don't get anything out of it . . ." "This doesn't do anything for me . . ." But the spiritual life is not just about "me" and "my" relationship with God; as Catholics, our spiritual life necessarily connects us with others—how we support the community in prayer, and then, by serving others in ministries. We start by spiritually strengthening our own family.

We can think about how our presence at Holy Mass deepens our relationship with God through confession and Holy Communion, and how our presence supports others through our prayers. We can take this further when we get involved in ministries including Bible studies, faith sharing, youth groups, devotional prayers, music ministry . . . Some parishes offer soup kitchens and street ministries both reaching out to the poor and marginalized. If none of the parish ministries offers what the parishioner is seeking, then a catechetical/virtue-building ministry can be proposed or discussed with the parish priest. I remember during my Dominican religious formation, I wanted to continue with a pastoral ministry I enjoyed. So, when I offered to help with RCIA, the priest at the parish where I hoped to get involved did not need help with RCIA, but they needed someone to lead a Bible study. And so, I offered my first parish Bible study.[1]

Some men hear a calling from God to give themselves to their community as priests and spiritual fathers. Men and women may also believe they have a calling to offer themselves as spiritual fathers and mothers—as religious. This total commitment of oneself to the salvation of others is indicative of the origins of religious orders, congregations, and societies of apostolic life. No one can doubt that the call to celibate life of a priest or the consecrated life as a religious expresses the radicality of Christian living.

Whether it's motherhood or fatherhood, natural or supernatural, the single life, the celibate, or the consecrated, the sacraments of confession and communion are our source of nourishment; the Bible, the rosary the armor for battle.

We depend on our Catholic community and hierarchy from the pope to the newly baptized. We depend on the Virgin Mary, on her intercessory role, and on each other for prayers; we are a community of Catholic faithful journeying together. We depend on Jesus, Son of the ever-living God, for our salvation and to lead us to his eternal Kingdom of Heaven. We are on our way.

---

1. Rite of Christian Initiation of Adults.

Bibliography

Alliata E. (OFM). In Pixner, *Paths of the Messiah,* 407.
Amorth, Gabriel. *Maria e Satana.* Milan: San Paolo, 2018.
Aquinas, Thomas. *The Summa Theologica of Saint Thomas Aquinas.* Translated by Fathers of the English Dominican Province. London: Burns Oates and Washbourne, 1920.
Augustine of Hippo. *Confessions* (Books I-VIII). Cambridge: Harvard University, 1999.
Bergsma, John, and Brant Pitre. *Catholic Introduction to the Old Testament.* San Francisco: Ignatius, 2018.
Bridget of Sweden (OSSS). *Revelations.* Charlotte: Tan, 2015. [Originally translated in English from Antwerp edition in 1611.]
Bunson, Margaret, and Matthew Bunson. *St. Damien of Molokai: Apostle of the Exiled.* Huntington, IN: Our Sunday Visitor, 2009.
Catechism of the Catholic Church. New York: Doubleday, 1995.
Destro, Robert A. "Genocide, Statecraft, and Domestic Geopolitics." In *The Persecution and Genocide of Christians in the Middle East,* edited by R. Rychlak and J. Adolphe, 59–92. Kettering: Angelico, 2017.
Dorcy, Mary Jean (OP). *Saint Dominic.* Rockford, IL: Tan, 1955.
Douay-Rheims Bible. American Edition, 1899. (First translated by the English College at Rheims and Douay 1582, 1609-10).
Egeria. *Egeria's Travels.* Translated by John Wilkinson. Oxford: Oxbow, 2013.
Graham, Henry Grey. *Margaret Queen of Scotland.* Milton Keynes: Oakpast, 2011.
Francis, Pope. *Patris corde* ["With a Father's Heart"]. Apostolic Letter. Rome, 2020.
Hahn, Scott, and Curtis Mitch. *The Ignatius Catholic Study Bible.* San Francisco: Ignatius, 2010.
"Jadwiga of Poland." https://military-history.fandom.com/wiki/Jadwiga_of_Poland.
John Paul II, Pope. *Fides et Ratio.* Boston: Pauline, 1998.
———. *Rosarium Viriginis Mariae* ["Rosary of the Virgin Mary"]. Apostolic Letter. Sherbrooke, QC: Mediaspaul, 2002.
———. *Theology of the Body.* Boston: Pauline, 2006.
Karlin, Louis W., and David R. Oakley. *Thomas More.* New York: Scepter, 2018.
Kilgallen, John J. *New Testament Guide to the Holy Land.* Chicago: Loyola, 1998.
Logan, Donald F. *A History of the Church of the Middle Ages.* London: Routledge, 2002.
Mother Teresa (MC). *Where There Is Love, There Is God.* Edited with introduction by Brian Kolodiejchuk (MC). New York: Image, 2010.

Murphy-O'Connor, Jerome. *The Holy Land: An Oxford Archaeological Guide from Earliest Times to 1700.* Oxford: Oxford University, 2008.
Paul VI, Pope. *Humanae Vitae.* Boston: Pauline, 1968.
Pixner, Bargil. *Paths of the Messiah.* San Francisco: Ignatius, 2010.
The Revised New Jerusalem Bible. Study Edition. London: Darton, Longman, and Todd, 2019.
Samson, Charles. *Come and See: A Catholic Guide to the Holy Land.* Steubenville, OH: Emmaus, 2018.
Vost, Kevin. *Hounds of the Lord.* Manchester NH, Sophia Institute, 2015.
Weidenkopf, Steve. *Timeless: History of the Catholic Church.* Huntington, IN: Our Sunday Visitor, 2018.

Subject Index

Abraham, 108, 223
Act of Contrition (prayer), 139
Adam, first man, 5–6, 8–9
addictions, 101–4, 181
Africa, Catholic practice in, 62–63
agony in the Garden
    agony, 134–35
    betrayal, 135–37
    contrition, virtue of, 139–143
    Father's will, 137–38
    Gethsemane, 131
    prophecies of Jesus's passion, 132–33
    will of God, conformity to, 139
Alexander of Cyrene (son of Simon), 176
Alexander VI, Pope, 257
Amorth, Gabriel, 61–62
ancient Christian communities, 231n5
angels
    announcing to shepherds, 35–36
    description of, 4n3
    fallen angel, Satan. *see* Satan
    Gabriel. *see* Gabriel (angel)
    Jóseph's escape to Egypt, 47
    Michael, 4
    Raphael, 4, 102, 102n9
Anne, Saint, 8, 70n6
annunciation, of Jesus birth, 3–15, 7n5, 62n5, 216–18
antichrist, 59
apostolic authority, 123, 193n7
apostolic churches, 193n7
Arianism, 78, 253, 253n4

Artaxerxes, King, 262–63
artificial contraception, 155n8
Assumption. *See* Mary, assumption of into heaven
Augustine of Hippo, Saint, 133
Ave Maria prayer, 20, 22

banqueting house, term usage, 83
baptism
    for adults, 213
    of disciples, 229
    Easter Vigil Mass reaffirmation of, 50
    Holy Trinity and, 75–76
    of infants/children, 42–44, 210
    of Jesus, 74–77
    original sin and, 188n3
    parents role in, 212–13
    sacrament of, 5, 75n10
Barluzzi, Antonio, 70, 106, 131
Bartholomew (Nathanael), apostle, 208
basilicas
    Basilica of Hagia Sofia, Turkey, 240
    Basilica of Santa Maria Maggiore, Rome, 250
    Basilica of the Dormition, Jerusalem, 189, 239–240
    Basilica of the Holy Sepulcher, Jerusalem, 178, 185, 187, 196–203, 200–201n3
    Basilica of the Nativity in Bethlehem, 28–29
    See also churches
Bathsheba, 113

SUBJECT INDEX

Battle of Hattin (1187), 3
Beatitudes, 101, 236–38, 265
Beheading of John the Baptist memorial observation, 73n9
Benedict XVI, Pope, 133
Benedictine monastery
    Dunfermline, Fife, Scotland, 254
    Monte Cassino, 95n3
Benedictus (hymn of Zechariah), 18, 18n4, 70n5
Benjamin, southern tribe of Israel, 108, 160
Bernard of Clairvaux, Saint, 259–260
Bethany, 68, 213
Bethlehem
    Christian presence in, 28–29
    David the Bethlehemite (King David), 8, 11, 33
    as "house of food," 35
betrayal, 135–37
biblical queens, 258–264
blasphemous demonstrations, 51
blessedness, 265–66
Boaz, Ruth and, 34
Boleyn, Anne, 258
Boniface IX, Pope, 256
Bridget, Saint, of Sweden, 255–56
Bridgettine Church, Rome, 256
burial practices, in Jesus day, 201

Caesar Augustus, 32–33
Caesarea Maritima, Judea capital, 148n4
Cain, 108
Caiphas' house, 146–47
Calvin, John, 256n8
Cana, Galilee. *See* miracle at Cana
cardinal virtues, 113, 114n8, 234
Cathedral of Turku, Finland, 249
Catherine of Aragon, 258
Catherine of Sweden, venerable, 255–56
Catholic schools, 210, 210n13
Central African Republic, Catholic practice in, 62–63
charity, 20–22, 26, 27
chastity, 31
children, looking for when lost, 54
Christ, term usage, 44
    See also Jesus

Christianity
    in ancient Christian communities, 231n5
    divisions among, 13–14
    fideistic, 211
    fragmentation of, 124, 163
    loss of Marian devotions, 90
    as a missionary religion, 232
    persecutions and executions of, 168, 170
    presence of in early stage of, 28–29
    proselytizing, 168–69n8
    two extremes of, 211
churches
    Bridgettine Church, Rome, 256
    Cathedral of Turku, Finland, 249
    Church of All Nations, Jerusalem, 131
    Church of England, 258
    Church of Saint Anne, Jerusalem, 70n6
    Church of Saint Joseph, Nazareth, 30
    Church of St. John the Baptist (Ein Karem, Jerusalem), 70
    Church of the Annunciation, Nazareth, 4
    Church of the Apostles, Jerusalem, 229
    Church of the Condemnation, Jerusalem, 151–52, 173
    Church of the Disciples, Jerusalem, 253, 253n2
    Church of the Flagellation, Jerusalem, 151
    Church of the Gallicantu, Jerusalem, 146, 146n2, 151, 152
    Church of the Holy Sepulchre, Jerusalem, 45
    Church of the Nativity, Bethlehem, 253
    Church of the Primacy of Peter, Tabgha, 209
    Church of the Transfiguration, Mount Tabor, 106
    Church of the Visitation (Ein Karem, Jerusalem), 17, 17n3
    See also basilicas

Cleopas, 206–7
Clotilda, Saint, Queen of France, 253
clouds, symbolism in Daniel, 216
Clovis, King of France, 253
collective disobedience, 51
collective sacrifice, 51–52
Columbus, Christopher, 257
Communion. *See* Eucharist
confession, sacrament of, 114, 123, 128, 140–42, 156–57, 179
Constantine the Great, 253
contrition, virtue of, 139–143
Council of Basel (1436), 256
Council of Ephesus (431 AD), 232n6, 242–43, 266
Council of Rome (382 AD), 162n2
covenantal oath, 35, 190
covenants
 ark of the covenant to Jerusalem, 17
 connection of old to new, 111–12
 movement from old to new, 70–72
 new covenant, initiation of, 117–19, 122
crucifix, meaning of, 174
culpability, 145–46

Damasus, Pope, 162n2
Damien of Molokai, Saint, 98
Daniel (prophet), 215–16
Daniel, Abbot, 70n7
darkness, spiritual, 127
darkness and light contrast, 202–3
David, King of Judah
 Bathsheba, 261–62
 brought the ark of the covenant to Jerusalem, 17
 David, house of, 8, 36, 159–161, 217–18
 as David the Bethlehemite, 8, 11, 33
 Jesus' ancestry, 29
 Nathan, son of, 29, 160
 Psalm of, 260–61
 Queen of Sheba and, 259
 throne of, 159–161
Day of Preparation, 202
Day of the Tomb, 201

death
 as absence of love, 26
 eternal life and, 245–46
 hope, for eternal life, 220–21
 of Jesus. *see* Jesus, crucifixion and death of
 Jesus condemned to, 26
 of persons, 245
 purgatory, 246
 raising from, 97–98
 sins, brought into the world, 244
Decalogue, 25
demons, casting out of, 99–100
 See also Satan
despair, 222
detachment, virtue of, 38–40
deutero-canonical books of scripture, 163n2
devotion to Mary, 90–91, 243–44, 248–251
disciples, at Cana, 80n1
discipline, 113–14
disobedience, communal level, 51–52
divinity, kingship and, 148–150
divisions
 in Christianity, 13–14
 tribes of Israel, 160
divorce, Jesus response to Pharisees, 141–42
Dominic, Saint, 187
"Dormition Abbey," 239, 240, 245
Douay-Rheims translation, 234n7
doubt, dealing with, 210–11

Ebionites
 founder of sect, 241
 Gospel of, 77n14
 heretical beliefs, 78, 189, 240–42
Ecumenical Church Councils, purpose of, 76, 76n12
 See also Council of Ephesus (431 AD)
Egeria (recording of Holy Land places), 3–4, 3n1
Ein Karem (Elizabeth's home), 16–17, 17n3, 31, 70–72

Elijah (prophet), 69, 71–72, 107–10, 192
Elisha (prophet), 67
Elizabeth (Mary's cousin)
    Ein Karem, home of, 16–17, 17n3, 31
    lineage of, 68
    Marian prayer, 19–20, 22, 247
    on Mary's conception, 23
    naming of John, 69
    visit from Mary, 11, 16–19
    See also John the Baptist; Zechariah
Elizabeth of Portugal, Saint, Queen, 257, 257n12
Emmaus, meeting Jesus, 206–7, 210
England, King of, Henry VIII, 258
Esau, Isaac's son, 35n6
Essenes, 163, 164n3, 241
Esther, Queen, 262–63
eternal happiness, 265–66
eternal life, 124, 220–21, 245–46
Eucharist
    body and blood of Christ, 124–25
    bread and wine, 124
    doubting Thomas, 125–26
    Eucharistic adoration, 126–28, 134
    Last Supper, 116–122, 189, 228–29
    priesthood of Jesus, 122–23
    spiritual communion, 226n1
Eve
    death because of sin, 244
    first woman, 5–6, 8–10
    Mary, as the second Eve, 6–10, 24, 43, 84, 244
Exodus, Passover ritual, 190–91
exorcism, 99–100
Ezekiel, prophet, 92–93

faith
    acts and, 194
    courage and, 169
    eternal life and, 124, 220–21
    obedience of, 52
    virtue of, 209–11
Fakhr al Din, emir of Mount Lebanon, 106
"false" preaching, 77
Fatebenefratelli Hospital, Rome, 95n3

"favored one" term usage, 8n6
Feast of Unleavened Bread, 118
Ferdinand II, King of Aragon, 257–58
fideistic Christianity, 211
fidelity, 35
Fides et Ratio (John Paul II), 211n14
Fisher, John, 49
flagellation of Jesus, 151–52
flogging, term usage, 151
forgiveness, 123, 125
four beasts (in Daniel), 215–16
four cups of wine, 117n1
France, Queen of (Saint Clotilda), 253, 253n3
Francis, Pope, 32n4, 38n8, 68n2, 206n6, 230n4, 231n5, 257n11
Franciscan, Third Order of, 255
Franciscan community, 4, 37, 70, 106, 172, 257n13
freedom
    of Mary's "yes," 9–10
    obedience and, 50–51

Gabriel (angel)
    Mary and, 3–5, 8, 9, 11, 17, 19, 159
    speaks of David and Jacob, 259
    Zechariah and, 21, 69
garden imagery, 84
gentile women, 113
Gethsemane, Garden of, 131
Gibson, Mel, 175
glorious, ascribed to Moses, Elijah, 110
Gnostic Gospels, writing of, 77n14
Gnosticism, 187–88, 189
God the Father
    conforming to will of, 139
    creator of life, 221
    hearing voice of, 128
    image of, 49, 59
    at Jesus' baptism, 74–75
    kingdom of proclamation, 92–104
    perversion of the image of, 133
    trust in, 101–4
    turning towards, 61
    will of, 137–38
Golgotha, Basilica (Church of the Holy Sepulchre), 28

Good Friday liturgy, 187
grace
    asking God for, 14–15
    of God, 194, 220
    need for, 98
grave sins, 140–41
Great Commission, 231
greed, 145
"greetings" term usage, 8n6
Gregory I, Pope, 95n3

Hadrian, Roman emperor, 28
Haggada (Jewish text), 241
Hail Mary prayer, 266
"hail" term usage, 8n6
Haman, chief officer (OT), 262
happiness, eternal, 265–66
Hasselblad, Saint Elizabeth, 256–57n9
Hattin, Battle of (1187), 3
heaven, desire for, 219–224
Helen, Saint (Empress), 28, 253
Helena of Constantinople, Saint, 178
Henry, Saint, 249
Henry VIII, King of England, 48–49, 258
heresy, postmodern context, 90
heretical movements
    Arianism, 78, 253, 253n4
    Ebionites, 78, 189, 240–42
    Gnostics, 187
    Manicheans, 187
    Nestorianism, 232n6
    Pelagians, 89n4
Herod Antipas, 71, 71n8, 72–73
Herod the Great, King, 47, 47n3, 72, 148n4
Herodias, Herod Antipas' wife, 72–73
hesed, term usage, 35
"highly favored one" term usage, 8n6
holiness, desire for, 112–13, 141–42, 227
Holy Innocents feast day, 47n3
Holy Saturday, 201
Holy Spirit
    descent of at Pentecost, 76, 226
    fruits of, 234–35
    gifts of, 233–34
    at Jesus' baptism, 71, 74–75
    languages and, 225–27
    in lives of apostles, 96
    in lives of individuals, 242
    openness to, 77–79
    other tongues speaking, 230–32
    the paraclete "counselor," 233
    at Pentecost, 145, 214
    role in bringing Jesus into the world, 5, 6
    Simeon's prophetic mission, 5
    Third Person of the Trinity, 226–28
    tongues of fire, 229–230
    in the upper room, 228–230
Holy Thursday, 189
Holy Trinity, 75–77
hope, virtue of, 219–224
hospice, term usage, 95n3
hospitals, 94nn3–4
human intelligence,, 59
Humanae Vitae (Paul VI), 141–42n7
humility
    of Elizabeth, 20–22
    of Mary, 11
    poverty and, 40
    purity and, 42
    virtue of, 12, 14, 50

idols, 12–13
impious, term usage, 60
India, Catholic practice in, 61
information, reliability of, 166–67
Isaac, Abraham's son, 35, 223
Isabel of Castile, Venerable, Queen of Spain, 257–58
Isaiah, prophesies, 30, 192, 216
Ishbosheth, King, 160
Israel, twelve tribes of, 108
Israelites, falling into pagan practice, 112

Jacob (NT), Joseph's father, 29
Jacob (OT)
    house of, 161–62, 218–19, 223, 259
    Isaac's son, 35, 35n6
Jadwiga, Saint, Queen of Poland, 254–55
James (apostle), Saint, 208
Jeroboam, King of Israel, 108
Jerome's Latin Vulgate, 234
Jesse, father of King David, 8, 29–30, 34

Jesus
  ancestry of, 29–30
  baptism of, 71, 74–77
  beginning of His ministry, 76
  birth of, 28–29, 29n2, 33–37
  breakfast with, 208–9
  consecration in the temple, 41–44
  descent into hell, 201
  divinity and kingship, 148–150
  Emmaus, meeting of Jesus, 206–7, 210
  finding of in the temple, 54–64
  flagellation of, 151–52
  fulfill the law, not abolish it, 189
  handed to Romans, 158–59
  healing power, 96
  human will/divine will, 137n4, 138
  humanity of, 187
  Joseph, spiritual father of. *see* Joseph (NT), Jesus' spiritual father
  kingdom of, 145, 162–66
  kingship of, 159, 216–18
  Last Supper, 116–122, 189, 228–29
  meetings after resurrection, 199–209
  named Immanuel, 36
  as new Adam, 84
  perfect obedience, 53
  prefigure of sacrificial Lamb, 43
  priesthood of J, 122–23
  prophesy of His passion, 132–33
  raising the dead, 97
  redemption accomplished by, 188n4
  resurrection of, 110
  Roman census, 32–33
  sacred heart of, 247
  as Savior, 124–25
  throne of the Word, 55–58
  timing of His coming, 7
  transfiguration and, 106–7
  trial of, 146–47, 158–59
  united with His Father's will, 56
Jesus, ascension of
  ascension, 212–15
  Jacob, house of, 218–19
  kingship of Jesus, 216–18
  son of man, 215–16

Jesus, carrying His cross
  condemned to death, 173
  consoling women of Jerusalem, 177–78
  first fall, 174
  meeting Blessed Mother, 174–75
  patience, virtue of, 179–184
  Simon of Cyrene, 175–76
  stripped of garments, 178
  taking up His cross, 173–74
  third fall, 178
  Veronica, wiping face of Jesus, 176–77
  Via Dolorosa, 172–73
Jesus, crowing of thorns
  Jacob, house of, 161–62
  Jesus, handed to Romans, 158–59
  kingdom come, 165–66
  moral courage, 166–171
  reign, with no end, 162–65
  throne of David, 159–161
Jesus, crucifixion and death of
  death of Jesus, 186–88
  Exodus, 190–91
  Isaiah, 192
  laid in tomb, 187
  law and prophets, 189–193
  lives forever changed, 185–87
  Mary at the cross, 192–93, 222
  nailed to the cross, 185–86
  Psalms, 191
  salvific act, 188–89
  self-denial, virtue of, 193–96
  taken down from cross, 186
  transfiguration and, 192
Joachim, Saint, 8, 70n6
Joanna, at Jesus' tomb, 202
Job, suffering of, 46
John (apostle), Saint, 193, 203–4, 208–9
John of God, Saint, 95n3
John Paul II, Saint (Pope), 141–42n7, 211n14, 255, 256
John the Baptist
  background, 68–71
  birthplace of, 70
  calls for repentance and conversion, 119

Ein Karem and, 70–72
Elijah and, 71–72
identifies Jesus as "Lamb of God," 87
imprisonment/execution of, 72–73
Jesus' baptism, 74–75
as Jesus' cousin, 71–72
making way for the Lord, 71
parents of, 18–20, 68
purity of, 72–73
Qumran communities, 163
role/mission of, 71
speaking to Jesus, 21
Jordan River, 67–68
Joseph (NT), Jesus' spiritual father
betrothed to Mary, 8
character of, 21, 34, 47
courage of, 169
divine mission, 45–47
escape to Egypt, 47
Jacob, father of, 29
at Jesus' birth, 37
as Mary's husband, 16n2, 30–32
message from an angel, 33–34
trust in God's messenger, 52–53
Joseph (OT), son of Jacob, 31, 223
Joseph of Arimathea, 186–87, 200, 202
Joshua, 67
Judah, house of, 7–8, 218, 223
Judaism, schools of biblical
interpretation, 162–63
Judas, betrayer of Jesus, 13, 135–37, 144–46, 223
Judith (OT), prefigures Mary, 243
Justinian, Byzantine emperor, 29

Kapiri Mposhi, Zambia, 194–95
Karlstadt, Andreas, 256n8
kingdom come, 165–66
kingdom of God proclamation
beatitudes of, 101
cast out demons, 99–101
cleanse the lepers, 98–99
heal the sick, 94–97
Jesus' proclamation, 145
raise the dead, 97–98
repentance, 101–4
two kingdoms, 92–94, 108

kiss, as sign of brotherhood, love, and
peace, 144–45
Knights Hospitallers, 95n3
Knights of Malta, 95n3
Knox, John, 256n8

language
importance of, 225–27
manipulation of, 9
other tongues, 230–32
Last Supper, 116–122, 189, 228–29
Law of Moses, 109–11
Lemech (OT), 108
Lent, season of, 127n5
Leo X, Pope, 256n8
lepers, cleansing of, 98–99
Levi, son of Jacob, 7–8, 218
Levites, collective sacrifice, 51–52
life, meaning of, 221
Lord's prayer, 165–66
lost sheep, 92–93
love
death, as absence of, 26
of God, 24–25
of neighbor as yourself, 24–25
true love, 26–27
truth and, 53, 127
Luke (disciple)
companion of St. Paul, 94n1
healing examples, 94–95
Mary as direct source of
information, 29, 174
lust, sins of, 6, 12, 102–3, 154–55, 236n9
Luther, Martin, 256n8

Maccabean revolt, 136
Maccabeus, Judas and Jonathan, 67
*Madonna della Seggiola with the Infant
Jesus and St. John* (Raphael
painting), 68
magisterial teaching, 14, 14n12
magisterium, 76, 76n12
Magnificat prayer, 23, 24, 247, 247n18
male-female complementarity roles,
88n3, 90
Manicheism, 187
Margaret, Saint, Queen of Scotland, 254

marriage
　commitments, 169–170
　oneness and, 14, 109–10, 109n6, 160–61
　significance of, 81, 102
　See also wedding
martyrs, 49, 168–69, 168n7
Mary (mother of Jesus)
　ancestry of, 29–30, 159, 218–19
　as bride in Song of Songs, 259
　at Cana wedding, 81, 260
　celestial queen in kingdom, 164
　chosen by God, 4–5
　with cousin Elizabeth. see Elizabeth (Mary's cousin)
　at the cross of Jesus, 192–93, 222
　devotion to, 90–91, 243–44, 248–251
　faithfulness of, 169
　first disciple of Christ, 49
　freedom to say "yes" to God, 9–10, 219
　Gabriel's announcement, 3–15, 7n5, 62n5, 216–18
　Holy Spirit and, 78, 241
　humility of, 11
　identity of Jesus, 78
　immaculate heart of, 247, 247n17
　intervention at wedding feast, 57
　Jesus, united at the cross, 46
　Joseph, betrothed to, 8
　Luke (disciple) and, 29, 174
　Magnificat prayer, 23, 24, 247
　Marian prayer, 19–20, 22
　Mary Mother of God, solemnity, 62n5
　as mediatrix, 84–85, 88–90
　meeting Jesus carrying His cross, 174–75
　as Mother of the Church, 230, 230n4
　Nazareth pilgrimage, 3–4, 4n2
　obedience of, 52
　parents of, 8
　at Pentecost, 226, 229–230
　Psalm of David and, 260–61
　Queen Esther as pre-figure of, 262
　Queen of Heaven, 263
　reflects and ponders, 57–58
　role of, 6–7
　as second/new Eve, 6–10, 24, 43, 84, 244
　seven sorrows of Mary, 45
　Simeon's prophetic words, 45–47
　Theotokos, "Mother of God," 189, 232n6, 242, 242n10, 243
　treasured things in her heart, 57, 247
Mary, annunciation of Jesus' birth, 3–15, 7n5, 62n5, 216–18
Mary, assumption of into heaven
　assumption of Mary, 245–48
　Council of Ephesus, 232n6, 242–43, 266
　devotion to Mary, 243–44, 248–251
　Ebionite heresy, 240–42
　immaculate conception, 246–48
　Mount Zion, 239–240
Mary, Immaculate Conception of, 7n5, 8–9, 8n6, 22–24, 23nn7–8, 62n5, 246–48
Mary, the wife of Clopas, 193
Mary Magdalene, 141, 193, 201–6, 206n6, 210
Mary Mother of God, solemnity, 62n5
Mary mother of James, 202
mass, active participation at, 124–28
Melchizedek, King of Salem, 85, 88, 122, 223
Memorial Church of Moses, Mount Nebo, 67–68
Messiah, term usage, 44
messianic prophesy, 32
Michael (archangel), 4
Michael IV Paphlagon (emperor), 207–8
Mignard, Pierre, 36
miracle at Cana
　fruits of, 89–91
　Mary, as mediatrix, 88–89
　Mary and Jesus, 84–86
　mystical interpretation, 260
　overview, 86–88
　problem at, 82
　purity, truth in, 83–84
　wedding, 80–81
　wine, significance of, 82–83
miracles, 80–91, 94–95

Missionaries of Charity, 98
moral courage, virtue of, 166–171
moral responsibility, 101
Mordecai (OT), 262
More, Thomas, Saint, 48–49
mortification, 152–55
Mosaic Law, 24–25, 41–42, 53, 141–42, 148
Moses
    journey of, 222
    leading the people, 51
    Memorial Church of Moses, 67–68
    Ten Commandments, 25, 109, 236
    at transfiguration, 109–11
Mother Teresa of Calcutta, Saint, 98
Mount Nebo, 67–68
Mount of Olives, Basilica (Jerusalem), 28
Mount Tabor, 105–6, 192
Mount Zion
    Basilica of the Dormition, Jerusalem, 239–240
    early church community, 78, 89
    Last Supper, 116–122, 189, 228–29
mystical theology, 259–260, 259–260n14

Naomi, Davidic ties to Bethlehem, 34, 35
Nathan (son of King David), 29, 160
Nathan, (prophet), 107, 159, 164, 216, 217–18
Nathanael (Bartholomew), apostle, 208
Nativity, Basilica of (Bethlehem), 28
natural law, 48, 114, 141–42
Nazareth
    Mary and Joseph's home, 30
    pilgrimage to, 3–4, 4n2
    as "stock of Jesse," 30
Nazirite vow, 69
Negretti, Jacoppo, 47, 47n4
Nero, Roman Emperor, 57n1
Nestorianism, 232n6
Nicene Creed, 201, 242
Nicodemus, the Pharisee, 187
Nizirite vow, 72
Noah, 108, 223

non-apostolic denominations, 193, 193n7
novena to the Holy Spirit, 227, 228n3
Nunc dimittis, term usage, 45n2

Oath/Act of Supremacy, England (1534), 48–49, 48n5, 258
Obed, Jesse's father, 34
obedience
    core virtue, 133n1
    in Garden of Gethsemane, 138
    of Jesus to parents, 57
    refusal to obey, 50
    to shatter pride, 13
    term usage, 52
    theological virtues, 43–44, 50
    virtue of, 47–53
    vow or promise of, 48
Obligatory Memorial of Mary, Martha, and Lazarus, 38n8
obligatory solemnities, 62n5
obstinacy, 142
Olive Grove Church, Jerusalem, 253n2
oneness
    of Catholicism, 160, 162n2, 242–43
    marriage and, 14, 109–10, 109n6, 160
    in the Scriptures, 108, 160–62, 264, 265
oral traditions, 174–77
Order of the Most Holy Savior, 255–56, 256nn8–9
original sin, 5
Our Father prayer, 165–66

pagan assimilation, 112n7
Papacy, Office of, 49
paraclete "counselor," 233
Passion Friday liturgy, 187
Passion of the Christ (movie), 175
Passover ritual (OT), 190–91
Passover supper (NT), 86–87, 117n1, 191
Pater Noster Church, Jerusalem, 253n2
patience
    description of, 179
    with God, 182–83
    with others, 180–82

patience *(continued)*
    with ourselves, 180
    in spiritual battle, 183–84
    virtue of, 179–184
Patris corde (Francis, Apostolic Letter), 32n4
Patroness of the Order of Preachers, 206n6
Paul VI, Saint (Pope), 141–42n7, 155n8
Pelagius, 89n4
Pentecost, 76, 226–28
Pentecost novena, 228n3
perversio voluntatis Dei, 133
Peter, Saint (apostle), 147–48, 203–4, 208–9, 223–24
Pharisees, 141–42, 163, 164n3, 189, 202, 204
piety, virtue of, 59–64
Pilate's dilemma, 150–51, 164
Pius IV, Pope, 254
Poland, Queen of (Saint Jadwiga), 254–55
popes, of the Roman Catholic Church, 78, 189
    See also specific popes by name
postmodern morality, 142–43, 196
post-truth era, 227
Potiphar's wife, 31
poverty, virtue of, 37–40
Praetorium, Herod the Great's fortress, 148n4
prayers, 165–66, 182–83
    See also specific prayers by name
pride, sin of, 6, 10, 12–15, 50, 133, 145
priesthood
    Catholic ministers in *persona Christi*, 125
    of Jesus, 122–23
prophecies
    fulfilled, 213
    of Jesus's passion, 132–33
Protestant Revolution, 256n8
Proto-Evangelium, 5–6, 222–23, 262
Psalm, as prefigure of Jesus, 191
Psalm of David, 260–61
purgatory, 246
purity
    humility and, 42
    of John the Baptist, 72–73
    steps toward, 155–57
    virtue of, 152–54

Queen Esther, 262–63
Queen of Sheba, 258–59
Quirinius, Governor of Syria, 32
Qumran, communities in, 163

Rahab (Old Testament), 113
Raphael (angel), 4, 102, 102n9
Raphael (Italian artist), 68
rationalism, 211
rebellion, human inclination toward, 50–51
reconciliation, sacrament of. *See* confession, sacrament of
Rehoboam, King of Judah, 108
reign, with no end, 162–65
relationships, 180–81
relativism, dictatorship of, 133, 133n1, 211
repentance, 101–4
resurrection
    Basilica of the Holy Sepulcher, 196–203
    Elijah and, 110
    Emmaus meeting, 206–7, 210
    faith, virtue of, 209–11
    Jesus, eating breakfast with apostles, 208–9
    Mary Magdalene, Jesus greeting, 203–6
    Moses and, 110
    Thomas, Jesus showing wounds, 207–8
Reuben, son of Jacob, 7–8, 218
rhythmic prayer, 166
Roman Catholic Church
    Annunciation of Mary, solemnity of, 7n5, 62n5
    apostolic authority, 123, 193n7
    apostolic penitentiary, 228n2
    Assumption of Mary solemnity, 246n16
    baptism, sacrament of, 5, 75n10
    beatifications and canonizations, 96n5
    Catholic schools, 210, 210n13

confession. *see* confession,
    sacrament of
core virtues, 133n1
crucifix and, 194
days prayers/abstinence/devotions,
    114
hospitals, 94nn3–4
Immaculate Conception, solemnity
    of, 7n5, 23n8, 62n5
Immaculate Heart of Mary
    Memorial, 247n17
Mary, as Queen Mother, 261–62
Mary Mother of God, solemnity of,
    62n5, 246n16
moral teaching, 266
Obligatory Memorial of Mary,
    Martha, and Lazarus, 38n8
oneness of the church, 160, 162n2,
    242–43
persecutions and executions, 168n7,
    170
popes, 78, 189. *see also specific popes
    by name*
on prayers, 165–66
priesthood, for males, 88n3
priesthood in *persona Christi*, 125
queens and saints, 252–58
Sacred Heart of Jesus Memorial,
    247n147
scriptures in, 164n3
spiritual life, formation of, 267–68
Transfiguration, solemnity of, 105n2
Roman Catholic Church of Moses,
    Mount Nebo, 67–68
Roman Catholics, executed in England,
    48n5, 49
Roman census, 32–33
Roman Martyrs memorial observation,
    170n9
rosary mysteries, as related events, 46
Rufus of Cyrene (son of Simon), 176
Ruth (OT), 34, 35, 113

sacraments, for obtaining purity, 156
    *See also specific sacraments, e.g.
    baptism, confession*
sacrifice, term usage, 118
sacrificial offering in the temple, 42–43

Sadducees, 163, 164n3
Saint Mary Magdalene feast day, 206n6
saints
    Catholic explorers naming places
        after, 257–58n13
    intercession of, 96
    See also specific saints by name
Salome (Herod Antipas' step-daughter),
    73
Salome, at Jesus' tomb, 202
salvific act, crucifixion as, 188–89
Samaritans, 163, 164n3
San Remo musical performance, 51,
    51n8
sanctification, 139
sanctity, path to, 12
Santa Maria Maggiore, Papal Basilica,
    29n2
Satan, 5–6, 9, 27, 51, 61–62, 142, 210,
    233, 262–63
Saul, King, 93, 108, 160
Scotland, Queen of (Saint Margaret),
    254
scourging, term usage, 151
scourging at the pillar
    Caiphas' house, 146–47
    divinity, kingship and, 148–150
    flagellation of Jesus, 151–52
    Judas' betrayal, 144–46
    Peter's threefold denial, 147–48
    Pilate's dilemma, 150–51
    purity, virtue of, 152–57
Scripture
    biblical queens, 258–264
    cannon of, 163n2, 164n3
    deutero-canonical books, 163n2
    Douay-Rheims translation, 234n7
    Exodus, 190–91
    Isaiah, 192
    Jesus' fulfillment of, 189–193
    levels of reading, 145n1
    oneness in, 108, 160–62
    Psalms, 191
    schools of biblical interpretation,
        162–63
    transfiguration, 192
Sea/Lake of Tiberias, 208–9, 210
secular humanism, 89n4

self-denial, virtue, 193–96
sensuous pleasures, 195
"Servant of God" Queen Isabel title, 257n11
Seth (OT), 223
seven sorrows of Mary, 45
sexual addiction/immorality, 102–3, 109n6, 141–42, 141–42n7, 154–55, 154n7, 167, 236n8
shepherds, 58–59
Shepherds' Fields, church of, 29
sick, healing of, 94–97
Simeon (OT) son of Jacob, 7–8, 218
Simeon, Prophet (NT) in the temple, 44–47, 247
Simon of Cyrene, 175–76
sins
    brought death into the world, 244
    confession of. *see* confession, sacrament of
    forgiveness of, 101, 227
    God's holy name and, 231
    grace of God and, 194
    grave sins, 140–41
    pride as, 6, 10, 12–15, 50
    as punishment, 46
    repetition of, 140, 179
    spiritual life and, 97–98
    types of, 6, 39
    venial sins, 179
"The Slaughter of the Innocents" (Negretti painting), 47n4
solemnities, obligatory, 62n5
Solomon, King
    Bathsheba and, 261
    Queen of Sheba and, 258–59
    Song of Songs, 259–260
Song of Songs, book of, 82–83, 87, 259–260
Spain, Queen of, Isabel of Castile, Venerable, 257–58
spiritual communion, 226n1
spiritual darkness, 127
spiritual healing, 96–97
spiritual life, 97–98, 127–28
spiritual reading, for obtaining purity, 156

spiritual training exercises, 195
St. John the Baptist Church (Ein Karem, Jerusalem), 70, 70n7
Stephen, Saint, 168, 168n5
strength, for obtaining purity, 155–56
subjectivism, in societies, 211
suffering, 46, 180
supernatural healing, 96n5

Tamar (Old Testament), 113
temple
    destruction of, 57, 57n1
    finding Jesus in, 54–64
    presentation in, 41–53
Ten Commandments, 25, 109, 236, 236nn8–9
Thebutis (founder of Ebionite sect), 241
theological virtues, 43–44, 50, 113, 114n8
Theology of the Body (John Paul II), 141–42n7
Theotokos, "Mother of God," 189, 232n6, 242, 242n10, 243
Thomas, Saint (apostle), 125–26, 207–8, 210
Thomas Aquinas, Saint, 4n3, 14, 59, 114n8, 128n6, 138n5, 141, 194, 201, 265n15
throne of the Word, 55–58
Tiberias, Sea/Lake of, 208–9, 210
Tobias and Sarah, 102
Tobit, Book of, 4
tomb
    Jesus laid in, 187, 200–202
    women at, 201–2
Tower of Babel, 108, 231
Transfiguration
    crucifixion and death of Jesus, 192
    discipline, 113–14
    Elijah, 107–10, 192
    glorious event, 106–7
    holiness, desire for, 112–13
    Law of Moses, 109–11, 192
    Moses, 192
    Mount Tabor, 105–6, 192
    My Beloved Son, 111–12

old/new covenant connection, 111–12
solemnity of, 105n2
virtue, striving for, 114–15
Trinity, Holy, 75–77
trust
　in God, 101–4
　in God's messenger, 52–53
truth
　crisis in modern society, 195–96
　happiness and, 265
　Jesus' trials, 151
　love and, 25–26, 53, 127
　mob rule and, 152–55
　as our nature, 59, 142
　post-truth era, 227
　spirit of, 145

unity, removal of barriers creating, 227
universality of church, 78
Unleavened Bread, Feast of, 118, 119
Urban V (Pope), 256

Vadstena Abbey, Sweden, 256
Vatican and Italian Episcopal Conference (2022), 51, 51n8
venial sins, 179
Venus, goddess, 28
Veronica, wiping face of Jesus, 176–77
Via Dolorosa, 172–73
vices, 140, 154
The Virgin of the Grapes (Mignard painting), 36
"virgin" term usage, 11n10
virtue-building, 155
virtues
　acquired learning of, 181
　cardinal virtues, 113, 114n8, 234
　striving for, 114–15

theological virtues, 43–44, 50, 113, 114n8
visitation, with Elizabeth
　Church of the Visitation, 17, 17n3
　Elizabeth and. *see* Elizabeth (Mary's cousin)
　feast of, 22n31

wedding
　at Cana, 80–82
　feast of the Lamb at, 86–88
　Tobias and Sarah, 102–3
　See also marriage
wine, significance of at Cana, 82–83
wisdom, 236–38
womanhood, 90, 90n5
women
　biblical queens, 258–264
　Catholic queens and saints, 252–58
　gentile presence of, 113
　Jesus consoling of, 177–78
　at Jesus' tomb, 201–2
　male-female complementarity roles, 88n3, 90
world, detachment from, 38–40
worship practices, public/private, 63–64

Xristokos, mother of Jesus, 189, 242

"young woman" term usage, 11n10

Zechariah
　Benedictus (hymn), 18, 70n5
　Elizabeth's husband, 16
　lineage of, 68
　naming of John, 69
　non-belief of, 21, 69
　role of, 21
Zimbabwe, Catholic practice in, 62
Zwingli, Ulrich, 256n8

Scripture Index

Genesis

1:1	108
1:27	49, 141, 153
1:27–28	81
1:28	14
2:15–17	9
2:16	6
2:17	245
2:24	14, 81, 90, 108, 109, 141, 160
3	5, 27, 48, 226, 228
3:1–5	9
3:3	245
3:4–5	6
3:6	6, 138
3:15	5, 223, 262
3:16–17	108
4	223
4:3–8	108
4:23	108
6:1–4	217n3
6:9—9:17	108
9	223
11	226, 228
11:1–9	108
11:4	231
11:6–8	231
12:1–3	35, 108
14	223
14:18	122
14:18–19	85
17:1–8	108, 219
17:21	35
19	228
22	223
22:6	35
25:27–34	35
26	223
28:13–15	35
34:24–25	218
34:25–26	7
35	223
35:22	7, 218
39:7–10	31
41:55	32
44	223
46	31
49	108, 223
49:8	218
49:9–10	160, 218
49:10	7, 218

Exodus

3:14	123
4:22	217n3
12:1–27	118
12:5–7	190
12:7	87
12:8	190
12:14	120
12:14–17	55
13:1–2	42
13:2	42
19:5	51

Exodus (continued)

19:8	51
19:16–19	230
20:1–18	109
20:1–21	25
20:2–17	236
21:24	237
24	35
24:3–8	118, 190
24:5	117
24:6	190
24:8	190, 191
32:1–6	51, 112
32:6	12
32:25–29	51
32:28	13

Leviticus

4	87
11:44	112
12:7–8	42
12:8	42
18:16	71
19:2	112
21:14	68
23:15–17	229
24:15–16	148

Numbers

32:13	182

Deuteronomy

5:6–21	109
9:28	33
34:1	67
34:4	222
34:5–6	67

Joshua

3:15–17	67
5:6	182

Judges

21:25	133

Ruth

1:1–5	34
1:16	34
2:8–9	34
3:7–9	34
4:13	34
4:18–22	34

1 Samuel

15:10–11	93
16:1–13	8
16:12–13	93
16:13	44
18:11	93

2 Samuel

2:8–11	108, 160
5:1–5	159
5:6	217
5:7	239
6:5	17
6:12	17
6:12–15	160
6:14	217
7:12–13	35, 36, 44
7:13	216
7:13–14	32, 217
7:14	191, 217
7:16	44, 107, 159, 191, 217
12:1–15	160

1 Kings

2:19	261
2:19–20	262
10:1–3	258
10:8	258
11:26–43	108
14:21–31	108

17:5	67	**Psalms**	
18:17–40	107	2:3	82
		22:16–17	191
2 Kings		45:6–7	260
1:8	72	45:9	260
2:11	107	45:10–12	260
5:9–10	67	45:13–14	261
5:14	67	45:15	261
		51 (50)	160n1
2 Chronicles		89:3–4	218n4
9:1–2	258	89:4	216
9:7	258	110:1	215
		113–114	117
		132:11–12	218n4
		132:12	216
Tobit			
5–8	4	**Ecclesiastes**	
6:13–14	101	3:1–9	166
6:18	101		
7:10–11	101	**Song of Solomon**	
		1:2	82
Judith		2:4	83
15:9	239, 242	4:7	259
		4:9–10	83
Esther		4:12	83
2:17	262	12	259
7:10	262		
		Isaiah	
1 Maccabees		2:3	231
5:24	67	7:14	11, 36, 108, 216
		9:6–7	217
2 Maccabees		11:1	30
8	136	11:2–3	233
12:40–42	246	53:3	132, 133
		53:3–5	138
Job		53:4–5	132
1:1	46	53:5	133
28:20–28	46	53:6	133
		53:7	133
		Jeremiah	
		50:6	92

Ezekiel

34:4	93

Daniel

3:52–90	166
7:1–12	215
7:13	214, 215
7:13–14	108, 215, 215n1
7:14	215
7:21–22	215
7:27	216
12:1	4

Hosea

1:2	13
2:1–5	92

Joel

2:12–13	127n5

Micah

3:12	239
5:2	33, 108

Malachi

4:5	72

Matthew

1:1–16	29
1:6	29
1:11	29
1:16	8, 29
1:18	31
1:19	30
1:20–21	32, 34
1:24	21
2:10–11	59
2:13–21	31
2:16	47n3
3:4	71, 72
3:11	71
3:13–17	71
3:14	74
3:15	74
3:16–17	74
5:1–12	264
5:3–12	236–37
5:8	153, 156, 248
5:15–16	153
5:17	107, 189, 214
6:1	60
6:6	63
6:9–12	165
6:10	165
7:21	14, 194
7:24–30	99
8:3	98
8:4	99
8:20	38
8:28–32	99
10:6	92
10:7	92
10:8	92
11:11	72
11:13–14	72
11:29	11
13:55	30
14:5	73
14:6–8	73
16:13–18	107
16:16–16	137
16:16–18	78
16:16–19	193n7
16:16–21	110
16:18	228
16:21	110
16:24	194
16:24–25	174
17:2	105
17:22–23	110
18:20	63
19:2–6	26
19:3–9	141
19:6	109
19:8	109
19:10	141
20:20–22	145
25:1–13	266

SCRIPTURE INDEX

25:31–46	94, 95n4, 104	14:15	229
26:12	118	14:22–24	118
26:26–28	189	14:44	144
26:26–29	116	14:48	144
26:28	134	14:49	145
26:29	86	14:60–64	148
26:36–38	106	14:61	214
26:37–38	64, 134	14:62	214
26:39	138	14:66–72	224
26:40	134	15:2	148
26:48	136	15:10	149
26:49	144	15:11	150
26:54	145	15:15	173
26:55	144	15:21	173, 175
26:57	146	15:24	185
26:64	215, 219	15:43	202
26:64–66	148	15:46	200
27:12	148	16:1	202
27:19	149	16:1–2	202
27:20	151	16:3	200
27:20–26	150	16:7	212
27:24	150	16:9	219
27:26	151, 173	16:14–16	212
27:28–29	158	16:19	212
27:32	173, 175		
27:35	185		
27:58	202	### Luke	
27:62–66	202		
28:1	201	1	263–64
28:19	264	1:5	68
28:19–20	77, 231	1:13	70
		1:15	69
		1:16–17	69
### Mark		1:18	21
		1:19–20	69
1:9	67	1:26	30
1:9–11	75	1:26–38	266
1:15	127n5	1:27	8, 30, 69
2:27	95	1:28	1
5:1–5	101	1:32	4
6:3	30	1:32–33	216, 263
6:17–28	71	1:32–35	32
8:31	109–10	1:33	161, 218
9:12	109–10	1:34	21
9:13	72	1:34–35	11
12:30–31	25	1:35	249
12:31	109	1:36	16
14:12	87, 118	1:38	10

Luke (continued)

1:39–40	16
1:41	70
1:42	19, 20, 58, 263
1:43	20
1:44	17
1:45	23
1:46–55	166
1:47	23, 24
1:48	11
1:49	247
1:60–63	70
1:68–79	18, 166
1:76–77	70, 72
2:4–5	30
2:6–7	34
2:11	28
2:11–12	35
2:22	41
2:22–24	42
2:25	44, 45
2:26	44
2:30	44
2:32	45
2:35	247
2:42	55
2:46	55
2:47	55
2:48	54, 55, 247
2:49	55, 57, 58
2:51	57, 175, 247
2:52	55
3:16	21
3:19–20	73
3:21–22	75
3:23–31	69
3:31	29
5:12–16	95, 98
5:17–26	95
6:6–11	95
7:1–10	95
8:29	99
8:40–42	97
8:49–56	97
9:2	92
9:22	110
9:28–36	134
9:29	106
9:35	111
9:44	110
10:9	92
13:10–17	95
17:11–19	98
17:22	215
22:7	119
22:7–8	87
22:15–20	119
22:18	117n1
22:19–20	116
22:20	117n1, 191
22:42	131, 137
22:44	137
22:48	144
22:51	144
22:53	144
22:63	146
22:63–65	158
22:66	146
23:3	148
23:4	149, 177
23:8–12	150
23:18–19	150
23:22	150
23:25	151, 173
23:26	173, 175
23:27	177
23:27–28	174
23:27–31	177–78
23:31	174
23:33	185
23:34	166
23:51	186
23:53	186, 187, 203
23:55–56	187
24:10	202
24:13–35	206
24:14	206
24:18	206
24:19	206
24:19–21	206
24:21	207
24:26–27	207
24:29	207
24:30–32	207
24:32	207

24:35	207	18:36	145, 150
24:36–43	209	18:37	151
24:44	213	18:39–40	150
24:47	213	19:1	144
24:50–51	213	19:2	158
24:51	213	19:5	151, 173
		19:16	152, 173
		19:17	172, 173

John

		19:18	176, 185
1	97	19:21–22	93
1:29–36	87	19:23	185
1:31	74	19:25	193
1:33	74	19:26–27	90
1:37–49	80	19:27	193, 240
2:1	80	19:30	111, 120
2:1–11	80, 89	19:33	186
2:1–12	266	19:34	186
2:4	57, 80	19:38	186, 187
2:10	85	19:39	187
2:19	55	19:40–42	187
3:5–6	226	19:42	202
3:16	138, 152	20:1	202, 203
6:38	97	20:2	203, 204
6:38–40	53	20:4–8	204
6:52	124	20:7	203
6:53–56	121	20:8	203
7:6	260	20:11	204
8	202	20:13	204
8:11	140	20:15	205
11:1–44	97	20:16	205
12:1–8	38	20:17	205, 206
12:5	145	20:18	199, 206
14:6	49, 151	20:19–20	207
14:12–17	214	20:21–23	123
14:16	228, 231	20:22	227
14:26	228, 231	20:23	228
15:13	95n4	20:24–31	124
16:13	145, 231	20:25	208
16:19	173	20:26–29	126
17:11	264, 266	20:27	205, 208
17:21	161, 242	20:28	208
18:3	13	20:29	208
18:10–11	144	20:809	204
18:11	136, 145	21:2–7	209
18:28	152	21:8	209
18:31	150	21:10	209
18:33	148	21:12	209
		21:12–13	212

John (continued)

21:13	209
21:15–16	147, 224
21:15–17	137

Acts

1:4–5	230
1:5	214
1:9	214
1:13–14	226, 229, 240
2:1	229
2:2	229
2:3	230
2:3–4	225
2:4	230
2:7–8	231
7:54–60	168
15:7–11	240

Romans

1:1–4	30
1:5	52
2:14	15
2:15	132
10:1–4	132

1 Corinthians

3:14–15	246
5:1	26
10:16	120, 122
11:23	121
11:23–25	120
15:45	84
15:54–55	223

Galatians

5:22–23	234

Ephesians

4:4–6	264
4:5	14, 227
4:5–6	160
4:14	49
5:21–28	90
5:23	14
5:26–28	88
5:31–32	160
5:32	86
6	157, 184

Colossians

1:13	99

1 Thessalonians

4:3	12, 139, 140
4:3–5	235

2 Thessalonians

2:15	120

1 Timothy

6:3–5	77

Hebrews

5:5–10	122
7:3	122
7:11–14	122
7:17	122
8:3	122
8:8	122
9:11–12	43
9:26	122
12:2	93

James

1:27	60
2:14–26	194
5:16	96

1 Peter

1:13–16	113

2 Peter

2:1–3	77
2:2	49

1 John

2:16	6
2:18	59
4:1–3	241
4:20	123

Revelation

3:20	128
12	264
12:1	250, 252, 263, 264
12:4–5	263
12:7	4
17:14	88
19:6–7	86
19:7–9	128
19:7–10	86
19:9	86

www.ingramcontent.com/pod-product-compliance
Lightning Source LLC
Chambersburg PA
CBHW071232230426
43668CB00011B/1396